"The editors have come up with a solid text that will prove useful for undergraduates and graduates alike. Its well-known contributors provide insight on a wide range of subjects, and the inclusion of nonviolent civil resistance as a key component of the field sets this text apart from many others. Overall, the text gives students a range of tools to handle international conflict and to work toward conflict transformation and global change."

– **Landon E. Hancock,** Kent State University, USA

"This book provides an exceptionally comprehensive and compelling collection of insights on international conflict management. Hallward and Butcher have brought together the voices of top contributors from around the world, who expertly integrate findings from theory and practice while grappling with both historical and newly emerging issues and ideas. The volume will be a must-read text for students and also a valuable resource for scholars and practitioners."

– **Julie M. Norman,** University College London (UCL), UK

"*Understanding International Conflict Management* is essential reading for anyone interested in the practical utility of peace and conflict studies. It is theoretically sophisticated and introduces readers to the fundamentals of negotiation theory, resistance studies, and long-term peacebuilding, justice, and reconciliatory processes. It does all of this while focusing a conflict-management lens on critical twenty-first century issues such as social media for the public good, gender-based conflict, refugees and migration, and the biggest existential dilemma of all: climate change and conflict. I heartily endorse it for everyone interested in peaceful social change and transformation."

– **Kevin P. Clements,** National Centre for Peace and Conflict Studies,
University of Otago, New Zealand

"*Understanding International Conflict Management* provides an exhaustive overview of international conflict management mechanisms ranging from negotiations to peacekeeping to transitional justice. Butcher and Hallward expertly tie together a wide array of perspectives on conflict management, helping readers to understand the current state of the field in an interdisciplinary way. For those seeking to understand conflict management mechanisms and the cross-cutting issues they help to address, this is an excellent resource."

– **Krista E. Wiegand**, University of Tennessee, USA

# Understanding International Conflict Management

This new textbook introduces key mechanisms and issues in international conflict management and engages students with a comprehensive interdisciplinary approach to mitigating, managing, and transforming international conflicts.

The volume identifies key historical events and international agreements that have shaped and defined the field of international conflict management, as well as key dilemmas facing the field at this juncture. The first section provides an overview of key mechanisms for international conflict management, such as negotiation, mediation, nonviolent resistance, peacekeeping, peacebuilding, transitional justice, and reconciliation. The second section tackles important cross-cutting themes, such as technology, religion, the economy, refugees and migration, and the role of civil society, examining how these issues contribute to international conflicts and how they can be leveraged to help address such conflicts. Each chapter includes a brief historical overview of the evolution of the issue or mechanism, identifies key theoretical and practical debates, and includes case studies, discussion questions, website links, and suggested further reading for further study and engagement. By providing a mixture of theory and practical examples, this textbook provides students with the necessary background to navigate this interdisciplinary field.

This volume will be of great interest to students of international conflict management, conflict resolution, peace studies, and international relations in general.

**Charity Butcher** is Associate Professor of Political Science in the School of Government and International Affairs at Kennesaw State University, USA.

**Maia Carter Hallward** is Professor of Middle East Politics in the School of Conflict Management, Peacebuilding and Development at Kennesaw State University, USA.

# Understanding International Conflict Management

**Edited by Charity Butcher
and Maia Carter Hallward**

Routledge
Taylor & Francis Group

LONDON AND NEW YORK

First published 2020
by Routledge
2 Park Square, Milton Park, Abingdon, Oxon OX14 4RN

and by Routledge
52 Vanderbilt Avenue, New York, NY 10017

*Routledge is an imprint of the Taylor & Francis Group, an informa business*

*British Library Cataloguing-in-Publication Data*
A catalogue record for this book is available from the British Library

*Library of Congress Cataloging-in-Publication Data*
A catalog record for this book has been requested

ISBN: 978-1-138-32953-9 (hbk)
ISBN: 978-1-138-32956-0 (pbk)
ISBN: 978-0-429-44816-4 (ebk)

Typeset in Times New Roman
by Apex CoVantage, LLC

# Contents

| | |
|---|---|
| HRW | Human Rights Watch |
| IAEA | International Atomic Energy Association |
| ICC | International Criminal Court |
| ICG | International Crisis Group |
| ICT | Information and Communication Technologies |
| ICTJ | International Center for Transitional Justice |
| ICTR | International Criminal Tribunal for Rwanda |
| ICTY | International Criminal Tribunal for the former Yugoslavia |
| IDP | Internally Displaced Person |
| IFOR | Implementation Force |
| ILO | International Labor Organization |
| IM | Instant Messaging |
| IMF | International Monetary Fund |
| INGOs | International Non-Governmental Organizations |
| IPRS | Interim Poverty Reduction Strategy |
| IRMCT | International Residual Mechanism for Criminal Tribunals |
| ISAF | International Security Assistance Force |
| ISF | Integrated Strategic Framework |
| ISPs | Internet Service Providers |
| ISIS | Islamic State of Iraq and Syria |
| IUCN | International Union for the Conservation of Nature and Natural Resources |
| LiDAR | Light Detection and Ranging |
| LGBTQI | Lesbian, Gay, Bisexual, Transgender, Queer, and Intersexed |
| LRA | Lord's Resistance Army |
| LTTE | Liberation Tigers of Tamil Eelam |
| MARO | Mass Atrocity Prevention and Response Operations |
| MDGs | Millennium Development Goals |
| MENA | Middle East and North Africa |
| MOU | Memorandum of Understanding |
| NAP | National Action Plan |
| NATO | North Atlantic Treaty Organization |
| NGOs | Non-Governmental Organizations |
| NEPA | National Environmental Policy Act |
| NSA | Non-state actor |
| NSM | New Social Movements |
| OMB | Office of Management and Budget |
| ONUC | UN Operation in the Congo |
| OPEC | Organization of the Petroleum Exporting Countries |
| PA | Palestinian Authority |
| PAPD | Pro-Poor Agenda for Prosperity and Development |
| PBC | UN Peacebuilding Commission |
| PBF | UN Peacebuilding Fund |
| PBSO | UN Peacebuilding Support Office |
| PD | Prisoner's Dilemma |
| PKO | Peacekeeping Operation |
| PLO | Palestinian Liberation Organization |
| PoC | Protection of Civilians |

# Abbreviations

| | |
|---|---|
| ACF | Apalachicola Chattahoochee Flint River |
| AI | Amnesty International |
| AIES | Arava Institute for Environmental Studies |
| BATNA | Best Alternative to a Negotiated Agreement |
| BCM | Billion Cubic Meters |
| BDS | Boycott, Divestment, and Sanctions |
| BLM | Bureau of Land Management |
| BRICS | Brazil, Russia, India, China, and South Africa |
| CAR | Central African Republic |
| CEESP | Commission on Environmental, Economic and Social Policy |
| CEQ | Council on Environmental Quality |
| CIMIC | Civil Military Coordination Officers |
| CMMRCs | Conflict Mitigation and Management Regional Councils |
| CPA | Coalition Provisional Authority |
| CPAN | Community Peace Action Network |
| CPCC | Community Peace Coordinating Centre |
| CPOs | Community Peace Observers |
| CSOs | Civil Society Organizations |
| CSSR | Civil Society Support Room |
| CST | Country Support Team |
| DDR | Disarmament, Demobilization, and Reintegration |
| DNH | Do No Harm |
| DOI | US Department of Interior |
| DPO | Department of Peace Operations |
| DRC | Democratic Republic of the Congo |
| ECCC | Extraordinary Chambers in the Courts of Cambodia |
| EITI | Extractive Industries Transparency Initiative |
| FARC | Revolutionary Armed Forces of Colombia |
| FOIA | Freedom of Information Act |
| FSC | Forest Stewardship Council |
| GATT | General Agreement on Tariffs and Trade |
| GBV | Gender Based Violence |
| GIS | Global Information System |
| GPPAC | Global Partnership for the Prevention of Armed Conflict |
| GPS | Global Positioning System |
| HRC | Human Rights Council |

| | |
|---|---|
| PPF | Production Possibility Frontier |
| PRIO | Peace Research Institute in Oslo |
| PSGs | Peacebuilding and Statebuilding Goals |
| PWEG | Palestinian Wastewater Engineers Group |
| R2P | Responsibility to Protect |
| SDGs | Sustainable Development Goals |
| SFOR | Stabilization Force (e.g., in Bosnia) |
| SIPRI | Stockholm International Peace Research Institute |
| SIT | Social Identity Theory |
| SMS | Short Messaging Service |
| TRC | Truth and Reconciliation Commission |
| UDHR | Universal Declaration of Human Rights |
| UN | United Nations |
| UNAMIR | United Nations Assistance Mission in Rwanda |
| UNDAF | United Nations Development Assistance Framework |
| UNDP | United Nations Development Program |
| UNEF | United Nations Emergency Force |
| UNHCR | United Nations High Commissioner for Refugees |
| UNITAF | Unified Task Force |
| UNMIL | United Nations Mission in Liberia |
| UNOSOM | United Nations Mission in Somalia |
| UNOY Peacebuilders | The United Network of Young Peacebuilders |
| UNPROFOR | United Nations Protection Force |
| UNSC | United Nations Security Council |
| UNTSO | UN Truce Supervision Organization |
| US | United States of America |
| USDA | US Department of Agriculture |
| VOIP | Voice Over Internet Protocol |
| VPN | Virtual Private Network |
| WAB | Syrian Women's Advisory Body |
| WTO | World Trade Organization |
| ZOPA | Zone of Possible Agreement |

# Figures

# Tables

# Textboxes

# Editors

**Charity Butcher, PhD** is Associate Professor of Political Science in the School of Government and International Affairs and is affiliated with the School of Conflict Management, Peacebuilding and Development at Kennesaw State University. She is currently on the Editorial Team for the *Journal of Peacebuilding and Development*. She is the author of *The Handbook of Cross-border Ethnic and Religious Affinities* (Rowman & Littlefield 2019) and has published numerous peer-reviewed articles in journals including *Journal of Human Rights, International Studies Perspectives, Terrorism and Political Violence, Democratization, European Political Science*, and *International Journal of Politics, Culture, and Society*.

**Maia Carter Hallward, PhD** is Professor of Middle East Politics in the School of Conflict Management, Peacebuilding and Development at Kennesaw State University and Executive Editor of the *Journal of Peacebuilding and Development*. Dr. Hallward is also on the Fulbright Specialist Roster for Peace and Conflict Resolution Studies. She has published five books, including *Transnational Activism and the Israeli-Palestinian Conflict* (Palgrave Macmillan 2013), *Struggling for a Just Peace: Israeli and Palestinian Activism in the Second Intifada* (University of Florida Press 2011), and, with Amanda Guidero, *Global Responses to Conflict and Crisis in Syria and Yemen* (Palgrave Pivot 2015) and over twenty peer-reviewed articles in journals including *Journal of Peace Research, Research in Social Movements, Conflict and Change, International Negotiation*, and *International Political Sociology*.

# Contributors

**Eric Abitbol, PhD** is Senior Consultant and Practice Leaders heading Universalia's Environment, Security, and Conflict Transformation (ENSECT) practice. He is a global environmental governance, sustainability, conflict transformation and evaluation practitioner, theorist, and innovator with more than 25 years of experience. Dr. Abitbol has notable thematic expertise in environmental peacebuilding, natural resources governance, water-food-energy nexus discourse and management, corporate social responsibility and philanthropy, and the cultivation of communities of practice. He continues to advise governments, international financial institutions, multilateral organizations, private foundations, civil society organizations, and grassroots communities in the Middle East, Africa, Asia, Latin America, Europe, and North America. Dr. Abitbol has delivered hundreds of lectures, presentations, training sessions, and dialogue processes and has written numerous articles for academic journals and magazines. He is an Adjunct Professorial Lecturer at the School of International Service, American University (SIS-AU), and is a Board Member with the Journal of Peacebuilding and Development.

**Mohammed Abu-Nimer, PhD** is Professor in Conflict Resolution and Peace Studies at American University in Washington, DC. He has worked for three decades on dialogue and peacebuilding research and training, including the application of conflict resolution models in Muslim communities, interreligious conflict resolution training, interfaith dialogue, and evaluation of conflict resolution programs. As a practitioner, he has been convening and conducting over 100 training workshops and courses all over the world on themes of community development, peacebuilding, reconciliation and development, training for trainers, interfaith and interethnic dialogue, intercultural training, conflict resolution and human rights in relief and development projects, and problem-solving workshops in conflict areas around the world, including Palestine, Israel, Egypt, Northern Ireland, the Philippines (Mindanao), and Sri Lanka.

**Joseph G. Bock, PhD** is Director of the School of Conflict Management, Peacebuilding and Development at Kennesaw State University. He was previously at the Eck Institute for Global Health at the University of Notre Dame. His humanitarian work has included directing Catholic Relief Services programs in Pakistan and Jerusalem/West Bank/Gaza Strip, and overseeing programs in Bosnia, Croatia, Guinea, Iraq, Kosovo, Liberia, Macedonia, Montenegro, Pakistan, Rwanda, Serbia, Sierra Leone, Thailand, and Uganda while serving as Vice President at American Refugee Committee. His articles on technology have appeared in the *Journal of Information Technology & Politics*, *Information Technology for Development*, and *Political Geography*. He is the author of three books. His most recent book, *The Technology of Nonviolence: Social Media and Violence Prevention*, was published by MIT Press in 2012.

**Thomas Doleys, PhD** is Associate Professor of Political Science and Director of the Master of Science in International Policy Management (MSIPM) at Kennesaw State University. His research focuses on the political dynamics of international organizations. Current projects explore the impact interinstitutional relations have on the design, negotiation, and implementation of competition and state aid policy in the European Union. His work has appeared in the *Journal of European Public Policy*, *Journal of European Integration*, the *Journal of Industry, Competition and Trade*, and *The Antitrust Review*.

**Brittany Foutz, PhD** is a faculty member in the Department of Conflict Analysis and Dispute Resolution at Salisbury University and a Senior Research Fellow with the Bosserman Center of Conflict Resolution. She received her PhD in International Conflict Management from Kennesaw State University's School of Conflict Management, Peacebuilding and Development. She has worked as the Program Manager for the United Nations Institute for Training and Research (UNITAR) and UNITAR's Centre for Authorities and Leaders (CIFAL), developing and facilitating international conflict management programs.

**Volker Franke, PhD** is Professor of Conflict Management at Kennesaw State University and the Founding Director of KSU's PhD program in International Conflict Management. Dr. Franke is also Founder and Chairman of TRENDS Global, an Atlanta-area-based nonprofit dedicated to research and engagement in diverse communities and a part-time Visiting Professor with the Peacekeeping and Stability Operations Institute at the U.S Army War College. He is the author of *Preparing for Peace: Military Identity, Value-Orientations, and Professional Military Education* (Praeger 1999) and more than 40 journal articles, book chapters, case studies and research reports on issues related to peace and security studies, conflict management, civil-military relations, development policy, and social identity.

**Karen Guttieri, PhD** is Associate Professor of Strategy at the Air University School of Graduate Professional Military Education, Maxwell Air Force Base, and has worked with humanitarian and international agencies throughout her career. With the Geneva Centre for Security Policy, she codeveloped and taught a multi-sector senior executive course on Leadership in Complex Operations for senior US military and Geneva-based humanitarian participants. She developed a complex operations teaching case study program, coedited *Understanding Complex Operations* (Routledge 2014), and has directed a multidisciplinary and interagency research project investigating civil affairs expertise requirements for Special Operations Command. She has published peer-reviewed articles on topics including evaluation metrics, civil information and communications technology innovation, civil-military relations, and cognitive preparedness for peacekeeping. Karen was recognized in 2014 as an Honorary Member of the Civil Affairs Regiment.

**Sherrill W. Hayes, PhD** is Professor of Conflict Management and Director of the PhD in Analytics and Data Science in the Graduate College at Kennesaw State University. Dr. Hayes (PhD, Newcastle University, UK; M.S. & B.S. University of North Carolina at Greensboro) has been working in conflict management since 1999. He has worked as a divorce and family mediator in the UK and US, designed and evaluated community conflict resolution programs for housing and refugee issues, and consulted with family-owned businesses. His recent research has focused on the impact of resettlement and host community programs on migrant children and families in the US. He serves on the Editorial Team of the *Journal of Peacebuilding and Development* and is the coeditor of *Atone: Religion, Conflict, and Reconciliation* (Lexington Books 2018).

**Timothy Hedeen, PhD** is Professor of Conflict Management at Kennesaw State University. His work examines conflict engagement in community, education, workplace, and court contexts. He serves on the editorial board of *Conflict Resolution Quarterly* and is an appointed member of the Commission on Dispute Resolution of the Georgia Supreme Court. He is a senior consultant to the National Center on Appropriate Dispute Resolution in Special Education, a former member of the Section Council of the American Bar Association's Section of Dispute Resolution, a former editorial board member of *Family Court Review*, and a past chair of the Board of Directors of the National Association for Community Mediation. Dr. Hedeen is an active member of the International Ombudsman Association, the American Bar Association Section of Dispute Resolution, the Association for Conflict Resolution, the National Association for Community Mediation, and the American Association of University Professors (AAUP). He is past president of the KSU chapter of AAUP, and served as University Ombuds for five years.

**Nicole Junker** is a Clendenin Scholar, holding degrees in history and Central and Eastern European Studies, and a post-graduate certificate in Post-Conflict Transitions and International Justice from the International Peace and Security Institute. She is completing her doctoral dissertation on the reintegration of conflict-related sexual violence victims in Nigeria. Her past research includes topics such as human trafficking in the Republic of Moldova and the impact of media on survivors of trafficking returning from Islamic State captivity in Iraqi Kurdistan. Ms. Junker has previously served as the Communications Specialist for the USAID-funded Access to Justice Program in Iraq and currently works as a Monitoring and Evaluation Specialist in Afghanistan.

**Kathleen Kirk** is Assistant Director of International Student and Scholar Services at the Georgia Institute of Technology, managing bilateral exchange programs for the Office of International Education. She earned bachelor's degrees in both philosophy and music from Valdosta State University, and a master's degree in musicology from Northern Arizona University. She is currently pursuing a PhD in International Conflict Management at Kennesaw State University, focusing her research on cultural exchange, adjustment, and needs-based assessment of first-year international student programming.

**Brandon D. Lundy, PhD** is Professor of Anthropology and Associate Director in the School of Conflict Management, Peacebuilding and Development at Kennesaw State University. He serves as the editor of the journal *Economic Anthropology* and is on the Editorial Team for the *Journal of Peacebuilding and Development*. Lundy's research focuses on sustainable livelihoods including ethnoeconomics, transnational labor migration, and entrepreneurship. He is the editor or coeditor of five books including *Atone: Religion, Conflict, and Reconciliation* (Lexington Books 2018), two on *Indigenous Conflict Management Strategies* (Lexington Books 2014, 2015), and one on *Teaching Africa* (Indiana University Press 2013). He has published in many edited books and journals including *Border Crossing* (2017), *African Arts* (2016), *African Identities* (2015), and *Migration*

*Letters* (2011). Lundy has also served the US Department of State as a country specialist (Guinea-Bissau).

**Marcus Marktanner, PhD** is Associate Professor of Economics and International Conflict Management at Kennesaw State University. He holds a joint appointment in the Department of Economics, Finance, and Quantitative Analysis and the PhD Program in International Conflict Management. He received his PhD from the Technical University of Ilmenau, Germany, where he examined the political economy of the economic transformation process of former socialist economies. Before joining the faculty of Kennesaw State University, Dr. Marktanner held teaching and research positions in Lebanon, US, and Germany. His research focuses on comparative economics, economic development, and conflict economics. He has consulted the United Nations Economic and Social Commission for Western Asia (ESCWA) and the World Food Program (WFP). He also regularly contributes to the work of the Konrad Adenauer Foundation as an author and speaker on the topic of the social market economy.

**Erin McCandless, PhD** is a widely published scholar and practitioner with over two decades of experience working on and in conflict-affected settings, broadly on issues of peacebuilding, statebuilding, governance, development, and resilience and their intersections. Dr. McCandless is cofounder of the international, refereed *Journal of Peacebuilding and Development*. She consults widely across the United Nations system and with other international organizations and is director of the research and policy dialogue project "Forging Resilient Social Contracts: States and Societies Building Sustainable Peace." She also serves as the first civil society Cochair of the New Deal Implementation Working Group, on behalf of the Civil Society Platform for Peacebuilding and Statebuilding. She has over 50 publications, including three books and several important United Nations policy reports.

**Almuth D. Merkel** is pursuing a PhD in International Conflict Management in the School of Conflict Management, Peacebuilding and Development at Kennesaw State University. She holds a bachelor's degree in ecotrophology (nutrition science and household economics) and a master's degree in food and agribusiness, both from Anhalt University of Applied Sciences in Germany. Her research focuses on the economic causes and consequences of conflicts, with a particular interest in food insecurity as a cause of conflict and the concept of the social market economy as a peacebuilding formula. Her research is applied in nature and data-driven, including economic impact studies, public policy simulations, policy programming, and country-risk assessments.

**Ilham Nasser, PhD** is Senior Researcher and Education Specialist at Salam Institute for Peace and Justice and previously an associate professor in Early Childhood Education at George Mason University in Virginia, United States. A Palestinian-American, Dr. Nasser holds a PhD in Human Development and Child Study and has spent over twenty-five years in teacher training and research in different educational settings in the US., Africa, and the Middle East. She has researched and published on the topic of teacher development, including teacher motivation, teacher preparation and professional development, and teaching for peace with focus on exploring classroom practices and pedagogues to promote peace and understanding. Her recent research on teaching for forgiveness in Arab schools includes five countries and more than 590 teachers.

**Edwin N. Njonguo** is a PhD candidate in International Conflict Management and teaches in the Interdisciplinary Studies Department at Kennesaw State University. He has published with the *International Journal on World Peace* and *Oxford University Press*. Edwin is a member of the scientific committee of the Peace and Conflict Resolution Conference. His research interests include transitional justice and human rights, alternative dispute resolution, conflict resolution and management, peacebuilding, and (un)constitutional political power change in Africa. He is presently researching how the power dynamics in the international geopolitical system impact decision-making and the situations that appear before the International Criminal Court. He received an MA in Conflict Analysis and Dispute Resolution from Salisbury University.

**Luc Noiset, PhD** is Associate Professor of Economics at Kennesaw State University. He has worked for the Office of Tax Analysis at the US Department of the Treasury in Washington, DC and was the Treasury's resident representative to the Latvian Minister of Finance and the resident Tax Policy Director of a large US government fiscal reform project advising the Russian government during the 1990s. Dr. Noiset has since worked as a tax policy advisor in many countries, including many countries of the former Soviet Union, as well as in Egypt and Vietnam. His research focuses on the role of government in free market economies.

**Thania Paffenholz, PhD**, is an internationally recognized expert in support of peace processes with 25 years of work experience as an academic, a policy advisor, and a practitioner. She is the Director of the Inclusive Peace and Transition Initiative (IPTI) at the Graduate Institute of International and Development Studies in Geneva. Dr. Paffenholz advises the United Nations, the European Union and other regional organizations, governments, non-governmental organizations as well as conflict parties, and has supported peace processes in over a dozen countries since 1992. Her main fields of expertise are mediation and peace process design, strategy development for actors involved in mediation and peacebuilding, inclusive peace negotiations and implementation including National Dialogues, civil society in peace processes, planning and evaluation of peace processes, and the development-peace nexus. Her publications are widely used by scholars and practitioners and include the books *Peacebuilding: A Field Guide* (Boulder 2000), *Aid for Peace* (2007), and *Civil Society and Peacebuilding: A Critical Assessment* (Boulder 2010). In recognition of her work, Dr. Paffenholz received the prestigious Wihuri International Prize in 2015.

**Madhawa "Mads" Palihapitiya** is the Associate Director at the Massachusetts Office of Public Collaboration at the John W. McCormack Graduate School of Policy and Global Studies at the University of Massachusetts Boston. From 2002 to 2006, Mads codesigned and implemented a unique "third generation," community-based conflict early warning system for Sri Lanka and managed a vast network of violence interrupters. The system used events data and local knowledge systems in communities to prevent and/or reduce violence. From 2013 to 2017, Mads was the lead consultant of a conflict early warning system designed and implemented as part of the Training of Leaders on Religious and National Coexistence (TOLERANCE) project in Nigeria, which was a five-year service and research project funded by the United States Agency for International Development (USAID). As part of this project, he was able to help the design and implementation of a community-based early warning system at the Interfaith Mediation Center in Kaduna,

Nigeria. Mads also designed a unique cloud-based conflict early warning database called "Waayama" for tracking violence using geospatial and events data.

**Pasan M. Palihapitiya** holds a master's degree in Network Systems Security from Swinburne University of Technology Australia and a Bachelor's degree in Information Technology from Deakin University Australia. An IT consultant and a cybersecurity researcher with over fifteen years of experience in the information communication and telecommunications industries, he worked with Ericsson in the 4G network rollout in Australia. Pasan has worked as a systems administrator and worked in IT incident management in large global organizations.

**Valerie Puleo** works at the Udall Foundation's US Institute for Environmental Conflict Resolution (USIECR). Her projects involve building consensus and enhancing collaboration in environmental, natural resource, and public lands issues. Valerie is also a trained mediator and provides community mediation services in Washington, DC, as well as reentry mediation for returning citizens at the DC jail. She also serves on the Leadership Council of the Association for Conflict Resolution's Environment and Public Policy Section. Before joining the Udall Foundation, Valerie worked on environmental peacebuilding issues in the Middle East, Europe, and Central America, and public housing and homelessness prevention issues in Boston. Valerie holds a dual MA in Natural Resources and Sustainable Development from the School of International Service at American University and the United Nations-mandated University for Peace and a BA in International Affairs and Middle East Studies from Northeastern University.

**Susan S. Raines, PhD** is Professor of Conflict Management at Kennesaw State University and the Editor-in-Chief of *Conflict Resolution Quarterly*. She owns Collaboration & ADR Services, LLC, through which she offers Conflict Management training and intervention services. She has mediated more than 15,000 cases around the world, including disputes involving trade, international migration, business-to-business issues, and environmental concerns. She is the author of *Conflict Management for Managers: Resolving Workplace, Client, and Policy Disputes* and *Expert Mediators: Overcoming Mediation Challenges in Workplace, Family, and Community Conflicts*, as well as dozens of peer-reviewed articles in a wide variety of journals.

**Debarati Sen, PhD** is a cultural anthropologist with training in sociology and gender and women's studies. She holds a dual appointment between School of Conflict Management, Peacebuilding and Development and the Anthropology program at Kennesaw State University. Her research takes place at the confluence of cultural anthropology, development studies, gender studies, and conflict studies. For fifteen years her research examined gendered mobilizations around sustainable development in rural India, culminating in her ethnographic monograph, *Everyday Sustainability: Gender Justice and Fair Trade Tea in Darjeeling* (Albany, NY: SUNY Press 2017). In 2018 her book won two major awards: the International Studies Association's Global Development Section Book Award and Gloria E. Anzaldúa Book Prize from National Women's Studies Association. Grants from the Wenner-Gren Foundation, the US National Science Foundation, Princeton University, and Columbia University funded her research. Dr. Sen serves pro bono on the American Association of University Women's (AAUW's) national fellowship review team. At KSU she cochairs the Presidential Commission on Race and Ethnic Diversity.

**Loubna Skalli Hanna, PhD** joined the American University in 2004 after teaching for 15 years at Moroccan Universities and Higher Institutes of Learning. Her research is grounded in the interdisciplinary tradition and examines issues at the intersection of development, politics, gender, youth, culture, and communication. She has published extensively in academic journals including *Gender and Society*, *Middle East Journal*, *International Feminist Journal of Politics*, *Journal of Middle East Women Studies*, and *Journal of Culture and Communication in the Middle East*. She has authored two books and has two forthcoming books with Columbia University Press (*Middle Eastern Youth*) and the Brandeis University Press (*Gender Politics and the Arab Spring*). An active member of international organizations, Skalli Hanna served on the Scientific Committee of the UNESCO Chair "Women and their Rights" (Morocco) and the Board of Directors of the Maghreb Center, a Washington-based think tank for policy research on North Africa. She has consulted with numerous development actors and agencies including World Learning, InterMedia and Broadcasting Board of Governors, the US Department of Labor, and the US Department of State.

**Lina Tuschling** is a PhD candidate in International Conflict Management at Kennesaw State University, where she also teaches International Relations. She holds a Masters degree in Peace and Security Studies from the University of Hamburg, Germany. Her current research focuses on national and military identities in the context of opposition movements. Other research interests include civil-military relations, divided societies, nonviolence, and the role of dissent in democratic societies. Geographically, her research focuses on the Middle East.

**Maureen Wilson** is a PhD candidate in International Conflict Management at Kennesaw State University. She received her MA in Social Science from Georgia Southern University. She teaches courses in international relations, comparative politics, and global issues. Her research interests include international law, international courts, and human rights. In her dissertation, she examines the influence of domestic legal traditions on transitional justice choices and outcomes.

# Part I

# Introduction to international conflict management

# 1 Introduction to international conflict management

*Charity Butcher and Maia Carter Hallward*[1]

## Introduction

World War I was called "the war to end all wars," and after the end of the Cold War, some scholars envisioned a *Pax Americana*, or a period of relative peace managed by the United States. However, violent conflict continues to plague the international system, demonstrating a great destructive capacity. War no longer affects only uniformed soldiers on the battlefield; instead, civilians are increasingly affected directly by inter- and intra-state wars. Advances in technology have resulted in changes in how wars are waged, how people learn about them, and how scholars, practitioners, and ordinary citizens can work to prevent, mitigate, and resolve violent conflict. Seemingly intractable conflicts with large numbers of domestic and international players, high death tolls and environmental fallout, and major negative impacts on neighboring (and distant) countries, such as those waged in Syria, the Democratic Republic of Congo (DRC), and Yemen at time of writing in 2019, have increasingly compelled the international community to explore methods beyond those in the traditional diplomatic toolbox. Civil society – which includes most of you reading this book – plays an increasing role in international conflict management, and any individual with a cell phone has the capacity to help track and respond to conflict at home and abroad. In a globally interconnected world, it is incumbent on all individuals to acquire the skills to actively promote and engage in constructive conflict management.

The desire to manage conflict peacefully is not new. World War I (1914–1918) and World War II (1939–1945) resulted in tens of millions of deaths around the world, including soldiers drafted from colonial holdings, those deemed politically or socially undesirable and who were murdered in Nazi work and death camps or in the Soviet gulags, and those exterminated by the nuclear bombs dropped on Hiroshima and Nagasaki. The destructive nature of World War I spurred the international community to create the League of Nations in 1920, a body that was intended to prevent another major war from occurring through institutionalizing the concept of collective security, whereby any member was obligated to come to the aid of any other member who was attacked. Although it was ultimately unsuccessful, in part due to the failure of the United States to join, the League of Nations specifically promoted a number of conflict management mechanisms that are now taken for granted in the international system, including efforts at disarmament and the management and settlement of disputes through negotiation and arbitration.[2] With the onset of World War II, the League of Nations collapsed, but the idea of an international organization designed to promote international peace and security continued. Following World War II, the international community created the United Nations, updated to reflect lessons learned as a result of the failures of the League and the devastation of World War II.

Created in 1945, the United Nations (UN) has evolved as the international community has expanded in size and is faced with new challenges. Reflecting the global power structure at the end of World War II, the United Nations is divided into the Security Council, with five permanent members (the nuclear powers and victors at the end of the war), and the General Assembly, in which every state has a vote. Article I of the United Nations Charter outlines the organization's purpose, which includes to work collectively to suppress acts of aggression, to help settle international disputes, to develop friendly relations based on equal rights and self-determination of peoples, and to promote cooperation on a range of international problems of an economic, social, cultural, or humanitarian character. This book takes as its starting point the international framework (albeit imperfect) established by the UN to examine a range of efforts taken since its creation to promote and maintain international peace and security.

## International law and organizations

In addition to the UN, a series of international laws and organizations were established with the intent of preventing atrocities seen during the two World Wars, including two major bodies of law: humanitarian law and human rights law. While agreements protecting the wounded and sick, as well as religious and medical personnel, during wartime go back to 1864, these laws were updated and expanded in 1949 in the Geneva Conventions, which codify international humanitarian law and regulate armed conflict. The Second Geneva Convention of 1949 expanded previous agreements, including the 1907 Hague Conventions, to protect wounded, sick, and shipwrecked members of the armed forces at sea. The Third Geneva Convention updated laws for treatment of prisoners of war, and a Fourth Geneva Convention was created specifically to protect civilian populations. While the first three Geneva Conventions of 1949 built on previous agreements protecting combatants, the fourth was new, aimed at addressing the dangers facing non-combatants due to new military techniques and challenges facing civilians in occupied territories.[3]

Over 190 countries have signed and ratified the Geneva Conventions, signaling a commitment to safeguarding wounded and civilian bystanders. These agreements, however, are specific to conduct once states are engaged in war. They do not adjudicate regarding a state's decision to go to war, which falls more under the purview of the United Nations Security Council, tasked with upholding international peace and security and determining whether a war was a justifiable act of self-defense or an act of aggression. Further, these Conventions do not address the treatment of civilians and issues of human rights outside of wartime. The United Nations Universal Declaration of Human Rights (UDHR) was drafted by representatives from around the world and proclaimed by the UN General Assembly on December 10, 1948. This declaration outlines political and civil rights, as well as social, economic, and cultural rights, that are considered fundamental rights of humankind. Unlike the Geneva Conventions, the UDHR considers rights more broadly and suggests that states are obligated to protect the rights of their citizens.

The international community has increasingly worked to protect populations from the most heinous acts of violence, including genocide, war crimes, crimes against humanity, and ethnic cleansing. The International Criminal Court (ICC) was established by the Rome Stature in 1998 and entered into force in 2002. This court was unique in the international system as individuals were the responsible agents to the court, not states. Prior to the ICC, international courts, such as the International Court of Justice, only held states accountable for war crimes. While individuals had been held accountable in ad hoc tribunals set up following major conflicts, such as the Nuremburg and Tokyo Tribunals following World War II, the ICC was the first large-scale international attempt to hold individuals accountable for their actions during war.

The movement toward protecting civilians from genocide, war crimes, ethnic cleansing, and crimes against humanity has led to the Responsibility to Protect (R2P) doctrine in the international community, which suggests that states are first responsible to protect their civilians from such crimes, but if states are unable or unwilling to take responsibility for their citizens, or are the perpetuators of these crimes, the international community has a responsibility to intervene to protect these individuals. The R2P doctrine is still quite controversial but has clear importance for any discussion of conflict management. On the one hand, the R2P doctrine can help protect civilians from significant human rights abuses. On the other hand, R2P could be used by the international community or individual states to justify interventionist policies that could escalate, or even instigate, conflicts, as was the case with the NATO intervention in Libya in 2011. Finding the right balance between protecting civilians and creating or escalating conflict is a challenge faced by the international community.

## Civil society approaches

Over the past decades civil society has played an increasing role in international conflict management, a complement to the state-based structure of the United Nations and its associated institutions. While civil society as a concept is quite diverse, it is generally understood to be comprised of voluntary activity between the state, the economic sphere, and the family/private sphere (Spurk 2010). Historically, civil society has been considered a Western notion, particularly with the professionalization of NGOs that had emerged with donor requirements for organizations receiving government aid. Civil society in other contexts has been comprised more of voluntaristic and charitable associations. While much of the scholarship has explored civil society in the context of democratization, an increased focus on the role of civil society in international conflict management and peacebuilding has occurred in the past decades, particularly since the end of the Cold War and an expansion of the scholarly focus beyond the dyadic rivalry between the United States and Soviet Union.

One of the first bodies of research on civil society and international conflict management focuses on Track II diplomacy, whereby a "second track" of influential members of society, such as academics and/or other socially engaged leaders, distinct from official Track I government representatives, from societies in conflict come together to problem solve and learn new communication and conflict management skills such as active listening. Often facilitated by trained conflict management scholar-practitioners, workshops have been held in interactable conflicts, such as the Israeli-Palestinian conflict and the Cyprus conflict (d'Estrée 2008; Kelman 2008; Rouhana 1995). According to an earlier generation of thinking by Lederach and others, Track II, or middle-level leaders, were able to connect government elites (Track I) and mass publics at the grassroots level (Track III) through their linkages to both constituencies (Lederach 1997). In practice, however, this assumption has not always resulted in tangible results, and many have criticized this triangle model and Track II workshops more broadly for failing to adequately delineate mechanisms for social change and social diffusion from the middle-level out. Further, a middle-level focus, particularly if it is donor-driven, can lead to the undue influence of outside actors, as well as the neglect of both the political process and grassroots needs and interests (Paffenholz 2015).

There is a long history of civil society engagement in conflict management and peace-building, from religious actors mediating conflict to actions taken by women or youth or artists to affect social change (Boulding 2000; Curle 1996). Several volumes document success stories of civil society efforts around the world, such as *People Building Peace I and II* collected by the European Centre for Conflict Prevention (van Tongeren et al. 2005). Civil society actors have also led the way in many civil resistance campaigns around the globe, most famously epitomized by Gandhi's movement for Indian independence, the US Civil Rights movement, and the student-led Otpor movement that brought down Milosevic in Serbia, which have also been documented in a range of volumes (see for example Ackerman and DuVall 2000; Schock 2015; Zunes, Kurtz, and Asher 1999).

## Current challenges for international conflict management

Despite the numerous efforts of state and civil society actors to create mechanisms for resolving and managing international conflict, complex and intractable conflicts continue to be waged by a range of actors around the globe. Further, with a recent rise in nationalist movements, states and non-state actors alike have exhibited decreased trust in international institutions and conflict management mechanisms. The United States withdrew from the Joint Comprehensive Plan of Action (JCPOA) in May 2018, for example, demonstrating a distrust in multilateral diplomacy as a means toward reducing tensions between Iran and its neighbors (Smith 2019). Further, conflict management mechanisms such as the adjudication leg of the World Trade Organization (WTO) have been undermined, as powerful members such as the United States have repeatedly blocked the appointment of new judges. While some statistics suggest that interstate war has declined, others point to the rise in intrastate conflict (SIPRI 2019). In July 2019, the International Crisis Group pointed to conflict risks in countries including Mali, the Democratic Republic of Congo (DRC), Malawi, Iran, Saudi Arabia, Yemen, and Algeria, with deteriorated situations in additional countries including Nagorno-Karabakh (Azerbaijan), Kazakhstan, Honduras, and Haiti (International Crisis Group 2019). There is increasing concern by many around the world that the key mechanisms developed to curb violent conflict at the international level are being systematically undermined. Knowledge of these mechanisms and their importance is critical to ensuring their survival in decades to come.

At the same time, many of the existing interstate mechanisms for international conflict management seem insufficient regarding several pressing global challenges, including climate change, terrorism, and the proliferation of non-state actors in the global arena. While none of these challenges is new, their reach has expanded, and their impacts resonate on a larger scale than they did previously. Accelerated effects of climate change impact livelihoods and patterns of migration, which in turn contribute to a variety of conflicts. Complex wars such as those in the DRC and Syria that involve myriad non-state armed groups (in addition to state parties) make the prospect of finding a negotiated agreement increasingly challenging. The current and new generations of scholars and practitioners must devote time and attention to refining existing mechanisms and developing new ones in order to effectively adapt skills and approaches to address the vital need for international conflict management in today's world.

## Organization of the book to follow

The field of international conflict management is interdisciplinary, with scholars approaching the field through a range of lenses shaped and informed by their disciplinary backgrounds. Chapter 2 introduces the diverse ontological and epistemological assumptions held by various scholarly disciplines and approaches to the field of study and provides a background for understanding some of the different theories and assumptions found in different approaches to international conflict management. The chapter also provides an introduction to the key concepts and terms in the field of international conflict management and a brief historical overview of the emergence of the field and introduces key concepts and the evolution of terms to describe and define the field.

Following Chapter 2, the remainder of the book is divided into two sections: one that considers the various mechanisms of managing international conflict, and a second that considers cross-cutting themes that are important in the field of international conflict management.

### *Mechanisms of international conflict management*

The section on mechanisms of international conflict management begins with traditional approaches to conflict management, including negotiation, mediation, peacebuilding, and peacekeeping, along with approaches that, while not new, are more recently added to the mainstream, such as civil resistance, transitional justice, and reconciliation. Negotiation is often used in diplomatic channels and between states in international bodies. In Chapter 3, Doleys and Hedeen examine various approaches to negotiation as an international conflict management mechanism, focusing on cases such as Great Britain's exit from the European Union (Brexit) to illustrate the role of negotiation in matters of security, trade, and human rights. Mediation theories, processes, and skills are increasingly applied to the resolution of conflicts within and between nation-states as well as between governmental and non-governmental organizations seeking to work together to provide humanitarian relief. *Mediation* has become a catchall term, often referring to collaborative problem-solving and consensus-building processes used to make collective decisions regarding a wide range of issues including the environment, trade, and diplomacy. In Chapter 4, Raines and Foutz examine the strategies and stages used in successful mediation, drawing on the cases of Northern Ireland and Colombia to illustrate.

The study and practice of nonviolent resistance, also called civil resistance, people power, and nonviolent revolution, has a long history in the field of peace studies, but has only more recently been deemed a subject worthy of serious study in mainstream social science scholarship. In Chapter 5, Hallward and Tuschling reflect on theoretical debates found in both classic and contemporary scholarship and practices of civil resistance and explore debates regarding the nature of power, the role of coercion, and the definition of *violence* used by scholars and practitioners to delimit what "counts" as civil resistance, focusing particularly on the Palestinian popular struggle in the first and second intifadas and the contemporary boycott, divestment, and sanctions (BDS) movement.

Peacekeeping as a construct has evolved with the configurations of international politics. In Chapter 6, Franke and Guttieri focus on how peacekeeping has been understood since World War II, examine the role of peacekeeping in international politics, and explore challenges regarding ethics, resources, and questions of might and right. Peacekeeping has increasingly expanded to incorporate elements of peacebuilding and other conflict management mechanisms. In Chapter 7, McCandless examines the history of peacebuilding itself, exploring the evolution of multiple generations of peacebuilding, including liberal, hybrid, and local approaches, using the case of Liberia as an example to illustrate many of the contemporary challenges facing peacebuilding scholars and practitioners.

For states emerging from periods of conflict and repression, transitional justice seeks to deal with legacies of abuse and to end impunity for those responsible for humanity's gravest crimes. Transitional justice aims to prevent future human rights violations, provide reparations for victims, and contribute to national reconciliation and peacebuilding processes. In Chapter 8, Wilson and Njonguo discuss the development of transitional justice mechanisms over time, emphasizing the distinction between domestic and international processes, the critiques of these various processes, and the application of multiple methods in the post-conflict period. Underlying some approaches to transitional justice is the desire for reconciliation, a complex process both conceptually and in practice. Distinct from but complementary to state-led transitional justice mechanisms, scholars and practitioners have identified several core components of the reconciliation process, including acknowledgement, apology, reparation, and forgiveness. In Chapter 9, Abu-Nimer and Nasser focus on the role of education in building societies open to the possibility of reconciliation and forgiveness, drawing on cases from the Arab Middle East to determine similarities and differences in teachers' willingness to teach reconciliation and forgiveness.

### Cross-cutting themes in international conflict management

Part III of the book highlights key cross-cutting themes within the field of international conflict management. These themes are chosen because they are complex, multi-faceted issues that are extremely important in the current international climate and consequently can benefit from an interdisciplinary lens.

Contemporary conflict management is a collective enterprise that requires broad participation by a multitude of local and international actors. In Chapter 10, Paffenholz outlines seven modalities for civil society participation in conflict management processes, using examples from Syria and elsewhere to show civil society peacebuilding efforts in action. The chapter also acknowledges that resistance to including civil society in negotiations persists, due to the fear that enhanced participation challenges the consensus-building process, and makes it more difficult to reach a peace agreement. However, even when civil society actors are included, Paffenholz cautions that it does not necessarily mean they will have an influence over the proceedings and outcomes of the negotiations.

Civil society actors can be involved in international conflict management outside formal negotiation channels. While it is commonly understood that Information and Communication Technologies (ICTs) serve to spread hatred, demonize others, and foment violence, they are also instrumental in mitigating tensions, preventing violence, and transforming conflict. Chapter 11, by Palihapitiya, Palihapitiya, and Bock, describes how ICTs can have a positive impact in reducing violent conflict. Comparing ICT usage to New Social Movements (NSMs), the authors examine the opportunities and challenges presented by digital technologies, including using social media for organizing and communicating, employing digital mapping and crowdsourcing to track events of cooperation and conflict, and texting large groups of people in counteracting rumors.

Identities are often viewed as important factors to consider within conflict contexts. The role of gender in conflict settings is an area of research that is ever evolving. Using feminist methodology in Chapter 12, Sen, Hanna, and Junker analyze research on how gender – the full range of sociological categorization ranging from hypermasculinity to hyperfemininity – impacts and is impacted by conflict. Going beyond the popular "women as victims in conflict" trope, this chapter explores the motivations, opportunities, and limitations that guide women's activities in conflict settings and considers how gender norms affect both women's and men's experiences during and following conflict. Ethnic and religious identities are often seen as drivers of conflict, and thus are important issues within the broader international conflict management field. In Chapter 13, Butcher and Kirk consider the causes of ethnic and religious conflicts and discuss case studies on the Uighurs in China as well as the Rohingya crisis in Myanmar to illustrate the theories and practices that help in preventing ethnic conflicts from beginning or recurring and help manage and mitigate these conflicts once they are underway.

While competition over resources can lead to violent conflict, cooperation around shared economic objectives can serve as a peacebuilding tool, as was the case in Europe after World War II. In Chapter 14, Marktanner, Merkel, and Noiset introduce key economic concepts and approaches to resolving such problems and discuss the theory and application of economic thought as it relates to contemporary international conflict management. Economic need and violent conflict are drivers for migration, the topic of Chapter 15, by Lundy and Hayes. Refugees and migrants can result from international conflicts, such as the millions of people affected by the wars in Syria and the Democratic Republic of the Congo (DRC), and such human displacement can also give rise to conflict, as evidenced in the European reaction to refugees or the destabilizing effect of displaced populations in neighboring countries. Using examples from Myanmar and Rwanda, the chapter explores the politics of migration from the perspectives of human needs, human rights, and security, highlighting the interdisciplinary nature of the dilemmas surrounding these issues.

In Chapter 16, Abitbol and Puleo examine the multiple ways that environment and conflict intersect, using a framework that examines the impact of conflict on the environment, as well as environment and environmental resources as both sources of conflict and potential opportunities for conflict resolution. The chapter presents two case studies that examine the complexity of the environment-conflict nexus, water relations between Israel and the Palestinians, and the complex and evolving relationship between the Federal Government of the United States and Tribal Nations, including the successes and limitations of environmental conflict resolution processes related to infrastructure, natural resources, and cultural and historic properties.

Finally, the book concludes by tying together the various chapters with a concluding discussion of the strengths and weaknesses found in existing conflict management mechanisms and an exploration of the interaction between the standard repertoire of international conflict management approaches with the complex array of issues facing international conflict management scholars and practitioners. After analyzing key themes and trends identified by the chapter contributors, the conclusion critically discusses key challenges and unanswered questions, including limitations of existing theories and the current policy climate in which trust in the global architecture of international organizations is waning and nationalist sentiment is rising.

## Notes

1 Authors have contributed equally to this chapter and are listed in random order.
2 The full Covenant of the League of Nations can be found here: Accessed July 31, 2019. http://avalon. law.yale.edu/20th_century/leagcov.asp.
3 For more on the Geneva Conventions, see the International Committee of the Red Cross (ICRC) website: Accessed June 26, 2019. www.icrc.org/en/war-and-law/treaties-customary-law/geneva-conventions.

## References and further reading

Ackerman, Peter, and Jack DuVall. 2000. *A Century of Nonviolent Conflict*. New York, NY: St. Martin's Press.

Boulding, Elise. 2000. *Cultures of Peace: The Hidden Side of History*. Syracuse, NY: Syracuse University Press.

Curle, Adam. 1996. *Another Way: Positive Response to Contemporary Violence*. Oxford: Jon Carpenter Publishing.

d'Estrée, Tamra Pearson. 2008. "Problem-Solving Approaches." In *The SAGE Handbook of Conflict Resolution*, edited by Jacob Bercovitch, Victor Kremenyuk, and I. William Zartman, 143–71. Thousand Oaks, CA: Sage Publications.

*International Crisis Group*. 2019. "CrisisWatch: Tracking Conflict Worldwide." Accessed August 1, 2019. www.crisisgroup.org/crisiswatch?utm_source=Sign+Up+to+Crisis+Group%27s+Email+Updates& utm_campaign=1e62c71ab4-EMAIL_CAMPAIGN_2019_07_01_06_33&utm_medium=email&utm_term=0_1dab8c11ea-1e62c71ab4-359776721#overview.

Kelman, Herbert C. 2008. "Evaluating the Contributions of Interactive Problem Solving to the Resolution of Ethnonational Conflicts." *Peace and Conflict: Journal of Peace Psychology* 14 (1): 29–60.

Lederach, John Paul. 1997. *Building Peace: Sustainable Reconciliation in Divided Societies*. Washington, DC: US Institute of Peace Press.

Paffenholz, Thania. 2010. *Civil Society and Peacebuilding: A Critical Assessment*. Boulder, CO: Lynne Rienner Publishers.

———. 2015. "Unpacking the Local Turn in Peacebuilding: A Critical Assessment Towards an Agenda for Future Research." *Third World Quarterly* 36 (5): 857–74.

Rouhana, Nadim. 1995. "The Dynamics of Joint Thinking Between Adversaries in International Conflict: Phases of the Continuing Problem-Solving Workshop." *Political Psychology* 16 (2): 321–45.

Schock, Kurt. 2015. *Civil Resistance Today*. Cambridge: Polity Press.

Smith, Dan. 2019. "The US Withdrawal from the Iran Deal: One Year On." *SIPRI*. Accessed August 1, 2019. www.sipri.org/commentary/expert-comment/2019/us-withdrawal-iran-deal-one-year.

Spurk, Christopher. 2010. "Understanding Civil Society." In *Civil Society and Peacebuilding: A Critical Assessment*, edited by Thania Paffenholz. Boulder, CO: Lynne Rienner Publishers.

Stockholm International Peace Research Institute (SIPRI). 2019. "Homepage." Accessed July 31, 2019. www.sipri.org/.

van Tongeren, Paul, Malin Brenk, Marte Hellema, and Juliette Verhoeven, eds. 2005. *People Building Peace II: Successful Stories of Civil Society*. Boulder, CO: Lynne Rienner Publishers.

Zunes, Stephen, Lester R. Kurtz, and Sarah Beth Asher, eds. 1999. *Nonviolent Social Movements: A Geographical Perspective*. Malden, MA: Blackwell Publishers.

# 2 Key theories of international conflict management

*Maia Carter Hallward and Charity Butcher*[1]

## Introduction

The field of international conflict management is interdisciplinary, with scholars approaching the field through a range of lenses shaped and informed by their disciplinary backgrounds. This chapter introduces students to the diverse ontological and epistemological assumptions held by various scholarly disciplines and approaches to the field of study and provides students with a background for understanding some of the different theories and assumptions found in different approaches to international conflict management. The chapter provides an overview of key theories that have been prevalent within the international conflict management field and that have shaped dominant approaches to approaching conflict, including the democratic peace theory, the contact hypothesis, social identity theory, greed vs. grievance, and human needs theory that stem from a variety of academic disciplines, including political science, sociology, economics, anthropology, peace studies, psychology, and geography. The chapter goes beyond the first- and second-generation thinkers in the field to engage with more recent developments including the idea of "new wars," the local turn in peacebuilding, the role of non-state actors, and the use of hybrid, cross-sectoral approaches. Underscoring the book's intention to link theory and practice, the chapter also explores the evolution in peace and conflict approaches in recent decades, including the evolution of the peacekeeping, peacemaking, and peacebuilding architecture of the United Nations and its attendant challenges.

## International relations paradigms relevant to international conflict management

Following thirty years of war that devastated the European continent, in 1648 the Peace of Westphalia created a new world order and what is known as the modern state system. One key concept that arose from the Peace of Westphalia was sovereignty, the idea that the supreme authority to rule within a state belonged solely to that state and its leader. This idea set the stage for the international relations concept of noninterference, where states do not interfere in the domestic politics of other states. While Europe was able to live in relative peace for quite some time, eventually conflict would rise again, with World Wars I and II once again devastating Europe. In the wake of the failed liberal institution of the League of Nations and the failure of peace in the interwar period, realism became the dominant paradigm in international relations.

### Realism

Realist theories have their roots in thinkers such as Thucydides, who wrote in the fifth century BCE about the struggles among Greek city-states in his *History of the Peloponnesian*

*War*, Niccolò Machiavelli in his work *The Prince* (2003 [1532]), and Thomas Hobbes in his *Leviathan* (2009 [1651]). Thucydides focuses on how powerful states will do what they are able in order to maintain their power and how weaker states will have little recourse against these powerful states. Machiavelli notes the importance of the military as a source of power and explains that leaders should be feared. Hobbes discusses the natural state of the world as one in which people are out to help only themselves, with some type of force (which he calls a "Leviathan") being required to keep people's human nature in check; otherwise there will be a constant state of conflict and war. For Hobbes, this Leviathan is government; people will need to give up some of their freedom to the government and their leaders in order to gain security.

These early thinkers perceive human nature as selfish and power-seeking. Early realist theorists extrapolate this idea of human nature to that of states, arguing that states are also power-seeking and self-interested. In such a system, where states are seeking only their own interests, states cannot rely on others to protect them. While individual states may have governments, or "Leviathans" as Hobbes might describe, to keep people and their human nature in check, there is nothing similar in the international system to keep states in check. Instead, the international system is characterized by anarchy, where every state must defend itself – what realists refer to as a self-help system. In such a system, realists argue that power becomes essentially important for states, as power is how states ensure their survival in such an anarchic world. Mercantilism, an economic concept in which countries promote trade but rely on protectionist strategies to create more profitable interactions, aligns with realist theory, as it promotes states acting based on their own national interests. Morgenthau (1948) argued that states should conduct their foreign policies based on their national interests, which were largely defined in terms of power, and that morals and ethical principles should not guide state behavior in the international system. This realist perception of ethical principles is certainly influenced by the failure of liberal principles and the League of Nations.

Owing to the importance of power for maintaining security, realists argue that states will build up their military power to be able to withstand an external attack and expand their own territory to create greater security. However, as states build up their military might, they make neighboring states more insecure about their own abilities, particularly because it is difficult to infer the intentions of other states with powerful militaries. As such, these states will also build up their military, in turn making their neighbors more insecure, and in the end create a security dilemma among states, where the very act of attempting to make their country more secure actually makes it less secure, because it encourages other countries to also build up their militaries. This security dilemma is a key part of realism, one that suggests that states generally find themselves in an uncertain world where they are unable to fully secure themselves. Such a security dilemma also makes cooperation between countries very difficult, as states tend to mistrust each other. Many of the conflict management approaches in this book are predicated on ways to reduce, or eliminate, this security dilemma through reframing conflict-related assumptions.

Further, realists see relations between states as zero-sum, where what is gained by one state will be lost by another. Consequently, realists focus on relative gain and are largely concerned with one state's gains relative to the gains of other states, as increases in one state's own power will give it an advantage in the international system. As a result, from a realist's perspective, a state should be skeptical of an agreement with another state where, even though both states gain, the other state gains more than your state. Such a situation would shift power in favor of your competitor, even though you may also gain. As discussed in subsequent chapters, conflict management approaches also challenge this zero-sum assumption, looking instead for what are called "win-win" solutions.

While traditional realists heavily emphasize the role of human nature in affecting the actions of states, neo-realists, or structural realists, like Kenneth Waltz (2001), focus more on the structure of the international system and how this structure creates an environment that affects the likelihood of conflict. Neo-realists tend to focus more on the distribution of power in the international system and how this might create greater security. Structural realists do not all agree on which kind of system is most stable. Some argue that a system in which power is balanced between major powers is most stable, as no single power can exert its will over others. When this balance of power shifts and a single state becomes a hegemon, these theorists argue that conflict is more likely. On the other hand, other structural realists argue that a system in which one state has a preponderance of power is the most stable, as no other state can challenge this hegemonic state, and the hegemonic state has a vested interest in maintaining peace and stability in the international system. These theorists argue that conflict is most likely as the hegemonic state declines relative to other states in the system, and that once another state reaches a place of parity in terms of power with the hegemon, there is likely to be conflict. While each of these theoretical perspectives has different prescriptions for what would make for a more peaceful world, they both emphasize the distribution of power within the international system, a structural element, as most important in determining peace and stability in the world.

## *Liberalism*

While realist theories often have a very conflictual view of the relations between states, liberal theories are more optimistic regarding the possibility of cooperation in the international system. Following World War I, the League of Nations was created to prevent another major war in Europe. The League was built on several key liberal ideas and principles, outlined in US President Woodrow Wilson's Fourteen Points (1918). Some of the key elements of Wilson's plan included open dialogue between states, free trade, a reduction in arms, and the formation of a collective security association of countries to guarantee the security of all states. The idea of collective security rests on the idea of strength in numbers – an "all for one" type of approach. In collective security organizations, such as the League of Nations, all countries agree to come to the defense of any country that is attacked, aiming to dissuade any country from attacking from fear of reprisal.

The idea that cooperation between states is not only possible, but helps provide security for the international system, is a key part of liberalism. Liberalism also views human nature more positively, with people seen as generally good and cooperative. Rather than focusing on relative gains, like realists, liberals tend to focus on absolute gains – situations where both parties might gain something at the same time. Such absolute gains can provide the foundation for cooperation among states, as states can pursue their own interests in ways that do not necessarily negatively impact others. Thus, liberals do not see the world in terms of a zero-sum game, where actors only win at the expense of others, but see that interactions can be mutually beneficial. Many of these liberal assumptions are embedded in conflict-resolution type approaches to international conflict management, including the quest for "win-win" solutions mentioned earlier.

For liberals, the international system is still characterized by anarchy, but this anarchy can be mitigated through cooperation. Liberals argue that cooperation between states, particularly over time as each state reciprocates positive interactions, can help build trust between states, which in turn helps overcome the security dilemma. In addition to the importance of cooperation for increasing security, liberals suggest that economic interdependence (particularly through free trade, where states are dependent upon each other economically) helps create some order in an otherwise anarchic international system. Further, the participation in international institutions can provide additional opportunities for cooperation among states and can also help socialize states into more cooperative norms in the system. Thus, for realists, free trade and interdependence, as well as participation in international institutions, are key factors to maintaining peace and security in the international system. The role of free trade in keeping peace is discussed further in Chapter 14 on economics.

Liberal theorists promote democratic peace theory, which is the idea that democratic countries are unlikely to go to war with each other. This is not to suggest that democracies are necessarily less war-prone than authoritarian countries, but that they appear unlikely to fight one another. This has led some states in the system to promote and even attempt to externally impose democracy on countries in hopes of increasing peace in the international system. Empirical studies have found significant support for democratic peace theory, though the theory does have some limitations. Democratic peace theory tends to only hold for strong, mature democracies. Mansfield and Snyder (1995) found that states that are in the process of democratizing are the most war-prone states in the entire system, particularly when the process of democratization, and elections specifically, occurred before the country was able to establish a strong and independent judiciary, set up a civilian-controlled military, and provide for the full protection of all citizens. In democratizing states without full internal security and rule of law, competing challengers in elections often rely on nationalist policies and tend to be overly expansionist and aggressive in their bid for power. Such a situation leads to a greater likelihood of aggressive foreign policies that will lead to conflict. Mansfield and Snyder's findings indicate that while democracies may be less likely to fight one another, the process of democratization can be wrought with conflict. As such, the imposition of democracy on other states to increase peace could be a dangerous and counterproductive policy. Some of these challenges will be discussed further in Chapter 6 on peacekeeping and Chapter 7 on peacebuilding.

### Alternative international relations theories

Realism and liberalism have been dominant within the international system for some time, but many people have pointed out that these various paradigms have limitations in explaining the international relations of states. Counter to both realism and liberalism, radicalism views international relations as a function of the unequal distribution of wealth and resources in the international system. Neo-Marxist in nature, radicalism sees the international system as hierarchically structured, with economic development unequal throughout the system. Those states that are the top of the hierarchy (core states) attain and maintain their status by extracting resources and wealth from those peripheral states on the bottom. The relationship between the core and periphery is one of exploitation, where the core exploits the periphery for its own benefit. This process of exploitation not only benefits the core, but it actively prevents the periphery from being able to develop. Further, since peripheral countries are often dependent upon the export of raw materials and agricultural goods while needing to import expensive manufactured goods, these countries often suffer from unequal terms of trade with core countries, perpetuating their dependent and underdeveloped nature. Multinational corporations are viewed as complicit and facilitating actors within this cycle of exploitation. One of the only ways to break out of this cycle of exploitation and dependency would be to change the hierarchical nature of the system, which is very unlikely. As such, while radical theory points to some key problems in the international system, it often is viewed as lacking

strong recommendations for how to address these problems. Structural approaches to conflict management often share many of these same assumptions regarding the need to addr
inequality in the global system as part of the quest for peace. One often hears the refrain
justice, no peace."

Constructivist theory, which gained prominence with social theorist Alexander Wendt
(1992), emerged in the wake of the Cold War to argue that the ways that states interact in
the international system are shaped by how states socially construct what they see as reality, including social structures such as anarchy. For some constructivists, the socially constructed norms of the international system shape the actions of actors. These norms can shape
and constrain the options that states see available to them and also shape their preferences
and interests. Other constructivists focus more on patterns of relationships, examining how
various actors interact with each other, as well as the nature of those interactions. For these
constructivists, not all actors in the international system interact with all others in the same
way, and some patterns of social ties may create different types of obligations or patterns of
reciprocity, while the absence of ties between some actors could contribute to conflict and/or
inequality. For both types of constructivists, power involves more than just military and economic might, which is more heavily promoted by realists and liberals, and encompasses ideas,
culture, language, and patterns of social ties – all of which shape norms and state behavior.

Feminist international relations theory also levies critiques at realism and liberalism, specifically related to the fact that women, their needs, and their actions are often left out of
the discussion of international relations and interactions between countries. J. Ann Tickner
(1992) was one of the early scholars to explore the role of gender in international relations. In
particular, she argues that realist views of national security are largely built from a consideration of the roles that men play within society, with little consideration of the roles that women
may play and the ways that women may be impacted by insecurity. Further, she discussed
the importance of considering both the conflictual and cooperative aspects of human nature
within discussions of how states may behave.

Another critique of realism and liberalism, also related to the critiques charged by feminists, is that both theories tend to take a very state-centric view of the world. While liberals
do also focus on actors outside the state, such as individuals and international institutions,
their approach to international relations is still quite state-centric, with considerations of
security and peace for both theories focusing on security and peace for states. Individuals
have increasingly noted that states are not the only actors to be affected by international
relations (especially war) and have advocated for a broader consideration of security, one
that encompasses the impact of conflict on the broader population of a country as well as
the environment. This turn toward human security has been seen throughout international
institutions such as the United Nations and ties security to more than the absence of war, or
negative peace, and begins to promote positive peace – where peace is tied to many other elements of human life, such as reduction in poverty, economic growth and development, and
equality. Peace-studies approaches to international conflict management often build on feminist assumptions by taking a more radical look at how power moves through the international
system and how individual, non-state actors can play a role in actively shaping processes
leading to a more holistic peace.

## Evolution of conflict management paradigms

The theory and practice of international conflict management has evolved along with international relations theories, reflecting changes in global politics and historical events. As noted

by Kriesberg (2009), the field of contemporary conflict resolution has a long history going back to Grecian times, but more recently rooted in the political philosophy of thinkers in the late eighteenth and nineteenth centuries, including Immanuel Kant and Jean Jacques Rousseau, who emphasized various moral and practical approaches to achieving perpetual peace. Kriesberg notes four main periods in the evolution of contemporary conflict resolution: 1914–1945, the period encompassing the two World Wars and the efforts to prevent war between them; 1946–1969, when a number of the international institutions such as the United Nations were created and scholarly outlets such as the *Journal of Conflict Resolution* and the International Peace Research Association were founded; 1970–1989, as the Conflict Resolution field became more established in university settings and the Cold War eased; and post-1989 as the field has expanded and diffused.

Scholarship and practice of international conflict management have evolved with changing international political currents. After World War I, deemed "the war to end all wars," the spirit was utopian, evident in Woodrow Wilson's Fourteen Points speech, which was designed to be "the programme of the world's peace" and included calls for disarmament, open diplomacy, and the removal of trade barriers.[2] After World War II and the start of the Cold War, theories dealt more with game theory, strategy (Axelrod 1980; Schelling 1981), and questions of disarmament (Benoit and Boulding 1963), as well as functional approaches that sought to build peace by focusing on cross-cutting issues of common concern, as was the case with the Coal and Steel Community that lay the groundwork for the European Economic Community, the forerunner of the European Union (Mitrany 1966). During this era several European peace research institutes were founded, notably the Peace Research Institute Oslo (PRIO), founded in 1959 and the Stockholm International Peace Research Institute (SIPRI), founded in 1966. Both of these Nordic-based institutes carry out rigorous research on the causes and consequences of armed conflict as well as make policy-relevant recommendations for building and sustaining peace.

Whereas European institutes such as PRIO and SIPRI focus on peace and well as conflict, examining structural and institutional approaches, approaches in the US have traditionally focused more on social-psychological and strategic dimensions, as evident in the 1979 founding of the Harvard Negotiation Project. The Harvard Negotiation Project has focused more on interpersonal and intergroup aspects of conflict management, publishing texts such as *Getting to YES* (Fisher and Ury 1981) and *Difficult Conversations: How to Discuss What Matters Most* (Stone, Patton, and Heen 1999). Theoretical models such as the dual-concern model, which sets forth approaches to conflict based on levels of concern for self and concern for others are associated with this approach to conflict management (Sorenson et al. 1999). In 1981, George Mason University launched the world's first Master of Science degree in Conflict Resolution, and in 1988 they awarded the world's first PhD in Conflict Resolution, paving the way for more of an academic and analytical approach to conflict resolution.

With the end of the Cold War, approaches to International Conflict Management expanded as (with the end of the UN Security Council stalemate) additional options were available for international action. A rise in UN peacekeeping action met with limited success and some dramatic failures, such as those in Rwanda – where peacekeepers left the country, thereby allowing a genocide to unfold – and Somalia, when peacekeepers were unable to prevent humanitarian disaster and political crisis. Further, the very limited mandate of peacekeeping missions in places like Bosnia, which in 1995 failed to prevent the Srebrenica massacre of more than 8,000 Bosniaks within an area that had been deemed a UN safe area, led to intense criticism of United Nations peacekeeping apparatus. Following these disasters, the United

Nations began to expand the nature and mission of its peacekeeping missions to include statebuilding and peacebuilding efforts. Despite these criticisms, research has indicated that peacekeeping is successful in increasing the duration of peace following peace agreements (Fortna 2008). More discussion on peacekeeping and peacebuilding can be found in Chapters 6 and 7.

In the context of expanding peace missions, Secretary-General of the United Nations Boutros Boutros-Ghali put forth his "Agenda for Peace" to the Security Council in January 1992, emphasizing the need for the UN to improve its work on conflict prevention as well as peacemaking, peacekeeping, and peacebuilding. Although Boutros-Ghali spoke of peacebuilding in the context of post-civil war agreements, the concept has been expanded and used in a wide variety of settings. In 2000, the Brahimi Report defined peacebuilding as "activities undertaken on the far side of conflict to reassemble the foundations of peace and provide the tools for building on those foundations something that is more than just the absence of war," tapping into positive conceptions of peace.[3] A Peacebuilding Commission was created in December 2005 to "bring together all relevant actors to marshal resources and to advise on and propose integrated strategies for post-conflict peacebuilding and recovery; to focus attention on the reconstruction and institution-building efforts necessary for recovery from conflict. . . . and to extend the period of attention given by the international community to post-conflict recovery." In 2015, a review of the UN peacebuilding architecture a decade after its founding asserted the importance of a strategic approach to peacebuilding, "noting that security, development and human rights are closely interlinked and mutually reinforcing."[4]

However, the peacebuilding arena has been fraught for the United Nations, and there are significant divides within the field regarding how to best approach peacebuilding. For some, peacebuilding as a concept was equated with statebuilding, particularly the liberal statebuilding project, in which democratic, free-market states were seen as necessary preconditions for peace. Thus, international donors and international NGOs pushed for a series of policies and institutions to be put in place in post-conflict states such as Bosnia-Herzegovina, East Timor, Afghanistan, and Liberia (Call and Wyeth 2008; Paris and Sisk 2009). Peacebuilding as state building has been roundly criticized by scholars, including Oliver Richmond and Roger MacGinty, and a more "local" turn to peacebuilding has been advocated. This approach builds on that of earlier scholar-practitioners such as John Paul Lederach, who emphasize the need for elicitive approaches that draw out local concepts of conflict, peace, and building on local needs (Lederach 1995). Firchow, Richmond, and others have developed an "Everyday Peace Indicators" research project to look at a bottom-up approach to measuring peace, seeking to move beyond externally imposed indicators that are tied into international policy agendas rather than local conceptions of peace.[5]

Also in 2015, the United Nations adopted the 2030 Agenda for Sustainable Development with 17 Sustainable Development Goals (SDGs), providing a follow-up to the Millennium Development Goals (MDGs) that were introduced in 2000. In addition to SDGs focusing on ending poverty and hunger, promoting gender equality, and implementing affordable and clean energy (among other goals), is Goal 16: Peace, Justice, and Strong Institutions, which seeks to "promote peaceful and inclusive societies for sustainable development, provide access for justice to all and build effective, accountable and inclusive institutions at all levels."[6] The targets of Goal 16 are far-reaching and wide-ranging, including efforts to "significantly reduce all forms of violence and related death rates everywhere," "promote the rule of law at the national and international levels and ensure equal access for all," and "strengthen relevant national institutions, including through international cooperation, for building capacity at all levels, in particular in developing countries, to prevent violence and combat terrorism and crime."[7]

## Basic conflict theory and analysis concepts

As elements of an interdisciplinary field, the concepts and terminology for international conflict management draw on a range of theoretical and practical vocabularies. While we cannot do justice to the entire field here in one chapter (or even in one textbook) we intend here to lay out some of foundational models upon which later chapters build. At a very basic level, it is important to differentiate between *conflict* and *violence*, as the two terms are often used interchangeably in popular parlance. In the field of international conflict management, conflict is often defined in terms of goal incompatibility, or more specifically, "perceived divergence of interest, or a belief that the parties' current aspirations cannot be achieved simultaneously" (quoted in Rubin, Pruitt, and Kim 1994, 5). As such, conflict is seen as a potential change agent, a breeding ground for potentially altering unjust practices. In the field of peace studies and in nonviolent resistance, conflict escalation is often seen as critical in making latent conflict overt, through processes of education and raising awareness. This is particularly true in contexts of unbalanced power relations, in which the problems of one party may be rendered "invisible" by those who benefit from the status quo. Related to conflict is the term *peace*, which in conventional international-relations scholarship is conceived of as the absence of war (negative peace). Within peace and conflict studies, however, peace is conceived of more positively, in terms of the absence of all forms of violence, as well as nonviolent conflict transformation (Galtung 1996, 9).

In contrast with conflict, direct violence causes harm and can be conceived in terms of verbal or physical violence that harms the body, mind, or spirit according to Galtung (1996). Galtung goes further, however, to also define *structural violence*, namely structures or oppression, exploitation, and/or marginalization that prevent individuals from reaching their potential, and *cultural violence*, or "those aspects of culture, the symbolic sphere of our existence – exemplified by religion and ideology, language and art, empirical science and formal science. . . . that can be used to justify or legitimize direct or structural violence" (Galtung 1990, 291). Galtung's typology of violence expands the concept of violence beyond what is typically used in international relations approaches and by including cultural and structural violence in his typology expands the concept of peace as well, considering positive peace to be the absence of all forms of violence, including those cultural forms that make direct and structural violence seem acceptable and "natural." While some may see positive peace as a utopia, or structural violence as such an inclusive category as to render "violence" analytically useless, these concepts have been broadly adopted as tools for thinking more holistically about peace and conflict resolution beyond the mere cessation of hostilities.

While Galtung is often associated with a more structural approach to peace and conflict resolution, another body of literature is rooted in sociology and psychology. From these disciplines come ideas such as the Social Identity Theory (SIT), human needs theory, protracted social conflict theory, and a range of problem-solving workshop approaches aimed at addressing them. Social Identity Theory (Tajfel and Turner 1986) suggests that humans have a need to identify with a group and that they also have a need to compare favorably against external others. For social identity theorists, this need for belonging and for positive association with self can lead to attributing negative stereotypes to "Other" groups. While there are limits to this theory (namely there is a big jump from comparisons between self and others to violent conflict, and any one individual belongs to numerous identity groups), the theory is still often implicit in many other identity-based approaches to resolving international conflict. Indeed, John Burton, a former diplomat who felt that power-based negotiations were insufficient in addressing intractable conflicts, saw identity as a critical factor in international conflict and asserted in his human needs theory that without finding a way to address the underlying human needs at play – primarily identity needs, security needs, recognition, and personal development needs – formal Track I negotiations would be inadequate for addressing such conflicts (Burton 1990). Although Burton's human needs theory has been criticized for not accounting enough for culture and for lack of specification regarding how appropriate satisfiers for underlying human needs should be identified, the field has generally moved toward an acceptance of the importance of differentiating between positions (stated demands that one holds as part of a negotiation process), interests (what one desires or the goals one may have), and needs (which are more fundamental and cannot be negotiated or relinquished). By focusing on needs, Burton and other human-needs theorists sought to connect conflict analysis, an examination of the sources and causes of conflict, with conflict resolution, ways to address those causes in a way that is mutually acceptable.

Burton's human needs theory, combined with Allport's contact hypothesis, has served as the basis for a range of Track II and problem-solving or interactive conflict resolution approaches. Allport's hypothesis basically states that intergroup contact, including informal, personal engagement with outgroup members, is the best way to help improve relations between communities in conflict, provided a series of conditions are met and the encounter is more positive than a reinforcement of negative assumptions. Allport suggests that parties should have equal status (i.e., relatively similar levels of education, profession, socio-economic class), a superordinate goal that they are working on cooperatively during the interaction, and support of authorities for the interaction to occur (Pettigrew and Troop 2005). By combining sustained interpersonal conflict between influentials or semi-influentials in their respective communities in pursuit of the superordinate goal of conflict analysis and problem solving regarding their shared conflict, problem-solving workshop organizers used both human needs theory and contact theory to seek to change conceptions of the "Other" and to find ways to satisfy the human needs underlying the violent conflict.

One of the main limitations of such Track II approaches is that they did not always have a specified mechanism of change for moving beyond the group engaged in contact to wider society and/or to the formal political process. Further, such social-psychological interventions do not always address power imbalances or some of the other structural drivers of conflict such as oppression, occupation, and economic marginalization. In contrast, theories of conflict transformation seek to "engage . . . the systems within which relationships are embedded" and "promote constructive change processes" (Lederach 2003). Conflict transformation, therefore, looks beyond immediate relationships and works to change structures, cultures, and systems in which such relationships are embedded.

Scholars from a variety of disciplines point to different drivers of conflict, however. While those listed thus far are primarily from sociology and psychology, as well as peace studies, some approach conflict from a more economics-focused perspective. Some scholars have suggested that conflict happens for reasons of greed, rather than grievances (Collier and Hoeffler 2004). In such cases, one argument is that conflict entrepreneurs seek to profit from natural resources available in a given area, such as so-called conflict diamonds in Sierra Leone, or lumber in the case of Liberia (Beevers 2016; Howard 2016). Others suggest that conflict parties and arms traders benefit from the perpetuation of conflict, and that unless the cost-benefit analysis of peace is more favorable than continuing war, then conflict will persist (Mason et al. 2011). The grievance side of this equation suggests that when parties feel that their economic needs or desires are unfulfilled, they are more likely to engage in acts of aggression (the so-called frustration-aggression hypothesis). A modified version of this suggests that it is not absolute measures of poverty or economic want that contribute to violent conflict, but rather a sense of relative deprivation, i.e., that a party feels it has less in comparison to other referent actors. In this manner, the theoretical assumptions of relative deprivation are similar to those of social identity theory wherein comparison between in-group and out-group can breed hostilities. For example, a study of Islamist terror attacks in Europe and the United States suggests that these were conducted by Muslims born and raised in Western societies and were due to their relative deprivation as compared to their peers in the majority group (Obaidi et al. 2019).

Increasingly, scholars and practitioners in the field are exploring ways to promote reconciliation and restorative justice in the wake of violence and to use terminology that goes beyond conflict management, conflict resolution, and conflict transformation. Reconciliation and transitional justice approaches work to do more than punish perpetrators of crimes or those responsible for atrocities in the course of armed conflict and to find a way for societies to heal and move forward without a recurrence of armed conflict. Debates around transitional justice include the repercussions of impunity on societies in the aftermath of civil conflict or grave human rights abuses under repressive regimes, as well as the importance of addressing economic, social, and cultural rights, not only political rights. While transitional justice mechanisms such as truth commissions and amnesty measures have their benefits, if done without the active participation of third-party states to ensure the process is credible and accountable, these mechanisms can fall short of their mission. Further, when victims are not active participants in the process, their stories can be ignored and voices silenced (Kiyala 2017). Impunity and failure to pursue justice along with peace is seen as a contributing factor for ongoing conflict in the Democratic Republic of the Congo (DRC) (Kiyala 2017). Surface level acts alone, however, are not sufficient for real healing to occur, as demonstrated in the stories of women whose needs were not actually met by the reparations program in Ghana (Baiden 2019).

## Challenges and future directions

As is discussed in the chapters to follow, numerous challenges face the field of international conflict management. One of the challenges that this text hopes to address is that the interdisciplinary nature of the field can contribute to a silo effect in which different disciplines approach and discuss similar problems using differing frameworks and terminology. More work is needed to integrate language and approaches across disciplines to build on collective wisdom and build appropriate models for addressing complex conflicts and so-called wicked problems. Another key challenge facing the field is the increase in non-state and transnational actors in an international system premised on states. Traditional realist and liberal theories are state-centric, and thus do not always provide appropriate means of engaging with conflicts involving non-state actors. Likewise, conflict management theories and approaches have often focused on the interpersonal or intersocietal levels without considering how those mechanisms of change could impact state practices.

An additional challenge, related to those mentioned above, deals with terminology, as terms such as *management*, *resolution*, and *transformation* can be ideologically loaded and can have different meanings to different people. Further, the diversity of actors and views in the broader conflict management field can include those with very strong anti-system inclinations, such as some of the more radical elements who use nonviolent resistance for changing systems of power and control in the international system (such as through the World Social Forum or Via Campesino movements) and those who seek to end interstate or intrastate conflict through more traditional means, which may involve providing amnesty to perpetrators of atrocities. Similarly, while international relations theories tend to seek generalizability, conflict resolution often underscores the unique features of individual conflict dynamics and the need to go beyond box ticking in conflict analysis and conflict resolution efforts. However, when one focuses only on the local or particular aspects of a conflict, it can be difficult to learn from and transfer lessons from one situation to help in another context. Thus, some balance between responsiveness to local needs and contexts and the ability to learn from and prevent the next conflict is required.

## Questions for further discussion

1   How does history affect conflict management theory? What might be changes we see to conflict theory based on current historical challenges?
2   What are the implications of different assumptions between European institutions that tend to be more peace-focused and US institutes that tend to be more conflict-focused?
3   Choose a current international conflict. Which of the theoretical approaches discussed in this chapter seems to be best suited for better understanding this conflict? Why? What are the strengths and limitations of this approach?

## Suggested resources

1   Stockholm International Peace Research Institute (SIPRI) hosts a wealth of research, databases, and publications on policy-relevant questions related to peace and security. www.sipri.org/.
2   The Peace Research Institution Oslo (PRIO) conducts research on the conditions for peaceful relations between states, groups, and people and has a range of publications and data available on its website. www.prio.org/.
3   Harvard Negotiation Project: www.pon.harvard.edu/research_projects/harvard-negotiation-project/hnp/.
4   Sustainable Development Goal 16: https://sustainabledevelopment.un.org/sdg16.

## Notes

1 Authors contributed equally to this chapter and are listed in random order.
2 "President Woodrow Wilson's Fourteen Points." 8 January 1918. Accessed July 4, 2019. https://avalon.law.yale.edu/20th_century/wilson14.asp.
3 "What Is Peacebuilding?" *UN Peacebuilding Fund.* Accessed July 4, 2019. www.unpbf.org/application-guidelines/what-is-peacebuilding/.
4 *UN Peacebuilding Commission Mandate.* Accessed July 4, 2019. www.un.org/peacebuilding/commission/mandate.
5 *Everyday Peace Indicators.* Accessed July 4, 2019. https://everydaypeaceindicators.org/publications/.
6 *Sustainable Development Goal 16.* Accessed July 4, 2019. https://sustainabledevelopment.un.org/sdg16.
7 *Sustainable Development Goal 16.* Accessed July 4, 2019. https://sustainabledevelopment.un.org/sdg16.

## References and further reading

Axelrod, Robert. 1980. "Effective Choice in the Prisoner's Dilemma." *Journal of Conflict Resolution* 24 (1): 3–25.

Baiden, Regina. 2019. "In the Aftermath of Reparations: The Experiences of Female Beneficiaries of Ghana's Reparations Programme." *Journal of Peacebuilding & Development* 14 (1): 22–35.

Beevers, Michael D. 2016. "Securing Forests for Peace and Development in Postconflict Liberia." *African Conflict and Peacebuilding Review* 6 (1): 1–24.

Benoit, Emile, and Kenneth E. Boulding, eds. 1963. *Disarmament and the Economy*. New York, NY: Harper and Row.

Burton, John. 1990. *Conflict: Basic Human Needs*. New York, NY: St. Martin's Press.

Call, Charles T., and Vanessa Wyeth, eds. 2008. *Building States to Build Peace*. Boulder, CO: Lynne Rienner Publishers.

Collier, Paul, and Anke Hoeffler. 2004. "Greed and Grievance in Civil War." *Oxford Economic Papers* 56 (4): 563–95.

Fisher, Roger, and William Ury. 1981. *Getting to YES: Negotiating Agreement Without Giving in*. New York, NY: Houghton Mifflin Company.

Fortna, Virginia Page. 2008. *Does Peacekeeping Work? Shaping Belligerents' Choices After Civil War*. Princeton, NJ: Princeton University Press.

Galtung, Johan. 1990. "Cultural Violence." *Journal of Peace Research* 27 (3): 291–305.

———. 1996. *Peace by Peaceful Means*. London: Sage Publications.

Hobbes, Thomas. 2009 [1651]. *Leviathan*. London: Oxford University Press.

Howard, Audrie. 2016. "Blood Diamonds: The Successes and Failures of the Kimberley Process Certification Scheme in Angola, Sierra Leone and Zimbabwe." *Washington University Global Studies Law Review* 15 (1): 137–59.

Kiyala, Jean Chrysostome K. 2017. "Combining Social Justice With Restorative and Transitional Justice: An Agenda for an Integrative Model in Transitional Societies." In *Restorative and Transitional Justice: Perspectives, Progress and Considerations for the Future*, edited by Jessica Evans, 81–177. [Place of publication not identified]: Nova Science Publishers, Inc.

Kriesberg, Louis. 2009. "The Evolution of Conflict Resolution." In *The Sage Handbook of Conflict Resolution*, edited by Jacob Bercovitch, Victor Kremenyuk, and I. William Zartman, 15–32. Thousand Oaks, CA: Sage Publications.

Lederach, John Paul. 1995. *Preparing for Peace: Conflict Transformation Across Cultures*. Syracuse, NY: Syracuse University Press.

———. 2003. *The Little Book of Conflict Transformation*. Intercourse, PA: Good Books.

Machiavelli, Nicolo. 2003 [1532]. *The Prince*. New York, NY: Penguin Classics.

Mansfield, Edward, and Jack Snyder. 1995. "Democratization and the Danger of War." *International Security* 20 (1): 5–38.

Mason, T. David, Mehmet Gurses, Patrick T. Brandt, and Jason Michael Quinn. 2011. "When Civil Wars Recur: Conditions for Durable Peace After Civil Wars." *International Studies Perspectives* 12 (2): 171–89.

Mitrany, David. 1966. *A Working Peace System*. Chicago, IL: Quadrangle Books.

Morgenthau, Hans. 1948. *Politics Among Nations: The Struggle for Power and Peace*. New York, NY: A.A. Knopf.

Obaidi, Milan, Robin Bergh, Nazar Akrami, and Gulnaz Anjum. 2019. "Group-Based Relative Deprivation Explains Endorsement of Extremism Among Western-Born Muslims." *Psychological Science (0956–7976)* 30 (4): 596–605.

Paris, Roland, and Timothy Sisk, eds. 2009. *The Dilemmas of Statebuilding*. New York, NY: Routledge.

Pettigrew, Thomas F., and Linda R. Tropp. 2005. "Allport's Intergroup Contact Hypothesis: Its History and Influence." In *On the Nature of Prejudice: Fifty Years After Allport*, edited by John F. Dovidio, Peter Glick, and Laurie A. Rudman, 262–77. Oxford: Blackwell.

Rubin, Jeffrey, Dean G. Pruitt, and Sung hee Kim. 1994. *Social Conflict Escalation, Stalemate and Settlement*, 2nd edition. New York, NY: McGraw-Hill.

Schelling, Thomas C. 1981. *The Strategy of Conflict*. Cambridge, MA: Harvard University Press.

Sorenson, Ritch, Eric Morse, and Grant Savage. 1999. "Underlying Choice of Conflict Strategies in the Dual-Concern Model." *International Journal of Conflict Management* 10(1): 25–44.

Stone, Douglas, Bruce Patton, and Sheila Heen. *Difficult Conversations: How to Discuss What Matters Most*. New York, NY: Viking Press.

Tajfel, Henri, and John Turner. 1986. "The Social Identity Theory of Intergroup Behavior." In *Psychology of Intergroup Relations*, edited by Stephen Worchel and William Austin, 276–93. Chicago, IL: Nelson-Hall.

Thucydides. 2003. *History of the Peloponnesian War*. Translated by Rex Warner. New York, NY: Penguin Classics.

Tickner, J. Ann. 1992. *Gender in International Relations: Feminist Perspectives on Achieving Global Security*. New York, NY: Columbia University Press.

Waltz, Kenneth. 2001. *Man, the State, and War: A Theoretical Analysis*, revised edition. New York, NY: Columbia University Press.

Wendt, Alexander. 1992. "Anarchy Is What States Make of It: The Social Construction of Power Politics." *International Organization* 46 (2): 391–425.

Wilson, Woodrow. 1918. "Fourteen Points." Accessed July 17, 2019. https://avalon.law.yale.edu/20th_century/wilson14.asp.

# Part II

# Mechanisms of international conflict management

# 3 International negotiation

*Thomas Doleys and Timothy Hedeen*

## Introduction

Negotiation is fundamental to how actors manage intercultural and cross-border relationships. When governments communicate in an effort to address a perceived difference, they are negotiating – whether or not they label the interaction as a negotiation. The contemporary international system is the result of governments engaging in dialogue, exchange, compromise, and concession to achieve outcomes that none could have attained alone.

Though negotiation is widely employed, success is never assured. The path from conflict to resolution is rarely straight. Negotiations are often complex and occasionally fraught. Talks fail, a lot, and for many reasons (Faure and Cede 2012). History is littered with the corpses – figuratively and literally – of conflicts left unresolved because the parties were unwilling or unable to find accommodation or reach agreement. The challenge for observers, scholars, and practitioners alike is to better understand the negotiation process and the role it plays in managing international conflict.

This chapter provides an overview of international negotiation as an instrument of international conflict management. The next section offers an overview of the wide range of issues governments address through negotiation. The third section provides an overview of three analytical frameworks that inform scholarly understanding of negotiation. The fourth section looks closer at the component elements of the negotiation process. The final section touches on several debates that shape scholarly discussion on the role and relevance of international negotiation as a tool of conflict management.

## International negotiation in global society

Societies have long used negotiation as a tool to manage conflict. Although it is common to think about negotiation as something undertaken between governments, the practice long predates the seventeenth-century origins of the modern nation-state (Cohen 1999). There is evidence that organized social units – be they city-states, kingdoms, or empires – have used dialogue, exchange, compromise, and concession to manage conflict and promote cooperation for at least 4,500 years (Cohen and Meerts 2008, 150).

Today, negotiation occupies center stage in affairs among states and is the principal means by which governments seek to resolve conflict with each other. Perhaps the most prominent expression of the preference for negotiation in global society is found in the *Charter of the United Nations*. Forged in the maelstrom of World War II, the founding states embedded within the UN Charter the precept that only through diplomacy and engagement can governments "save succeeding generations from the scourge of war" (Preamble). Article 2 (3) of the

Charter explicitly obliges governments to resolve disputes by peaceful means. Though the Charter lists a number of conflict management tools – including negotiation, enquiry, mediation, conciliation, arbitration, and judicial settlement – experience demonstrates that negotiation has been "the predominant, usual and preferred method" to resolve disputes (Bilder 1986, 20). So important has negotiation been to the post-World War II international order that some have dubbed the era as the "age of negotiations" (Zartman and Berman 1982, 3).[1]

### *Armed conflict*

Armed conflict, and the threat of such, is the most significant issue that states address through negotiation. Governments negotiate to end wars, settle militarized disputes, and manage the proliferation of weapons. America's ten-year armed conflict in Vietnam came to an end not through victory or defeat on the battlefield, but through compromise at a Paris negotiating table. Negotiation has also been critical to managing violence in conflict-prone regions. In the Middle East, Israel secured a formal peace with regional rivals Egypt (1979) and Jordan (1994) through negotiation.

States also use negotiation as a tool to forestall violence. During the Cold War, Berlin was an omnipresent flashpoint in US-Soviet relations. Located geographically in East Germany, but politically and administratively part of West Germany, the US and Soviet Union sparred continually over its status. Although numerous crises erupted, tensions between the heavily armed adversaries never escalated to war. Governments on both sides of the Iron Curtain repeatedly demonstrated a preference for negotiation over direct military confrontation.

### *Commerce*

Negotiation has proved to be an important tool not just to *reduce violence*, but also as a means to *build cooperation* (Zartman 2007). To many, the seeds of World War II were sown by the rivalry and conflict born of the eroding economic conditions of the late 1920s and early 1930s. The foundations of today's global economy were fashioned in direct response to the lessons learned. Shortly after the end of the war, the world's dominant economic powers negotiated a framework to govern the post-war trading order. One outgrowth of these efforts was the General Agreement on Tariffs and Trade (GATT). By joining the GATT, governments commit to progressively reduce trade barriers through negotiation. They also commit to use negotiation as the principal means to settle trade conflicts. Negotiation was also critical to the establishment of the global financial system. The World Bank, International Monetary Fund, and Bank of International Settlements all emerged from negotiation and all function on the principle that the individual and collective needs of member states are best met through negotiation-driven decision-making processes.

### *Global society*

Governments have used negotiation as the chief means to address an array of technical, regulatory, and social challenges. Interstate negotiation was the wellspring from which a rich web of global organizations has emerged. The World Health Organization, the Food and Agriculture Organization, the World Meteorological Organization, the International Labor Organization, the International Organization for Migration, and many others emerged from negotiation and exist to serve as a forum for states to resolve differences and promote cooperation on issues that bear directly on the health and welfare of people the world over.

Negotiation has also been central to the emergence of the body of legal rules that govern how states behave both toward one another and their own citizens. In 1948, member governments of the newly established United Nations laid the foundations of international human rights law when they negotiated the UN Universal Declaration of Human Rights. This agreement has since served as the lodestar for the negotiation of a large number of human rights conventions, including inter alia the Convention on the Elimination of All Forms of Racial Discrimination, the Convention on the Elimination of All Forms of Discrimination against Women, the Convention on the Rights of the Child, and the Convention on the Rights of Persons with Disabilities.

The International Criminal Court (established by the Rome Treaty) illustrates the important role negotiation plays in the evolution of international law. Spurred to act by the atrocities in Rwanda and the former Yugoslavia, members of the international community agreed on the need for a permanent institution to prosecute individuals guilty of heinous crimes, but they differed, sometimes greatly, on what crimes should be covered and how the Court should function. Negotiations took four years, concluding in 1998. In the end, no single state got everything it wanted, but almost every state got enough to be satisfied with the outcome. Now, individuals accused of the most heinous crimes – genocide, crimes against humanity, and war crimes – can be held to account. This was possible only because states resolved their conflicting positions through negotiation.

---

## Textbox 3.1  Negotiating Brexit

Brexit is the term used to describe the decision by the United Kingdom to leave the European Union. The Brexit process is dizzyingly complicated. But of all the issues the UK has had to negotiate, none has proved more challenging than the post-Brexit status of the 310-mile border between the Republic of Ireland and Northern Ireland.

While the UK was a member of the EU, EU law ensured the border was open for the free movement of goods and persons between the countries. As part of Brexit, the British government sought to take back control over the cross-border movement of persons while preserving the free movement of goods. EU negotiators came to the table with a different end-goal in mind. For the EU, free movement of both goods and persons was an all-or-nothing proposition. Importantly, though the sides held contrasting views on preferred outcomes, negotiators shared the view that some agreement was better than no agreement. If negotiations failed, the result would be a "no deal" Brexit and the immediate reimposition of a hard border on the Irish frontier. From the perspective of negotiators, this was the worst possible outcome.

After months of fraught negotiations, the two sides reached an accord: in exchange for continued access to the EU market (something the British valued highly), the British government agreed to the EU demand that people be allowed to continue to move freely across the border (something the EU negotiators valued highly). To appease those in the British government who preferred greater border controls, the arrangement – known as the Irish Backstop – was cast as temporary. It would govern the Irish frontier only until such time as UK and EU negotiators agreed on a replacement. EU member states, although preferring a more permanent solution, signed off on the arrangement. The agreement fared less well in the UK parliament. Much to the dismay of negotiators on both sides, British legislators voted down the agreement. They argued that their negotiator betrayed them and that the Irish Backstop amounted to a capitulation to the EU.

At the time of this writing, the EU and UK still have no agreement. Each day that passes it grows more likely that the outcome negotiators on both sides fought hard to avoid – a "no deal" Brexit – will occur. This fact points to a critical lesson for international negotiators and for students of international negotiation – no international agreement, however hard-found and artfully crafted by negotiators, will resolve conflict if it does not adequately account for the broader political and institutional context within which those negotiations take place.

## Theoretical approaches

Negotiation is a complex social phenomenon. To understand this complexity, scholars have developed a range of theories and frameworks to provide insight, offer explanation, and generate understanding by focusing on particular features of the phenomenon. Three prominent approaches are examined below. The first emphasizes the structural features of a negotiation situation, the second focuses on negotiators' strategic choices, and the third examines the influence of culture on negotiators and the negotiation process.

### *Structural approaches*

Structural approaches explain outcomes as a function of the characteristics of a given negotiation context. A key variable in such explanations is the role of *power*. But what is power? For some, power is synonymous with capability – the real or symbolic assets, elements, and resources that a party can use to influence others (Telhami 1990). For others, power is defined in relational terms: power is the ability of Actor A to change the behavior of Actor B (Baldwin 2013). However defined, structural approaches share the view that the greater a party's power, the greater its ability to shape negotiations, and the greater the likelihood that it will achieve its objectives.

But what about those situations where weaker parties prevail? To explain these outcomes, structural approaches focus on how weaker parties overcome structural impediments through tactical maneuvering (Habeeb 1988). A weaker state might refuse to make concessions, or it might make unreasonably high demands, until it is convinced that the stronger party is willing to make concessions (Zartman and Berman 1982, 205–7). A weak state might use linkage strategies across issues to increase bargaining leverage. It might work in coalition with others to "borrow" the power required to level the playing field (Zartman and Rubin 2000, 277–81). Finally, a weak state might have a particularly strong BATNA, an acronym for the "best alternative to a negotiated agreement" (Fisher, Ury, and Patton 1991). The stronger a party's BATNA, the better that party's *alternatives* to a negotiated outcome, and thus the greater that party's leverage to make demands *during negotiations*.

Another point emphasized by structural approaches is that context matters. For instance, it is common to make a distinction between immediate context and the broader environment in which negotiations take place. The immediate context is comprised of things over which negotiators have control and that can be manipulated to advance a negotiator's objectives. They include a negotiating party's interests, resources, and relationships. The broader environment includes negotiation-relevant factors that are beyond an actor's immediate control. They cannot be controlled, but they must be accounted for just the same. For example, in Brexit negotiations (see Textbox 3.1), British negotiators had no control over the actions of the Parliament. They negotiated with a view to the action parliamentarians might take, but they had no ability to affect those actions. They would only later come to find that their efforts fell short.

### Strategic approaches

Strategic approaches to negotiation have their roots in mathematics and game theory (Raiffa 1985). Whereas structural approaches focus on *means* of negotiating (such as power), strategic approaches focus on the *ends* (preferred outcomes) (Zartman 1988). Negotiators are understood to be "rational actors" – those who evaluate options seeking to maximize their gains and minimize their losses.

Strategic approaches often use models to depict the essential features of negotiations. Two prominent models are the Prisoner's Dilemma and the Chicken Game. The Prisoner's Dilemma (PD) is named for a hypothetical situation in which two individuals – let's call them Actor A and Actor B – are arrested following a bank robbery. While in custody, Actors A and B are held in separate cells. The prosecutor explains to each that she already has enough evidence to convict on the lesser crime of possessing a weapon. What she does not say is that she does not have enough evidence to convict on the robbery charge. She needs one of the two to turn state's evidence. The prosecutor indicates to each that she is willing to show leniency to the individual who confesses. She said to each, "If you confess and the other stays silent, I will drop the weapons charge. However, if you stay silent, I will seek the maximum punishment for the crimes you've committed." In their respective cells, and unable to speak to one another, Actor A and Actor B consider the possible outcomes: *if both keep quiet and do not confess*, each will each go to jail but only for a short period of time since the weapons charge carries little jail time; *if both confess*, each will go to jail, but for a longer period of time since the evidence each gives will lead to a lot of jail time on the robbery charge; *if one confesses while the other denies and stays quiet*, the confessor will go free (!) and the one who stayed quiet will receive a very lengthy prison term since he would be convicted for both weapons possession *and* robbery. If you were Actor A, what would you do?

The logic of games indicates that Actor A will defect and turn state's evidence. Actor B will do the same. The reason for this outcome is illustrated in the payoff matrix (Table 3.1). Both Actor A and Actor B have the same preferences over outcomes (4>3 > 2>1). Each prefers the outcome corresponding with a "4" more than he does one with a "3," and so on. Actor A's *most* preferred outcome (Outcome = 4) is achieved when he defects (i.e., confesses and rats out Actor B) but Actor B does not confess, as this will allow Actor A to go free. Actor A's *least* preferred outcome (Outcome = 1) occurs when he cooperates with Actor B by denying the crime only to find Actor B has confessed and turns state's evidence. This result is sometimes termed the "sucker's payoff," and is the outcome Actor A wishes to avoid *above all else*. Faced with the prospect of being played the sucker, Actor A rationally chooses to defect. Actor B does the same thing, for the same reason. The resulting joint defection means that both go to jail for a long time (since each turned state's evidence against the other).

The PD is important because it shows why even though Actor A and Actor B *together* prefer the outcome where nobody confesses (3,3), not knowing what the other will do combined

*Table 3.1* The Prisoner's Dilemma Payoff Matrix

| | | Actor B (preferences = second #) | |
| --- | --- | --- | --- |
| | | Cooperate (do not confess) | Defect (turn state's evidence) |
| **Actor A** **(preferences = first #)** | Cooperate (do not confess) | 3,3 (Most preferred *joint* outcome) | 1,4 (Actor A = the sucker) (Actor B = best outcome) |
| | Defect (turn state's evidence) | 4,1 (Actor A = best outcome) (Actor B = the sucker) | 2,2 (Least preferred joint outcome) |

with the fear of being "played the sucker" leads each to defect (2,2). The tragedy of the situation – and the key insight of the model – is that this outcome could be avoided if only Actor A and Actor B had agreed not to confess and/or figured out a way to insure the other would not confess. The challenge for criminals – and negotiators – is to find ways to overcome the individually rational strategy to defect (i.e., cheat, lie, etc.) in order to reach a joint outcome that everyone prefers.

The second model is the Game of Chicken. Like the PD, scholars use the game to illustrate why cooperation can be difficult. In the axiomatic version of the game, two drivers head toward each other at a high rate of speed. The winner is the driver who holds her nerve longer (Outcome = 4). The problem is, if both drivers hold their nerve (i.e., neither swerves) the result is the worst possible outcome, a head-on collision (1,1). Interestingly, while being the only driver to swerve makes one "the loser," if both drivers should swerve, both are quite satisfied in the result. Mutual swerving is, in fact, a desirable outcome, both individually and collectively (3,3). The importance of the game lies in its ability to show that if one actor should approach the contest (negotiation) with a single-minded determination "to win," such an approach leads to that actor's most preferred outcome *only* if the other party "chickens out" (4,2). Unfortunately for that driver, she only won't know whether the other party will chicken out until it is too late. In view of this, it is better to find ways to agree on "mutual swerve." At least that way everyone lives to drive another day.

The chicken game is sometimes used to model trade negotiations. Trade theory posits that the maintenance of open global trade is good for individual countries and, importantly, open trade is the best countries can achieve collectively. However, an individual country can

*Table 3.2* Chicken Payoff Matrix

| | | Actor B (preferences = second #) | |
| --- | --- | --- | --- |
| | | Swerve | Do Not Swerve |
| **Actor A** **(preferences = first #)** | Swerve | 3,3 (Optimal *collective* outcome) | 2,4 (Optimal outcome for Actor A) |
| | Do Not Swerve | 4,2 (Optimal outcome for Actor B) | 1,1 (CRASH!) |

achieve a strategic advantage by introducing trade barriers, but it gains this advantage *only* if others don't introduce trade barriers of their own. If everyone responds in kind, the result (that no one swerves) is a potentially catastrophic trade war. Chapter 14 on the economics of conflict discusses this issue further.

### Cultural approaches

Apart from power, culture is perhaps the most often-discussed single factor presumed to influence negotiation (Faure and Rubin 1993; Brett 2007). Defined as "[the] set of shared and enduring meanings, values, and beliefs that characterize national, ethnic, or other groups and orient their behavior" (Faure and Sjostedt 1993, 1), *culture* pertains to relationship between people and their environment, as well as to the way people understand nature, space, time, or major events of one's life.

Culture influences negotiation in a number of ways (Faure 1999; Salacuse 2003; Brett 2000), including how parties communicate, how they expect themselves and others to negotiate (Brett et al. 1998), and even how they understand the nature and function of the negotiation process (Rubin and Sander 1991). It influences what sorts of issues parties regard as subject to negotiation and how negotiators understand what is at stake in any proposed negotiation. For instance, culture can influence whether negotiators perceive a negotiation as an exercise in distributing something desirable among the parties (like land or natural resources, such that anything gained by one party is lost by the other) or an opportunity to find mutual benefits for gains for all parties, like a unified currency or addressing humanitarian needs (Thompson and Hastie 1990). Culture can also shape a negotiator's willingness to accept risks, such as when she has limited information (Foster 1992). Cultures also differ in the status and meaning they ascribe to a negotiated agreement (Foster 1992). In some societies, a finalized agreement is regarded as a contract to be interpreted and applied strictly. In others, a negotiated agreement is viewed as an open-ended, impermanent arrangement that may be changed easily.

Although many negotiation-relevant cultural attributes have been identified, those who study the impact of culture still do not agree on its precise influence. One perspective holds that cultural differences can act as *an obstacle*, as negotiators from different cultures think differently and conduct themselves differently at the negotiating table (Berton, Kimura, and Zartman 1999). This leads to the potential for misunderstandings that create barriers to deal-making. Another perspective holds that culture can serve as *a bridge* between parties who might otherwise find it difficult to reach agreement. Salacuse (1993) argues that by showing sensitivity and respect for another's culture, a skillful negotiator can create goodwill between the parties, enhancing the likelihood of a negotiated outcome. Finally, there are those who argue that, in any given negotiation, culture might have *no impact at all*: just because negotiators have different cultural backgrounds does not mean that culture will be meaningful. Overall, the position advanced by proponents of cultural explanations is not that culture *always* impacts negotiation. Rather, the position is that culture *can* impact negotiations, and it does so in ways that cannot be adequately explained or understood by other analytical or theoretical approaches.

## The negotiation process

Another approach to understanding international negotiation is to examine it as diplomats and negotiators experience it – as a *process* that unfolds over time and through a sequence of phases (Berridge 2010). Each phase has distinct characteristics and functions.[2] There are several phase models in the literature (e.g., Gulliver 1979; Zartman and Berman 1982; Druckman 2007). The one discussed below is comprised of four phases: *a pre-negotiation phase*, *a formula phase*, *a details phase*, and *a ratification phase*. Similar phases can be found in mediations, which are discussed in Chapter 4.

### Phase #1: pre-negotiation

Pre-negotiation is "talks about talks" (Saunders 1985). The phase comprises "the span of time and activity in which the parties move from conflicting unilateral solutions for a mutual problem to a joint search for cooperative multilateral or joint solutions" (Zartman 1989, 4). It *begins* when one or more parties consider negotiation as an alternative to continued conflict and communicates this intention to other parties. The phase *ends* when parties to a conflict agree to the agenda and procedures necessary to complete for conducting talks, or, alternatively, when the parties rule out negotiation as a viable path forward (Gross Stein 1989, X).

During this phase parties engage in two sets of activities: diagnosis and preparation. The core diagnostic activity is *problem identification*, where parties seek to define a dispute and consider whether it can be redefined into a set of issues amenable to a negotiated outcome (Tomlin 1989). They examine each other's capabilities and desires, as well as their own goals and expectations, and consider whether a negotiated settlement is likely.

Once a problem is identified, parties begin to *search for options*. Parties may not initially consider negotiation the preferred way to address the problem; they might yet see unilateral action as preferable. The decision to choose negotiation becomes more likely, however, if parties find that the potential benefits of joint action outweigh those associated with unilateral moves or the status quo. Zartman (2006) describes the process as "ripening." Ripening involves both push and pull factors. One of the ways parties feel themselves "pushed" toward negotiation is when they see themselves in a *mutually hurting stalemate* – a politically painful deadlock in which neither side believes it can win, but from which neither side is willing to back down. The situation becomes fully ripe, however, when the perceived benefits "pull" parties toward negotiation as the preferred way out of the situation in which they find themselves.

It can take time for a situation to ripen. In the Arab-Israeli conflict, it took four wars before Egypt and Israel agreed to meet at the table to negotiate a permanent peace. It is perhaps not surprising, therefore, that former President Jimmy Carter identified the process of agreeing on the need for talks as the "most difficult" step in negotiation process (Carter 2003, 13). Until parties come to "recognize that an unacceptable situation exists, that unilateral action cannot resolve it, and that one's overall circumstances will not improve without negotiation," there is little reason to believe talks, were they somehow to take place, would be productive (Carter 2003, 20).

Once parties acknowledge that negotiations are fitting, the pre-negotiation phase proceeds from "diagnosis" to "preparation." At this point, the conversation shifts from *whether to negotiate* to *what will be negotiated* (Tomlin 1989, 23). An important step in this process is setting the *agenda* for talks (Gross Stein 1989). Parties use discussions to identify the boundaries of negotiation. They identify issues to be included on the negotiating agenda and, equally important, issues that should be excluded. The parties also look to settle matters such as the order in which the issues will be discussed and whether issues can be added and/or subtracted.

The pre-negotiation phase can serve more purposes than simply "setting the stage" for formal talks. Pre-negotiation contacts can be used to open channels of communication and build rapport between parties who might otherwise have little contact. Pre-negotiation interactions may "build bridges from conflict to conciliation" (Zartman 1989, 13). For example, parties can temporarily suspend conflict activities, such that ceasefires can be arranged or economic sanctions can be suspended. Such actions function as "down payments on confidence," providing parties an opportunity to demonstrate the capacity for reciprocity and trust – resources on which they can draw in formal talks (Zartman 1989, 13). Finally, the process of pre-negotiation can provide a means to manage domestic politics (Gross Stein 1989). Reflecting the two-level nature of international negotiation contexts, in which negotiators must manage the expectations both of their national constituents and their opponents in the international realm, the pre-negotiation phase provides leaders an opportunity to seek political support and build national or transnational coalitions needed to credibly commit to a negotiated outcome (Putnam 1988).

Brexit negotiations raise this final issue to high relief (see Textbox 3.1). Negotiators representing the government of British Prime Minister Theresa May believed her governing parliamentary majority would support any agreement it was able to reach with EU negotiators. That belief proved misguided when a majority of legislators, many of which were members of the Prime Minister's own party, refused to endorse the agreement reached. This has led to recriminations within Prime Minister May's government as she failed to do precisely the coalition building required to shield a negotiated outcome from this sort of revolt.

### Phase #2: the formula phase

The second phase begins when parties convene "at the table." This phase of negotiations rarely unfolds quickly or in a straight line. Negotiators often find it impossible to identify a comprehensive solution on the basis of an exchange of initial positions. Instead, parties find themselves engaging in an incremental process of narrowing differences and identifying commonalities. One way parties do this is by crafting a *formula* that then serves as a framework for negotiations.

Negotiators look to craft one of two types of formulas, depending on the nature of the issue and the degree to which parties differ (Zartman 2016). The first type is a *minimal agreeing formula*. The primary aim of such a formula is to end or suspend the conflict, emphasizing conflict management over conflict resolution. The other type of formula is the *resolving formula*, by which the parties engage conflict issues directly with the goal of addressing the core issues underlying the conflict.

Formulas take many forms. Parties can craft a formula as a statement of principles, the first draft of a negotiating text, or just about anything in between. For example, the People's Republic of China and the United Kingdom agreed that the "one country, two systems" principle would guide negotiations on the status of Hong Kong. In the case of the International Criminal Court, pre-negotiation discussions undertaken by the aptly named Preparations Committee (PrepCom) resulted in a draft treaty text (Kirsch and Holmes 1999). The draft identified through bracketed text specific points of contention that would later be the focus of negotiations at the Rome Conference.

It can be difficult to identify an acceptable formula. The parties seek, generally by trial and error, to identify the range of outcomes that are acceptable to the all parties and that all parties also prefer to the status quo – what negotiation scholars term the *zone of possible agreement* (ZOPA). Parties indicate what they would like to see in a final agreement (and what must be left out), and what each is willing to give or receive. The process continues until all sides conclude that their needs are satisfied. In the case of the International Criminal Court, it took representatives of PrepCom over fifteen weeks to negotiate a formula text that was broadly acceptable (Kirsch and Holmes 1999).

### Phase #3: the details phase

If and when parties agree on a formula to guide talks, negotiations move to the *details phase*. In this phase, negotiators seek to translate the set of broad concepts and guiding principles into a set of specific mutual commitments (Zartman and Berman 1982). The details phase can be long and the atmosphere more hostile than in the formula phase. Finalizing details often entails that each party make substantive compromises and commitments that have real costs. Controversial issues that were addressed broadly when looking for an acceptable formula can reemerge as sticking points.

In final negotiations over the Rome Treaty, which established the International Criminal Court, there were sharp differences between countries on a number of issues (Lee 1999). Parties differed on the types of crimes that would fall within the Court's purview. While negotiators generally agreed that genocide, crimes against humanity, and war crimes should be included, some delegations advocated for the inclusion of crimes of aggression, while others held that drug trafficking and terrorism should be included. Negotiating delegations also differed sharply on whether a state must accept the court's jurisdiction before the court could prosecute one of its citizens. The United States argued that state recognition was essential. Others, including Germany, argued that no such acknowledgement should be required (Scheffer 1999).

Nailing down agreement on details is made more challenging when one or more parties regards the details phase as an opportunity to revisit, rebalance, or otherwise alter the contents of the resolving formula. In the final hours of the Rome Conference, both the United States and India offered proposals that would alter core provisions of the emerging treaty text. These proposals were decisively defeated, as the prevailing view was that to alter the text at that point would undermine the delicate balance that had been achieved over months of talks (Kirsch 1999).

The details phase continues until all parties acknowledge agreement on all outstanding issues or until parties acknowledge that agreement is not possible. Acknowledgement can take a number of forms. The parties might issue a joint statement in which they indicate that all matters have been resolved, or they may stage a photo opportunity in which the parties signal final agreement through a handshake. In the case of the ICC, the draft treaty was put to formal vote. At 10 p.m. on the last day of the conference, the text was put before the assembled delegations. By a vote of 120 for and 7 against (with 21 abstentions), the text was formally adopted.

### Phase #4: the ratification phase

The last step of the negotiation process is ratification. Ratification is not always addressed in discussions of international negotiations. This is due, at least in part, to the fact that ratification is not always a relevant consideration. Sometimes negotiators want agreements to be informal (Lipson 1991). But often in negotiations between sovereign states, the parties expect the agreement to have binding legal and political effect (Berridge 2010). In some contexts, a signature by the chief negotiator or senior politician (such as a head of state) is sufficient. In other cases, though, those who negotiated (and perhaps even signed) an agreement may be required to have that agreement endorsed by another constitutionally assigned authority. Such is the case in the US, where treaties negotiated by the executive branch do not have legal effect until ratified by the Senate.

Ratification is more than just a formality. Until such time as a negotiated agreement receives the required endorsement, there remains the possibility that one or more parties will seek to revise, alter, or otherwise change the terms of a negotiated outcome. Negotiators who give insufficient attention to the importance of this step risk seeing their hard-won agreements threatened or undermined altogether. This point is illustrated poignantly in the failure of the British parliament to endorse the Irish Backstop negotiated between Prime Minister May and her EU counterparts (see Textbox 3.1).

## Challenges and future directions

Three debates animate discussion among scholars and practitioners of negotiation. These concern the role of justice, the issue of ethics, and the thorny issue of whether there are contexts in which a party should not negotiate.

How to deal with issues of *justice* in international negotiation is a matter of considerable interest (Zartman et al. 1996; Albin 2001). What, precisely, does one mean by justice in this context? One way to understand the role justice plays is to think about it as part of the mental map individual negotiators bring to the negotiating table. It is the basis on which certain actions are justified and others are not. The challenge is that each party to a negotiation tends to prefer a notion of justice that favors its own cause. A second way justice is talked about in international negotiations is as the basis on which to assess aspects of the negotiation process. Do negotiations unfold in a way that comports with some notion of process-related or procedural justice? A third way to think about justice is with reference to negotiated outcomes. A key challenge facing those who would adjudge outcomes is the standard against which such a judgement is made. *What* standard of justice? *Who* determines?

A second area of debate concerns the role *ethics* play, or should play, in negotiations. Is it OK to lie or deceive? If so, under what circumstances? How should one respond when confronted with tactics one perceives to be unethical? Some studies have explored the ethics of various negotiating tactics. Studies have found different cultural preferences around deception (Rivers and Lytle 2007), information gathering (Lewicki and Robinson 1998), and performance on commitments (Cohen 1997). Like notions of justice, it is difficult to identify clear standards of behavior against which the rightness of actions can be judged (Barry and Robinson 2002). It is equally unclear as to the appropriate response when faced with tactics one perceives as ethically problematic.

A third topic is whether negotiations may be an *inappropriate* method to address some conflicts (Miller 1993; Spector 1998, 2004; Mnookin 2010). Many governments pledge not to negotiate with hostage takers, and yet some countries end up doing so. Is it ever appropriate to negotiate with rogue states, terrorists, extremist groups, or other unsavory actors? If so, under what circumstances? In other cases, a large difference in the relative power of the parties may suggest that any "negotiation" would conclude with the more powerful party dictating terms to its counterpart, without needing to compromise meaningfully. And finally, in those instances where one or more important players will be absent from the negotiation, will the outcome be stable or recognized as legitimate?

## Questions for further discussion

1   How, if at all, are negotiations between governments different from those involving non-state actors?
2   Which of the theoretical approaches discussed in the chapter do you find most compelling? What do you see as the strengths and weakness of each?
3   Which of the four phases of the negotiation process pose the greatest challenge for negotiators? Why?

4    Are there issues for which negotiation is an inappropriate or ill-advised conflict manage-
     ment tool?
5    Which of the key debates poses the greatest challenge to those seeking to understand
     international negotiation?

## Suggested resources

1    Fisher, Robert, Andrea Kupfer Schneider, Elizabeth Borgwardt, and Brian Ganson.
     1997. *Coping With International Conflict: A Systematic Approach to Influence in Inter-
     national Negotiation*. Upper Saddle River, NJ: Prentice Hall.
2    Kremenyuk, Victor A., ed. 2002. *International Negotiation: Analysis, Approaches,
     Issues*, 2nd edition. San Francisco, CA: Jossey Bass.
3    Moore, Christopher, and Peter Woodrow. 2010. *Handbook of Global and Multicultural
     Negotiation*. San Francisco, CA: Jossey Bass.
4    Institute for the Study of Diplomacy (ISD). Case Study Library, Georgetown University.
     https://casestudies.isd.georgetown.edu/.
5    Harvard University Law School Program on Negotiation (PON). www.pon.harvard.edu/.
6    United States Department of State. "Discover Diplomacy." www.state.gov/
     discoverdiplomacy/diplomacy101/.
7    Art of Diplomacy Lecture Series, John's Hopkins School of Advanced International
     Studies (SAIS). www.fpi.sais-jhu.edu/art-of-diplomacy-lecture-series.
8    Ury, William. 2016. "The Art of Negotiation." Talk given at the University of Geneva.
     https://youtu.be/sajCKwxXG_g.

## Become engaged!

1    Join or create a Negotiation Club, Model United Nations Team, or similar club at your
     university.
2    Organize a roundtable at your university to discuss and evaluate an ongoing interna-
     tional negotiation.
3    Consider a dispute in your past that reached a stalemate. How did it "ripen" to a point
     where each party chose to negotiate? Make a plan for how you will deal with a similar
     dispute in the future, using what you have learned in this chapter.

## Notes

1  According to one study, more than 90 percent of international conflicts between 1945 and 1995 were
   addressed through negotiation (Bercovitch and Jackson 2001).
2  While each phase corresponds to the reality that negotiators encounter, the idea that phases stand
   apart from one another is far sharper in concept than in reality. Not only is the dividing line between
   phases blurred in practice, but negotiators can (and do) move back and forth between them as circumstances require.

## References and further reading

Albin, Cecilia. 2001. *Justice and Fairness in International Negotiation*. New York, NY: Cambridge
     University Press.
Baldwin, David. 2013. "Power and International Relations." In *Handbook of International Relations*,
     edited by Walter Carlsnaes, Thomas Risse, and Beth A. Simmons, 177–91. Los Angeles, CA: Sage
     Publications.

Barry, Bruce, and Robert J. Robinson. 2002. "Ethics in Conflict Resolution: The Ties that Bind." *International Negotiation* 7 (2): 137–42.

Bercovitch, Jacob, and Richard Jackson. 2001. "Negotiation or Mediation? An Exploration of Factors Affecting the Choice of Conflict Management in International Conflict." *Negotiation Journal* 17 (1): 59–77.

Berridge, Geoff R. 2010. *Diplomacy: Theory and Practice*, 4th edition. New York, NY: Palgrave Macmillan.

Berton, Peter, Hoshi Kimura, and I. William Zartman, eds. 1999. *International Negotiation: Actors, Structure/Process, Values*. New York, NY: St Martin's Press.

Bilder, Richard. 1986. "An Overview of International Dispute Settlement." *Emory Journal of International Dispute Resolution* 1: 1.

Binnendijk, Hans. 1987. *National Negotiating Styles*. Washington, DC: Foreign Service Institution, US Department of State.

Brett, Jeanne. 2000. "Culture and Negotiation." *International Journal of Psychology* 35 (2): 97–104.

———. 2007. *Negotiating Globally*, 2nd edition. San Francisco, CA: Jossey Bass.

Brett, Jeanne, Wendi Adair, Alain Lempereur, Tetsushi Okumura, Peter Shikhirev, Catherine Tinsley, and Anne Lytle. 1998. "Culture and Joint Gains in Negotiation." *Negotiation Journal* 14: 55–80.

Carter, Jimmy. 2003. "Negotiation: The Alternative to Hostility." In *Negotiation: The Alternative to Hostility*, edited by Jimmy Carter, 1–26. Macon, GA: Mercer University Press.

Cohen, Raymond. 1997. *Negotiating Across Cultures: International Communication in an Interdependent World*, revised edition. Washington, DC: United States Institute of Peace Press.

———. 1999. "Reflections on the New Global Diplomacy: Statecraft 2500 BC to 2000 AD." In *Innovation in Diplomatic Practice*, edited by Jan Melissen, 1–20. New York, NY: St Martin's Press.

Cohen, Raymond, and Paul Meerts. 2008. "The Evolution of International Negotiation Processes." *International Negotiation* 13 (2): 149.

Druckman, Daniel. 2007. "Negotiating in the International Context." In *Peacemaking in International Conflict: Methods & Techniques*, revised edition, edited by William Zartman, 111–62. Washington, DC: United States Institute of Peace.

Faure, Guy Oliver. 1999. "Cultural Aspects of International Negotiations." In *International Negotiation: Actors, Structure/Process, Values*, edited by Peter Berton, Hoshi Kimura, and I. William Zartman, 11–32. New York, NY: St. Martin's Press.

Faure, Guy Oliver, and Franz Cede. 2012. *Unfinished Business: Why International Negotiations Fail*. Athens, GA: University of Georgia Press.

Faure, Guy Oliver, and Jeffrey Z. Rubin. 1993. "Lessons for Theory and Research." In *Culture and Negotiation*, edited by Guy Oliver Faure and Jeffrey Z. Rubin, 209–31. Newbury Park, CA: Sage Publications.

Faure, Guy Oliver, and Gunnar Sjostedt. 1993. "Culture and Negotiation: An Introduction." In *Culture and Negotiation*, edited by Guy Oliver Faure and Jeffrey Z. Rubin, 1–16. Newbury Park, CA: Sage Publications.

Fisher, Roger, William Ury, and Bruce Patton. 1991. *Getting to Yes: Negotiating Agreement Without Giving in*, 2nd edition. New York, NY: Penguin Books.

Foster, Dean A. 1992. *Bargaining Across Borders: How to Negotiate Business Successfully Anywhere in the World*. New York, NY: McGraw-Hill.

Gross Stein, Janice, ed. 1989. *Getting to the Table: The Processes of International Prenegotiation*. Baltimore, MD: Johns Hopkins University Press.

Gulliver, Phillip H. 1979. *Disputes and Negotiations: A Cross-Cultural Perspective*. New York, NY: Academic Press.

Habeeb, William Mark. 1988. *Power and Tactics in International Negotiation: How Weak Nations Bargain With Strong Nations*. Baltimore, MD: Johns Hopkins University Press.

Kirsch, Philippe. 1999. "The Development of the Rome Statute." In *The International Criminal Court: The Making of the Rome Statute: Issues, Negotiations, Results*, edited by R.S. Lee, 451–61. Boston, MA: Kluwer Law International.

Kirsch, Philippe, and John T. Holmes. 1999. "The Rome Conference on an International Criminal Court: The Negotiating Process." *The American Journal of International Law* 93 (1): 2–12.

Lee, Roy S., ed. 1999. *The International Criminal Court: The Making of the Rome Statute: Issues, Negotiations, Results*. Boston, MA: Kluwer Law International.

Lewicki, Roy J., and Robert Robinson. 1998. "A Factor-analytic Study of Negotiator Ethics." *Journal of Business Ethics* 18: 211–28.

Lipson, Charles. 1991. "Why Are Some International Agreements Informal." *International Organization* 45 (4): 495–538.

Miller, R. Reuben. 1993. "Negotiating With Terrorists: A Comparative Analysis of Three Cases." *Terrorism and Political Violence* 5 (3): 78–105.

Mnookin, Robert. 2010. *Bargaining With the Devil: When to Negotiate, When to Fight*. New York, NY: Simon and Schuster.

Putnam, Robert. 1988. "Diplomacy and Domestic Politics: The Logic of Two-Level Games." *International Organization* 42 (3): 427–53.

Raiffa, Howard. 1985. *The Art and Science of Negotiation*. Cambridge, MA: Harvard University Press.

Rivers, Cheryl, and Anne Louise Lytle. 2007. "Lying, Cheating Foreigners! Negotiation Ethics Across Cultures." *International Negotiation* 12: 1–28.

Rubin, Jeffrey Z., and Frank E.A. Sander. 1991. "Culture, Negotiation, and the Eye of the Beholder." *Negotiation Journal* 7 (3): 249–54.

Salacuse, Jeswald W. 1993. "Implications for Practitioners." In *Culture and Negotiation*, edited by Guy Oliver Faure and Jeffrey Z. Rubin, 199–208. Newbury Park, CA: Sage Publications.

———. 2003. *The Global Negotiator: Making, Managing, and Mending Deals Around the World in the Twenty-First Century*. New York, NY: Palgrave Macmillan.

Saunders, Harold H. 1985. "We Need a Larger Theory of Negotiation: The Importance of Pre-Negotiating Phases." *Negotiation Journal* 1 (3): 249–62.

Scheffer, David J. 1999. "The United States and the International Criminal Court." *The American Journal of International Law* 93 (1): 13–22.

Spector, Bertram I. 1998. "Deciding to Negotiation With Villains." *Negotiation Journal* 14 (1): 43–59.

———. 2004. "Negotiating With Villains Revisited: Research Note." *International Negotiation* 8: 613–21.

Telhami, Shibley. 1990. *Power and Leadership in International Bargaining: The Path to the Camp David Accords*. New York, NY: Columbia University Press.

Thompson, Leigh, and Reid Hastie. 1990. "Judgment Tasks and Biases in Negotiation." In *Research on Negotiations in Organizations*, Vol. 2, edited by Blair H. Sheppard, Max H. Bazerman, and Roy J. Lewicki, 31–54. Greenwich, CT: JAI Press.

Tomlin, Brian W. 1989. "The Stages of Prenegotiation; the Decision to Negotiate North American Free Trade." In *Getting to the Table: The Processes of International Prenegotiation*, edited by Janice Gross Stein, 18–43. Baltimore, MD: Johns Hopkins University Press.

Zartman, I. William. 1988. "Common Elements in the Analysis of the Negotiation Process." *Negotiation Journal* 4 (1): 31–44.

———. 1989. "Prenegotiation: Phases and Functions." In *Getting to the Table: The Processes of International Prenegotiation*, edited by Janice Gross Stein, 1–17. Baltimore, MD: Johns Hopkins University Press.

———. 2006. "Timing and Ripeness." In *The Negotiator's Fieldbook*, edited by Andrea Kupfer Schneider and Christopher Honeyman. Washington, DC: American Bar Association.

———. 2007. *Peacemaking in International Conflict: Methods & Techniques*, revised edition. Washington, DC: United States Institute of Peace.

———. 2016. "Diplomacy and Negotiation." In *The Sage Handbook of Diplomacy*, edited by Costas Constantinou, Pauline Kerr, and Paul Sharp, 207–19. Los Angeles, CA: Sage Publications.

Zartman, I. William, and Maureen Berman. 1982. *The Practical Negotiator*. New Haven, CT: Yale University Press.

Zartman, I. William, Daniel Druckman, Lloyd Jensen, Dean Pruitt, and Peyton Young. 1996. "Negotiation as a Search for Justice." *International Negotiation Journal* 1 (1): 79–98.

Zartman, I. William, and Jeffrey Z. Rubin. 2000. *Power and Negotiation*. Ann Arbor, MI: University of Michigan Press.

# 4 International mediation

*Susan S. Raines and Brittany Foutz*

## Introduction

International mediation is a nonviolent conflict resolution process in which a third party (or parties) assists disputing states or intrastate actors as they seek to negotiate a resolution to their conflict. Mediation is an attempt to prevent or end violence through negotiation assisted by an outside third party, even though it often occurs in the shadow of threatened or ongoing violence. Mediation theories, processes, and skills are increasingly applied to the resolution of conflicts within and between nation-states as well as amongst governmental and nongovernmental organizations seeking to work together to provide humanitarian relief or end violent conflict. *Mediation* has become a catchall term, often referring to collaborative problem-solving and consensus-building processes, led by a mediator, and used to make collective decisions regarding a wide range of issues including the environment, trade, and diplomacy. The majority of the mediations occurring internationally involve trade matters – virtually every treaty on trade contains dispute resolution provisions, often including arbitration and mediation options – yet the bulk of academic interest and literature focuses on diplomatic mediations (i.e., country-to-country). This chapter will provide an overview of all arenas in which international mediation is commonly used.

In the past twenty-five years, the use of mediation has increased rapidly as has the depth of scholarly research. A rich body of research has increased our ability to predict the best timing for a mediation intervention, known as "ripeness" (Coleman et al. 2008). Other authors focus on mediator styles and strategies (Kressel 2007), the use of mediator power vs. neutrality (Cohen et al. 1999), and the ways in which third party states can play critical roles during all stages of the mediation process (Bercovitch 2004, 2007). Unfortunately, a striking disconnect remains between those engaged in the practice of international mediation and scholars producing new knowledge. To address this gap, this chapter includes information from the literature as well examples of two successful uses of international mediation: the Good Friday Accords in Northern Ireland (mediated by George Mitchell of the US) and the ceasefire and surrender of the FARC rebels in Colombia (mediated by Cuba and Norway). Both cases involved state and non-state actors as influencing forces and potential negotiation partners. This chapter examines the historical and contemporary uses of international mediation, and then discusses some of the challenges facing the future use of international mediation. The world is becoming a less violent place (Pinker 2011; Russett and O'Neal 2001), and mediation is a critical tool in the march toward preventing and resolving international conflict.

## The evolution and current state of international mediation

Mediation is simply negotiation that occurs with the assistance of a third party. International mediation commonly occurs on matters of trade and the environment because these matters cannot be addressed unilaterally, meaning they require collaboration between nation-states. Yet, disputes involving the political security of states tend to occupy the headlines and garner more attention from academic researchers. Mediators are generally brought in once the parties have failed to reach a negotiated settlement on their own. The longer a dispute has festered, the harder it may be for mediators to overcome the history of poor relationships and mistrust. In fact, there is a deep literature analyzing "ripeness" in mediation (Coleman et al. 2008). This term refers to the extent to which the parties are ready to come to the negotiating table due to the presence of a mutually-hurting stalemate as well as incentives or pressure from third-party states or international organizations (such as the United Nations). Powerful states can provide enticements or otherwise foster ripeness through security guarantees or amnesty/sanctuary to leaders accused of criminal acts. While the literature on ripeness indicates that the likelihood of successful mediation increases under certain conditions (e.g., before the conflict escalates to violence, when the cost of continued conflict gets high for all sides), critics of ripeness theory assert it has been unfairly used to justify inaction in the face of violent intergroup or interstate conflict.

While some violent conflicts involve states, increasingly, the parties taking part in mediation include non-state actors such as rebel groups and/or ethnic minorities fighting for political power, autonomy, or economic resources. The inclusion of non-state actors reflects the fact that stakeholders to a conflict often exist within states, rather than merely between them. In these instances, it can be difficult to determine who is the legitimate spokesperson or delegate to the mediation from a specific group, especially when internal divisions within a rebel group leave doubt as to who the legitimate leader may be.

### *The pre-mediation phase: convening*

Prior to the commencement of mediation, peacemakers must undertake an analysis of the potential parties to the conflict (also known as stakeholders) and seek to understand their interests and any obstacles they face to participating in mediation. Next, the peacemaker decides whether or not mediation is likely to make the problem better or worse and ensures he is invited and welcomed as a legitimate mediator in the eyes of the primary disputants. Third, he must lay the groundwork for a successful process by securing necessary funding, determining the logistics of the process (e.g., when, where, who), and decide whether and when to announce the mediation effort to the public through the strategic use of the media. Whom to invite to the table becomes a critical question for all international mediators at the convening stage. The more participants in the process, the more unwieldy the mediation becomes, with consensus becoming less likely. On the other hand, any stakeholder group with the power to block or delay the implementation of an agreement needs to be included at some level during the negotiations in order to garner buy-in. Each decision made by the mediator comes with difficult trade-offs. For example, some stakeholders will argue for the exclusion of others from the negotiation process, yet their absence could undermine the legitimacy of any agreements reached. Mediators must use their influence to persuade parties to accept some reasonable compromises in order to gain commitment to the mediation process itself.

*Early mediation phase*

Next, mediators typically engage in "shuttle diplomacy" by meeting with each side's represent-atives separately while carrying messages or applying appropriate pressure or inducements for collaboration and compromise. This is common prior to the commencement of official media-tion efforts. Parties begin with a general dialogue, designed to deepen each side's understand-ing of the other's perspective, to build relationships and trust in both the mediator and the other parties. Only after trust has been established do they begin negotiating. While exceptions to this exist, this is the common trajectory when using mediation to resolve long-standing ethnic or international disputes: "Dialogue is required before negotiation" (Corry 2012a).

International mediators often communicate or collaborate with civic groups or non-gov-ernmental actors (e.g., religious leaders, celebrities, or other public figures) to build public support for the peace process and ask them to apply pressure to those at the negotiating table. If these groups work against peace, the mediators or their emissaries must address the parties' fears or concerns so as to remove any obstacles to reaching agreements. In terms of mediation logistics, most mediation occurs away from the glare of public scrutiny. By the time a mediation effort is announced, usually it has been underway for many months or even years (Sparks 1996).

*Late mediation phase*

Once an agreement in principle is reached, the mediator must work with the parties to put their agreement into language that clarifies their specific duties and obligations. They "word-smith" each phrase and clause of the treaty so as to elicit consensus among the negotiators, and plan for the implementation of the agreement including the timeline and terms of any ceasefire, disarmament, resettlement, or return of displaced peoples, ownership of contested land, and the safeguarding of civilians and human rights. Many treaties include provisions for monitoring and enforcement in case either side defects from the agreements.

Most mediation and negotiation happens away from the limelight and public view. Official representatives typically come to the mediation table, in the view of the media and public, only after the outlines of an agreement have been reached. Why? There will always be power-ful individuals and groups who benefit from the continued conflict or who hold extreme views that will reduce the chance of settlement. For example, diaspora communities commonly hold more extreme views and are less willing to compromise to reach agreements than those living with the violence of conflict on a daily basis. For example, Irish-American communities were less supportive of the Good Friday Agreement than Irish Catholics living in the six counties of Northern Ireland. Diaspora communities often spend money or engage in political lobby-ing designed to "hold out" or avoid reaching agreements until all their demands are met. By engaging in quiet diplomacy and negotiations, mediators are able to get the primary parties closer to agreement before making the negotiations public, thereby drawing the attention of secondary stakeholders and outside influences that might derail agreements.

## Strategies for successful mediation

At every stage of the process, the mediator must ensure that each official negotiator is not overpromising or reaching agreements that his or her constituency will not support. These are multistep, multilevel negotiations that often last for years. International mediation takes a team, patience, and great stamina. It also requires a "moral imagination," meaning the boldness and creativity necessary to envision a peaceful future and to create a process designed to help disputants escape the quagmire of intractable conflict and violence of their present (Lederach 2010). Some of these conflicts have raged on for generations. Envisioning a different future is often difficult for those who have never known peace. International mediators must be able to engender such a vision and convey it to others in a way that builds hope and commitment to work and even sacrifice for peace.

## Case study: international mediation in the Good Friday Agreement

In the late 1960s, Northern Ireland fell into a 30-year cycle of sectarian conflict and violence known as "The Troubles." In 1998, the Good Friday Agreement was signed between the British government, the Irish government, and most of the political parties in Northern Ireland to set up a power-sharing assembly to govern Northern Ireland. In a conflict that was once deemed intractable, international mediation proved to be the key to success leading to this international agreement.

The effective mediation effort can be attributed to the significant role played by external actors serving as catalysts and drivers of resolution and agreement. With its large diasporas from both Britain and Ireland, the United States had the most prominent role in the Northern Ireland peace process, with two years of negotiations chaired by the United States Special Envoy for Northern Ireland and one of the key architects of the agreement, George Mitchell. Mitchell's best skills as a mediator were his patience and ability to build trust and confidence in all parties. His commission established the principles of nonviolence and democracy that were expected of all parties before, during, and after the negotiations (White 2013, 8, 231). This created the safe space needed for negotiations to make progress.

There are three noticeable characteristics of effective mediation that were prominent in this conflict and are common in most other successful international mediations as well. First, the actual negotiations and mediation occurred away from the public view, as parties did not come to the official mediation table until the outlines were in place, leaving only the final discussions and changes in a public forum (White 2013, 19). Second, the agreement took years of patience, as the mediator and parties built trust and interpersonal relationships. Third, the mediator encouraged and helped the parties to keep their constituencies informed and supportive along the way as the negotiations proceeded. These factors led to the successful resolution of a conflict involving concern for ideology, security, and independence (White 2013, 49, 190, 218).

## Who mediates?

Mediators generally lack the formal power to force parties to accept concessions or come to the negotiating table, so how do they succeed? International mediators sometimes apply pressure or inducements, but cannot force parties to reach agreements. For example, a mediator may obtain promises of sanctuary or immunity from prosecution for war crimes in exchange for the peaceful surrender of power from a dictator or warlord. Mediators must be invited or at least accepted by all disputing parties as "neutral enough" or otherwise able to act as a legitimate mediator at the behest of all parties to the negotiation. This means that complicated networks of alliances come into play in determining who will be accepted as a mediator and who will not. Most state-sponsored mediation is done out of self-interest. For example, the US has large Irish and British diaspora communities as well as long-standing trading relationships in the region. These longstanding, deep connections had fueled the conflict for years, with Irish-Americans supplying funds and political support for the Irish Republican Army (IRA) and related organizations. Yet those same connections lent greater legitimacy to the US role as trusted friend and mediator.

Peace in Northern Ireland was attractive for both humanitarian and political-economic reasons. In fact, the term *peace dividend* became popularized by the American President George H.W. Bush and British Prime Minister Margaret Thatcher in the early 1990s to describe the positive economic benefits stemming from the end of violent conflict, including increased trade, decreased government spending on security, and increased foreign investment which comes only once stability is established. In other words, peace is better for the economy than war. Sometimes, countries like Cuba or Norway volunteer to mediate on largely humanitarian grounds, without any clear national self-interest, but this is less common than mediation by economically or politically interested third parties (Zartman and Touval 2007). Disputants can end their participation in mediation at any time, therefore mediators must tread carefully as they seek to reason with all sides and to encourage both collaboration and compromise, often reminding disputants of the peace dividend and related benefits of ending the conflict.

How does one become a famous mediator like Special Envoy for Northern Ireland George Mitchell or former President Jimmy Carter? George Mitchell was elected to the US Senate, from Maine in 1980 and eventually became the Senate Majority Leader. In 1995, when he left the Senate, President Clinton appointed him as Special Envoy for Northern Ireland where he played the role of international mediator leading up to the Good Friday Peace Agreement. He was later tasked with writing a report with recommendations for the Middle East (in 2001) and even weighed in on the matter of doping in baseball in 2007. He developed his negotiation skills while in the Senate and applied those key skills in his mediation work. Former President Jimmy Carter became famous as a humanitarian and international mediator both during and after his time in office. While President, he mediated the Camp David Accords, which brought together the President of Egypt and the Prime Minister of Israel to negotiate peace between these two countries in September of 1978. Unfortunately, the assassination of Prime Minister Begin and the complicating network of shifting alliances in the region disrupted the ability of these Accords to fully realize broader peace in the region. Yet, these Accords stand as a testament to the ability of international mediators to bring together adversaries in order to endeavor to work together toward peace in spite of vast differences.

In both examples the US was not a third-party "neutral." Unlike court-based mediation in which the mediator has no preexisting relationship with the parties and exercises no leverage or power over them, in both of these cases the US had significant political and economic interests in promoting peace. In fact, the US had the ability to offer financial aid and other inducements to all sides for their willingness to reach important compromises, and the US could pressure parties to comply with agreements, once reached, including threatening to invoke trade or other sanctions if necessary. When choosing a mediator or accepting an offer of mediation, disputing states often make a trade-off between neutrality and influence. A third-party state viewed as more neutral to the conflict, such as Norway, might be more objective but less likely to invoke needed influence that could assist the parties to reach agreements.

## Track I, II, and III diplomacy and mediation

Mediation can occur in Track I, II, or III. What does this mean? Track I diplomacy and mediation involves high-level political and military leaders working on issues of cease-fires, political boundaries, treaties, and peace agreements (Usip.org/glossary for more definitions).

For example, the US Secretary of State might serve as a mediator for matters involving two or more allies in dispute. It should be noted there is an almost complete absence of female international mediators at the Track I level (O'Reilly 2013), despite UN resolution 1325 calling for involvement of more women in mediation. Track II diplomacy and mediation involves dialogue and problem-solving interventions aimed at improving relationships between two or more countries, usually undertaken by influential leaders who are not members of the government, such as academics, religious leaders, non-profit organizations, business owners, and even well-known athletes or celebrities (Jones 2015). Mediation and diplomacy between and within these groups can be used to inform policymaking at the Track I level as well as to resolve trade disputes of interest to all parties. Track III diplomacy and mediation involves people-to-people efforts undertaken by individuals and small groups designed to build understanding and draw attention to important causes of international conflict such as refugees or the environment. Track III pressure can force governments to the mediation table, when large numbers of citizens and groups demand efforts to de-escalate tensions or to restart peace negotiations as has happened in Liberia with the Women for Peace movement headed by Leymah Gbowee and in North and South Korea, where individuals and groups on all sides responded to growing tensions between Kim Jong-Un and President Trump with demands for more engagement and peace efforts (PeaceAction 2011). In reality, these tracks overlap, with pressures from Track II and III forcing government officials to engage in negotiations with or without a mediator, in the hope of addressing popular demands for peace and collaboration on matters like trade and the environment.

## Contending approaches to international mediation

Early scholarship on mediation emphasized the diversity of approaches, techniques, and strategies utilized by mediators, arguing that each approach was idiosyncratic to the individual and to the dispute at hand, thereby making analysis meaningless. "The variables are so many that it would be an exercise in futility to describe typical mediator behavior with respect to sequence, timing or the use or non-use of the various functions theoretically available" (Simkin 1971, 118). The small number of international mediations hampered the use of statistical analysis as well. As time passed and the use of international mediation grew, scholars discarded this view and began to look for patterns of behaviors and correlations to the conclusion and durability of peace agreements. In the past thirty years, scholars of mediation have approached their analyses from various lenses, including psychology, communications, international law and institutions, and political science.

How often is international mediation used? When examining armed conflicts that ended between 1946 and 1990 (during the Cold War), peace agreements made up 8.4 percent and victories 57.2 percent. Since 1990, these percentages have changed to 18.4 percent and 13.6 percent, with many settling due to mediation (Wallensteen and Svensson 2014, 317). Experts estimate that between 1990 and 2013, 64 percent of all armed conflicts were resolved through international mediation efforts (Wallensteen and Svensson 2014, 317). But the use of mediation is not uniform across regions, with Europe and Africa being more likely to use mediation for their conflicts than Asia or the Middle East. While mediators have historically come from the United Nations or from a great power, mediation is increasingly supplied by a regional organization such as the African Union or the European Union. In addition to the support of regional organizations, Europe and Africa have recognized mediation at an early start due to the need to fight the long backlog of court actions and to lower the expenses of litigation. If regional mediation fails, then superpowers or the UN may get involved.

Intervention from regional actors is often viewed as more legitimate than intervention from distant powers.

According to Zartman and Touval (2007, 447) there are five sources of power for international mediators: persuasion, the ability to paint a picture of a better future; extraction, the ability to elicit positive proposals from each party; termination, the ability of the mediator to threaten to end his or her participation in mediation; deprivation, the mediator's capacity to withhold resources from an intransigent party; and gratification, the ability to supply resources to induce agreements. "There is, however, no consensus among researchers and practitioners as to which strategy is used the most and which is most effective" (Wallensteen and Svensson 2014, 319).

Scholars are divided as to how forceful or directive (e.g., pushy) mediators should be in their efforts to push the parties toward a resolution. When states or non-state actors are strongly pressured into reaching agreement, there is a general belief that these agreements may be less durable once the international attention and pressure is gone. On the other hand, there seems to be an element of "stickiness" when it comes to peace, meaning that once warring factions put down their weapons and a feeling of normalcy resumes, citizens generally do not support a return to violence, thereby making even imperfect agreements "stick." Bosnia is one clear example of ethnic conflict in which external actors pressured all parties to accept a ceasefire and a peace treaty that was, at the time, deeply criticized for being imposed by powerful outsiders. In 1994, NATO began air strikes against the Bosnian Serbs. In December 1995, US-led negotiations in Dayton, Ohio (the Dayton Peace Accords) ended the violent conflict in Bosnia, with the requirement of a monitoring presence stationed in Bosnia to assure that all sides respected the peace agreement. Researchers have noted that these forcing or directive strategies often coexist with the softer strategies of fostering ripeness and facilitating communication between the parties, so it is difficult to determine which strategies are most effective under specific circumstances (Wallensteen and Svensson 2014).

Can mediation make a conflict worse? Yes. "Spoilers" (those who enter into mediation with no intention of seeking a true resolution) can use the mediation process to avoid a ceasefire as they gain increased territory or other goals. As the spoilers talk and talk, people suffer from unresolved conflict. Before beginning the process, mediators must undertake a thorough analysis to ascertain the true interests of all parties in the pursuit of mediation to ensure the process is not used to further the aims of violence. If any parties benefit from the status quo, then mediators must seek to change that equation if they wish to see that party undertake meaningful negotiations.

## Contemporary international mediation: regional mediators and international organizations

Sometimes the most contentious question in international mediation is whether or not to mediate. For example, should the US engage in mediation with the Taliban? Qatari officials have been working behind the scenes to negotiate a cease-fire in Afghanistan and the withdrawal of US troops, but the use of mediation in this case has drawn criticism from all sides within the US domestic political arena. Article 2 (3) of the United Nations Charter requires that "All member states shall settle their international disputes in such a manner that all international peace and security, and justice, are not endangered." Yet, since 9/11, the US media and government have portrayed the Taliban as terrorists, even though the Department of State does not list the Afghan branch of the Taliban as a recognized terrorist organization (U.S. Department of State, Bureau of Counterterrism 2019). Listing the Taliban as a terrorist organization would make it illegal for the US to engage with them in peace talks. In the end, the decision to enter into mediation with other state(s) and non-state actors is a politically complicated matter, often influenced by the tangled web of alliances on all sides.

When selecting a mediator, there are costs and benefits to using either a mediator from the region versus one from further afield. For example, when Cuba was selected to assist with the peace talks to end the civil strife in Columbia, it did so from a place of overlapping historical and linguistic identities: Cuba and Columbia shared the same language, Spanish colonial heritage, and regional identities. On the other hand, sometimes one or more parties seek a mediator from outside the region to increase perceptions of neutrality and objectivity. Regional mediators may come from countries impacted by refugee flows and economic interdependence more so than mediators from outside the region. Yet, sharing a language and some aspects of culture may enhance the mediator's ability to relate to the parties and build trust. In the example of Columbia, selecting mediators from both Cuba and Norway allowed for the best of both worlds.

---

**Textbox 4.1  Sustaining peace: Cuba and Norway in the Colombian peace process**

As a revolutionary icon in Latin America, Cuba may seem like an unlikely mediator of negotiations between the Colombian government and the Revolutionary Armed Forces of Colombia, known as FARC (a non-state actor). However, the government of Cuba was of great assistance in mediating the end of the longest-running armed conflict in the Western Hemisphere, leading to the Colombian peace process and the signing of a historic accord on June 23, 2016, in Havana, Cuba.

In the spring of 2011, numerous secret exploratory meetings occurred between Colombian and FARC representatives to agree on upcoming negotiations, including the appointment of Cuba and Norway as international mediators and guarantor countries (Acuerdo 2012). With the assistance of these international mediators, secret negotiations began in February 2012, followed by four years of public talks before resulting in the final agreement.

Cuban and Norwegian mediators served as buffers between representatives from Columbia and the FARC, which was particularly critical since ongoing incidents of violence occurred throughout the negotiating period. Cuba has been referred to as the "unsung star of the peace process" (Arias 2017). Not only did Cuba host the negotiations but its government was also essential in pressuring the FARC to enter into the negotiations. In his book, Peace in Colombia, Cuban President Fidel Castro publicly urged the FARC to disarm and to become a political party (Castro 2008). Since Norway is not part of the European Union, it was able to perform the role of mediator without being encumbered by the slow process of reaching internal consensus within European states.

Norway brought extensive experience as an international mediator as well as the funding necessary to complete the mediation process. The dual contributions of Norway and Cuba, as cultural outsider and insider, helped ensure that the parties would remain committed, foster confidence, and contribute to the successful resolution of this previously intractable conflict in Colombia.

Increasingly, international organizations play an important role in reducing international conflict through the establishment of agreed-upon rules and expectations amongst members (Russett and O'Neal 2001). Organizations and agreements like the European Union (EU) and North American Free Trade Agreement (NAFTA) create shared expectations for the behaviors of member states, businesses, and citizens. Mediation or arbitration can be applied when conflicts cannot be avoided (Dispute Settlement Without 2018). Arbitration, unlike mediation, involves the use of a third-party decision maker (or a panel of decision makers) to determine which party is "right" under international laws, treaties, or agreements. For example, under the World Trade Organization's rules, mediation can be used in order to resolve disputes prior to requesting arbitration. The same is true for members of the African Union (Dispute Mechanisms 2018). In 2009, the EU took steps to create a roster of expert mediators to intervene in disputes between member states at the earliest stages, in the hope of diffusing and de-escalating conflict before escalation leads to outright violence or even trade wars (European Union 2009). Mediation through a trusted local or regional institution, under familiar rules and processes, preserves the ability of the parties to work together successfully in the future, which is important for trade and diplomatic relationships. Mechanisms for mediation through regional institutions are increasingly being created and used for the prevention or early resolution of conflicts that might otherwise escalate and come to the attention of the global community.

## *Challenges and future directions*

When we think of international mediation, we imagine foreign representatives shaking hands and smiling after signing a peace agreement, basking in the glory of success. However, this image hides the vast amount of effort undertaken in the mediation process. International mediation can be overwhelming, takes a whole team of support staff and allies working behind the scenes, and does not always end well. In fact, there are often years of failure before agreements are reached. Once reached, not all agreements are kept. "The mediator's challenge is to lead the parties where they do not want to go in order to talk about what they do not want to discuss with interlocutors they do not want to recognize" (Crocker, Hampson, and Aall 2004, 150).

Furthermore, international mediation seems to be getting more complicated due to the increased involvement of non-state actors and intrastate conflict. Contemporary non-state armed groups, such as al-Qaeda in the Islamic Maghreb, the Revolutionary Armed Forces of Colombia (FARC), and the Taliban have multiplied and developed greater complexity (Briscoe 2013, 3). National leaders often object to mediation for cases of civil unrest or ethnic conflict within their borders, since any official negotiations could lend legitimacy to these groups or signal weakness on the part of the national government. Going further, governmental leaders may "crack down" or engage in human rights abuses as they seek to dominate or extinguish competing internal groups. The participation of non-state actors in a conflict (such as ethnic minority leaders, gangs, or warlords) often makes it unclear as to who can speak for the group or exercise legitimate control over their own constituencies. Some parties to conflict benefit from the status quo and actively act as "spoilers" to the peace process. They delay talks, make outrageous demands, or pretend to go along with concessions, only to withdraw from an agreement at the final stages. International mediators must ask themselves, "Who benefits from the conflict and how do I overcome their resistance or, if need be, meet their interests?" The latter option raises serious ethical dilemmas, but is often a necessary step on the path to peace. This is why war criminals sometimes receive pardons or amnesty as part of a peace process: without these painful concessions, the violence might continue.

Future research can expand on addressing the blurred lines between the actors of Track I and Track II mediation and further develop a comprehensive framework to include unofficial and nontraditional actors at the table as appropriate and helpful to the process of reaching durable agreements. As the peacemaking process moves "upstream," mediators may undertake the role of mediating between contesting intranational groups in order to reach agreements as to who will come to the table with the legitimacy to make and enforce agreements within their diverse and contested constituencies. With each success, we learn more about the strategies employed by mediators in order to increase the frequency and success of international mediation.

## Questions for further discussion

1   What are the trade-offs between neutrality and influence for international mediators?
2   Discuss the concept of ripeness in international mediation. Why and how does the timing of mediation influence the chance of reaching an agreement?
3   What are the benefits of having a regional mediator (e.g., from the African Union or a nearby state) rather than asking the United Nations to mediate?
4   What role do non-state actors and Tracks II and III play in influencing the use and outcomes of international mediation?
5   Why were Cuba and Norway a good mediation team in the Columbian/FARC peace talks? Why was the US a good choice to mediate an end to "The Troubles" in Northern Ireland?

## Suggested resources

1   United States Institute of Peace: videos, articles and more. www.usip.org/issue-areas/mediation-negotiation-dialogue.
2   Smith, Amy, and David R. Smock. 2008. *Managing a Mediation Process*. Washington, DC: United State Institute of Peace. www.usip.org/sites/default/files/managing_mediation_process.pdf.
3   Mediators Beyond Borders International: https://mediatorsbeyondborders.org/.
4   Mediate.com: Articles, blogs, videos and more. Posted by mediators: Mediate.com.
5   United Nations Peacemaker Support. Resources on mediation at Track I, II and III: https://peacemaker.un.org/mediation-support.
6   Conflict Resolution Quarterly. Search for articles by keyword "International Mediation": https://onlinelibrary.wiley.com/journal/15411508.

## Become engaged!

1   Annual conference of the Association for Conflict Resolution and various resources: https://acrnet.org.
2   Internships and Careers at United Nations: https://careers.un.org/lbw/home.aspx?viewtype=ip.
3   Peace & Collaborative Development Network Jobs, universities, and internships advertise mediation and conflict resolution opportunities: https://pcdnetwork.org/.
4   Mediation Skills Training: http://conflict.hss.kennesaw.edu/training/.

## References and further reading

"Acuerdo General para la Terminación del Conflicto y la Construcción de una Paz Estable y Duradera." 2012. Report Published from Government of Colombia, Revolutionary Armed Forces of Colombia, and People's Army on August 24, 2016. *UN Peacemaker* online. Accessed August 1, 2019. http://peacemaker.un.org/colombia-generalaccordendconflict2012.

Arias, Gerson. 2017. "Made in Havana: How Colombia and the FARC Decided to End the War." Interview by Renata Segura and Delphine Mechoulan. International Peace Institute. Accessed August 1, 2019. www.ipinst.org/wp-content/uploads/2017/02/IPI-Rpt-Made-in-Havana.pdf.

Bercovitch, Jacob. 2004. "International Mediation and Intractable Conflict." *Beyond Intractability*. Accessed August 1, 2019. www.beyondintractability.org/essay/med_intractable_conflict.

———. 2007. "Mediation in International Conflicts: Theory, Practice & Techniques." In *Peacemaking in International Conflict: Methods & Techniques*, edited by William Zartman, 163–94. Washington, DC: United States Institute of Peace.

Briscoe, Ivan. 2013. *Non-Conventional Armed Violence and Non-State Actors: Challenges for Mediation and Humanitarian Action*. Norwegian Peacebuilding Research Centre (NOREF), GrØnland.

Castro, Fidel. 2008. *La paz en Colombia*. Havana: Editora Política.

Cohen, Orna, Naomi Dattner, and Ahron Luxenburg. 1999. "The Limits of the Mediator's Neutrality." *Mediation Quarterly* 16 (4): 341–48.

Coleman, Peter T., Atony G. Hacking, Mark A. Stover, Beth Fisher-Yoshida, and Andrzej Nowak. 2008. "Reconstructing Ripeness I: A Study of Constructive Engagement in Protracted Social Conflicts." *Conflict Resolution Quarterly* 26 (1): 3–42.

"Concept on Strengthening EU Mediation & Dialogue Capacities." 2009. *European Union*. Database online. Accessed August 1, 2019. http://eeas.europa.eu/archives/docs/cfsp/conflict_prevention/docs/concept_strengthening_eu_med_en.pdf.

Corry, Geoffrey. 2012a. Personal Interview conducted by Susan S. Raines. October 16.

———. 2012b. "Political Dialogue Workshops: Deepening the Peace Process in Northern Ireland." *Conflict Resolution Quarterly* 30 (1): 53–80.

Crocker, Chester, Fen Osler Hampson, and Pamela Aall. 2004. *Taming Intractable Conflicts: Mediation in the Hardest Cases*. Washington, DC: United States Institute of Peace Press.

"Dispute Mechanisms for Trade Agreements." 2018. Training Manual Published from TradeMark South Africa in 2014. *African Union* online. Accessed August 1, 2019. https://au.int/en/documents-3.

"Dispute Settlement Without Recourse to Panels and the Appellate Body." 2018. *World Trade Organization "Handbook on the WTO Dispute Settlement System online"*. Accessed August 1, 2019. www.wto.org/english/tratop_e/dispu_e/disp_settlement_cbt_e/c8s1p1_e.htm.

"Foreign Terrorist Organizations." United States Department of State. Accessed August 1, 2019. www.state.gov/j/ct/rls/other/des/123085.htm.

Jones, Peter. 2015. *Two Track Diplomacy in Theory and Practice*. Stanford, CA: Stanford University Press.

Kressel, Kenneth. 2007. "The Strategic Style in Mediation." *Conflict Resolution Quarterly* 24 (3): 251–83.

Lederach, John Paul. 2010. *The Moral Imagination: The Art and Soul of Building Peace*. Oxford: Oxford University Press.

O'Reilly, Marie. 2013. "Issue Brief: Women in Conflict Mediation: Why It Matters." *International Peace Institute*. Accessed August 1, 2019. www.ipinst.org/2013/09/women-in-conflict-mediation-why-it-matters.

*PeaceAction*. 2017. "In a Letter to Trump, Over 200 Organizations and Individuals Call for Maximum Engagement in Korea." Written and Published March 8, 2017. Accessed August 1, 2019. www.peaceaction.org/news-posts/in-letter-to-trump-over-200-organizations-and-individuals-call-for-maximum-engagement-in-korea/.

Pinker, Steven. 2011. *The Better Angels of Our Nature: Why Violence Has Declined*. New York, NY: Viking Press.

Russett, Bruce Martin, and John R.R. Oneal. 2001. *Triangulating Peace: Democracy, Interdependence, and International Organizations*. New York, NY: W.W. Norton & Company.

Segura, Renata, and Delphine Mechoulan. 2017. *Made in Havana: How Colombia and the FARC Decided to End the War*. New York, NY: International Peace Institute.

Simkin, William E. 1971. *Mediation and the Dynamics of Collective Bargaining*. Washington, DC: Bureau of National Affairs.

Sparks, Allister. 1996. *Tomorrow Is Another Country: The Inside Story of South Africa's Road to Change*. Chicago, IL: University of Chicago Press.

Stewart, Phil. 2018. "US Detecting Taliban Interest in Afghan Peace Talks: Mattis." *Reuters World News*. Accessed August 1, 2019. www.reuters.com/article/us-afghanistan-usa/u-s-detecting-taliban-interest-in-afghan-peace-talks-mattis-idUSKCN1GP0EL.

Themnér, Lotta, and Peter Wallensteen. 2013. "Armed Conflicts 1946–2012." *Journal of Peace Research* 50 (4): 509–21.

"Tracks of Diplomacy." 2011. In *Peace Terms: Glossary of Terms for Conflict Management and Peacebuilding*, edited by Dan Snodderly, 50. Washington, DC: United States Institute of Peace Press. Accessed August 1, 2019. www.usip.org/sites/default/files/files/peaceterms.pdf.

U.S. Department of State, Bureau of Counterterrism. 2019. Accessed October 6, 2019. https://2009-2017.state.gov/j/ct/rls/other/des/123085.htm.

Wallensteen, Peter, and Isak Svensson. 2014. "Talking Peace: International Mediation in Armed Conflict." *Journal of Peace Research* 51 (2): 315–27.

White, Timothy J. 2013. *Lessons from the Northern Ireland Peace Process*. Madison, WI: University of Wisconsin Press.

Zartman, William, and Saadia Touval. 2007. "International Mediation." In *Leashing the Dogs of War: Conflict Management in a Divided World*, edited by Chester A. Crocker, Fen O. Hampson, and Pamela Aall, 437–44. Washington, DC: United States Institute of Peace Press.

# 5 Nonviolent (civil) resistance and international conflict management

*Maia Carter Hallward and Lina Tuschling*

## Introduction

Although, as a field, nonviolence studies is relatively new to the academic mainstream, the study and practice of nonviolence dates back to ancient times. Western audiences may be most familiar with the nonviolent efforts of Mahatma Gandhi for Indian independence from Great Britain or with Martin Luther King Jr.'s leadership of the US civil rights movement, but the strategy of nonviolent resistance has been documented at least as far back as the Greeks, and examples can be found in many religious scriptures. Civil disobedience, one form of nonviolent action, is a regular occurrence in the Hebrew Bible. King Saul, for example, instructs his guards to kill all priests who helped David escape, but the guards refuse. Nonviolence has been used to counter oppressive leaders, unjust laws, and bring attention to a wide variety of social injustices. Changes in different parts of the world that were made with the help of nonviolence include many types of political regimes, democracies as well as autocracies, and were even waged against the Nazis and Communist systems (Sharp 2005).

Often inaccurately called "passive" resistance, nonviolent resistance is an active approach to challenging war and oppression. Because of confusion surrounding the term, including the fact that it is named by what it is *not* rather than what it *is*, some scholars and practitioners eschew the term *nonviolence* and use terms such as *civil resistance*, *popular struggle*, and *unarmed insurrections*. Nonviolent resistance, in all its different forms and names, gains its power from collective action, starting with the collective withdrawal of consent. Expanding on Gandhi's statement that "even the most powerful cannot rule without the cooperation of the ruled" (Gandhi 1958, 8), Gene Sharp defines nonviolent action as "the belief that the exercise of power depends on the consent of the ruled who, by withdrawing that consent, can control and even destroy the power of their opponent" (1973, 4). Power is central to the study and practice of nonviolence; according to Sharp, power is pluralistic, and governments cannot operate without the consent – tacit or otherwise – of the people. Further, nonviolent resistance is *active*, a "method for transforming latent conflicts into manifest ones, as well as a method of waging or prosecuting a struggle, and increasing the leverage of marginalized groups" (Schock 2015, 12). A paradigmatic shift is needed that "moves away from the traditional focus on structures, conditions, processes, military power, violence, and political elites" (Bartkowski 2013, 3) and shifts the focus instead to the power of collective action waged by ordinary people.

This chapter first provides a definition of nonviolent resistance and how its assumptions differ from other forms of international conflict management. It then provides a historical overview of nonviolence and then discusses the strategies and tactics used as part of this approach to international conflict management. Next, this chapter outlines key theories of nonviolent resistance and differentiates between principled and pragmatic variants. Finally, using examples from Israel/Palestine, the chapter examines how nonviolent resistance works in practice, including the controversies and debates surrounding its use.

### *Defining nonviolence*

Nonviolent resistance is used by a wide range of groups and movements around the world – across cultures, nationalities, regime types, and religions. While perhaps nonviolent efforts to achieve self-determination (as in the case of Gandhi) or to overthrow an oppressive government (as in the ousting of Ferdinand Marcos in the Philippines) are most visible in the headlines, nonviolent resistance also takes the form of economic noncooperation through boycotts and reform efforts more commonly associated with social movements. Nonviolent resistance can occur through actions of *commission*, by taking actions that one may not normally take or that are forbidden, or *omission*, the refusal to act in a way that is expected, such as boycotting a product or staying home from a political rally. To be considered an act of nonviolent resistance, the action must be free of violence or the threat of violence and must be outside of the channels of routine politics; this means that in an established democracy, although the act of voting is nonviolent, it does not represent a form of extra-institutional political action (Schock 2015, 3). Further, while there are many forms of violence and exact definitions vary among approaches to nonviolence, this text adopts Sharp's (2005, 552) definition of violence: "Physical violence against other human beings that results in injury or death, or threatens to cause injury or death, or any act dependent on such infliction or threat."

For scholars and practitioners of nonviolence, conflict (as distinct from violence) is not to be avoided. Instead, conflict is inherent in human interaction and should be embraced as a mechanism for drawing attention to issues of structural and cultural violence. Galtung (1969) argues that institutional structures and cultural patterns and assumptions can prevent marginalized groups from achieving their full potential, thus contributing to the oppression of certain segments of society. Distinct from direct violence, which is generally a form of physical harm committed by individual agents, cultural and structural violence is built into societal structures, supported by laws and regulations, engrained into culture, and/or perpetuated through customs and traditions. Such structures prevent marginalized groups from influencing resource allocation in their favor and perpetuate asymmetric power relations. According to peace scholar Adam Curle (in Curle and Dugan 1982), in situations of asymmetric power and relatively unpeaceful relations between parties, actors should engage in education (methods of protest and persuasion) during periods of latent conflict and nonviolent confrontation (methods of noncooperation and nonviolent intervention) and advocacy in periods of overt conflict as important stages prior to negotiation or mediation and sustainable peace.

## History of nonviolence

Nonviolence has a long history, and its tenets can be found in many religions, from the Buddhist imperative to do no harm to the Christian message of turning the other cheek. However, collective resistance against unjust laws and oppressive rulers is not merely a religious, nor modern, phenomenon; the first documented incidence of nonviolent resistance dates back to the Roman Republic, predecessor of the Roman Empire from 509 to 527 BC. Various acts of nonviolent resistance and public self-sacrifice were used to object to participation in defensive wars (Howes 2014). Many secular groups are also strong proponents of nonviolent principles based on ethical values, for example treating all humans with respect and dignity and the commitment to upholding human rights. Henry David Thoreau's foundational work *Civil Disobedience* (2008 [1849]) argues for accountability of political leaders to counter the temptation to misuse power and resort to corruption and tyranny. Individuals should trust their conscience and oppose unethical government action with civil disobedience. This includes in democracies, because the principles and beliefs of the majority are not necessarily just or ethically correct and can lead to oppression of minorities. Similarly, Leo Tolstoy's (1967) *Civil Disobedience and Nonviolence* emphasizes the responsibility of the individual to resist unjust laws and practices. Theoretical and philosophical approaches to nonviolence are complemented by scholarship examining empirical data to provide "lessons learned" and best practices.

Two well-known nonviolent movements of the twentieth century, Gandhi's struggle for Indian independence and the Civil Rights movement in the US, had significant impact on world politics and influence scholarship to this day. However, many lesser-known civil resistances resulted in positive change as well. For example, in 1942 Norwegian teachers resisted Nazi Germany's occupation by refusing to teach fascism or join a fascist organization for teachers. The Nazi regime responded with harsh countermeasures, and many teachers were arrested and sent to concentration camps or to the Arctic. Parents' support of the resistance and the teachers' firm stance eventually led to the dissolution of the fascist teacher organization before Norwegian schools could be used for fascist propaganda (Sharp 2005, 135–42). In 2003, thousands of women organized in Liberia to end the civil war. Through demonstrations, dancing, singing, and praying in the streets dressed in white, they raised awareness and eventually met with President Taylor to advocate for peace. Contacting stakeholders, including rebel factions and the US government, increased their agency and when the warring parties met for peace talks in Ghana, a delegation of Liberian women traveled there. When peace talks moved slowly, they blocked the doors to prevent anyone from leaving until an agreement was reached (Theobald 2012, 52–3).

### Strategy and methods

Nonviolence is often dismissed as naïve, utopian, or unrealistic by advocates of the realist school of international relations that sees states as central actors that behave rationally to maximize their power in an otherwise anarchic world. However, nonviolent activism is not simply a spontaneous display of people power, an indication of weakness, nor one that throws caution to the wind. Instead, nonviolent resistance reflects courage, strength, perseverance, and a conscious choice to resist through means that are a) generally accessible to all, b) aligned with the desired end goals of the movement, c) respectful of the humanity of the opponent, and d) strategic. At the core of nonviolence is the idea that it is a "weapon of the weak," meaning that individuals in asymmetric conflicts (i.e., who are oppressed or disadvantaged in the social, economic, or political system) can use nonviolent activism to advance their concerns. From a pragmatic or strategic perspective, choosing nonviolent action can benefit groups who would never be able to match their opponents on the physical or metaphorical battlefield due to power differences. The so-called Arab Uprisings in Egypt and Tunisia in 2010 and 2011, for example, are often incorrectly characterized as spontaneous protests. In reality, leaders of the movement had been part of youth movements that engaged in nonviolent training for years prior to the nonviolent demonstrations they helped orchestrate. However, as actions in which everyone can participate, civil resistance campaigns can conscript more people than those who meet the criteria for enlisting in the armed forces.

*Table 5.1* Select Nonviolent Methods (based on Sharp 2005)

| Nonviolent method | Protest and Persuasion | Noncooperation | Nonviolent intervention |
|---|---|---|---|
| Examples | *Public speeches* | *Boycotts* | *Pray-in, sit-in, walk-in* |
| | *Mock elections* | *Strikes* | *Stay-in strike* |
| | *Wearing symbols* | *Rent withholding* | *Seizure of assets* |
| | *(buttons, patches,* | *Refusal to pay fees and* | *Establishing alternative* |
| | *symbolic colors)* | *dues* | *institutions* |
| | *Singing* | *Blacklisting of traders* | *Seeking imprisonment* |
| | *Marches* | | *Overloading* |
| | *Walk-outs* | | *administrative systems* |

By including individuals regardless of age, gender, race, physical ability, social class or educational achievement, nonviolent action is more widely available than the traditional warrior archetype dominating many narratives of struggles for liberation and justice. Sharp (1973, 2005) names almost 200 different types of nonviolent methods, organized by three categories: protest and persuasion, nonviolent noncooperation, and nonviolent intervention. Examples of each method can be found in Table 5.1. These methods differ in the degree of risk undertaken as well as the level of effectiveness or impact. While nonviolent interventions such as accompaniment, sit ins, civil disobedience, and hunger strikes require a greater degree of risk-taking and therefore may not be suitable for all, methods of protest and persuasion – including displaying of symbols, humorous skits, marches, and teach-ins – are lower risk in many contexts. Collective banging of pots and pans as a sign of solidarity or protest, for example, is something even the smallest child can do. Political, economic, and social acts of noncooperation, such as boycotts of various types, can be done individually or collectively, but have greater impact when done in a coordinated fashion.

Given that civil resistance efforts often seek to raise awareness about sociopolitical and economic oppression, nonviolent activists may engage in civil disobedience by intentionally breaking laws considered unjust and facing the consequences, including imprisonment without violence or refusal, openly proclaiming their reason for breaking the law. Rosa Parks famously broke US segregation laws on a Montgomery bus in 1955 when she refused to give up her seat to a white passenger. Dr. Martin Luther King Jr. wrote, "an unjust law is a code that is out of harmony with the moral law" (King 1963, 3). While nonviolent activists may pay a significant cost for their acts of civil disobedience, they also attract media attention to their causes while shifting sympathies of some audiences. Commitment to nonviolent action specifically in threatening and intimidating situations is at the core of a successful movement, and "discussing nonviolence when things are going smoothly does not carry much weight. It is precisely when things become really difficult, urgent, and critical that we should think and act with nonviolence" (Dalai Lama 2006, XIV).

By modeling respect for the humanity of the opponent through the refusal to engage in physical violence – even when threatened – nonviolence helps create the foundations for systems based on respect for fundamental human rights and diversity of perspectives. One of the oft-cited benefits of nonviolent action is that it is a form of prefigurative politics; that is, it seeks to model the world they wish to create, through more democratic, egalitarian methods. Further, when an oppressor responds to nonviolent action with violent force, more people may sympathize with the cause and even join the movement. Such acts can also undermine the opponents' sources of power, especially if security forces or key leaders shift their loyalties as a result (Sharp 2005, 47; Nepstad 2011) but are more likely when parties feel they are not physically threatened and can envision living in a context governed by their erstwhile opponent.

---

**Textbox 5.1  Surprising with creativity**

Nonviolent resistance takes many forms at different times and places and utilizes different forms of power. Ideally, campaign organizers select methods and tactics designed to achieve short-term objectives along the way to longer-term social change goals and conduct power-mapping activities to determine who holds which kinds of power in the community of interest. Although marches and demonstrations are perhaps the most familiar forms of nonviolent activism to general audiences, there are scores of other available methods. Creativity and comedy are assets in civil resistance campaigns, as is the element of surprise. Set in 411 BCE, Aristophanes' play Lysistrata tells the story of Greek women who withhold sex from all men in an effort to end the Peloponnesian war, utilizing the power available to them in a male-dominated society. As documented in "The Wanted 18," Palestinians in the town of Beit Sahour bought a small herd of cows to avoid buying Israeli milk during the first intifada in the late 1980s. However, Israel declared owning cows to be illegal, and thus producing milk became an act of civil disobedience and the 18 cows became "wanted." Although humorous in its portrayal of the animated cows' efforts to hide from the military, the story illustrates the quest of popular campaigns to defeat arbitrary and unjust laws. A third example of humor in protest comes from Siberia in 2012, where the government banned opposition protests and activists set up a display of small dolls and toys holding signs calling for clean elections and opposing acts of corruption. Unable to arrest the organizers for a protest, the authorities grasped at straws, suggesting that activists should have rented the plot of snow where the toys were displayed before they put them there.[1] This exaggerated response to the protest of dolls and toys underscored the activists' message regarding the regime's closing of space for opposition.

---

## Theories related to nonviolence

Nonviolent resistance is distinct from what Kenneth Boulding termed "unviolence" in that it is purposeful, organized effort to undermine the power of an oppressive regime or socioeconomic system. While it is unarmed and refrains from physical violence, it is neither passive nor the simple avoidance of force.

### *Reconceptualizing power dynamics*

Power is sometimes falsely equated with the capacity to use force, or possession of economic or political authority. The phenomenon of power is crucial to nonviolent movements because "non-violent action is . . . about depriving the power-holders of the deepest sources of their power, outflanking their more visible coercive instruments" (Roberts and Ash 2009, 375). Nepstad (2015) distinguishes between elite-based and citizen-based power structures. In the former, elites monopolize power, leaving ordinary citizens with limited agency to voice their concerns and influence change. In the latter, the public has significant tools at its disposal to bring about change. Nonviolence theory assumes that rulers are powerful only because the ruled obey and consent to being ruled. Refusing to obey, withdrawing consent, and realizing the power of the collective reverses this perceived power dynamic (Sharp 2005). People power works because of masses of individuals as well as strategic leaders who provide guidance, direction, and inspiration. As Roberts and Ash (2009, 384) observe: "on the one hand, there are very large numbers of individual people acting collectively, directly, publicly, and unpredictably; on the other, there are great or less great individuals who . . . play a decisive role in human history." Sharp's (2005) pluralistic approach assumes power is dispersed throughout society, with distributions changing over time based on a range of tangible and intangible factors, including access to resources, skills and knowledge, and ideological/cultural beliefs related to cooperation and obedience.

### (When) does nonviolence work?

Despite the long history and documented successes of nonviolent action, its effectiveness is regularly questioned. In a widely acclaimed study, Chenoweth and Stephan (2011) empirically examine the effectiveness of 323 violent and nonviolent campaigns from 1900 to 2006, finding that nonviolent campaigns were twice as likely to achieve a measure of success as violent campaigns. Maybe even more surprisingly, they found the rate of success was unaffected by opposing regime type, regime capabilities, and repression. Specifically for antiregime efforts, nonviolence has a significantly higher likelihood of success than violence, and even in territorial conflicts, which are often associated with wars fought by militaries and militias, nonviolence is slightly more successful. The authors attribute this success to the exposure and undermining of power structures when masses are mobilized.

Critics of nonviolent action often suggest it takes too long to achieve change, is not appropriate to the circumstances or that power imbalances are too great. However, using violent means, as evidenced by Chenoweth and Stephan, does not guarantee success or shorter duration. The introduction of violence to the Syrian protests of 2011 has made the conflict more intractable and more difficult to resolve; the introduction of more and greater powers has only further entangled and entrenched the Assad regime rather than achieved the aims of the protestors. While it is true that Assad massacred protestors, the regime's violence has not lessened with the introduction of armed actors, and now hundreds of thousands of Syrians have been killed with hundreds of thousands more displaced.

### Mechanisms for nonviolent change

Strategically analyzing and deploying citizen power to undermine the power of one's opponent is vital to the success of nonviolent action. Sharp (2005) identified three key mechanisms for political change: conversion, accommodation, and nonviolent coercion and disintegration. Opponents are rarely "converted" to agree with the opponents' point of view, but frequently accommodate some demands because of the high cost to maintain the status quo. However, when the oppressor is not willing to make concessions, nonviolent coercion can be an effective tool. Coercion occurs when change is forced against the will of the opponent; it requires a significant loss of power on the opponent's side and the inability or unwillingness to maintain the status quo (Sharp 2005; Schock 2015).

Scholars and activists often differentiate between principled (moral/ethical) and pragmatic (strategic) approaches to nonviolence. While both approaches are unarmed and draw on the same list of methods, their philosophical differences can lead to varied strategic and practical considerations. Principled nonviolence is characterized by religious and moral convictions that prohibit any type or threat of physical violence and for some, a firm belief that the process needs to meet ethical standards of pacifism. The most prominent advocate of principled nonviolence was Gandhi, who appealed to the morality and conscience of his oppressors. From this perspective, persuading and changing the opponent's views is just as important as changing societal structures and norms, and the preference is for solutions that are beneficial for both sides. Those engaged in civil resistance for moral or religious reasons emphasize the synergy between means and ends in respecting the humanity of the enemy. In contrast, pragmatists do not oppose violence in all cases; pragmatic use of nonviolence results from strategic consideration of available options and the determination that nonviolent resistance is the most realistic and efficient path to change. Pragmatic nonviolence may rely on coercion, albeit unarmed varieties, to undermine the pillars of support of an unjust or oppressive individual, institution, or regime. In practice, the distinction is not always so stark; activists who engage in civil resistance for pragmatic reasons may have moral reasons for their choices, and principled activists also act strategically.

In comparison to mediation and negotiation, which are designed to reduce or ameliorate conflict, nonviolent resistance often intentionally provokes and/or creates conflict. While this conflict may be creatively orchestrated and is unarmed, there are debates within the field regarding the boundaries of nonviolent action. As Kurt Schock (2015, 3) observes, "Implementing nonviolence does not mean that opponents, third parties, or bystanders will not be inconvenienced, distressed, or nonviolently coerced, or that they will not respond with violence." Successful campaigns require significant strategic planning, power mapping, and coalition building. Prior to the lunch counter sit-ins in Nashville, for example, students underwent extensive nonviolence training to develop the skills and discipline necessary for reacting calmly to the anticipated threats, insults, and physical attacks they would receive from bystanders and authorities. Activists also identified the pillars of support within the community and nurtured those relationships, even as they also sought to identify and strategically undermine the pillars of support for the racist system they were targeting. Nonviolent organizers can build their support base through strategically emphasizing their respectability, legitimacy, or moral stance in their appeals. The Mothers of the Plaza de Mayo in Argentina, for example, emphasized their motherhood by wearing white headscarves displaying the names of their "disappeared" children to protest against the military junta. Demanding answers and accountability, they used their status as mothers to appeal to a large audience and managed to mobilize domestic and international support.

Many movements benefit from the "radical flank effect," a more radical arm of the movement with more extreme goals and demands, sometimes even with the use or threat of violence. This can make the mainstream movement appear more reasonable, increase its legitimacy, and advance the movement's overall goals. However, activities of the radical flank can also undermine the credibility of the whole movement, alienate potential allies, and jeopardize concessions made by the oppressor (Schock 2015). In Chenoweth and Stephan's (2011) estimation, this holds true in particular when loyalty shifts of military or other high-ranking security personnel are required to interrupt the oppressor's sources of power.

Because the practice of nonviolent resistance is typically used in asymmetrical contexts, it often confronts and challenges existing power structures. Consequently, those engaged in nonviolent resistance are often maligned, portrayed as hooligans, imprisoned, or denounced for failing to compromise or act peaceably. Nonviolent campaigns may focus on structural and cultural violence – aspects of culture that help legitimize direct or structural violence – that are frequently invisible to those benefitting from them, whether that be the dominant racial, ethnic or linguistic group, or those in the upper and middle socioeconomic classes. Because those benefiting from such structures – akin to "white privilege" or "male privilege" – may not have experienced or understand the injustices challenged by nonviolent movements, activists may need to engage in awareness-raising efforts to help shift the spectrum of allies such that those who passively oppose the movement or are neutral are convinced to become neutral or passive allies. Scholar-activist George Lakey designed the "spectrum of allies" tool to help organizers identify allies, potential allies, and opponents to the movement so they can consider how actors might be shifted closer to the activists' perspective and farther from their opponent's, even if a move is from active to passive opponent. Although active opponents are unlikely to move to a supportive position, some passive adversaries might be convinced to move to a neutral position, such as when Delta Airlines canceled its discounts for National Rifle Association (NRA) members after they were approached by gun-control advocates. Although this decision had a limited economic impact, the symbolism involved drew national attention to the issue. Shifting opponents often requires extensive research, analysis of power structures, examination of points of leverage, and assessment of networks and relationships with influential contacts.

## The case of nonviolent resistance in Israel/Palestine

Palestinians have a long, if relatively unknown to Western audiences, history of civil resistance, which has been documented by scholars, including Mazin Qumsiyeh (2011), Mary King (2007), Mohammed Abu-Nimer (2003), Julie Norman (2010), Wendy Pearlman (2011), and Maia Carter Hallward (2011). While the specific strategies and tactics have varied over time and place, Palestinians have drawn from all three categories of methods outlined by Sharp, have engaged in both acts of omission and commission, and have illustrated through their resistance some of the tensions involved in maintaining strategic nonviolent discipline and dealing with the radical flank effect. The case that follows explores these issues, as well as debates surrounding whether the civil resistance efforts of Palestinians have consistently met the criteria of being 1) generally accessible to all, 2) aligned with the desired end goals of the movement, 3) respectful of the humanity of the opponent, and 4) strategic.

Palestinians and solidarity activists have used a wide range of methods of protest and persuasion over the years. One such example is graffiti artist Banksy, who painted the iconic imagery of balloons lifting a girl over the eight-meter-high concrete wall Israel built around Bethlehem and other parts of the West Bank. Marches, parades, religious processions, and the Palestinian marathon that raises awareness for their lack of freedom of movement all fall into this category. During the first intifada and before, when it was illegal to fly the Palestinian flag, symbolic displays of the Palestinian colors also fell into this category, as did the series of papers written by Jonathan Kuttab and Mubarak Awad for the Palestinian Center for the Study of Nonviolence.

### *The first intifada (1987–1991)*

Palestinians have used a wide range of methods of social, economic, and political noncooperation. Indeed, the methods used by BDS (discussed in depth later) fall into this category of nonviolent action. During the first *intifada*, literally "shake off," the Palestinians sought to rid themselves of Israeli occupation through a variety of means, including general strikes, boycotts of Israeli goods, planting their own gardens, and producing their own milk (see Textbox 5.1). When Israeli authorities closed Birzeit University and other schools, Palestinians created alternative educational institutions, secretly, in peoples' homes. An entire generation of political prisoners was self-educated in Israeli jails, another form of alternative institution-building, and the Unified National Leadership Command that coordinated actions among the four main secular factions in the West Bank was established. Yitzhak Rabin responded to unarmed protestors – often young boys – with his infamous "break their bones" policy directing Israeli soldiers to break the arms and legs of Palestinians for anything from writing graffiti on walls during curfew to throwing stones at armored tanks.

The largely nonviolent resistance (since many consider rock-throwing violent, even if it is unarmed) conducted on a broad scale strengthened Palestinian collective identity and posed a challenge not only to the Israeli military occupation, but also to the exiled Palestinian leadership in Tunis, who saw the strong, grassroots character of the movement as a threat. Failure of support for the nonviolent activists from the PLO, as well as the use of violence by some Palestinian factions, particularly in the later years of the uprising, undermined the popular struggle and counteracted the effort to elicit a loyalty shift among Israeli soldiers. Although some Israeli soldiers refused to respond to unarmed boys with brutal force, mixed messages from the PLO and the grassroots committees, as well as the collapse of nonviolent discipline failed to convince a critical mass of soldiers – or Israeli civilians – that Israel's interests were better served by withdrawal. Thus, the first intifada was a) generally accessible to all, and b) a grassroots movement that led to the creation of thousands of committees that included broad swathes of the population and laid the foundations for a vibrant and democratic civil society, which was aligned with the state-building goals of the popular struggle. However, although many aspects of the first intifada were c) respectful of the humanity of the opponent, and Israeli and Palestinian activists coordinated through groups such as Committee of the Iron Fist, the organizers did not always strategically and intentionally seek to engage with the humanity of Israeli society – in part due to the fact that Palestinians primarily engaged with Israeli soldiers occupying their towns and cities. Finally, elements of the first intifada were d) strategic, such as the creation of coordinating committees, an intellectual think tank that formulated and disseminated ideas and led to the creation of the Unified National Leadership Command; however, some tactics were not targeted enough, and the lack of support of the PLO undermined their efforts.

### The second intifada (2000–2005)

Although the second Palestinian intifada is most commonly known for the suicide attacks used by Hamas, internal conflict among Palestinian factions and the Palestinian Authority, and a brutal Israeli response, including reinvasion, extensive curfews (when individuals are not allowed out of their homes for days), and the erection of hundreds of barriers prohibiting movement between Palestinian areas, nonviolent popular struggle continued. During this period, many methods were limited due to restrictions on Palestinian movement. Some Palestinian and Israeli activists, however, joined forces in nonviolent actions along the route of the separation barrier Israel began constructing and engaged in strategic efforts to resist construction of the wall.

Through creative protest, such as dressing in blue to represent the indigenous peoples displaced in the popular Avatar movie and building and occupying their own "settlement" in the olive groves per the army's specification, Palestinians, often accompanied by Israeli and international solidarity activists, drew attention to the issue and routinely disrupted the construction efforts (Hallward 2009). Although such actions – due to the time and risks involved – were not widely accessible, they demonstrated a popular organization and inclusion at the village level that crossed lines of division. Coordination with Israeli activists illustrated the capacity of Palestinians and Israelis to work together when power balances were equal and goals were aligned. However, the fragmentation of Palestinian society – politically, economically, and geographically – challenged efforts to coordinate the village level protests into a national movement. Further, the Palestinian Authority again failed to mobilize in support of the protestors, widening the gap between the people and the governing body. Although villages such as Budrus and Bil'in managed to move the route of the wall through their popular resistance, legal cases, and efforts to raise international awareness, they still lost hundreds of olive trees – a key economic resource – and have not yet achieved self-determination.

### The boycott, divestment, and sanctions movement

In 2005, over 170 Palestinian civil society organizations came together to issue a call for boycott, divestment, and sanctions (BDS), asking for global civil society pressure on Israel until it complies with international law and universal principles of human rights. Although Palestinians and Israeli peace activists have long called for boycotts of Israeli settlement goods, the 2005 call targets not only settlement products, but also companies that violate the rights of Palestinian refugees and Palestinians holding Israeli citizenship, as well as those who support the occupation more broadly, such as Motorola Solutions and HP, which provide surveillance equipment and technology used at the separation barrier and Israeli checkpoints.[2] It is also an example of nonviolent coercion, as it attempts to change government action through collective economic pressure. Modeled on the BDS campaign targeting South African anti-apartheid, the Palestinian BDS movement is a decentralized, transnational movement, with an organizing hub in Palestine and networks promoting and supporting BDS in countries around the world.

Because anyone can choose to buy a non-HP printer or to boycott Ahava cosmetics, BDS is widely accessible to individuals living globally; it is more difficult for Palestinians living in the West Bank, who are a captive market for Israeli products and subject to Israeli controls on the Palestinian economy and border crossings. The movement also seeks to be strategic, selecting campaign targets that are of symbolic importance or where individuals and collectives may be capable of leveraging change. While critics of BDS suggest that it is impossible to boycott all Israeli products given the ubiquity of Intel processors and other technical products produced in Israel, BDS organizers do not advocate for a blanket boycott, but rather selection of targets that comprise the pillars supporting the Israeli occupation regime, where strategic leverage exists, and that resonate with international audiences. In addition, Palestinian organizers encourage international activists to choose issues and campaigns that link to struggles facing their local communities, for example connecting environmental movements in their hometown with the environmental impact of various occupation policies, from uprooting trees to building the separation barrier to the dumping of Israeli garbage in West Bank territory.

In contrast to the Otpor! campaign in Serbia that sought to bring down Milosevic, or the California grape boycott that sought better pay and working conditions in the late 1960s, the BDS movement does not articulate a clear end goal, but rather seeks implementation of international law. Opponents of BDS argue that because this opens up a range of possible scenarios, including the creation of a single state between the Mediterranean and the Jordan River, it is a form of "terrorism by other means" that seeks to destroy the existence of a Jewish state. However, while for opponents of BDS the lack of a specified end goal suggests a disjuncture between ends and means, supporters of BDS posit that the target of their actions is a series of discriminatory, oppressive, and racist policies – more than 65 Israeli laws discriminate against Palestinian citizens of Israel and Palestinian residents of the Occupied Palestinian Territories[3] – and that by having an unspecified end goal they leave open political possibilities that uphold international principles of freedom, justice, and self-determination.

The power of the BDS movement, which has relied on economic, political, and discursive forms of leverage rather than rockets, suicide bombs, or airplane hijackings, is evident in the tens of millions of dollars poured into anti-BDS campaigns by casino magnate Sheldon Adelson and the Israeli government, including anti-BDS public relations campaigns, highly punitive laws forbidding Israeli citizens from engaging in BDS, and the denial of entry to diaspora Jews who have supported even limited boycotts of products made in Israeli settlements.[4] It also supports efforts to criminalize boycotts at the state and federal level in the United States. Opponents also seek to undermine the legitimacy of BDS by refusing to recognize it as nonviolent. To be clear, the methods listed by Sharp are not inherently nonviolent; it is their use that determines whether they are an act of civil resistance. Johan Galtung, for example, argues that if doctors boycotted a particular hospital it could lead to widespread death and the Nazi boycott of Jewish businesses was part of a racist ideology and was used to shore up, not to undermine, an oppressive regime. The decentralized nature of the BDS movement, while enabling multiple leverage points and synergistic actions, makes enforcing nonviolent discipline and building a collective identity and unified message difficult. Further, the use of tactics deemed physically violent or anti-Semitic by even a small number of activists can damage the credibility of the whole movement. However, despite the asymmetrical nature of the conflict, strategic planning and careful targeting has afforded the BDS movement with significant symbolic victories. For example, pressure on high profile musicians not to perform in Israel shifts big name stars from active supporters of Israel to passive or neutral ones on the spectrum of allies. Musicians such as Elvis Costello, Lorde, Santana, and Lana Del Ray have all cancelled shows in Israel, although not all have stated they did so for political reasons, raising awareness among common Israelis regarding the impact of their government's policies.

## Challenges and future directions

A number of ongoing debates face the field of nonviolent resistance, including ethical questions regarding whether, when, and why activists should engage in nonviolent resistance. Some, such as Gelderloos (2007), argue that the call for oppressed groups to use nonviolence is hypocritical, as it does not make the same request of powerful parties who use violence at will to control and dominate others domestically and internationally. Further, nonviolent movements often express the moral obligation to exclusively use nonviolent means and do not consider violent, perhaps more efficient, alternatives to advance their cause. This, following Gelderloos' argument, too often leads to concessions on the oppressors terms and time, and ultimately reinforces structures and mechanism that nonviolence seeks to change. Why should Palestinians use nonviolent resistance when international law recognizes the legitimacy of armed struggle in cases of occupation and when no one is calling on Israel, the fourth most powerful military in the world, to use nonviolence? While Israel carries out armed attacks daily on Palestinians with little to no consequence and the occupation epitomizes structural and cultural violence, the unarmed BDS movement is targeted for not being nonviolent enough.

At the same time, ongoing questions regarding the boundaries of nonviolent action and the limits of acceptable coercion in terms of harm to self and others remain. Hunger strikes, for example, are a form of nonviolent action, but also cause harm – even death – to those deploying the method. Similarly, while property destruction does not cause direct harm to people, it is often still considered violence because it causes economic harm, may be indiscriminate in nature, and can alienate potential allies. However, dismantling roadblocks that prevent civilians from accessing their homes and/or places of business does not cause harm, is targeted, and removes a form of harm imposed by an oppressive system.

The large-scale protest movements that occurred in Tunisia, Egypt, and elsewhere in 2010 and 2011 highlighted the power of collective action, but also the challenges facing such movements as they transition from protest movement to political actor seeking to shape new constitutions and political systems. While nonviolent action can be accessible to all, political campaigns and constitution-writing require specific skills and resources available only to a few. Further, questions remain regarding how to best respond to the challenge of external military intervention and support for armed actors, as in the case of Syria, where a nonviolent movement was overtaken by armed actors funded by an array of regional and world powers. Changing the widely held assumption that governments hold a legitimate monopoly on the use of force and that power stems from this capacity remains a challenge.

Recent nonviolent movements display new and creative ways to engage in nonviolent struggle. The nonprofit organization Nonviolence International now documents over 300 nonviolent methods, and future campaigns will likely think of additional ways to disrupt the status quo. The study of nonviolence has moved into the academic mainstream in recent years, and a burgeoning literature has emerged focusing not only on historical and contemporary case studies, but also on theory, strategy, and methods. While some large-scale studies have been conducted, additional quantitative analysis of a larger numbers of campaigns will improve knowledge on effective methods and strategy. Further, while scholars of nonviolent struggle have largely focused on removing and changing unjust laws and furthering democratic transitions, more studies are needed to investigate the deployment of civil resistance to address structural and cultural violence connected to environmental challenges and economic disparities.

## Questions for further discussion

1  Why are there so many different approaches and respective terminologies to discuss the field of "nonviolence" studies? What is the underlying logic of some of the varying names for the field?

2  How does the concept of power factor into the study and practice of nonviolence?

3  Why might someone seek to delegitimize a nonviolent campaign for being "strategic" rather than "principled"? To what extent does this distinction matter? Should campaigns be judged on their actions (i.e., are they nonviolent) or their broader views (i.e., if they reject all forms of violence always)?

4  Consider the following quote: "*nonviolence does not mean the mere absence of violence. It is something more positive, more meaningful than that. The true expression of nonviolence is compassion, which is not just a passive emotional response, but rather a*

*rational stimulus to action"* (The Dalai Lama). In what ways is nonviolence more than what Kenneth Boulding calls "unviolence"?

5　If you were a campaign organizer for a nonviolent campaign, how would you go about determining the pillars of support of the target regime? What research might you undertake? How might that information be leveraged into strategic actions?

## Suggested resources

1　Chenoweth, Erica, and Maria J. Stephan. 2008. "Why Civil Resistance Works: The Strategic Logic of Nonviolent Conflict." *Security Studies* 33 (1): 7–44. www.belfercenter. org/sites/default/files/legacy/files/IS3301_pp007-044_Stephan_Chenoweth.pdf.

2　Hallward, Maia Carter, and Julie M. Norman, eds. 2015. *Understanding Nonviolence: Contours and Contexts*. Cambridge: Polity Press.

3　King, Martin Luther Jr. 1963. *Letter from Birmingham Jail*. Stanford, CA: The Martin Luther King, Jr. Research and Education Institute.

4　Schock, Kurt. 2015. *Civil Resistance Today*. Cambridge: Polity Press.

5　Sharp, Gene. 2005. *Waging Nonviolent Struggle: 20th Century Practice and 21st Century Potential*. Boston, MA: Extending Horizons Books.

6　International Center on Nonviolent Conflict: www.nonviolent-conflict.org/. Extensive case studies and online courses.

7　Center for Applied Nonviolent Action and Strategies: http://canvasopedia.org/. Country Analysis, Glossary, lectures on how to make nonviolent movements successful.

8　Nonviolence International: http://nonviolenceinternational.net/wp/. Collection of nonviolent methods, training and educational resources.

9　Nathan, Thrall. "BDS: How a Controversial Non-Violent Movement Has Transformed the Israeli-Palestinian Debate." *The Guardian*, 14 August 2018. Accessed September 4, 2018. www.theguardian.com/news/2018/aug/14/bds-boycott-divestment-sanctions-movement-transformed-israeli-palestinian-debate.

10　Global Nonviolent Action Database by George Lakey, Swartmore: https://nvdatabase. swarthmore.edu/content/uses-database-0. Extensive collection and analysis of nonviolent movements.

11　*A Force More Powerful*. Documentary featuring many nonviolent movements of the past one-hundred years. https://vimeo.com/112189700.

12　*5 Broken Cameras*. Documentary about nonviolent struggle in Bil'in, the West Bank. https://vimeo.com/groups/51228/videos/58596849.

13　*Budrus*. Documentary about nonviolent struggle in the village of Budrus, West Bank.

14　*Pray the Devil Back to Hell*. Documentary on the peace movement lead by women in Liberia.

## Become engaged!

1　Volunteer to be a marshal at a demonstration or event in your community. To receive the training necessary for this job, see the following online resources that offer free courses/ trainings:

International Center for Nonviolent Conflict: www.nonviolent-conflict.org/.
James Lawson Institute: http://jameslawsoninstitute.org.
Nonviolence International: http://nonviolenceinternational.net/wp/.

2  Be part of a nonviolent peace force through some of the following organizations, after receiving training, or seek out an internship in one of these organizations:

Christian Peacemaker Teams: www.cpt.org/about.
Nonviolent Peace Force: www.nonviolentpeaceforce.org/.
Peace Brigades International: www.peacebrigades.org/.

3  Become a facilitator to do conflict resolution work in communities and prisons through the Alternatives to Violence Project: https://avpusa.org/.

## Notes

1  Photos of the display of toys can be seen in "Toy Figure Protests in Barnaul, Russia-Gallery." *The Guardian*, 26 January 2012. Accessed September 12, 2018. www.theguardian.com/world/gallery/2012/jan/26/russia-human-rights?INTCMP=ILCNETTXT3487#/?picture=385070067&index=0.
2  To see the full BDS call see: https://bdsmovement.net/call. Accessed September 10, 2018.
3  Adalah, an Isareli Human Rights NGO, documents these laws in a database accessible here: www.adalah.org/en/law/index
4  Under international law, all Israeli settlements are illegal as they violate the Fourth Geneva Convention that prohibits permanently moving civilian populations into occupied territory. The international community, and until very recently the US government, holds that settlements are an obstacle to a two state solution to the Israeli-Palestinian conflict.

## References and further reading

Abu-Nimer, Mohammed. 2003. *Nonviolence and Peace Building in Islam: Theory and Practice*. Gainesville, FL: University of Florida Press.

Bartkowski, Maciej J., ed. 2013. *Recovering Nonviolent History: Civil Resistance in Liberation Struggles*. Boulder, CO: Lynne Rienner Publishers.

Chenoweth, Erica, and Maria J. Stephan. 2011. *Why Civil Resistance Works*. New York, NY: Columbia University Press.

Curle, Adam, and Marie Dugan. 1982. "Peacemaking: Stages and Sequence." *Peace & Change* 8 (2-3): 19–28.

Dalai Lama XIV. 2006. "Foreword." In *Nonviolence: The History of a Dangerous Idea*, edited by Mark Kurlarnksy, XIII-XIV. New York, NY: Random House.

Galtung, Johan. 1969. "Violence, Peace, and Peace Research." *Journal of Peace Research* 6 (3): 167–91.

Gandhi, Mahatmas. 1958. *The Collected Works of Mahatma Gandhi*. Ahmedabad: Ministry of Information and Broadcasting, Government of India.

Gelderloos, Peter. 2007. *How Nonviolence Protects the State*. Cambridge, MA: South End.

Hallward, Maia Carter. 2009. "Creative Responses to Separation: Israeli and Palestinian Joint Activism in Bil'in." *Journal of Peace Research* 46 (4): 541–58.

———. 2011. *Struggling for a Just Peace*. Gainesville, FL: University of Florida Press.

Howes, Dustin Ells. 2014. "Defending Freedom With Civil Resistance." In *Comparative Perspectives on Civil Resistance*, edited by Kurt Schock, 282–311. Minneapolis, MN: University of Minnesota Press.

King, Martin Luther. 1963. "Letter from a Birmingham Jail." Accessed October 9, 2019. https://www.africa.upenn.edu/Articles_Gen/Letter_Birmingham.html.

King, Mary Elizabeth. 2007. *A Quiet Revolution: The First Palestinian Intifada and Nonviolent Resistance*. London: Nation Books.

Nepstad, Sharon Erickson. 2011. *Nonviolent Revolutions: Civil Resistance in the Late 20th Century*. New York, NY: Oxford University Press.

————. 2015. *Nonviolent Struggle: Theories, Strategies, and Dynamics*. New York, NY: Oxford University Press.

Norman, Julie M. 2010. *The Second Palestinian Intifada: Civil Resistance*. London: Routledge.

Pearlman, Wendy. 2011. *Violence, Nonviolence, and the Palestinian National Movement*. Cambridge: Cambridge University Press.

Qumsiyeh, Mazin B. 2011. *Popular Resistance in Palestine: A History of Hope and Empowerment*. London: Pluto Press.

Roberts, Adam and Timothy Garton Ash, eds. 2009. *Civil Resistance and Power Politics*. Oxford: Oxford University Press.

Schock, Kurt. 2015. *Civil Resistance Today*. Malden, MA: Polity Press.

Sharp, Gene. 1973. *Politics of Nonviolent Action: Power and Struggle*. Boston, MA: Porter Sargent Publishers.

Theobald, Anne. 2012. *The Role of Women in Making and Building Peace in Liberia: Gender Sensitivity Versus Masculinity*. Stuttgart: ibidem-Verlag.

Thoreau, Henry David. 2008 [1849]. *Civil Disobedience: Resistance to Civil Government*. Reprint, Auckland, New Zealand: The Floating Press.

Tolstoy, Leo. 1967. *On Civil Disobedience and Nonviolence*. New York, NY: Bergman Publishers.

# 6 United Nations peacekeeping in international conflict management

*Volker Franke and Karen Guttieri*[1]

## Introduction

In 1945, delegates from 50 nations gathered in San Francisco to establish the United Nations as an organization dedicated to the management of international conflict and the enhancement of peaceful relations among member states, "determined to save succeeding generations from the scourge of war . . . and to promote social progress and better standards of life in larger freedom . . ." (Preamble of the UN Charter 1945). Since its founding, the UN's most visible and arguably its most important responsibility is to keep and, since the end of the Cold War, to enforce the peace between warring states and conflicting groups. As of 2019, the United Nations is currently leading 14 peacekeeping operations and has completed 57 for a total of 71 peace operations (United Nations Peacekeeping 2019a, 2018). The UN budget for Peacekeeping operations July 2019 – June 2020 is $6.5 billion for missions involving more than 100,000 uniformed personnel (United Nations Peacekeeping 2019b). Today, most international conflicts, and increasingly also many intrastate conflicts, involve UN civilian and military peacekeepers who interdict violence, demobilize combatants, monitor peace agreements, stabilize post-conflict environments, help reconstruction and reintegration efforts, and assist in the transition to sustainable peaceful relations. With the number of member states steadily growing to a total of 193 in 2019 and an ever-expanding portfolio of projects and initiatives, the reach of the United Nations has become both comprehensive and truly global.

This chapter discusses peacekeeping as a tool of conflict management that has evolved over time. Although referencing numerous cases, the discussion features the 1960 UN mission in the Congo and the 1990s UN and NATO missions in the former Yugoslavia, focusing on quandaries and dilemmas related to authorizations and mandates, state sovereignty and human security, and increasingly ambitious, multi-organizational and civil-military missions. The chapter closes with some projections about the future of peace operations and a list of questions and recommended readings.

## Peacekeeping as conflict management in theory and practice

Shifts in the meaning and practice of peacekeeping over time coincided with significant developments in international politics such as decolonization, the end of the Cold War, and the initiation of the United States' global war on terror. Recent developments include the emergence of a UN doctrine on the Protection of Civilians (PoC); greater engagement by civilian agencies; and the addition of regional peacekeepers such as the North Atlantic Treaty Organization (NATO), the African Union, and the European Union, leading their own missions, often with UN approval.

Peacekeepers put military force behind conflict management, aiming to deter conflict by providing an external source of observation or even coercion. In the recent era, peacekeepers work more directly in affected societies alongside local and external military and civilian agencies to combat the drivers of conflict and to support social and institutional elements to build peace. UN missions pursue objectives in five broad categories: maintaining international peace and security, protecting human rights, delivering humanitarian aid, promoting sustainable development, and upholding international law.

Although the focus here is on the practice of peacekeeping, it is worth noting that international relations theory provides competing views on it. Peacekeeping is fundamentally a liberal project associated with nation or state building, promotion of pluralist self-governance, and market economics. Constructivist accounts highlight the emergence of global norms around development, democracy, and human rights that inform peacekeeping missions (Finnemore 2003; Barnett and Finnemore 2004). This normative evolution culminated in a challenge to peacekeeping's statist orientation after 2000 by the PoC doctrine that shifted the UN focus from state to human security. Meanwhile, realpolitik approaches by the United States and others in the name of counterterrorism may also be considered challenges to a liberal peacekeeping paradigm (Karlsrud 2015). A pragmatic approach depicts peacekeepers as a means to mitigate security dilemmas for warring parties seeking conflict resolution, reducing their vulnerability as they disarm, for example (Posen 1993). In response, some critical theorists depict peacekeeping instead as a project that reinforces power imbalances in the international system (see Paris 2000; Pugh 2004).

An essential paradox of involving military personnel in peacekeeping is encapsulated in a comment frequently attributed to former UN Secretary General Dag Hammarskjöld: "peacekeeping is not a job for soldiers, but only soldiers can do it."[2] That said, governmental and non-governmental civilian agencies have in recent times deepened their reach into conflict zones. Rivalries and coordination challenges among civilian and military participants followed (Guttieri 2005a). The UN has its critics, and UN peacekeeping reform is itself something of an academic cottage industry (Boutellis and Novosseloff 2017). In recent times, UN peacekeeping has been criticized for inadequately resourced missions, convoluted management of peacekeeping, underrepresentation of women, and crimes (including sexual exploitation and abuse) committed by UN military personnel (Díaz 2016).

## The United Nations as peacekeeper

In 1945, the victors of World War II created the UN as an institution for international conflict management that acknowledged the sovereign equality among states but gave the Security Council – in which they held veto power – authority for the "pacific settlement of disputes."

Believing colonialism had been a factor in global conflict, the UN initially envisioned a Trusteeship Council to assist with decolonization. That plan was overtaken by events as former colonies rushed to independence in frequently turbulent transitions. The UN turned to peacekeeping as a stopgap (Claude 1995). The ghosts of colonial rule plague peacekeeping efforts to this day.

The first UN peacekeeping effort was an unarmed UN Truce Supervision Organization (UNTSO) in 1948 to monitor a plan approved by the UN General Assembly for the partition of Palestine. In 1956, Canadian foreign minister Lester B. Pearson took this idea a step further in proposing the UN Emergency Force (UNEF), the first armed UN peacekeeping mission, to de-escalate tensions among the United Kingdom, France, and Egypt in their conflict over the Suez Canal. The UN did not establish its own peacekeeping force but drew its personnel from member states that wore blue berets or helmets to signify a UN mission.

### The Cold War: Chapter VI peacekeeping

Rivalry between the United States and the Soviet Union, both with permanent seats on the Council, long restrained UN action. Peacekeeping missions throughout the Cold War (1945–1990), with some notable exceptions, were based on "classical" or "traditional" peacekeeping mandates as stipulated by Chapter VI of the UN Charter. Advocating peaceful means of conflict resolution, Article 33 specifies mechanisms for the peaceful settlement of a dispute. Should these fail, the Charter authorizes the Security Council to "recommend appropriate procedures or methods of adjustment" (Art. 36) including the use of force to interdict the conflict and keep fighting parties apart.

---

**Textbox 6.1  Principles of Chapter VI peacekeeping**

Traditional UN peacekeeping authorized under Chapter VI is grounded in three related and mutually reinforcing principles (United Nations 2019a):

1   Consent of the parties. UN peacekeepers deploy only after the main parties to the conflict agree to the UN mandate and the presence of peacekeeping troops in the country.
2   Impartiality. To maintain the consent and cooperation of the main parties[3]
3   Non-use of force except in self-defense and defense of the mandate. Force may only be used minimally and as a last resort to "deter forceful attempts to disrupt the political process, protect civilians under imminent threat of physical attack, and/or assist the national authorities in maintaining law and order."

Chapter VI missions during the Cold War monitored truces and peace treaties aimed at the immediate cessation of hostilities by using a combination of military and diplomatic means. The major powers in this era did not contribute troops to UN peacekeeping missions. Most peacekeepers came from mid-level powers such as Canada and Belgium, who were perceived to be more impartial, or from developing countries such as Nigeria, Ghana, Pakistan, or Bangladesh. Typically, UN peacekeepers are vastly outnumbered by local military forces. Their safety depends upon their legitimacy – the premise that the parties have reached a conflict resolution agreement, consent to UN presence, and promise no harm.

---

### Case study: decolonization, democratization, and intervention – the Congo in 1960[4]

The 1960 UN intervention in the Congo was an exception for its era because it involved the UN in active hostilities, but it actually foreshadowed the more robust UN peacekeeping of the 1990s. In this case, and many to follow, decolonization and turbulent nation-building preceded intervention. The Congo declared independence on June 30, 1960, ending eighty years of Belgian rule. However, the nation was divided, and an estimated 8,000–11,000 were killed in the Congo's first civil war (1960–1964), involving government officials, secessionists, Belgian forces, European mercenaries, and UN peacekeepers, including UN civilians (for more detail see Rikhye 1995; BBC 2018).

Congolese security forces mutinied right after independence was declared. Prime Minister Patrice Lumumba as a concession named his rivals Victor Lundula and Joseph Mobutu as force commander and chief of staff, respectively (Rikhye 1995, 207–27). Political parties formed along ethnic rather than policy lines (a common dilemma of democratization). Ideological disputes exemplified the legacies of colonial rule: the merits of capitalism or socialism, whether to break with the West, and what to do with the country's natural resource wealth including diamonds, gold, cobalt, copper, and tin. The leaders of the resource-rich Eastern provinces resented unitary government control of their endowments and sought more autonomy, resulting in a war of open secession in the resource-rich Katanga province.

Belgium sent troops in response to the violence and danger to Belgian nationals. Prime Minister Lumumba requested help from the United Nations. UN Security Council Resolution S/4387 on July 14 called upon Belgium to withdraw its forces and authorized "necessary steps," including technical and military assistance, until "the national security forces may be able . . . to meet fully their tasks." The UN Operation in the Congo (ONUC) rapidly brought peacekeepers to Leopoldville (Kinshasa). UN Secretary General Dag Hammarskjöld arrived in Katanga's capital with a Swedish contingent of peacekeeping troops to replace Belgian soldiers. Lumumba, frustrated with the lack of progress against Katanga's secession, attempted – with Soviet support – to send a force to quash the Katanga secession, but became embroiled in tribal warfare when it landed in neighboring Kasai province due to lack of access to airfields in Katanga. President Joseph Kasavubu opposed the action and dismissed Lumumba, who dismissed the president in return. Colonel Mobutu staged a successful coup, removing both. The UN recognized Kasavubu, but Lumumbu continued to have a loyal following until he was arrested and killed on February 13, 1961. This prompted the UN Security Council to issue Resolution S/4741 regretting the killing of Lumumba and other leaders, expanding the mandate to "take immediately all appropriate measures to prevent the occurrence of civil war in the Congo" and authorizing "the use of force, if necessary, in the last resort." The UN was prepared for peace*making* to manage the conflict.

The UN force sought to create neutral zones, secure the safety of government leaders and refugees, and address the collapse of public services, health crises, and other humanitarian issues. The UN took measures to remove European mercenaries, including mercenary leaders of secessionist gendarmes fighting against UN forces. UN Secretary General Dag Hammarskjöld traveled to the Congo for talks with the Katangan rebels, but was killed on September 17, 1961, en route by plane. By February 1963, the Katanga province was reintegrated, and UN troops began to withdraw. At its maximum strength, ONUC comprised 19,828 peacekeeping troops from thirty nations. Two more Congolese civil wars have occurred to this date. ONUC came to be regarded as a misstep and served for many years as a cautionary tale for the UN to avoid intervention amidst active hostilities.

### After the Cold War: expanding peace operations

With the end of the Cold War came hope for a new era of global peace. However, during the 1990s, a rising number and intensity of socio-ethnic conflicts and civil wars prompted UN missions in Somalia, Rwanda, Sierra Leone, Cambodia, Haiti, East Timor, and the

Balkans, necessitating expanding UN engagement beyond Chapter VI peacekeeping to Chapter VII peace *enforcement* missions. Chapter VII authorizes "such action by air, sea, or land forces as may be necessary to maintain or restore international peace and security" (Art. 42, UN Charter), effectively accepting UN forces to becoming parties to the conflict. Increasingly, the UN faced a dilemma between respecting the sovereignty of its member states and the need for engaging in humanitarian missions to protect civilians when states fail to do so.

In 1992, UN Secretary General Boutros-Ghali introduced the term *peacebuilding*, defined as "action to identify and support structures which will tend to strengthen and solidify peace in order to avoid a relapse into conflict"(Boutros-Ghali 1992, 5). Peacebuilding introduced more comprehensive civil and military initiatives at the social, political, and economic levels (Bellamy, Williams, and Griffin 2004). Peacekeepers, working closely with many civilian partners, expanded goals beyond purely military issues such as the disarmament, demobilization, and reintegration of former combatants to now also include support to reform of governance and security systems as well as economic and political institutional reforms (Franke 2006). In 1992, the UN established the Department of Peacekeeping Operations (DPKO) – since renamed as the Department of Peace Operations (DPO). This era of "expanded" UN peace operations included:

- Traditional *peacekeeping* designed to preserve the peace once the active fighting has stopped and to assist in implementing peace agreements, increasingly relying on cooperation between military, police, and civilian actors.
- *Peace enforcement*, following authorization by the Security Council, which permits a range of coercive measures, including the use of military force to stop active fighting and restore peace and security.
- *Peacebuilding*, which involves a range of measures aimed at reducing "the risk of lapsing or relapsing into conflict by strengthening national capacities at all levels for conflict management, and to lay the foundation for sustainable peace and development" (United Nations Peacekeeping 2019c).

The UN role in international conflict management now involved a complex, long-term process intended to create the necessary conditions for comprehensively addressing deep-rooted, structural causes of violent conflict. Peacebuilding phases often overlap and occur simultaneously (Warnecke and Franke 2010; de Coning 2006):

- *Initial response or short-term stabilization*, establishing a safe and secure environment and managing the immediate consequences of the conflict through emergency humanitarian assistance
- *Transformation or transition phase*, where the focus shifts from emergency relief to recovery, rehabilitation, and reconstruction including the appointment/election of a (interim) government
- *Sustainability or consolidation*, where the emphasis lies on reconciliation and nation-building, strengthening the rule of law, security sector reform, and socio-economic recovery

Despite organizational refinements to address changing global security requirements and improve coordination, UN peace missions suffered notable failures. For example, the presence of UN troops was insufficient to halt violence in the former Yugoslavia.

### Case study: dilemmas of transition to democracy

The former Yugoslavia unraveled in 1991 in ethno-nationalist violence among its republics.[5] Bosnia and Herzegovina, once models of tolerance and diversity, became divided among Orthodox Christian Serbs, Roman Catholic Croats, and Muslim Slavs (later self-identified as "Bosniaks"). The international community supervised a referendum in early 1992, after which Bosnia declared independence and its Serb population (who had boycotted the referendum) declared their own republic. The international community, seeking to stabilize borders, rejected partition. The ensuing Bosnian civil war included "ethnic cleansing," the killing or forced removal of people based on perceived ethnicity. Public acts of terror against other groups, even against one's own people, aimed to induce people to leave or occupy an area. The International Criminal Tribunal for the Former Yugoslavia (ICTY) later indicted participants from all parties to the conflict. The crimes, many by irregular forces, included systematic rape, torture, and arbitrary killing.

In February 1992, the UN Security Council authorized a United Nations Protection Force (UNPROFOR) and negotiated takeover of the Sarajevo airport. Because impediments to aid convoys persisted, the UN increased UNPROFOR numbers to protect food and medical aid and operations of the UN Refugee Agency and the International Committee of the Red Cross (Res. 776). In 1993, the UN authorized NATO forces from France, Turkey, the United Kingdom, the Netherlands, and the United States to enforce a no-fly zone. Under Chapter VII, the UN established "safe areas" declared off-limits from attack by any party. By 1994, there were as many as 22,000 UN troops in Bosnia.

UNPROFOR lost credibility as personnel were taken hostage and safe areas were targeted. In July 1995, Bosnian Serb troops commanded by General Ratko Mladić overran the UN safe-area in Srebrenica, killing more than 8,000 Muslim men and boys (Lamy 2001). A lightly armed battalion of Dutch peacekeepers was later sued for liability in the deaths of 300 men turned away from the compound. The tragedy raised questions of troop-contributor responsibility in UN peacekeeping. Violence and human suffering not seen since World War II prompted wide-ranging calls for and promises of reform.

### Dilemmas of mandates and resources

The United States began taking on peacekeeping roles when a UN Chapter VII mission in Somalia (UNOSOM) was unable to create a secure environment for relief supplies. The Somali government had fallen apart, and violence constrained humanitarian action, including access to ports and airfields. Looting, extortion, and general lawlessness kept relief supplies from reaching the starving population. US President Bush authorized a US-led Unified Task Force (UNITAF) that deployed in 1992. President Clinton inherited the situation, which worsened when Blackhawk helicopters were shot down in an ambush and the bodies of US soldiers were dragged through the streets of Mogadishu, leading the US to withdraw. Because many Americans had seen the deployment as a humanitarian effort, the US discourse on peacekeeping after Somalia was punctuated by critiques of "mission creep" – a gradual shift in military objectives leading to unplanned long-term commitment.

Consequently, US policymakers became hesitant to intervene in the genocide in Rwanda in 1994 that resulted in the deaths of 500,000 to 1,000,000 people. The United Nations authorized its Assistance Mission in Rwanda (UNAMIR) as a Chapter VI mission to assist the implementation of a peace accord, but UNAMIR was unable to stop the killing (Gourevitch 1998; Power 2003). To this day, a question lingers whether 5,000 more peacekeepers, as requested by UNAMIR's force commander General Romeo Dallaire, could have saved thousands of lives (Dallaire 2003; Feil 1997).

The US and other influential states in the international community nonetheless rallied to address the escalating Bosnia conflict. After the leaders of Bosnia, Croatia, and Serbia signed a settlement in November 1995, the US and NATO allies assembled a 60,000-strong Implementation Force (IFOR) that arrived in January 1996 (under Chapter VII authorization). The agreement, known as the Dayton Accord, made Bosnia into one country with two parts, including three major ethnicities (and armies). UNPROFOR troops were absorbed into IFOR or withdrawn. A robust military force had now become a more frequent characteristic of peacekeeping.

The international community post-Dayton took on responsibility for building peace in Bosnia. However, unclear allocation of agency responsibilities and conflicting agendas created coordination difficulties. An Office of the High Representative (OHR), nominated by the President of the European Union and approved by the UN Security Council, became responsible for civilian implementation of the Dayton Accord. The OHR had no executive authority over the other civilian agencies and was prohibited from interfering in military operations or the chain of command. The UN remained involved, and a Special Representative of the Secretary General ran the UN Mission in Bosnia-Herzegovina (UNMiBH). However, the UN Refugee Agency, despite its name, operated along separate lines of authority from the Special Representative. The Organization for Security and Cooperation in Europe (OSCE), also separate from the UN, took responsibility for human rights monitoring, arms control, and confidence-building measures. An International Criminal Tribunal for the former Yugoslavia was formed to investigate war crimes, issue indictments, and prosecute war criminals. International financial institutions focused on reconstruction. Finally, many non-governmental organizations supported humanitarian efforts as well as political and economic programs to strengthen institutions and manage conflict in Bosnia. While these civilian agencies brought expertise, resources, and legitimacy, they also complicated for the military participants what had previously been a simpler concept of peacekeeping.

NATO authorized only a one-year commitment to IFOR and considered its main military tasks – separation and initial demobilization of the warring forces – to be completed in the first six months. However, economic reconstruction, rehabilitation, and the return of refugees and displaced persons were far from complete. Therefore, NATO military forces remained, and in 1997 rebranded as a stabilization force (SFOR). SFOR at various points provided election security, took over television broadcasts from Republika Srpska, and arrested persons indicted for war crimes. The military's goal became assurance of a "safe and secure environment" for the return of displaced people and for civilian agency operations (Guttieri 2005b). Civilian and military elements together developed a "Multi-year Roadmap" for peace that identified the tasks, the timelines, and the agency primarily responsible for each line of effort. In 2004, the European Union took over peacekeeping duties in Bosnia.

### Dilemmas of might and right

The UNPROFOR effort in the former Yugoslavia had lacked both local consent and military capability. Absent consent, UN peacekeepers became themselves targets. The US answer to this dilemma was to step up coercion until consent might be attained. Peacekeeping became increasingly fraught with reliance on military might to force or enforce conflict resolution, in violation of the UN principle of attaining consent of the parties.

Dilemmas around the use of force came to a crisis point in another part of the former Yugoslavia. Western powers and the UN could not establish whether or how to intervene to prevent yet more ethnic cleansing in Kosovo, as it sought independence from Serbia. Russia objected to a Security Council resolution authorizing the use of force to protect the ethnic Albanian population of Kosovo. NATO intervened without UN authorization. This intervention was deemed *illegal*, yet in a fine parsing of language, it was nonetheless determined to have been *legitimate* because it was undertaken after all other avenues had been exhausted (Kosovo 2001). The United States, in a historical moment of preponderance of power after the collapse of the Soviet Union, set the agenda for intervention in the years that followed.

Afghanistan-based terrorists attacked the United States on September 11, 2001. US and NATO allies invaded Afghanistan in October 2001. The US, declaring a "global war on terror," became party to the conflict. The UN Security Council authorized the Assistance Mission in Afghanistan (UNAMA) in S/Res/1401 on March 28, 2002, to promote reconciliation and manage "all United Nations humanitarian relief, recovery and reconstruction activities in Afghanistan," even as US and NATO allies fought the Taliban government. Then, in March 2003, Washington invaded Iraq without UN approval. UNSG Kofi Annan called the action "illegal" (Tyler 2004, A11). In August 2003, Iraqi resistance fighters bombed the UN headquarters in Baghdad, killing UN Secretary-General Special Representative Sergio Vieira de Mello and 20 members of his staff. The tragic incident symbolized for many that international conflict management had been effectively replaced by great power management.

### *Responding to protect*

As the examples from Somalia, the Democratic Republic of Congo, Rwanda, and the former Yugoslavia show, fragile, failing, or failed states cannot always protect their citizens from violence and harm. Following the genocides of the 1990s, the international community began to seriously consider how to respond to civil wars, ethnic cleansing, and the mass atrocities resulting from them and, ultimately, how to prevent their future occurrence. Much of the debate and, indeed, the reasons for UN inaction in these cases revolved around desires to uphold state sovereignty, i.e., the principle that self-governing states have primacy over their internal affairs and that any outside interference would be considered a breach of international norms (Thakur and Schnabel 2001; Orford 2011). In his 2000 *Millennium Report*, then UN Secretary-General Kofi Annan recalled the failures of the Security Council to act in a decisive manner in Rwanda and the former Yugoslavia and appealed to member states to come up with a response reflecting "our common humanity" (Annan 2000).

The Canadian government likewise perceived that crises in fragile states were overtaking the paradigm of security that had informed traditional peacekeeping. Canada, acclaimed for contributions to UN peacekeeping, convened the International Commission on Intervention and State Sovereignty (ICISS). Its 2001 report entitled "The Responsibility to Protect" (R2P) affirmed two core principles:

1   State sovereignty implies responsibility, and the primary responsibility for the protection of its people lies with the state itself.
2   Where a population is suffering serious harm, as a result of internal war, insurgency, repression or state failure, and the state in question is unwilling or unable to halt or avert it, the principle of non-intervention yields to the international responsibility to protect (ICISS 2001, XI).

Implementation of R2P requires coordination among member states based on a shared understanding of the key actors and the sources and drivers of violent conflict or civil strife. Since 2006, a number of UN Security Council resolutions have invoked the responsibility to protect to justify the use of force in humanitarian interventions in general and condemning all acts of violence or abuses committed against civilians in situations of armed conflict (UNSC Res. 1674). These applications included conflicts in Darfur (UNSC Res. 1706), Libya (UNSC Res. 1970), Côte d'Ivoire (UNSC Res. 1975 and 2062), South Sudan (UNSC Res. 1996), Yemen (UNSC Res. 2014), and the Central African Republic (UNSC Res. 2121).

The UN conducted numerous reforms to better respond to the needs of civilians. In 2008, the UN created the role of a "Civil Affairs Officer." Unlike the US model of Civil Affairs Officers who are in military uniform, UN Civil Affairs Officers are civilians who perform local liaison, monitoring, and facilitation; participate in conflict management, reconciliation, and confidence-building among the population; and provide support to formal state authority (UNDPKO 2012). Separately, military peacekeepers who provide civil-military coordination in UN missions are called Civil Military Coordination Officers (CIMIC).

The UN and several national militaries developed doctrines around the protection of civilians. In a newly inclusive approach, the US military worked with academic experts and civilian government agencies to develop two significant doctrines: *Guiding Principles of Stabilization and Reconstruction* (USIP and PKSOI 2009) and *Mass Atrocity Prevention and Response Operations* (MARO) (PKSOI 2012). *Guiding Principles* is a peacebuilding guide that identifies drivers of conflict and principles of action across five sectors: governmental, economic, judicial or rule of law, societal, and military. MARO defines genocide, war crimes, and crimes against humanity. It is a military guide that identifies seven forms of military intervention and the factors shaping decisions about the use of force in such situations to prepare military forces for complex multiagency operations that may escalate across the conflict spectrum.

## Challenges and future directions

The key challenges for peace operations in the future will likely revolve around commitments and capabilities. Peacekeeping commitments put strains on the United Nations machinery and state participation in the global peacekeeping partnership (UN News 2009). The collective nature of peacekeeping requires the UN to share the burdens among contributing members and to establish regional security centers for quick response and rapid deployment. In 2009, UN Secretary General Ban Ki-moon identified governance priorities, including more immediate support to core functions and support for transitional arrangements and constitutional processes. He also identified socio-economic priorities, such as the reintegration of returnees, economic revitalization, employment generation, and infrastructure rehabilitation (UNSG 2009).

Since 2009, the gap between UN commitments and capabilities has continued to grow. In June 2015, a High-level Independent Panel on UN Peace Operations issued a report finding that "changes in conflict may be outpacing the ability of United Nations peace operations to respond" and that "there is a clear sense of a widening gap between what is being asked of United Nations peace operations today and what they are able to deliver" (United Nations General Assembly and Security Council 2015, 9). The Panel recommended a comprehensive focus of UN operations on conflict prevention and mediation, the protection of civilians, clarity of the mandate, and caution to remain impartial and not engage in offensive warfare. Of particular note, it called for a sustained "high-level political engagement in support of national efforts to deepen and broaden processes of inclusion and reconciliation, as well as address the underlying causes of conflict" (12).

In 2019, UN Secretary-General Antonio Guterres reorganized UN peacekeeping and its peacebuilding structure overall (United Nations 2019b). The UN co-located two departments: a Department of Political and Peacebuilding Affairs (DPPA), responsible for electoral assistance, decolonization, mediation, and other functions; and a Department of Peace Operations (DPO), including an Office of Military Affairs, Office of Rule of Law and Security Institutions, a Policy, Evaluation, and Training Division, and Office of Peacekeeping Strategic Partnerships. The DPO structure includes an assessment and planning unit as well as a gender unit.

Increased responsibilities for international and regional peace also come with increased resource commitments. Between 2007 and 2014, the UN peacekeeping budget soared from US $5.2 billion to US $7.8 billion. But even this increased budget could not match the challenges, as peacekeepers are continuously pressured to do more with less. The 2018 announcement by the Trump administration to limit US financial contributions to UN peacekeeping to no more than 25 percent, combined with its decision to reduce multilateral assistance by US-$253 million, indicates that resource pressures will likely remain a key challenge for peacekeeping in the future.

Apart from UN-led peacekeeping, the past two decades have also seen a surge in non-UN peacekeeping operations led by the North Atlantic Treaty Organization (NATO), the African Union (AU), the Economic Community of West African States (ECOWAS), and individual countries, including the Stabilization Force (SFOR) in Bosnia and Herzegovina, the Kosovo Force (KFOR), the International Security Assistance Force (ISAF) in Afghanistan, the Multinational Force – Iraq, US-led Operation Northern Watch in Iraq, an ECOWAS mission in Liberia, and an AU mission in Sudan (Sandler 2017). In general, countries participating in non-UN peacekeeping operations "cover their own troop and equipment costs; hence, such missions impose greater expense on participating countries than UN PKOs [peacekeeping operations]" (Sandler 2017, 1882). The fact that the rising demand for peacekeeping globally cannot be met even with increasing budget allocations for UN operations will put greater responsibility for all types of peace operations on regional organizations and individual states. Peacekeeping in the future may become more fragmented. This may allow for more cultural and regional sensitivity but comes at a higher financial cost and with less normative cohesion than is provided by UN-authorized peace operations. Despite its soaring cost, peacekeeping is still the most, if currently not the only, effective and efficient alternative to stop the fighting and to prevent war from escalating or recurring.

## Questions for further discussion

1   What, in your opinion, are the most important changes in UN peacekeeping since World War II? What is changing in the world today that may affect peacekeeping as an instrument of conflict management?

2   How effective an instrument of conflict management has UN peacekeeping been? How has peacekeeping contributed to international peace and security since the end of the Cold War? Since 2001? What are some of the problems associated with peacekeeping as a practice?

3   What are the circumstances, contexts, and conditions that merit international intervention in a crisis or conflict? How should the participation of the UN, regional organizations, or other configurations be determined? How should the civilian and military

elements be determined? Does it matter whether the conflict is inter- or intrastate? Why? How would the intervention differ?

4   Select a conflict or crisis, past or ongoing, and determine whether it merits an intervention by the international community. What kind of intervention? What are the legal (e.g., UN Charter), political, economic, social, and cultural factors that determine the type and size of the mission needed? Consider the likely support and opposition, and provide a recommendation as to whether the mission should be conducted as a UN-led mission or a non-UN-led mission.

5   The United Nations has recognized the importance of addressing the specific role of women in peace and security. Using the crisis or conflict selected in question 4 above, describe the specific challenges faced by women and children and explore the contributions women and girls can make to conflict prevention, peacekeeping, conflict resolution, and peacebuilding in the crisis you selected.

## Suggested resources

1   "Ambush in Mogadishu." 1998. *PBS Frontline WGBH Educational Foundation*. [warning: graphic content]. Website available online at: www.pbs.org/wgbh/pages/frontline/shows/ambush/. The documentary explores an intervention that began as a humanitarian mission and escalated and highlights the difficulties of coordination between UN and national military forces.

2   de Coning, Cedric, and Peter Mateja, eds. 2018. *United Nations Peace Operations in a Changing Global Order*. Cham, Switzerland: Springer. Open Access available at: https://link.springer.com/book/10.1007%2F978-3-319-99106-1. Experts discuss context and particular issues for UN peacekeeping, such as its interface with diplomacy, changes in the nature of war, the use of force, the role of regional organizations, and the balance of people-centered and state-centered approaches.

3   "Ghosts of Rwanda." 2004. *PBS Frontline WGBH Educational Foundation*. [warning: graphic content]. Video excerpts available online at: www.pbs.org/wgbh/pages/frontline/shows/ghosts/video/. Links to analysis, interviews, timeline, viewers guide and teacher's guide available at: www.pbs.org/wgbh/pages/frontline/shows/ghosts/.

4   International Commission on Intervention and State Sovereignty, Gareth J. Evans, and Mohamed Sahnoun. 2001. *The Responsibility to Protect: Report of the International Commission on Intervention and State Sovereignty*. Ottawa: International Development Research Centre. https://web.archive.org/web/20070731161527/www.iciss-ciise.gc.ca/report2-en.asp.

5   UN spokesman Farhan Haq on rape allegations in Searcey, Dionne. 2016. "UN Peacekeepers Accused of Rape in Central African Republic." *New York Times Online*, February 4. https://nyti.ms/1L0VwhQ.

6   Sengupta, Somini. 2016. "What Can the United Nations Do When Its Troops Can't, or Won't, Protect Civilians?" July 12. www.nytimes.com/2016/07/14/world/africa/un-peacekeepers-south-sudan-massacre.html. [warning: graphic content].

7   Snodderly, Dan, ed. 2011. *Peace Terms: Glossary of Terms for Conflict Management and Peacebuilding*. Washington, DC: United States Institute of Peace. www.usip.org/sites/default/files/files/peaceterms.pdf.

8   United Nations Peacekeeping. 2018. "Under the Blue Helmet: Life as a UN Peacekeeper." 360VR Film, May 29. https://youtu.be/MJ_bvC9Efuc.

9  United Nations Department of Peace Operations. "Historical Timeline of UN Peacekeeping." https://peacekeeping.un.org/en/un-peacekeeping-70-years-of-service-sacrifice.

10  United Nations Department of Peace Operations. "Women, Peace and Security." https://peacekeeping.un.org/en/promoting-women-peace-and-security.

## Become engaged!

1  Volunteer opportunities for democratic governance and capacity support, emergency health, and human rights monitoring are available also at www.unv.org/partners/un-peacekeeping-partnering-un-volunteers.

2  USAID careers in economic and political development are possible as direct-hire or by contract at www.usaid.gov/work-usaid/careers.

3  Internship opportunities at the Stimson Center provide experience in the work of non-governmental organizations in peace and security.

4  The US Institute of Peace and the Carter Center offer internship and employment opportunities.

5  The online game Statecraft Model UN (involves a per-student fee) provides an interactive environment simulating the UN Resolution process. www.statecraftsims.com/model-united-nations.

## Notes

1  The views expressed in this publication are those of the author and do not reflect the official policy or position of the Department of Defense, the United States Government, or of the Air University.

2  This is an often-attributed comment, but a citation is elusive. The introduction of military forces of any type can add to the dangers for human security. See, for example, Franke and Guttieri (2009) and Guttieri (2004, 79–85).

3  Impartiality should not be confused with neutrality. Like a good arbiter or referee, UN peacekeepers are authorized to penalize infractions or violations of a peace agreement, but any action taken must remain impartial so as not to undermine the objectives of the mission and jeopardize the consent of the parties.

4  For further detail see Rikhye 1995 and for a timeline of the conflict see BBC. "Democratic Republic of Congo Profile – Timeline." Accessed September 28, 2018. www.bbc.com/news/world-africa-13286306.

5  This discussion draws from a prior case study (Guttieri 2005b).

## References and further reading

Annan, Kofi. 2000. *We the People: The Role of the United Nations in the 21st Century*. New York, NY: United Nations. www.un.org/en/events/pastevents/pdfs/We_The_Peoples.pdf.

*BBC*. 2018. "Democratic Republic of Congo Profile – Timeline." Accessed September 28, 2108. www.bbc.com/news/world-africa-13286306.

Barnett, Michael N. and Martha Finnemore. 2004. *Rules for the World: International Organizations in Global Politics*. Ithaca, NY: Cornell University Press.

Bellamy, Alex J., Paul Williams, and Stuart Griffin. 2004. *Understanding Peacekeeping*. Cambridge: Polity Press.

Boutellis, Arthur, and Alexandra Novosseloff. 2017. *Road to a Better UN? Peace Operations and the Reform Agenda*. New York, NY: International Peace Institute. Boutros-Ghali, Boutros. 1992. *An Agenda for Peace: Preventive Diplomacy, Peacemaking and Peace-Keeping: Report of the*

*Secretary-General Pursuant to the Statement Adopted by the Summit Meeting of the Security Council on 31 January 1992 (A/47/277 – S/24111)*. New York, NY: United Nations.

Chopra, Jarat, and Tanja Hohe. 2004. "Participatory Intervention." *Global Governance* 10 (3): 289.

Claude, Inis L., Jr. 1995. "The United Nations of the Cold War: Contributions to the Post-Cold War Situation." *Fordham International Law Journal* 18 (3): 789–93.

Dallaire, Roméo. 2003. *Shake Hands with the Devil*. Toronto: Random House Canada.

de Coning, Cedric. 2006. "Civil-Military Coordination and UN Peacebuilding Operations." *The Journal of Humanitarian Assistance*: 89–118.

Díaz, Pablo-Castillo. 2016. "Where Are the Women? The Missing Question in the UN's Response to Sexual Abuse in Peacekeeping Operations." *Security & Human Rights* 27 (1): 28–44.

Feil, Scott R. 1997. "Could 5,000 Peacekeepers Have Saved 5,000 Rwandans?" *ISD Reports* III (2). Accessed August 1, 2019. https://isd.georgetown.edu/sites/isd/files/ISDreport_Could_5000_Feil.pdf.

Finnemore, Martha. 2003. *The Purpose of Intervention: Changing Beliefs About the Use of Force*. Cornell Studies in Security Affairs. Ithaca: Cornell University Press.

Franke, Volker C. 2006. "The Peacebuilding Dilemma: Civil-Military Cooperation in Stability Operations." *International Journal of Peace Studies* 11 (2): 5–25.

Franke, Volker C., and Karen Guttieri. 2009. "Picking up the Pieces: Are Officers Ready for Nation Building?" *Journal of Political and Military Sociology* 37 (1): 1–25.

Franke, Volker C., and Andrea Warnecke. 2009. "Building Peace: An Inventory of UN Peace Missions Since the End of the Cold War." *International Peacekeeping* 16 (3): 407–36.

Gourevitch, Philip. 1998. *We Wish to Inform You That Tomorrow We Will be Killed with Our Families*, 1st edition. New York, NY: Farrar, Straus and Giroux.

Guttieri, Karen. 2004. "Civil-Military Relations in Peacebuilding." *Security and Peace* 2: 79–85.

———. 2005a. "Humanitarian Space in Insecure Environments: A Shifting Paradigm." *Strategic Insights* IV (11). www.ccc.nps.navy.mil/si/2005/Nov/guttieriNov05.asp.

———. 2005b. "Gaps at the Seams of the Dayton Accord: A Role Play Scenario." In *Case 279 Pew Case Studies in International Affairs*. Washington, DC: Institute for the Study of Diplomacy, Georgetown University.

International Commission on Intervention and State Sovereignty, Gareth J. Evans, and Mohamed Sahnoun. 2001. *The Responsibility to Protect: Report of the International Commission on Intervention and State Sovereignty*. Ottawa: International Development Research Centre. www.iciss-ciise.gc.ca/report-e.asp.

Karlsrud, John. 2015. "The UN at War: Examining the Consequences of Peace-Enforcement Mandates for the UN Peacekeeping Operations in the CAR, the DRC and Mali." *Third World Quarterly* 36 (1): 40–54.

Kosovo, Independent Commission on. 2001. *Kosovo Report*. London: Oxford University Press.

Lamy, Steven L. 2001. "The Dutch in Srebrenica: A Noble Mission Fails." *Pew Case Studies in International Affairs* Case 241.

Orford, Anne. 2011. *International Authority and the Responsibility to Protect*. New York, NY: Cambridge: Cambridge University Press.

Paris, Roland. 2000. "Broadening the Study of Peace Operations." *International Studies Review* 2 (3): 27–44.

Posen, Barry R. 1993. "The Security Dilemma and Ethnic Conflict." *Survival* 35 (1): 27–47.

Power, Samantha. 2003. *A Problem from Hell*, 1st Perennial edition. New York, NY: Perennial.

Pugh, Michael. 2004. "Peacekeeping and Critical Theory." *International Peacekeeping* 11 (1): 39–58.

Rikhye, Indar Jit. 1995. "The United Nations Operation in the Congo: Peacekeeping, Peacemaking and Peacebuilding." In *Beyond Traditional Peacekeeping*, edited by Donald C.F. Daniel and Bradd C. Hayes, 207–27. New York, NY: St. Martin's Press.

Ruggeri, Andrea, Han Dorussen, and Theodora-Ismene Gizelis. 2017. "Winning the Peace Locally: UN Peacekeeping and Local Conflict." *International Organization* 71 (1): 163–85.

Sandler, Todd. 2017. "International Peacekeeping Operations: Burden Sharing and Effectiveness." *Journal of Conflict Resolution* 61 (9): 1875–97.

Searcey, Dionne. 2016. "U.N. Peacekeepers Accused of Rape in Central African Republic." *New York Times Company*. https://nyti.ms/1L0VwhQ.

Snyder, Jack L. 2000. *From Voting to Violence*. New York, NY: W.W. Norton & Company.

Thakur, Ramesh, and Albrecht Schnabel. 2001. "Cascading Generations of Peacekeeping." In *United Nations Peacekeeping Operations*, edited by Ramesh Thakur and Albrecht Schnabel, 3–26. Tokyo: United Nations University Press.

Tyler, Patrick E. 2004. "U.N. Chief Ignites Firestorm by Calling Iraq War 'Illegal'." *New York Times* 153 (52975): A11. https://aufric.idm.oclc.org/login?url=http://search.ebscohost.com/login.aspx?direct=true&db=f5h&AN=14661302&site=ehost-live&scope=site&custid=airuniv.

United Nations. 2019a. "Principles of Peacekeeping." https://peacekeeping.un.org/en/principles-of-peacekeeping.

————. 2019b. "United to Reform." Accessed April 19, 2019. https://reform-un-org.aufric.idm.oclc.org/news/peace-and-security-pillar.

United Nations Peacekeeping. 2019a. "Where we Operate." Accessed October 8, 2019. https://peacekeeping.un.org/en/where-we-operate.

————. 2019b. "How we are funded." Accessed October 8, 2019. https://peacekeeping.un.org/en/how-we-are-funded.

————. 2019c. "Terminology." https://peacekeeping.un.org/en/terminology.

————. 2018. "UN peacekeeping brochure" https://peacekeeping.un.org/sites/default/files/dpko-brochure-2018v17.pdf

————. 2012. *Civil Affairs Handbook*. New York, NY. https://peacekeeping.un.org/sites/default/files/civil_affairs_handbook.pdf.

United Nations General Assembly and Security Council. 2015. "Report of the High-level Independent Panel on Peace Operations on Uniting Our Strengths for Peace: Politics, Partnership and People." https://www.un.org/en/ga/search/view_doc.asp?symbol=S/2015/446.

United Nations Regional Information Center for Western Europe. "Responsibility to Protect." www.unric.org/en/responsibility-to-protect?layout=default.

United Nations Secretary General. 2009. *Guidance Note of the Secretary General on Democracy*. https://www.un.org/democracyfund/sites/www.un.org.democracyfund/files/un_sg_guidance_note_on_democracy.pdf.

United States Army Peacekeeping and Stability Operations Institute. 2012. *Mass Atrocity Prevention and Response Options (MAPRO): A Policy Planning Handbook*. Carlisle, PA: PKSOI. www.ushmm.org/m/pdfs/MAPRO-091117.pdf.

United States Institute of Peace and United States Army Peacekeeping and Stability Operations Institute. 2009. *Guiding Principles for Stabilization and Reconstruction*. https://www.usip.org/sites/default/files/guiding_principles_full.pdf.

United States Joint Staff JP 3–07.3. 2012. *Peace Operations*. 1 August, B-10.

Warnecke, Andrea, and Volker C. Franke. 2010. "Sustainable Conflict Transformation an Analytical Model for Assessing the Contribution of Development Activities to Peacebuilding." *International Journal of Peace Studies* 15 (1): 71–93.

# 7  Peacebuilding

*Erin McCandless*

## Introduction

Peacebuilding as a concept emerged in the 1970s and was institutionalized in United Nations policy and practice in the 1990s. Yet the question of how to build and sustain peace has captured the attention of philosophers and politicians for centuries. Peacebuilding now constitutes a dominant international mechanism of conflict management. This has much to do with the fact that violent conflict is increasingly difficult to transform, and peace more difficult to achieve and sustain. A global commitment to preventing violent conflict and sustaining peace is now reflected in United Nations' twin Security Council and General Assembly Resolutions, signed April 27, 2016. In 2015, a new global development framework was also adopted, "Transforming our World: the 2030 Agenda for Sustainable Development." Unlike the prior Millennium Declaration, this agenda places peace concerns at its core, both as a cross-cutting pillar identified in the Preamble and through Goal 16, which draws attention to peace, justice, and strong institutions as necessary to meet development goals. This chapter examines the theory and practice of peacebuilding as a mechanism for international conflict management. It reflects on shifts in thinking, policy, and practice over time, as well as strategic tensions, dilemmas, and debates captivating the field.

## History of peacebuilding and evolution of contending approaches

Peacebuilding theory and practice is situated academically within the field of peace studies – an interdisciplinary field inspired by compelling historical questions and shaped by historical events and global processes, as well as ongoing engagement with policy and practice. As described in earlier chapters, realpolitik approaches in international relations eventually met competition with rising awareness of the interdependence of states and pressing global issues. This fostered a greater sense of international responsibility to become more involved in civil wars, particularly where large-scale human rights and humanitarian disasters were in play (Schwoebel and McCandless 2002).

The discipline of peace studies (or peace and conflict studies) began flourishing within this contested terrain of international affairs from the 1970s, though peace-studies programs were present in Scandinavia from the late nineteenth century. Situated first in traditional programs in international relations and political science, as awareness of the complexity of conflict dynamics grew, so did the demand for multi-faceted, -sectoral and -disciplinary approaches within peace studies. Streams of conflict management also evolved, influenced in the United States in particular by organizational theory and practice and social psychology.

In the 1990s, peacebuilding was institutionalized through United Nations policy and practice. Conceptualized by the Norwegian sociologist Johan Galtung (1976), peacebuilding, as part of a tri-partite classification including peacemaking and peacekeeping, was infused within Boutros-Boutros Ghali's *Agenda for Peace* (1992). The *Agenda* suggested that peacebuilding is a post-conflict tool to follow peacekeeping, a "process that facilitates the establishment of durable peace and tries to prevent the recurrence of violence by addressing root causes and effects of conflict through reconciliation, institution building, and political as well as economic transformation." The *Supplement* (1995) to this agenda expanded the notion to address all phases of conflict. This institutionalized a major debate that continues to challenge coherent peacebuilding policy and practice.

As attention to peacebuilding grew in the policy realm, numerous United Nations agendas aligned with the notion, as evident in the Agenda for Development (1994), Agenda for Democratization (1996), and the UNDP Report on Human Security (1994) (Pouligny 2009). While this supported greater integration of efforts in theory, in practice international peacebuilding still tended to be too compartmentalized, involving everything and lacking in strategy. This led to greater attention to questions of coherence, integration, and strategy. A growing concern around how to operationalize peacebuilding came with widening alarm over the propensity for war reversion; there is 18 percent chance of conflict relapse in year one post conflict (United Nations and World Bank 2018, 84). Ninety percent of countries with war in the last decade also experienced war in the past 30 years (World Bank 2011, 2). In response, existing efforts of United Nations funds, agencies, and programs targeting peacebuilding were deemed insufficient, leading to the adoption of a new peacebuilding architecture. The Peacebuilding Commission (PBC), Peacebuilding Support Office (PBSO), and Peacebuilding Fund (PBF) broadly aimed, respectively, to bring all relevant actors together and advise on integrated strategies for post-conflict peacebuilding and recovery, to provide financial resources, and to support the PBC in managing the PBF while advising the Secretary General on UN system-wide strategies and policies.

Other core concerns and debates that gripped the international peacebuilding community over decades and influenced the policy and practice trajectory of peacebuilding, include: 1) the question of whether peacebuilding is fundamentally political or developmental – representing different United Nations agency perspectives and prominent positions of member states of the global North and South, respectively; 2) whether peacebuilding should be targeted towards negative peace or positive peace (or minimalist/maximalist positions), and related, whether it should be targeting stabilization or transformation and addressing root causes; 3) what the core components of peacebuilding practice are, and whether it should focus on broad or targeted efforts, and the nature and role of sequencing; 4) when peacebuilding should end, including the question of when peacekeepers should leave a country, and the nature and processes of transition; 5) how to assess progress; and 6) appropriate roles for international actors (McCandless 2013; Pouligny 2009).

Throughout the evolution of United Nations policy and practice, peacebuilding was taking shape in and through many other international organizations, non-governmental organizations, with scholar-practitioners innovating in ways that would be picked up and mainstreamed in policy many years, if not decades, later. A major player attempting to change international norms and practices of peacebuilding over the last decade has been the International Dialogue on Peacebuilding and Statebuilding, a policy dialogue of three actors: civil society; northern donors; and notably, the g7+ (an intergovernmental voluntary organization of 20 countries affected by conflict and fragility). Its guiding framework "The New Deal for Engagement in Fragile States" lays out principles and a strategic roadmap to change the way aid to fragile and conflict-affected states is delivered. Attention is also being directed at the BRICS (Brazil, Russia, India, China, and South Africa), and other "rising powers" also present new thinking for peacebuilding. As Call and de Coning (2016) argue, rising powers have different understandings of what peacebuilding means and different theories of change for its realization.

Much has been written about the evolution of peacebuilding (i.e., Pouligny 2009); the conceptual debates (i.e., Barnett 2007); the relationship with conflict and how to resolve, manage, and transform it (i.e. Azar, Lederach, Galtung); and assessment of practice (i.e., Paris 2004; Call 2012) and its measurement (i.e., McCandless 2013; Caplan 2019) that is simply too voluminous to edify here. Suffice it to say that the persistence and growth of peacebuilding as a field is well evidenced by the fact that building and sustaining peace remains a "wicked problem"[1] for the global community (McCandless 2013, 1) – yet positively, one that there is increasing policy consensus on the need to collectively act upon.

### Generations of theorizing about peacebuilding

Building on the conceptualization by McCandless and Donais (forthcoming), various "generations" of peacebuilding theorizing can be identified that reveal much about the evolution of thinking and practice and the normative debates underpinning these. These are: structural peacebuilding, liberal peacebuilding, integrated peacebuilding and conflict sensitivity, the local turn, hybridity, and transformative/post-colonial.

### Structural peacebuilding

Early peace theorists promoting a structuralist perspective on peacebuilding advanced a framing of peace rooted in notions of transforming power relations, structures and systems, and promoting distributive justice, equitable development, and just institutions. While much Northern attention toward peace focused on issues perceived relevant to the security of the industrialized world, i.e., denuclearization and weapons control, structuralist peace thinkers such as Elise Boulding, Adam Curle, Emmanuel Hansen, and Johan Galtung spearheaded policy-oriented theory to reframe the concept and its operationalization, making it relevant for marginalized people globally (Fuller 1992; McCandless 2007). Attention, they argued, should be placed on changing asymmetrical power relations through varying interventions; different approaches were needed at different stages of conflict and its transformation. For Curle (1990), education and conscientization are vital during latent conflict; heightened awareness of the structural roots of conflict fuels a desire for social change, motivating advocacy. Successful confrontation advances awareness of power-holders of need for (and benefits to) restructuring rules and relationships to promote fairness and improve relations. Galtung, often recognized as a "father" of peace studies, concurred (1996, 93). He set forth the notion of the *structure* of peace and thinking around how ideas, interests, and behaviors can align to transform root causes of violence. With peace mechanisms also built into the peace structure, sustainability was more secured (1976). He spotlighted the need for international actors to be cognizant of how their efforts might reinforce structures of violence, undermining the potential for transformation.

Structural theories of conflict, differentiated from psychosocial theories (with more emphasis on emotions, attitudes, behaviors), flourished anew through literatures of war economy and political economy in the 1990s (McCandless 2007, 95), reigniting attention towards the contributions of global political and economic processes, in domestic power asymmetries and structural sources and drivers of conflict and violence (Keen 1997; Duffield 1998). Structural peacebuilding today remains highly relevant in amongst many theorists and practitioners, adapting to new contexts and complexities, and providing insight into the interconnections of violence, conflict, and fragility.

## *Liberal peacebuilding*

Liberal peacebuilding arose in practice in the early 1990s following the collapse of the Soviet Union and the liberal triumphalism that followed – though as a scholarly term, much later. This agenda – rooted in Liberal peace theory of the Enlightenment – was premised on the assumption that the broadening and deepening of political democratization and marketization through norms and institutions offered a path to peace. Roland Paris' (2004) examination of 14 countries with international peace missions between 1989 and 1999 documents the implementation of liberal peacebuilding and its failures. In most cases, peace efforts were undermined rather than advanced, with democracy diverted in some and the sources of conflict reproduced in others. Overall, the cases illustrate the ways in which processes of economic and political liberalization are inherently tumultuous – a poor fit in particular, for conflict settings, which, he suggests, need "institutionalization before liberalization."

Scholarly critiques of liberal peacebuilding over the last decade have meanwhile flourished. Critics argue that mainstream interventions have failed to understand and respond to the complexity of conflict and transitional contexts. They have relied too heavily on templated, externally driven approaches modeled on Western institutions insufficiently sensitive to – and engaging with – local realities, values, and needs. A key concern has focused on the propensity for peacebuilding (much like development aid) to weaken the state and its institutions. As Paris astutely observed (2004), while classical philosophers including Kant and Hobbes assumed that functioning states did not exist and needed fostering to achieve peaceful, cosmopolitan federations of states, the state in the liberal peacebuilding agenda was effectively being hollowed out and left behind. The rise of statebuilding as an alternative policy agenda is a result, which is influencing, and in many ways now conflated and intertwined with, peacebuilding practice efforts. Other scholarly critiques have focused on "ideological supremacy" to open space for other understandings of politics, the state, and peace, while others have targeted the unresolved structural issues of political economy, historical injustices, and consequences of power – rooted in colonial history, which is now accommodated in the liberal peace system (Mac Ginty and Richmond 2013).

The appropriateness and efficacy of liberal peacebuilding has led to deep disillusionment among a wide swath of scholars and national actors who are recipients of aid around the world. Yet, much of the western policy community remains largely attached to the values and norms underpinning these approaches. The growing tide of critiques has, however, opened pathways for new thinking and practice.

## *Integrated peacebuilding and conflict sensitivity*

Over the last two decades, efforts have been underway to achieve "integration" through peacebuilding within the UN, and "coordination and coherence" more widely across humanitarian, security, political, and development interventions – with and between governments and other international organizations globally (McCandless and Tschirgi 2010, 21). This movement can be seen as emerging from wider international policy efforts to ensure aid effectiveness, as witnessed, i.e., in the Paris Declaration. Scholar-practitioners have also adopted the concept and utilized it to shape their work, contributing to its evolution with emphasis on ensuring that it does no harm and contributes to positive results in challenging environments (Zellizer 2013).

In response to a perceived strategy deficit in UN peacebuilding action (i.e., Smith 2004; UN 2000) in 2008, the Secretary General's Policy Committee heralded integration as the guiding principle for all multi-dimensional peacekeeping operations or political mission contexts. Integrated Missions, then Integrated Peace Support Operations, were designed to ensure a system-wide UN response, and the UN's peacebuilding architecture was designed as a structure to integrate the many sectoral peacebuilding efforts. The preparation of an Integrated Strategic Framework with shared objectives and delivery plan for consolidating peace would bring coherence amongst the many competing frameworks in play in these contexts.

Conflict sensitivity grew as a key practice within integrated peacebuilding out of the "do no harm" (DNH) movement emerging within the humanitarian aid industry. Mary Anderson's pathbreaking book *Do No Harm* (1999) challenged a core premise of humanitarian aid: that it could be neutral. This forced critical reflection on the impacts (both positive and negative) of aid in settings affected by conflict. Building on these and other important works, i.e., Peace and Conflict Impact Assessment (Bush 1998), the field of "conflict sensitivity" began flourishing. Tools and methodologies to assess the drivers of conflict and peace, and to infuse this assessment into programming and policy design, were developed. The expansion and use of conflict sensitivity can now be seen across sectors and policy frameworks.

Integrated peacebuilding remains a work in progress, particularly in the UN, where cohering every agency, fund, and program to work in ways that are responsive to local context, not overly technical, and that genuinely put local actors in the driver's seat remains a challenge (McCandless and Tschirgi 2010; Zellizer 2013). Building coherence across departments is similarly a challenge for other international organizations and governments. Where security actors are concerned this is particularly challenging, given the propensity for this sector to *not* work in deeply consultative manners within a local context. This should not however, lend cause to conflate integrated, with liberal, peacebuilding.

## The "local turn"

The idea that peacebuilding should be driven at the local level and by local actors is not new. Another regarded "father" of the field, John Paul Lederach (1997, 94), famously observed "the greatest resource for sustaining peace in the long term is always rooted in the local people and their culture." Building upon and growing out of the critiques of the liberal peacebuilding and statebuilding projects, critical scholars began crafting the "local turn" as an alternative, seeking to emancipate peacebuilding from its liberal hegemony and create space for organic, more grounded forms of peace to emerge (Richmond 2009). This fresh investigation into the local turn in peacebuilding has reignited attention to local context, and local level actors, including their agency in change, the effectiveness and durability of local traditions, their legitimacy, and the relevance of all of this for peacebuilding. A focus on the local narratives, dynamics, conditions, and lived experiences of what has come to be known as the "everyday" is presenting a critical alternative to the top-down, externally driven and templated practices common with the liberal paradigm.

Scholars have produced important conceptual and empirical research over the last decade on this topic (i.e., led by Roger MacGinty and Oliver Richmond). In her critical assessment of this literature Paffenholtz (2015) highlights that despite the importance of this literature in shifting attention in peacebuilding from the international to local actors as the most important drivers of peace, there are weaknesses. These include an essentializing of the local and overstating of local resistance, which underplays the roles of local elites and overstates local resistance. Greater nuance is needed to understand the dynamics of peace processes and the power relationships informing and underpinning them.

The scholarly and policy attention to resilience – relatively new in peacebuilding but grounded across disciplines over decades – provides a variant on the local turn literature that also challenges the liberal paradigm (see McCandless and Simpson for review erature 2015). Like the notion of "peace capacities" that rose within the DNH mover resilience lens identifies the endogenous local and societal capacities that drive local actor agency – in absorptive, adaptive, and ideally transformative (for peace) ways. Its focus is on system functioning and complexity, directing attention beyond linear interpretations of context, conflict, and fragility. "Adaptive peacebuilding" is another variant growing from these trends, referring to a pragmatic, systematic, and iterative learning by peacebuilders who work closely with local communities in contexts affected by conflict. Here, efforts focus on peacebuilding processes rather than end-states, and building local and national institutional resilience (de Coning 2018).

---

**Textbox 7.1   Peacebuilding in Liberia: a sustained challenge**

Liberia, a small country of 4 million, is a recipient to considerable international peacebuilding efforts and financial investments. While considerable progress has been made on numerous fronts in its war-to-peace transition, expansive challenges lie ahead.

Efforts across numerous generations of peacebuilding took place in Liberia. As described later in more detail, integrated peacebuilding and conflict sensitivity efforts were comprehensively and innovatively employed in the country, well before many other countries with UN missions. To promote conflict sensitivity, analysis of conflict was infused within policy frameworks and linked with mission benchmarking systems – taking this work beyond its usual program-level focus. Myriad efforts were also made to localize peacebuilding efforts, departing from traditional liberal peacebuilding approaches.

Liberia also shows how incredibly challenging sustaining peace can be. Despite many efforts to date, the resilient and deep-rooted issues and challenges, described in the case that follows, illustrate that there is no magic bullet for sustaining peace. Structural issues remain – around the sluggish economy, poverty and inequality, and governance, which will demand ongoing attention – and need to be seen fully as lying at the core of sustaining peace. Further, the deep fragility that many countries emerging from conflict face and their vulnerability to other forms of crisis that can derail successful transition, need to be viewed critically as international issues requiring international attention, particularly in the realm of prevention.

---

*Hybrid peacebuilding*

The rising scholarly attention to hybridity as a lens through which to view and approach peacebuilding offers an alternative to the previous two generations – the local turn and liberal peacebuilding. It may also better account for the dynamics of peace processes and the evolution and contestation of norms underpinning them. Building upon Mac Ginty and Sanghera (2012), hybridity is a lens through which the dynamics and significance of multidirectional (international, national, local, transnational) processes of interaction and negotiation can be captured, understood, and developed. It can counter the weaknesses of both liberal peacebuilding (which fails to engage local agency) and the local turn (which fails to engage the power and agency of the external/international), capturing the nuances of this interaction.

While there is wide awareness that hybridity is present across institutions, cultures, and social processes over time, much peacebuilding scholarship has concentrated on the international (liberal)-local interaction. This focus tends to insufficiently acknowledge the hybridity of the multileveled endogenous systems, institutions, and processes in play that interact, adapt, and evolve over time (McCandless et al. 2019). It also tends to deny attention to the role of the state – a mistake that liberal peacebuilding also made – and work on statebuilding sought to amend. Boege et al. (2008, 10), however, point to hybrid political orders in fragile contexts "in which diverse and competing claims to power and logics of order co-exist, overlap and intertwine" across formal and informal, local and global, and varying forms of social fragmentation. This focus is vital in contexts of fragility where the state often does not have reach across its territory, and non-state actors can be playing vital governance, security, and service delivery roles. Understanding how such actors' interests, skills, and efforts can be harnessed and harmonized lies at the core of peacebuilding. The importance of these actors should not be underestimated: the data across many countries worldwide on citizen trust for customary leaders, for example, reveals higher percentages than trust for government (McCandless 2014).[2]

Hybridity occurs naturally, and it can also come through design; this constitutes a growing debate amongst peacebuilding scholars. Increasingly we see hybridity by design in peace operations, i.e., Afghanistan's Loya Jirga[3] and Rwanda's gacaca courts, in efforts to enhance legitimacy, acceptance, and sustainability of international interventions. Some argue that such forms of "hybrid peace governance" hold promise (Belloni 2012), while others suggest that this hybrid peacebuilding amounts to cooptation, or instrumentalize hybridity with shallow insight into the local can have misplaced outcomes (Mac Ginty and Richmond 2016, 220; Peterson 2012). While both perspectives undoubtedly hold value, hybridity is a fact, and ignoring hybrid orders undermines the potential for building and sustaining peace – one rooted in and engaging the realities on the ground.

## Application: peacebuilding in Liberia

### Background and evolution of peacebuilding efforts

Liberia emerged from two consecutive civil wars in 2003, with an estimated 250,000 mostly civilian deaths, leaving the country deeply traumatized. Many were victims of torture, rape, and abduction, amongst other human rights violations that were committed by all armed factions. This devastation was compounded by the decimated infrastructure countrywide, which left the legal system and security sector in tatters, and massive displacement. The conflict's roots lay in deep-rooted historical patterns of exclusion. Established in 1847 by freed, former United States slaves, Liberia's "Americo-Liberian" minority elite ruled the 95 percent indigenous population through systematic economic, political, and social exclusion (Shilu and Fagen 2014; United Nations n.d.). These patterns continue to lie at the heart of Liberia's fragility and division.

In 2003, the United Nations Mission in Liberia (UNMIL) was established, and over the 14 years of its mandate (renewed 16 times, ending in March 2018), 180,000 peacekeepers were deployed, including military, police, and civilian staff, and US $7.5 billion were spent (United Nations n.d.). Peacebuilding activities progressively became part of UNMIL's mandate through this time. Liberia's peacebuilding process also paralleled advancements in UN peacebuilding at the global level, and in fact, inspired and informed learning and new practice that would take root and evolve in other settings. Liberia has also been a major recipient of UN Peacebuilding Support Office (PBSO) funds, amounting to US $65 million between 2008 and 2018.

### *History of peacebuilding in post-conflict Liberia*

In the first of what can be viewed as three phases of peacebuilding efforts (McCandless and Tschirgi 2010), between 2003 and 2005, the Liberian government and international partners sought to build a common understanding around sources of insecurity and how to address them. This occurred through the development of integrated needs-assessment processes and related strategic-planning frameworks. Efforts to articulate national priorities through strategic frameworks thereafter grew rapidly, with awareness of the need to consolidate the many humanitarian and development-oriented frameworks and to infuse peacebuilding efforts and priorities within them.

In the second phase, four processes drove the expansion of peacebuilding awareness and strategic efforts within and between the UN and government (McCandless 2007). First, there was awareness generation of conflict analysis and the peacebuilding process, marked by a participatory conflict analysis workshop with government, UN and civil society in 2006. Second, conflict and peacebuilding analysis was then refined and infused within the UN's Development Assistance Framework (UNDAF) and the government's Interim Poverty Reduction Strategy (iPRS), alongside efforts to cohere cross-cutting issues to reduce demands on the capacity-strapped government. Third, critical interventions to address conflict issues (absent in existing frameworks) informed a US $15 million proposal to the newly set up UN Peacebuilding Fund. Fourth, conflict analysis was linked to mission benchmarking, or what is termed "drawdown for withdrawal" of troops, and was aimed at sustaining peace beyond UNMIL's exit.

In the years following, integrated peacebuilding efforts bore fruit. UNMIL worked more closely with the UN country team through an integrated strategic framework (ISF) and a Liberia Peacebuilding Priority Plan, developed through support from the PBF, was implemented. Later PBF funding supported efforts to decentralize security and rule of law to the regions, reconciliation activities, and youth employment, amongst other issues. A Liberia Peacebuilding Office was set up within the Ministry of Internal Affairs to run the program, building national leadership and ownership in these processes.

From the UN's entry into Liberia in 2003, efforts were made to engage at the local level, notably through Civil Affairs officers in each county. At the heart of their work was "restoring state authority," and with time and consolidation of UN presence across the country, concerted efforts were made to ensure local participation and buy-in into policy frameworks. The UN County Support Team (CSTs) mechanism was developed in 2006, the first major integrated project involving political/security sides of the UN Mission and development/humanitarian UN Country Team. The CSTs brought the UN together at local (county) level, building local administrative capacity, a key to restoring the state and providing a vehicle for service delivery.

Liberia was also a pilot country of the New Deal process and was heavily involved in the establishment of the tri-partite global dialogue overall. President Sirleaf launched the Monrovia roadmap, where the New Deal's peacebuilding and statebuilding goals (PSGs) were formulated and endorsed – goals that the three constituencies felt were more context-relevant for countries affected by conflict and fragility than the MDGs. In Liberia, government and civil society worked together to adhere to the New Deal principles and benchmarks by developing a fragility assessment, a compact with international partners, a set of peace-building and statebuilding indicators, and by ensuring the infusing and aligning of plans to reflect analysis and agreements. Liberia's Pro Poor Agenda for Prosperity and Development (PAPD), also embodying its Vision 2030 goals, embraces "sustaining the peace" as one of four pillars, with strong attention to addressing absolute poverty through inclusive growth.

## Achievements and challenges

Achievements in Liberia's peace efforts are many and include:

- Disarmament of over 100,000 ex-combatants' collection of weapons;
- Transferring of security responsibilities to the Government of Liberia (June 2016);
- Conduct of peaceful presidential (2005, 2011, 2017) and legislative elections (2011, 2014);
- Development of key national policy frameworks and initiatives (Liberia Rising: Vision 2030; the Agenda for Transformation (2012–2017); the Strategic Road Map for National Healing, Peacebuilding, and Reconciliation (2013–2030);
- A constitutional review process, a Land Rights Act (LRA), and Local Government Act (LGA), and numerous other pieces of legislation that were in process by the time UNMIL left, i.e., around justice and security sectors, civil service reform;
- An improved sub-regional situation (Côte d'Ivoire, Guinea and Sierra Leone).

(UN 2017; UN ND; AllAfrica 2019)

Nonetheless, as Liberia's Peacebuilding Plan highlights (2017, 4), despite many achievements, root causes of the 14-year war remain unaddressed. These include: slow progress on critical government reforms and notably public institutional reforms, i.e., the delivery of the national legislative agenda. Key triggers of violence, as in the early post-conflict years, include land, boundary, and concession-related disputes and corruption. Economic growth has been deeply challenged by both low prices for primary exports and the Ebola Virus Disease (EVD) crisis (2012–2015), which infected 11,000 people. Challenges are compounded by capacity constraints across and lack of trust in security and justice institutions, where presence is limited outside of the capital, Monrovia.

The Ebola crisis revealed the weakness of national institutions and state-society relations. A reliance on international actors and a dearth of structures and processes for communication, inclusive participation, and decision-making at sub-national levels revealed great lack of trust in the state and in its response mechanisms. The crisis also revealed how fragile contexts are particularly vulnerable in humanitarian crises and how easily hard-won progress can be so easily derailed with debilitating effects on public morale.

Reconciliation remains a stark challenge. The Truth and Reconciliation Commission (TRC) completed its mandate in 2010, highlighting key issues in need of addressing to heal wounds and ensure responsibility and reparations. President Sirleaf, in her State of the Nation address, admitted that her government had failed to reconcile Liberians across the deep divides (Shilu 2017). Farid Zarif, the last UNMIL Special Representative to the Secretary-General, suggested that the international community did not come with a unified voice to address the deep-rooted challenges. The UN, in the interests of honouring sovereignty and the alignment of UN with national priorities, also did not hold the government accountable to "a higher standard of social and rights-based responsibilities" (UN 2018).

Economic challenges are profound, and addressing them lies at the heart of sustaining peace. The year 2018 saw economic slowdown (1.2 percent in 2018, from 2.5 percent in 2017), an all-time high of inflation (28.5 percent), while 70.1 percent of Liberians were rated as "multi-dimensionally poor" (deprived of development) (Republic of Liberia 2018, 6). Poverty and vulnerability manifest varyingly across regions, while 28 percent of Liberians in Monrovia live in poverty, 89 percent in the Southeastern B region do (Republic of Liberia 2018, 6). Various issues have undermined ambitious economic reform plans, including a drastic fall of Liberia's traditional export commodities and the Ebola crisis – illustrating the ways in which international drivers of conflict and fragility impact national peacebuilding.

Against the critiques of liberal peacebuilding, in Liberia there were strong efforts to contextualize and localize efforts. The UN in Liberia pursued the strengthening of local administration and infrastructure for peacebuilding. Development planning processes employed strong consultation with local populations, and still do. Inevitably more can be done to localize peacebuilding in Liberia; notably, traditional and local structures can be better integrated into peacebuilding efforts, and civil society can be better engaged as a peacebuilding partner. Localizing peacebuilding, much like decentralization generally, is not sufficiently valued at national level (Neumann and Nagelhus Schia 2012, 10). There remains a wide gulf – both perceived and in fact – between the national-level elites running the country and the realities on the ground, at local levels, and countrywide.

There remain questions about whether Liberia is safely on a path to sustaining peace. As highlighted in Liberia's Peacebuilding Plan and pointing to a key driver of a resilient social contract, this will require "long-term investment in national institutions that are inclusive, accountable, and responsive, with a government that is committed to providing opportunities and services to all Liberians" (UN 2017).

## Challenges and future directions

As the previous discussion of "generations" of peacebuilding reveals, considerable attempts have been made to learn and adapt to the evolving realities facing our field. There is now widespread agreement that there are no fixed models for success in peacebuilding, that context is a paramount concern, and that existing local, national, and endogenous systems and capacities must be at the forefront of peacebuilding efforts. Peacebuilding, however, confronts innumerable challenges in transforming the conflict and security landscape and in finding agreed methods for effective practice that bring sustained results. A selection of key challenges and promising directions is highlighted here.

A first key issue involves the persistence and evolving nature of conflict. While this is not a new challenge per se, fragility and violence are also evolving and intermingling with conflict, expanding complexity and making it ever more difficult to find trusted responses to social problems. While there were advances in peace up until the mid-2000s, since 2007 intrastate conflicts have illustrated a steady upward trend (UN-WB 2018, 12). Since 2007, "wars" with at least 1,000 battle deaths have tripled, and by 2014, global annual battle deaths were over 100,000 for the first time since the end of the Cold War. As discussed previously, war reversion is far too common. Further, the nature of conflict continues to evolve in complex ways, ensuring its intractability and the widening and deepening of suffering from its consequences. The trends of "new wars" that Mary Kaldor articulated in 2001 – war without military borders and propensity for regionalization, financed through war economies and targeting citizens – are simply worsening. Numbers of violently displaced people and refugees are over 50 million – the highest since the end of World War II.

Other factors driving these trends include expanding violent extremism, the internationalization of wars, interventions by more and different types of actors, expanding links between illicit markets and organized crime, and the continued proliferation of small arms and light weapons (UN-WB 2018). Violent extremism is expanding in terms of numbers of countries and people affected, and the devastating impacts it has, including innocent lives affected. Extremist groups have wider appeal as they connect their grievances with wider struggles, capitalize on technology, and use international financing to expand their networks (UN-WB 2018, 22). Proliferation of non-state actors (NSAs)[4] is also rising, and with it the number of armed groups in conflict. A key challenge lies in their informality and fragmentation, lacking connections to the state and often resisting rule-based processes and solutions, and alarmingly, rejecting international humanitarian law (UN-WB 2018, 6) – all profoundly challenging traditional approaches to peacemaking, peacekeeping, and peacebuilding (Department of Peacekeeping Operations 2009).

Critically, violent conflict, violence, and fragility are intermixing in ways that deeply challenge peacebuilders – demanding the field to expand in scope and sophistication to grapple with these realities. This is consistent with the very focus of peacebuilding, which demands attention beyond negative peace.

While the concept of fragility has historically focused around states lacking capacity, legitimacy or will to deliver basic services, carry out needed functions across their territory, and maintain constructive relations with society, increasingly it is seen as multidimensional and linked to risk and coping capacity of the state.[5] State fragility is often linked with flawed or failed political settlements, particularly where exclusion is a factor (Rocha Menocal 2017, 4). Conflict and fragility links are clear: Since 1989, approximately 70 percent of fragile states have experienced conflict.[6] Nine of fifteen extremely fragile contexts in 2018 are experiencing conflict – and often fall prey to extended time stuck in a "fragility trap" (OECD 2018, 15).

The wide consensus that peacebuilding engages positive peace – one free of structural and cultural violence – directs focus toward the pervasiveness of violence. Armed conflict accounts for a relatively low portion of death; only 18 percent of 560,000 violent deaths in 2016, 26 percent of which were considered terrorism-related (McEvoy and Hideg 2017, 92, in OECD 2018, 51). Violence and fragility also share an interdependent relationship: fragile contexts are more associated with violence, with higher homicide rates, social violence, gender violence, armed conflict, and terrorism (OECD 2016).

Too often overlooked and critical for peacebuilding, given its common orientation as an internal pursuit within states, is the fact that many drivers of fragility and conflict have transnational and international origins and require partnership with international actors to address. The SDGs move helpfully in recognizing external drivers of violent conflict and fragility, i.e., aiming to address, illicit financial arms flows, organized crime and corruption, terrorism, exclusive global governance (Goal 16) and long-term debt, unfavorable terms of trade, and global macroeconomic stability (Goal 17). While the international community continues to be challenged by manifesting integrated approaches, new efforts to advance a humanitarian-peace-development nexus approach to address complexity are promising.

The rise and rapid advancement of authoritarian populism and atavistic nationalism is a second critical issue generating profound challenges for states and societies globally, advancing destruction of the rule-based systems underpinning many hard-fought-for social and political rights and aspirations that lie at the heart of liberal traditions (Clements 2019). The Trump presidency, the Brexit vote, and like-minded movements gaining traction across Europe and beyond are fueling authoritarian politics and knitting supportive social fabrics, resulting in deeply polarizing dynamics across societies. While populist concerns are often drawing attention to social justice concerns, including adverse economic effects of neoliberalism in the form of poverty, unemployment, and labor migration, the atavistic nationalist tendencies are serving divisiveness. Other implications threatening peacebuilding include increasing lack of truthful access to information through the media and an assault on multilateral institutions (within which lie our collective peace and security response mechanisms).

A related issue involves the implications of who is included or excluded from peace and development processes. The now-strong consensus of exclusion as a key driver of conflict and fragility is rooted in a wide base of evidence, where exclusion emanating from the state reinforces perceptions that there is no other alternative for expressing grievances and frustration (UN-WB 2018, XXII). Inclusion, on the other hand, is becoming a norm in international peacebuilding (Donais and McCandless 2016, 291). This rising practice of making peacemaking and peacebuilding processes more inclusive rests on a growing evidence base that shows both that exclusive agreements do not sustain, and that more inclusive agreements stand a greater chance of success.[7] Ensuring inclusive political settlements ultimately transition into inclusive, resilient social contracts constitutes a further area of policy and research interests (McCandless et al. 2019). These discussions have roots in scholarship and policy, i.e., on the importance of local actors in peacebuilding (discussed previously), as well as the profound need for national ownership in peacebuilding. Inclusion can support more societally owned processes, particularly where youth, women, and wider social movements engage and participate in peace processes, building legitimacy in the process and providing greater opportunities towards ensuring implementation. The importance of inclusion as a peacebuilding policy priority can be evidenced by its centrality in the New Deal for Engagement in Fragile States, across the Agenda for Sustainable Development, and in the twin Security Council and General Assembly Resolutions (A/RES/70/262 and S/RES/2282) on preventing conflict and sustaining peace.

Finally, while preventing violent conflict and sustaining peace has always been a focus area for peacebuilding scholarship and practice, policy attention, new policy efforts have revitalized global attention to these issues. These include the United Nations 2016 twin Security Council/General Assembly resolutions, buttressed by supportive analysis and focus in the 2030 Agenda for Sustainable Development and a major United Nations-World Bank study, *Pathways for Peace* launched in 2018, both of which involve the search for appropriate policy and practice to address the contemporary contexts described previously. These agendas remake the case for the value of prevention and the need to redirect dwindling resources in this direction, prioritizing the need to build inclusive ownership around a national vision, address root causes of conflicts and grievances that undermine peace, place politics at the center of analysis and response, and utilize frameworks and tools that reinforce synergies across approaches, sectors, and pillars. Despite member state consensus as never before on these agendas, overcoming differing conceptual, political, ideological, and operational notions of how to achieve these profound goals cannot be underestimated. Simply gaining agreement on what constitutes a threat to peace and when and how sovereignty can and should be transgressed in the interests of protecting lives are issues that have divided actors globally and historically, be they states and societies, Northern and Southern actors, or identity groups within and across borders.

## Questions for further discussion

1   What lessons can we derive from past peacebuilding efforts about peacebuilding as a tool of international conflict management?
2   What insight do the varying "generations" of peacebuilding scholarship and practice provide for addressing contemporary challenges?

3   What have we learned about the roles of different actors engaged in peacebuilding, for effectiveness and appropriateness in particular?
4   How can root causes and drivers of violence, conflict, and fragility be addressed and prevented in integrated ways?
5   Reflecting on lessons of peacebuilding, what does a sustaining peace and conflict-prevention agenda need to prioritize and uphold?

## Suggested resources

1   Video: A Discussion on Peacebuilding and Sustaining Peace: www.ipinst.org/2018/02/unsg-report-peacebuilding-and-sustaining-peace#10.
2   Security Council/General Assembly Resolutions on Sustaining Peace: www.un.org/en/ga/search/view_doc.asp?symbol=S/RES/2282(2016)&referer=www.un.org/en/sc/documents/resolutions/2016.shtml&Lang=E.
3   UN Agenda for Sustainable Development Agenda 2030, Particularly Goal 16: https://sustainabledevelopment.un.org/post2015/transformingourworld.
4   White Paper on Peacebuilding: www.gpplatform.ch/content/white-paper-peacebuilding-0.
5   Pathways for Peace: www.pathwaysforpeace.org/.
6   The Missing Peace: Independent Progress Study on Youth, Peace and Security: www.un.org/peacebuilding/ar/news/missing-peace-independent-progress-study-youth-peace-and-security.
7   Handbook on Conflict Prevention: https://igarape.org.br/wp-content/uploads/2018/12/The-Handbook-of-Conflict-Prevention.pdf.
8   International Alert: www.international-alert.org/publications.
9   Collaborative for Development Action: www.cdacollaborative.org/publications/peacebuilding-effectiveness/.

## Become engaged!

1   Join a voluntary organization such as the Peace Corps that allows you to do lengthy work abroad.
2   Investigate PCdnetwork.org and its career pages: https://pcdnetwork.org/the-social-change-career-helping-line-main-page/.
3   Attend annual meetings of key associations and networks. There are often opportunities, aside from presenting in formal panels, for students, including presenting posters and volunteering. These include:

   • Geneva Peace Week
   • Alliance for Peacebuilding (AfP)
   • Academic Conference of the United Nations (ACUNS)
   • The Fragility Forum, World Bank
   • The International Studies Association

## Notes

1  For Horst Rittel, these are an ill-formulated class of social system problems, with confusing information and many actors involved with conflicting values, with system-wide ramifications of great confusion and complexity (Churchman 1967).
2  Afrobarometer surveys have documented this trend in African countries. See also McCandless (2014) for supporting data and analysis.

3  A traditional assembly of leaders meeting that make decisions by consensus in Pashtun tradition. Afghanistan's *Loya Jirga* brought state and non-state institutions (customary, civil society, warlord) into critical conversation—actors with considerable legitimacy with populations.

4  NSAs include rebels, militias (i.e. pro-government, or community, drug-cartel or international actor/ government-sponsored), armed trafficking groups, and violent extremist groups.

5  This can be witnessed in consecutive OECD States of Fragility reports, the most recent in 2018.

6  IDPS website.

7  See McCandless (2018) for a review of the literature on this.

## References and further reading

Anderson, Mary. 1999. *Do No Harm*. New York, NY: Lynne Rienner Publishers.

Barnett, Michael, Hunjoon Kim, Madalene O'Donell, and Laura Sitea. 2007. "Peacebuilding: What Is in a Name?" *Global Governance* 13 (1): 35–58.

Belloni, Roberto. 2012. "Hybrid Peace Governance: Its Emergence and Significance." *Global Governance* 18 (1): 21–38.

Boege, Volker, Anne Brown, Kevin Clements and Anna Nolan. 2008. "On Hybrid Political Orders and Emerging States: State Formation in the Context of 'Fragility'." *Berghof Handbook Dialogue No. 8, Berghof Research Center for Constructive Conflict Management*.

Bush, Kenneth. 1998. *A Measure of Peace: Peace and Conflict Impact Assessment (PCIA) of Development Projects in Conflict Zones*. (Working Paper No. 1.) Ottawa: International Development Research Centre. Accessed October 9, 2019. http://www.idrc.ca/peace/p1/working_paper1.html

Call, Charles. 2012. *Why Peace Fails: The Causes and Prevention of Civil War Recurrence*. Washington, DC: Georgetown University Press.

Call, Charles, and Cedric de Coning. 2016. *Rising Powers and Peacebuilding: Breaking the Mold?* London: Palgrave Macmillan.

Caplan, Richard. 2019. *Measuring Peace: Principles, Practices, and Politics*. Oxford: Oxford University Press.

Churchman, West C. 1967. "Wicked Problems." *Management Science* 4 (14): B141-B142.

Clements, Kevin P. 2019. "Authoritarian Populism and Atavistic Nationalism: 21st Century Challenges to Peacebuilding and Development." *Journal of Peacebuilding and Development* 13 (3): 1–6.

Curle, Adam. 1990. *Tools for Transformation*. London: Hawthorne Press.

David, Chandler. 2013. "Promoting Democratic Norms? Social Constructivism and the 'Subjective' Limits to Liberalism." *Democratization* 20 (2): 215–39.

Donais, Timothy, and Erin McCandless. 2016. "International Peacebuilding and the Emerging Inclusivity Norm." *Third World Quarterly* 38 (2): 1–20, 291–310.

de Coning, Cedric. 2018. "Adaptive Peacebuilding." *International Affairs* 94 (2): 301–317.

Department of Peacekeeping Operations. 2009. *Second Generation DDR Practices in UN Peace Operations: A Contribution to the New Horizon Agenda*. New York: United Nations.

Duffield, Mark. 1998. *Aid Policy and Post-Modern Conflict: A Critical Review*. Occasional Paper 19. Birmingham, UK: University of Birmingham, School of Public Policy.

Fuller, Abigail. 1992. "Toward an Emancipatory Methodology for Peace Research." *Peace and Change* 17 (3): 286–311.

Galtung, Johan. 1969. "Violence, Peace and Peace Research." *Journal of Peace Research* 16 (3): 167–91.

———. 1976. "Three Approaches to Peace: Peacekeeping, Peacemaking, and Peacebuilding." In *Peace, War and Defense: Essays in Peace Research*, Vol. II, edited by Johan Galtung. Copenhagen: Christian Ejlers.

———. 1996. *Peace by Peaceful Means*. Oslo: Sage Publications.

Hansen, Emmanuel. 1988. *Africa: Perspectives on Peace and Development*. London: United Nations University and Zed Books.

Kaldor, Mary. 2012. *New and Old Wars: Organized Violence in a Global Era*, 3rd edition. Cambridge: Polity Press.

Keen, David. 1997. "The Political Economy of War." In *The Social and Economic Costs of Conflict in Developing Countries*, edited by Frances Stewart. London: Economic and Social Research Programme, Department for International Development.

Lederach, John Paul. 1997. *Building Peace: Sustainable Reconciliation in Divided Societies*. Washington, DC: United States Institute of Peace Press.

Mac Ginty, Roger, and Oliver Richmond. 2013. "The Local Turn in Peace Building: A Critical Agenda for Peace." *Third World Quarterly* 34 (5): 763–83.

———. 2016. "The Fallacy of Constructing Hybrid Political Orders: A Reappraisal of the Local Turn in Peacebuilding." *International Peacekeeping* 23 (2): 219–39.

Mac Ginty, Roger, and Gurchathen Sanghera. 2012. "Hybridity in Peacebuilding and Development: An Introduction." *Journal of Peacebuilding and Development* 7 (2): 3–8.

McCandless, Erin. 2008. *Integrated Approaches to Peacebuilding in Transitional Settings: Lessons from Liberia*. South Africa: Institute for Security Studies.

———. 2013. "Wicked Problems in Peacebuilding and Statebuilding: Making Progress in Measuring Progress in Peacebuilding and Statebuilding." *Global Governance* 19 (2): 227–48.

———. 2014. "Non-state Actors and Competing Sources of Legitimacy in Conflict Affected Settings." In *Building Peace: A Forum for Peace and Security in the 21st Century*, September. http://buildingpeaceforum.com/2014/09/non-state-actors-and-competing-sources-of-legitimacy-in-conflict-affected-settings/.

McCandless, Erin, with Rebecca Hollender, Marie-Joel Zahar, Mary Hope Schwoebel, Alina Rocha Menocal, Alexandros Lordos and case study authors. 2019. "Forging Resilient Social Contracts: Preventing Violent Conflict and Sustaining Peace." Summary Findings, and Full Report, United Nations Development Program. Accessed October 9, 2019. http://www.undp.org/content/undp/en/home/librarypage/democratic-governance/oslo_governance_centre/forging-resilient-social-contracts--preventing-violent-conflict-.html.

McCandless, Erin, and Abdul Karim Bangura. 2007. *Peace Research in Africa: Critical Essays on Methodology*. Geneva: UN University for Peace.

McCandless, Erin, and Timothy Donais. Forthcoming. "Generations of Constructing Peace: The Constructivism Paradigm and Peacebuilding." In *Peacebuilding Paradigms*. Cambridge: Cambridge University Press.

McCandless, Erin, and Graeme Simpson. 2015. *Assessing Resilience for Peacebuilding*. Geneva: Interpeace. www.interpeace.org/resource/assessing-resilience-for-peacebuilding-executive-summary-of-discussion/.

McCandless, Erin, and Necla Tschirgi. 2010. "Strategic Frameworks that Embrace Mutual Accountability for Peacebuilding: Emerging Lessons in PBC and non-PBC Countries." *Journal of Peacebuilding and Development* 5 (2): 20–46.

Mc Evoy, Claire, and Gergely Hideg. 2017. *Global Violent Deaths 2017: Time to Decide, Small Arms Survey*, Geneva. http://www.smallarmssurvey.org/fileadmin/docs/U-Reports/SAS-Report-GVD2017.pdf.

Neumann, Hannah, and Niels Nagelhus Schia. 2012 "Contextualizing Peacebuilding Activities to Local Circumstances: Liberian Case Study Field Report." *Security in Practice* 6. Norwegian Institute of International Affairs. https://core.ac.uk/download/pdf/52113773.pdf.

OECD. 2016. *States of Fragility*. Paris: OECD.

———. 2018. *States of Fragility*. Paris: OECD.

Paffenholtz, Thania. 2015. "Unpacking the Local Turn in Peacebuilding: A Critical Assessment Towards an Agenda for Future Research." *Third World Quarterly* 36 (5): 857–74.

Paris, Roland. 2004. *At War's End: Building Peace after Civil Conflict*. Cambridge: Cambridge University Press.

Peterson, Jenny. 2012. "A Conceptual Unpacking of Hybridity: Accounting for Notions of Power, Politics and Progress in Analyses of Aid-Driven Interfaces." *Journal of Peacebuilding and Development* 7 (2): 99–22.

Pouligny, Beatrice. 2009. "Introduction to Peacebuilding." Peacebuilding Initiative, Humanitarian Policy and Conflict Research (HPCR), Harvard University & HPCR International. www.peacebuilding-initiative.org.

Republic of Liberia. 2018. "Pro-poor Agenda for Prosperity and Development." Liberia. http://liberianconsulatega.com/wp-content/uploads/2017/07/PAPD-Pro-Poor-Agenda-for-Prosperity-and-Development.pdf

Rocha Menocal, Alina. 2017. " Political Settlements and the Politics of Transformation: Where Do "Inclusive Institutions" Come From?". *Journal of International Development* 29 (5): 559–75.

Richmond, Oliver. 2009. "A Post-liberal Peace: Eirenism and the Everyday." *Review of International Studies* 35: 557–80.

Schwoebel, Mary-Hope, and McCandless, Erin. 2002. "From Making to Building Peace in the 21st Century: New Approaches for New Conflict Contexts." In *Global Almanac*. Washington DC: CQ Press.

Shilu, Jimmy. 2017. "Election and Democracy in Liberia." *The African Bulletin*. http://mediablackberry.com/election-and-democracy-in-liberia/.

Shilue, James, and Patricia, Fagen. 2014. *Liberia: Links Between Peacebuilding, Conflict, Prevention and Durable Solutions to Displacement*. Washington, DC: Brooking Institution. https://www.brookings.edu/research/liberia-links-between-peacebuilding-conflict-prevention-and-durable-solutions-to-displacement/

Smith, Dan. 2004. "Towards a Strategic Framework for Peacebuilding: Getting Their Act Together." *Overview Report of the Joint Utstein Study of Peacebuilding*, Norwegian Ministry of Foreign Affairs, Oslo.

United Nations. n.d. "UNMIL Facts." https://peacekeeping.un.org/en/unmil-facts

———. 2000. *Report of the Panel on United Nations Peace Operations*. New York, NY: UN. www.un.org/peace/reports/peace_operations/.

———. 2017. "Sustaining Peace and Securing Development: Liberia Peacebuilding Plan." https://unmil.unmissions.org/sites/default/files/liberia_peacebuilding_plan_-_20_march_2017.pdf.

———. 2018. "Mutual Accountability Must Be Fundamental to Peacekeeping." https://unmil.unmissions.org/mutual-accountability-must-be-fundamental-peacekeeping-farid-zarif-under-secretary-general-special.

United Nations and World Bank. 2018. *Pathways for Peace: Inclusive Approaches to Preventing Violent Conflict*. Washington, DC: World Bank Group.

World Bank. 2011. *World Development Report 2011: Conflict, Security, and Development*. Washington, DC: World Bank.

Zellizer, Craig. 2013. "Introduction to Integrated Peacebuilding." In *Integrated Peacebuilding: Innovative Approaches to Transforming Conflict*, edited by Craig Zelizer. New York, NY: Avalon Publishing.

# 8 Transitional justice

*Maureen Wilson and Edwin N. Njonguo*

## Introduction

In the aftermath of violent conflict and political transitions, societies face the challenge of coping with legacies of widespread human rights abuses and dealing with accountability and justice issues. Inadequate or broken institutions, insecurity, political and social conflict, and histories of repression set the stage for human rights abuses and the eventual need for reconciliation and peacebuilding. For states emerging from periods of conflict and repression, *transitional justice* mechanisms seek to address past conflicts and atrocities.

Given that the field of *transitional justice* is interdisciplinary, scholars vary in how they define the term. However, there is general agreement that transitional justice takes place in post-conflict or transitional contexts, whereby societies strive to attain a point of political stability from a period of violence and repression. The scope and severity of such abuses are widespread and grave and can range from torture to mass incarceration, maiming, sexual and gender-based violence, political disappearance, and genocide. The United Nations defines *transitional justice* as "the full range of processes and mechanisms associated with a society's attempts to come to terms with a legacy of large-scale abuses, in order to ensure accountability, serve justice and achieve reconciliation" (United Nations Security Council 2004). Because transitional justice seeks to address such extraordinary abuses, ordinary institutions and justice systems are "not able to provide an adequate response," according to the International Center for Transitional Justice (International Center for Transitional Justice 2019). Reasons for inadequate responses include, amongst others, the lack of capacity or will to investigate, seek, and implement justice mechanisms.

It is generally accepted by the international community that in the wake of events that result in the commission of major human rights abuses, impunity – the act of perpetrating atrocities against humanity without being held accountable – is not an option, and that states must address humanity's gravest crimes. Popularized in the twentieth century in the aftermath of World War II, which saw some of the worst atrocities against humanity in history, transitional justice practices have grown to include a variety of legal and non-legal methods to help societies remember and deal with past trauma. These methods include prosecutions in domestic courts, ad hoc tribunals, the International Criminal Court (ICC), amnesties, reparations, truth commissions, memorialization, and lustration or vetting policies, as discussed later in this chapter. The adoption and implementation of transitional justice is a complicated process that is dependent on political and economic factors. Questions of how to deal with the aftermath of conflict are critical to victims, practitioners, scholars, donors, and the international community at large in order to prevent future conflict.

This chapter explores the background and history of transitional justice as it is known today, presents current theoretical understandings and applications, examines contending approaches and key challenges to the notion of transitional justice, and discusses the cases of Rwanda, Chile, and Iraq, which highlight the variations and complexities of the transitional justice question.

## History of transitional justice in the twentieth century

International conflict management has witnessed the increasing application of transitional justice mechanisms in addressing local and international conflicts, especially since the late 1980s and early 1990s. The notion of transitional justice as it exists today can be traced back to the Paris Peace Conference of 1919, convened by the victorious Allied powers (France, Great Britain, Italy, Japan, and the United States) to address the atrocities of World War I. The Geneva Conference of 1937, which was held by the League of Nations, advanced transitional justice by defining the crimes that are today addressed using transitional justice approaches, including crimes against humanity, war crimes, and genocide. Whereas the post-World War I era saw the conceptualization of the jurisdiction and mechanisms of transitional justice, the post-World War II period was characterized by the creation of specialized institutions to deal with the identified atrocities as well as to advance international criminal justice.[1]

Before World War II, individuals, especially those in power, were not held accountable for heinous crimes. The establishment of criminal tribunals for the prosecution of leaders of the Nazi party in Germany and political and military leaders of Japan (commonly referred to as the Nuremberg Trials and the Tokyo Tribunals) were the first to seek accountability from those responsible for planning and carrying out war crimes and crimes against humanity. After the devastation of World War II, and specifically the genocide of the Holocaust, in which over 6 million civilians were intentionally killed by the Nazis, the international community determined that impunity was not an option.[2]

Held under the auspices of the Allied forces, the Nuremberg trials were an important milestone in the development of transitional justice, but also in international law more broadly. The proceedings helped in the development of the jurisprudence, the theoretical or philosophical study of international humanitarian law, specifically relating to war crimes, crimes against humanity, and genocide. Critics referred to the tribunals at Nuremberg as a form of "victor's justice,"[3] because the defendants were indicted on crimes *ex post facto*; the crimes were not legally defined as crimes during their commission. Further, the United States killed significant numbers of people in the bombing of Hiroshima and Nagasaki, yet was not held accountable. The legacy of the tribunal however, is undeniable. Twenty-four members of Nazi leadership were prosecuted and many received death penalties or long prison sentences. While the most prominent Nazi leaders such as Adolf Hitler, Heinrich Himmler, and Joseph Goebbels committed suicide prior to capture, thus avoiding any accountability or prosecution, the trials nonetheless sent an important message: humanity's gravest crimes are punishable, and political and military leaders are held accountable.

The term *transitional justice* came to the forefront of post-conflict and international conflict management discourse in the 1980s and 1990s. As many states began political transitions from authoritarianism towards democracy in the aftermath of the Cold War, greater emphasis was placed on the promotion of human rights across the world. Greece (1975), Argentina (1983), and Chile (1990) were the first to establish trials to hold former members of their military juntas accountable for repression and violations of human rights.

In the 1990s, two specific civil wars necessitated the creation of international tribunals to address massive violations of international humanitarian law. The dissolution of Yugoslavia resulted in a series of violent wars between the successor states, and rising ethnic tensions in Rwanda ended in genocide of 1 million people. The scope and gravity of the violations

national humanitarian law in both of these cases were such that the United Nations
...ed two ad hoc tribunals to address these crimes: the International Criminal Tribu-
...al for the former Yugoslavia (ICTY) and the International Criminal Tribunal for Rwanda
(ICTR).

The ICTY, established under United Nations Security Council (UNSC) Resolution 827
in 1993, had jurisdiction over breaches of the Geneva Conventions,[4] violations of the laws
or customs of war, genocide, and crimes against humanity committed on the territory of the
former Yugoslavia since 1991. There was no capital punishment under the statute of the
ICTY; instead, the maximum sentence one could receive was life imprisonment. Similar to
the Nuremberg Tribunals, the ICTY indicted many of the top political and military leaders of
the former Yugoslavia. Former president Slobodan Milošević was the first head of state to be
indicted on charges of war crimes, crimes against humanity, and genocide. In 2001, he was
extradited to the ICTY; however, in 2006 he died in the tribunal's detention center before the
conclusion of his trial.

The Rwandan Civil War (1990–1994) between the Hutu-led Rwandan Armed Forces and
the majority Tutsi Rwandan Patriotic Front culminated in horrific violence and destruction of human lives and property. Estimates suggest that between 800,000 and one million

---

### Textbox 8.1   Transitional justice in Rwanda

In November 1994, the United Nations Security Council, expressing "grave concern"
for the commission of genocide and other systematic and widespread abuses, adopted
Resolution 955 establishing the International Criminal Tribunal for Rwanda (ICTR). It
is interesting to note that Rwanda, a non-permanent member of the UNSC at the time,
ultimately voted against Resolution 955 citing issues including the inadequacy of the
period covered by the tribunal (ratione temporis) and the disparity in possible sentenc-
ing between the ICTR and the Rwandan penal code. The ICTR, for example, did not
include the death penalty as a possible sentence while the Rwandan penal code does
have provisions for capital punishment.

One of the reasons the ICTR was significant was the case of Jean-Paul Akayesu, in
which the legal precedent for the inclusion of rape as an act of genocide was established. It is estimated that up to 250,000 women were raped during the Rwandan Genocide. Rape, when used as a weapon of war, inflicts physical and psychological harm
and destroys families and communities. Prior to the Akayesu case, rape had never been
included in prosecutions for crimes against humanity or genocide. Akayesu was found
guilty on 9 of 15 counts, including rape as a crime against humanity and was sentenced
to life in prison.

In addition to the ICTR, Rwanda also implemented a form of community-based
justice, known as gacaca courts, after the conflict. In these courts, community leaders
serve as judges and the process emphasizes conflict resolution, reconciliation, revela-
tion of the truth, and promoting healing within the community. Given the large number
of participants in the genocide, neither the ICTR nor the national court system was
equipped to handle such a caseload.

Rwandans lost their lives. Many of them belonged to the Tutsi population, however many Pygmy Batwa and so-called moderate Hutus were also killed between April and July 1994. The scale of violence was so great that the UN estimates "a rate of killing four times greater than at the height of the Nazi Holocaust" (International Residual Mechanism for Criminal Tribunals 2019).

Jurisdiction of the ICTR included the crimes of genocide, crimes against humanity, and violations of Common Article III of the Geneva Convention, which is applicable to non-international armed conflicts of high intensity and requires that non-combatants be treated humanely. Located in Arusha, Tanzania, the first case in the ICTR began in 1997, and the Court was set to complete all work by 2012. The Tribunal indicted a total of 96 individuals, acquitted 14 individuals, transferred the cases against 10 individuals to national jurisdictions, and convicted 61 individuals.

Due to the large number of individual cases and the nature of the ICTR's work, the anticipated conclusion of the Court was unrealistic. With similar issues facing the ICTY, the United Nations Security Council established the International Residual Mechanism for Criminal Tribunals (IRMCT) in 2010. With locations in both Arusha and The Hague, each branch was tasked with completing the remaining work of both the ICTR and ICTY and will continue to work until the UNSC deems otherwise. More recently, special courts have been established in Sierra Leone, Lebanon, Cambodia, and East Timor to address specific conflicts, with the United Nations playing a role in the establishment of each of these courts.

### Transitional justice in the twenty-first century – the international criminal court

After the growing use of mechanisms for transitional justice in the late twentieth century, the international community recognized a need for a more permanent solution to ad hoc tribunals. In 1998, the Rome Statute of the International Criminal Court (ICC) was adopted and it entered into force in 2002. The ICC has the strength of a broader geographical reach, almost global, over its predecessors – the Nuremberg trials, ICTY and ICTR. The ICC is the first and only permanent treaty-based international criminal court. The ICC, a court of last resort,[5] has jurisdiction over four international crimes: war crimes, crimes against humanity, genocide, and most recently, the crime of aggression, which refers to the use of armed force by one state against another state. These are the violations of international law and norms that the international community generally agrees to be the gravest and most serious. A substantial difference between the ICC and its predecessor institutions is that membership to the Court is voluntary, while the ad hoc tribunals were imposed on states either by international bodies or powers. States are not automatically party to the Court, nor does the Court have automatic jurisdiction. The ICC operates on the principle of complementarity, meaning that they only step in when and if a state is either unable or unwilling to investigate and prosecute alleged crimes.

To date, 122 countries are States Parties to the Rome Statute. *States Parties* refers to sovereign countries that have signed and ratified the Rome Statute, which is the founding treaty of the ICC, thereby accepting jurisdiction of the Court over their territories. Since its establishment, the ICC has been highly controversial and faced criticism for Western imperialism in Africa, where several states have either withdrawn or threatened to withdraw from the Court, including South Africa, The Gambia, and Burundi (though The Gambia and South Africa later rescinded their withdrawal). Russia announced the withdrawal of its signature in November 2016, after the ICC Prosecutor suggested that the Russian annexation of Crimea constituted an armed conflict between Russia and Ukraine.[6] In 2018, the Philippines also announced its intention to withdraw from the Court after preliminary investigations into President Duterte's efforts to rid the country of drugs through a violent crackdown that included extrajudicial killings and gross human rights abuses. The Philippines officially withdrew from the ICC in March 2019, making it the second state after Burundi to officially withdraw after ratification.

While the ICC is one option available to states, criminal trials and tribunals at the domestic level are another method that can be conducted with the assistance of the international community if necessary. For example, the Extraordinary Chambers in the Courts of Cambodia (ECCC), also known as the Khmer Rouge Tribunal, is a hybrid court established at the domestic level and created with the help of the United Nations. The Court, however, operates independently from the UN. Established in 1997, the ECCC is tasked with trying the most senior members of the Khmer Rouge that were responsible for crimes committed during the Cambodian genocide in the 1970s.

## Contending approaches of transitional justice

### *Global versus local justice*

While international trials receive a great deal of exposure and have played a historically important role in the development of transitional justice, more localized transitional justice can provide access and agency to people who might otherwise be excluded from the process. Hinton (2011, 1) describes local justice as being "concerned with the ways in which justice is experienced, perceived, conceptualized, transacted, and produced in various localities." Both the ICTY and ICTR took place outside of the territory in which the respective conflicts occurred; the tribunals were located in The Hague, Netherlands, and Arusha, Tanzania respectively. The alternative locations provide a level of security and independence from any pressures that may arise in the post-conflict area. However, holding tribunals elsewhere also distances the process from those most impacted by the conflict, which may reinforce a sense of injustice.

International processes have come under scrutiny as most international justice mechanisms were created based on Western conceptions of justice. As previously mentioned, the ICC faces harsh criticisms of neocolonialism in the selection of situations that the Court takes on, since the vast majority of cases that have been considered by the court are in Africa. The application of Western norms of justice in non-Western contexts is often considered problematic. Muvingi (2016) points out that post-conflict societies vary, but a transitional justice international template has developed to attract international support and resources in a way that negates the history, culture, and context of the local societies. Zartner (2012, 298) argues that transitional justice can be more effective if "closer attention be paid to the local understandings of law in making assessments about justice and the best way to achieve peace and harmony in post-conflict societies." The increasing use of community-based justice reinforces this claim. For example, Rwanda held gacaca courts and Sierra Leone adopted traditional reintegration and *Fambul Tok* (translated as "family talk" in Krio), a community program that brings victims and perpetrators together to deal with past events through traditional ceremonies aimed at "confession, apology, and forgiveness" (Fambul Tok International 2019). *Reintegration* refers to the process of bringing individuals back into their communities. Traditional reintegration emphasizes cultural practices and rituals

such as cleansing ceremonies and healing practices aimed at community participation
reconciliation.

The inclusion of civil society actors in determining transitional justice practices is
increasing importance. By consulting with the public and those most affected by conflict,
new governments can increase buy-in to the transitional justice process and trust of public
institutions. Consultation with civil society groups can help create a transitional justice process that is unique to both the cultural context in which the conflict occurred and that has
local legitimacy. For example, the Mothers of the Plaza de Mayo formed in Argentina in the
late 1970s to find out what happened to their children who had "disappeared" during the
Process of National Reorganization, more commonly known as the Dirty War. This movement was one of the first in Argentina to pressure the government to reveal the truth about
the massive human rights violations that had occurred. Hayner (2004) emphasizes that civil
society actors often have a positive effect on transitional justice outcomes because of their
expertise and advocacy; they are able to articulate the goals of transitional justice, which can
better serve the needs of broader populations.

### Transitional justice and gender

Gender-sensitive approaches to transitional justice recognize the unique experiences of
women in conflict. Women are often targeted by conflict belligerents because of their gender
and experience sexual violence as a tool of war. Further, women experience a broad range
of consequences from conflict that can lead to instability in the post-conflict period. For
example, some women are victims of rape during conflict, and as a result may suffer rejection from their spouses. The rejection fragments family structures and poses more challenges
to post-conflict peacebuilding initiatives. Structural inequalities in many societies serve to
reinforce the hardship experienced by women as their ability to seek assistance may be hin-
dered by both institutional rules and cultural norms. In addition, many traditional transitional
justice mechanisms do not adequately engage with women. Many of these practices are
dominated by patriarchy, and women feel unable to speak publically about indignities that
they have suffered for fear of shame. For example, women have a minor role in *mato oput*,
a traditional Acholi reconciliation practice, and are unable to participate in certain aspects
of the ceremony (Ensor 2013). Women are often asked to let go of their rights by relegating
gender issues to be dealt with at a later time in order to achieve peace and justice (Hellsten
2012), or gender concerns are "sacrificed in order to not offend those cultural and religious
views which maintain the suppression of women" (Stewart 2013).

Gender sensitive transitional justice is not focused only on the needs of women, but rather
seeks to include voices of men and LGBTQI individuals and communities who have experienced targeted abuse and violence specific to their gender. In Latin America, for example,
many truth commissions are investigating gender-based crimes. The Commission for Clari-
fication of the Truth, Coexistence and Non-Repetition in Colombia, launched in 2018, will
investigate and report on over 50 years of conflict. The president of the Commission has
stated that they will "focus on the most fragile of victims – women, children, old people,
indigenous and Afro-Colombian groups and LGBT people" (Moloney 2018). Truth commissions in Brazil, Peru, Paraguay, and Ecuador have included the experiences and documented
crimes against members of the LGBTQI community to varying degrees. The Brazilian Truth
Commission (2012–2014), for example, placed a strong emphasis on these issues, while The
Peruvian Truth and Reconcilliation Commission (2001–2003) reduced the matter to a note in
the final report (Bueno-Hansen 2018).

## Transitional justice mechanisms and their applications

While criminal prosecutions and tribunals tend to have more visibility, there is a range of mechanisms for transitional justice that is implemented regularly in post-conflict and transitional contexts. Aside from trials, which were previously discussed, other mechanisms include amnesties, reparations, truth commissions, and lustration and vetting policies. The following section discusses these transitional justice mechanisms in more detail.

### *Amnesties*

Amnesties are a commonly used method of transitional justice. *Amnesty* derives from the Greek word *amnesia*, meaning "forgetfulness." It refers to the extension of pardon by a sovereign power to persons who should otherwise be prosecuted for political crimes (Garner and Black 20014). As Scharf (1999) has observed, the goals of peace and justice, however complementary, are sometimes incompatible. Often, negotiations to end international and domestic conflicts must happen with the very leaders who perpetrated war crimes and crimes against humanity. In such cases, capitalizing on criminal prosecutions has the adverse effect of prolonging conflicts and deepening their consequences, especially human suffering and death. Amnesty therefore serves the purpose of achieving durable peace where governments decide that reconciling citizens who comply with the law is more important than punishing individuals for offenses committed. Critics of this mechanism, however, argue that perpetrators are likely to use amnesty as a shield. Further, many would argue that amnesties do not actually serve justice to individuals.

With the rise in the practice and utility of transitional justice in the last two decades, the UN has recognized, endorsed, and/or helped to negotiate the granting of amnesty as a way of achieving durable peace and reinstating democratic government in Cambodia, El Salvador, Haiti, and South Africa. In addition to these countries, other countries such as Argentina, Chile, Guatemala, and Uruguay have each granted amnesty, as part of a peace agreement, to perpetrators of the former regime that committed international crimes within their states.

### *Reparations*

*Reparation* is a form of social and transitional justice defined as "policies and initiatives that attempt to restore to victims, their sense of dignity and moral worth and eliminate the social disparagement and economic marginalization that accompanied their targeting, with the goal of returning their status of citizens" (Verdeja 2008, 1). Whereas most of the long-term goals of transitional justice are intangible, such as fostering inclusiveness, material reparations can have a direct, tangible impact on victims.

The 1993 UN document on The Right to Reparation for Victims of Gross Violations of Human Rights and Humanitarian Law, otherwise referred to as the Van Boven Principles, identifies four categories of reparation: restitution, compensation, rehabilitation, satisfaction, and the guarantee of non-repetition. Some examples of how reparations may be provided to victims include the restitution of lost rights or property, monetary compensation for material damage or lost income, and psychological or medical rehabilitation from trauma. Further, taking measures to provide satisfaction to victims and their families through apologies, memorialization and commemorations, and the identification and recovery of bodies as well as implementing measures to ensure the prevention of future human rights violations are also part of reparation programs.

Despite its strengths, reparations bring to the fore a moral dilemma. The conflict management and transitional justice literature has largely represented any attempts at monetizing mass atrocities as ethically problematic. Reparations become trivial in the aftermath of mass violence, with their incommensurate ability to compensate for human lives and the value of property. Also, reparations, more especially material compensations, have the tendency of shifting the issue from moral to interest-based dimensions. Material compensation results in what Chaumont (2010) has termed "victim's competition" by questioning the victim's real motivations when he or she seeks reparations. At best, it is interpreted as a form of payment, and at worst, blood money. Reparations raise the question of whether any price can be placed on the horrors of mass atrocities. More so, the timing of reparations can be problematic by raising the question of when one can stop compensating or being accountable for the commission of mass atrocities.

### Truth commissions

The purpose of truth commissions is to investigate and report on past wrongdoings related to widespread conflict and repression. Hayner (2010), a leading expert on the study of truth commissions defines of the scope and function of truth commissions in *Unspeakable Truths: Transitional Justice and the Challenge of Truth Commissions*. She writes,

> A truth commission (1) is focused on the past, rather than ongoing, events; (2) investigates a pattern of events that took place over a period of time; (3) engages directly and broadly with the affected population, gathering information on their experiences; (4) is a temporary body, with the aim of concluding with a final report, and; (5) is officially authorized or empowered by the state under review.
>
> (Hayner 2010, 12)

Truth commissions became more common in the 1980s in Latin America where political disappearances were frequently carried out by ruling militaries. Some of the early commissions were not necessarily referred to as truth commissions but were established to serve the same purpose of revealing past wrongdoings. Examples include Bolivia's 1982 National Commission of Inquiry into Disappearances and Argentina's 1983 National Commission on the Disappearance of Persons.

Truth commissions are often used in conjunction with other transitional justice mechanisms such as amnesties or reparations. For example, the South African Truth and Reconciliation Commission (TRC), established in 1995 in the post-apartheid period, was permitted to grant amnesty to those who fully disclosed their wrongdoings. Amnesties were not available for all crimes; amnesties were limited to human rights violations that occurred in a specified period as part of a political objective, and the perpetrator had to admit his or her fault and be willing to provide complete information regarding the offense (Promotion of National Unity and Reconciliation Act 34 of 1995). The TRC received thousands of applications for amnesties from both sides of the conflict, with most being rejected and less than 1,000 amnesties ultimately being granted. In this case, the TRC utilized amnesty as an incentive to gather information that contributed to the historical record and promoted reconciliation.

Truth commissions take a more reconciliatory approach to transitional and post-conflict justice, emphasizing restorative justice rather than the retributive justice associated with criminal trials. Restorative justice refers to an approach whereby the response to a crime is to organize a meeting between the victim and the offender, with the possibility of a third party,

ually to share experiences of what happened, discuss who was harmed by the crime and w, and create a consensus for what the offender can do to repair the damage.

The ICTJ and Kofi Annan Foundation (2016) cautioned that setting unrealistic expectations for truth commissions, as well as the ever-increasing mandates of the commissions, is likely to frustrate affected communities. It is important to keep in mind the dangers of applying a uniform approach while overlooking the cultural dynamics of the affected community, the need for independent and capable commissioners and staff, the repercussions of aiming to reconcile a divided society, and the criticality of timing and strategies in ensuring accountability. These factors together determine the extent to which truth commissions can succeed or fail.

## The national commission for truth and reconciliation in Chile

Between 1973 and 1990, Chile was governed by a military dictatorship under General Augusto Pinochet. The Pinochet regime was characterized by extreme repression of political dissidents, the dissolution of congress, and the suspension of the constitution. Human rights abuses were widespread as political prisoners were detained, tortured, disappeared, and killed. The regime established detention and torture centers across Chile and it is estimated that approximately 1,200 individuals were disappeared. To this day, it is still unknown what became of many of those people, as tens of thousands of people were detained and tortured.

Chile began its transition to democracy in the late 1980s. Although Pinochet and his Junta suspended the 1925 constitution, between 1973 and 1980 a new constitution was drafted by a junta commission. The new constitution, which established Pinochet's executive power for the next eight years, was approved in a referendum by 67 percent of voters. Eight years later in the mandated "plebiscite" or referendum to "elect" a new president, the continuation of Pinochet's rule was voted down by 56 percent of voters. Presidential and Parliamentary elections took place three months later in December 1989. In March 1990, the newly and democratically elected president, Patricio Aylwin, and parliament took office.

In 1991, President Aylwin established The National Commission for Truth and Reconciliation, also known as the Rettig Commission. The Commission was tasked with establishing the truth regarding the abuses of the Pinochet regime, gathering evidence to identify victims and their whereabouts, recommending reparations, and recommending legal and/or administrative actions to prevent the recurrence of these events. The final report recommended the establishment of a National Corporation for Reparations and Reconciliation to provide support and assistance to victims who provided testimony, and the adoption of human rights legislation.

Pinochet was arrested in 1998 while seeking medical treatment in London after a Spanish judge issued an arrest warrant related to an investigation of the death of Spanish citizens in Chile during Pinochet's rule. This event was notable as it was the first application of universal jurisdiction, in which states may claim jurisdiction regardless of where and who committed the alleged crime. Further, this was the arrest of a former dictator and head of state. Pinochet was extradited back to his native Chile and placed under house arrest.

The mandate of the Rettig Commission was limited to abuses that resulted in death or disappearance and did not take into account the thousands of individuals who were subjected to torture and sexual abuse in state-run detention facilities. Later in 2003, President Ricardo Lagos established The National Commission on Political Imprisonment and Torture to further document abuses that occurred, achieving a more comprehensive account of the extent of repression and abuse under the Pinochet regime.

### Lustration or vetting policies

From the Ancient Greek *lustratio*, referring to purification ceremonies, contemporary lustration is the purging of party members and government officials associated with the previous regime from the new administration. In post-Soviet Eastern Europe, as democratically elected governments came to power, new laws were enacted disqualifying members of the communist party from holding public office. Lustration policies were implemented throughout the region after the fall of communism in the late 1980s and early 1990s. Poland (1992 and 1996), Czechoslovakia (1991), and Romania (2012) are all examples of states that adopted lustration as a means to prohibit the participation of former communist party members from public service positions. Further, these policies meant that public employment would require screening or vetting to determine if an individual had any previous or current ties to the Communist party or collaborated in prior repressive regimes.

Post-war Germany experienced a denazification process to remove all forms of Nazism not only from government, but other areas of German and Austrian life. A massive undertaking considering the extent of the influence of the Nazi party in Germany at the time, it was impractical to investigate every individual who may have supported or collaborated with the party. Further, had every former party member been banned from public service or any professional service, there would be a shortage of doctors, teachers, lawyers, and other professionals. Other efforts to remove remnants of the Nazi regime from public life included the destruction of physical symbols.

### De-Ba'athification in Iraq

Similarly, in 2003, the Coalition Provisional Authority (CPA) in Iraq adopted a policy to remove members of the Ba'ath Party, which had dominated Iraqi politics under deposed dictator Saddam Hussein, from power. Under this policy members of the Ba'ath Party who held public office were removed from their positions. Further, according to Order 1 of the policy, "Individuals holding positions in the top three layers of management in every national government ministry, affiliated corporations and other government institutions (e.g., universities and hospitals) shall be interviewed for possible affiliation with the Ba'ath Party, and subject to investigation for criminal conduct and risk to security" (Coalition Provisional Authority Order 1 2003a).

Lustration policies have been met with controversy. In the Iraqi example, while the Ba'ath Party was in power, many people had to join the party in order to gain employment or university admission despite any ideological agreement. Under the de-Ba'athification policy, many people were removed and banned from their previous employment. This meant not only did the government lose institutional knowledge that could be beneficial in a political transition, but also that hospitals lost doctors and schools lost teachers. Further, Iraq experienced economic and social consequences as a result of this policy. The loss of public services, high unemployment rates, and the loss of social safety nets like pensions were all attributable to de-Ba'athification.

A major consequence of de-Ba'athification was the power vacuum that was created as a result of these purges and attempts to rid the state of all remnants of the Hussein regime. In addition to personnel and administrative purges, the CPA dissolved the Iraqi military, the Ministry of Defense, and the Iraqi Intelligence Service among other state entities (Coalition Provisional Authority Order 2 2003b). An inadequate security sector as well as unemployment, especially among youth, helped set the stage for the development of insurgency and the rise of the Islamic State of Iraq and Syria (ISIS) or *Da'esh*, as it is commonly known in Arabic.

## Challenges and future directions

Originally situated in the discipline of law, transitional justice scholarship has expanded rapidly in recent years to include approaches from sociology, psychology, anthropology, gender studies, international relations, and political science, among others. One of the primary challenges faced by transitional justice scholars is the conceptualization of the term itself. We know broadly that it includes a number of legal and non-legal methods to "deal with the past," which usually describes periods of conflict, repression, and widespread abuses of human rights. Conceptions of transitional justice are often shaped by Western assumptions of what justice is and ought to be. Further, the historical experiences of transitional justice that have shaped global norms are based in Western experiences. Increasingly, scholarship is taking into account the need for a diversity of voices and experiences in transitional justice as highlighted in the discussion above regarding local or traditional justice practices and gender-sensitive approaches to transitional justice. Some scholars (Bell 2009; Fletcher and Weinstein 2015) have attempted to fill in these gaps by critically examining the overall state of the "field" of transitional justice.

Transitional justice operates on the core assumption that impunity is unacceptable. Something must be done to address violations of human rights and state repression. However, one of the major challenges of transitional justice is the lack of any unified conception. There are several core documents such as the UN Secretary General's Report, "The Rule of Law and Transitional Justice in Conflict and Post-Conflict Societies" and the Guidance Note of the Secretary-General, "United Nations Approach to Transitional Justice," both of which provide a definition of transitional justice as well as outline the various components and offer direction for implementation. However, as De Greiff (2012, 32) points out, "The consensus around any given understanding of transitional justice and its components is far from complete." As such, there are volumes dedicated to the conceptualization of transitional justice and its lack of theoretical frameworks. What we do know about transitional justice is driven by the practice itself; observing and describing the ways in which states confront legacies of conflict and repression. From this, practitioners and scholars attempt to prescribe measures to achieve the goals of transitional justice and the means.

Relatedly, one of the primary points of contention surrounding both the study and practice of transitional justice is the relationship between peace and justice. In post-conflict and transitional contexts, is it more important to establish peace or achieve justice? Can these two goals be achieved simultaneously? If not, which one must or should necessarily take precedence? In some cases, justice has been compromised to achieve peace, and perpetrators of violence and human rights abuses have negotiated amnesties in order to end a conflict. Those opposed to this approach remind us that without addressing the needs of victims there is a threat of violent conflict recurring. Others argue, however, that the pursuit of transitional justice mechanisms can jeopardize efforts towards peace when perpetrators still have power and can act as veto players. Former military or armed resistance leaders may find other ways to maintain their power and influence in the post-conflict state through political positions or business.

Increasingly, international norms are shifting away from granting amnesty to those responsible for international crimes (war crimes, genocide, and crimes against humanity).

However, the question of amnesties remains unsettled. The ICC provides no provisions for amnesties; amnesties are seemingly antithetical to the mission of the Court. Yet national jurisdictions may enact amnesty laws for a number of reasons, including reaching a cease-fire and handing over of power. Transitional justice has evolved dramatically since the post-World War II period. Permanent international institutions and laws exist where there once were none, and norms have shifted away from impunity and towards accountability. The various transitional justice options that are available in the wake of political transition and conflict have increased the accessibility of justice and visibility of important issues related to conflict management.

## Questions for further discussion

1   What is or should be the role of the international community in the establishment and practice of transitional justice?
2   What are the goals of transitional justice? How do the various transitional justice mechanisms support these goals?
3   Should amnesties be considered as part of the transitional justice toolbox? Why or why not?
4   Describe the peace versus justice debate. Can these goals be achieved simultaneously? If not, which one takes precedence?
5   What are the strengths and limitations of each transitional justice mechanism?

## Suggested resources

1   Guidance Note of the Secretary General: United Nations Approach to Transitional Justice: https://un.org/ruleoflaw/files/TJ_Guidance_Note_March2010FINAL.pdf.
2   International Center for Transitional Justice: www.ictj.org. An NGO dedicated to advancing the cause of transitional justice through research, advocacy, and education.
3   International Journal of Transitional Justice: https://academic.oup.com/ijtj. A peer-reviewed academic journal for the study of transitional justice.
4   United Nations – The Rule of Law and Transitional Justice in Conflict and Post-Conflict Societies: https://digitallibrary.un.org/record/527647.
5   *The Reckoning: The Battle for the International Criminal Court.* 2009. Directed by Pamela Yates. Skylight Pictures. A documentary film that follows the work of the first Prosecutor of the ICC, Luis Moreno Ocampo, and challenges of the Court faces.
6   *Prosecuting Evil: The Extraordinary World of Ben Ferencz.* 2018. Directed by Barry Avrich. Melbar Entertainment Group. A documentary film documenting the life and work of Benjamin Ferencz, who served as the Chief Prosecutor at one of the Nuremberg trials at the age of 27.

## Become engaged!

1   The Cres Summer School – Transitional Justice & Memory Politics: https://summer-schoolcres.org/.
2   Ulster University Transitional Justice Institute – Summer School on Transitional Justice: www.ulster.ac.uk/research/institutes/transitional-justice-institute/study/summer-school.
3   International Center for Transitional Justice Internships: www.ictj.org/job-type/internship.

## Notes

1 For a more detailed history of transitional justice prior to the twentieth century see Jon Elster. 2004. *Closing the Books: Transitional Justice in Historical Perspective*. New York, NY: Cambridge University Press.
2 In fact, the term *genocide* became popularized because of the events of the early 1940s and is credited to Raphael Lemkin, a lawyer of Polish-Jewish descent who also contributed to the writing of the Convention on the Prevention and Punishment of the Crime of Genocide.
3 A form of injustice whereby a victorious entity applies arbitrary sets of rules or principles to judge themselves differently from the defeated entity. Victor's justice generally results in excessive and or unjustified punishment of the defeated while the victor receives clemency or light punishment.
4 Rules exclusively applicable in times of armed conflict to protect people who are not or are no longer taking part in hostilities, such as civilians, prisoners of war, the sick and wounded of armed forces on the field, and wounded, sick, and shipwrecked members of armed forces at sea.
5 A Court of last resort, meaning the ICC operates on the principle of complementarity: jurisdiction over a specific case is not automatic, and the Court may exercise its jurisdiction or get involved only when states are unable or unwilling to investigate and prosecute alleged crimes.
6 Russia initially signed, but never ratified the Rome Statute of the International Criminal Court.

## References and further reading

Bell, Christine. 2009. "Transitional Justice, Interdisciplinarity and the State of the 'Field' or 'Non-Field'." *International Journal of Transitional Justice* 3 (1): 5–27.
Bueno-Hansen, Pascha. 2018. "The Emerging LGBTI Rights Challenge to Transitional Justice in Latin America." *The International Journal of Transitional Justice* 12 (1): 126–45.
Chaumont, Jean-Michel. 2010. *La concurrence des victimes: génocide, identité, reconnaissance*. Paris: La Découverte.
Coalition Provisional Authority. 2003a. "Coalition Provisional Authority Order Number 1: De-Ba'athification of Iraqi Society." May 16. Accessed July 30, 2019. https://nsarchive2.gwu.edu/NSAEBB/NSAEBB418/docs/9a%20-%20Coalition%20Provisional%20Authority%20Order%20No%201%20-%205-16-03.pdf.
———. 2003b. "Coalition Provisional Authority Order Number 2: Dissolution of Entities." May 23. Accessed July 30, 2019. https://nsarchive2.gwu.edu/NSAEBB/NSAEBB418/docs/9b%20-%20Coalition%20Provisional%20Authority%20Order%20No%202%20-%208-23-03.pdf.
De Greiff, Pablo. 2012. "Theorizing Transitional Justice." *Nomos* 51: 31–77.
Ensor, Marisa O. 2013. "Drinking the Bitter Roots: Gendered Youth, Transitional Justice, and Reconciliation Across the South Sudan-Uganda Border." *African Conflict and Peacebuilding Review* 3 (2): 171–94.
Fambul Tok International. 2019. "What Is Fambul Tok?" Accessed August 1, 2019. www.fambultok.org/what-is-fambul-tok.
Fletcher, Laurel E., and Harvey M. Weinstein. 2015. "Writing Transitional Justice: An Empirical Evaluation of Transitional Justice Scholarship in Academic Journals." *Journal of Human Rights Practice* 7 (2): 177–98.
Garner, Bryan A., and Henry Campbell Black. 2014. *Black's Law Dictionary*. Tenth edition. Toronto: Thompson Reuters.
Hayner, Priscilla B. 2004. "Responding to a Painful Past: The Role of Civil Society and the International Community." In *Dealing with the Past: Critical Issues, Lessons Learned, and Challenges for Future Swiss Policy*, edited by Mô Bleeker Massard and Jonathan Sisson. KOFF Series Working Paper. Bern: Swiss Peace.
Hayner, Priscilla B. 2010. *Unspeakable Truths: Transitional Justice and the Challenge of Truth Commissions*. New York, NY: Routledge.
Hellsten, Sirkku K. 2012. "Transitional Justice and Aid." WIDER Working Paper 2012/006. Helsinki: UNU-WIDER.

Hinton, Alexander Laban. 2011. "Introduction: Toward an Anthropology of Transitional Justice." In *Transitional Justice: Global Mechanisms and Local Realities After Genocide and Mass Violence*, edited by Alexander Laban Hinton, 1–22. New Brunswick, NJ: Rutgers University Press.

International Center for Transitional Justice. 2019. "What Is Transitional Justice?" Accessed July 29, 2019. www.ictj.org/about/transitional-justice.

International Center for Transitional Justice, and Kofi Annan Foundation. 2016. "Challenging the Conventional: Can Truth Commissions Strengthen Peace Processes?" Accessed April 24, 2019. www.ictj.org/publication/challenging-conventional-can-truth-commissions-strengthen-peace-processes.

Moloney, Anastasia. 2018. "New Colombia Truth Commission to Focus on Society's 'Most Fragile'." *Reuters*, May 16. Accessed July 31, 2019. www.reuters.com/article/us-colombia-truth-commission-conflict-in/new-colombia-truth-commission-to-focus-on-societys-most-fragile-idUSKCN1IH2S8.

Muvingi, Ismael. 2016. "Donor-Driven Transitional Justice and Peacebuilding." *Journal of Peacebuilding & Development* 11 (1): 10–25.

Scharf, Michael P. "The Amnesty Exception to the Jurisdiction of the International Criminal Court." *Cornell International Law Journal* 32 (3): 507–28.

South African Truth and Reconciliation Commission. 1995. "Promotion of National Unity and Reconciliation Act 34 of 1995." Accessed July 31, 2019. www.justice.gov.za/legislation/acts/1995-034.pdf.

Stewart, James. 2013. "Gender and Transitional Justice." *United Nations University*, April 25. Accessed July 30, 2019. https://unu.edu/publications/articles/gender-and-transitional-justice.html.

United Nations, Security Council. 2014. "The Rule of Law and Transitional Justice in Conflict and Post-conflict Societies: A Report of the Secretary-General, S/2004/616 (23 August 2004)." undocs.org/s/2004/616.

United Nations International Residual Mechanism for Criminal Tribunals. 2019. "The Genocide." Accessed August 1, 2019. https://unictr.irmct.org/en/genocide.

Verdeja, Ernesto. 2008. "A Critical Theory of Reparative Justice." *Constellations* 15 (2): 208–22.

Zartner, Dana. 2012. "The Culture of Law: Understanding the Influence of Legal Tradition on Transitional Justice in Post-Conflict Societies." *Indiana International and Comparative Law Review* 22 (2): 297–315.

# 9 Reconciliation and forgiveness

## Theoretical and research-based interactions

*Mohammed Abu-Nimer and Ilham Nasser*

## Introduction

When examining the history of many national and international conflicts, temporary agreements and settlements of conflict issues such as land sovereignty, water, and oil rarely end the conflict. Violent conflict often resumes, triggered by another set of issues. However, when parties engage in the process of reconciliation and forgiveness, it is more likely that they will maintain peace and stability in their relationships. Unfortunately, there are few examples of times when such processes have been applied at the national and international political levels. For the purposes of this chapter, *forgiveness* is defined as "the act of letting go of hurt and hard feelings toward a wrongdoer." It is defined in various ways and disciplines as the ability to unconditionally relieve the self from the need to seek revenge (Nasser and Abu-Nimer 2014). *Reconciliation* is defined by de Waal (2000) as "a friendly reunion between former opponents not long after an aggressive confrontation" (586).

For reconciliation and forgiveness values and processes to become part of cultural and political institutions, it is necessary for members of society to be aware of and understand their importance in building and rebuilding cohesive societies. Thus, education becomes the main venue to broadly introduce these values in society. Scholars are confident about the role education might play in transforming societies, yet few educational experts are investing in researching forgiveness and reconciliation education as an alternative path to address violence and combat bullying. There is a scarcity of studies examining perceptions and attitudes of educators on forgiveness and its effect on students' behavior, particularly regarding teachers and educational counselors in conflict areas (Ahmed, Azar, and Mullet 2007; Nasser and Abu-Nimer 2014).

This chapter examines the importance and role of reconciliation and forgiveness in responding to international and national conflicts, specifically examining the role of educators in addressing these topics in schools. The main assumption is that without integrating these values in the fabric of the society, it is difficult and unrealistic to expect genuine transformation of conflicts. Human political and social systems will continue to be dominated by the principle of "power politics" (win-lose framework) until values and practices of reconciliation and forgiveness become an integral part of these systems. Teachers are key in this vision to transform social and political systems and how they deal with conflict and violence. To understand the prospects and challenges of educating for forgiveness and reconciliation in conflict areas, examples from case studies from the Arab region are highlighted throughout this chapter to explore teachers' reasoning on teaching forgiveness. These cases add to our understanding of the social, cultural, and religious factors at play when teachers consider whether to integrate forgiveness and reconciliation in schools, and help construct a possible framework for engaging educators in these types of conversations and learning activities.

Contextual factors such as social and political conflicts, whether between nations or communities, have an impact on schools, families, and the fabric of society. The "Arab Spring" and its concomitant revolutions that have swept the region since 2011 are examples of the type of changes that can affect everyone's life in a given society. In many countries, where there is an ongoing conflict such as the civil wars in Syria, Yemen, and Libya, there is a need for immediate educational interventions to rehabilitate and reconcile communities and individuals. Investing in forgiveness and reconciliation education should be part of the post-conflict plan in such contexts. To do so, researchers need to understand the variables at play in forgiveness education, including teachers' attitudes and perceptions of forgiveness along with the cognitive processes involved in rationalizing forgiveness and its applicability in their lives. To begin a genuine process of conflict transformation and move beyond the temporary political agreements drawn up by the negotiators, society has to engage in the process of peacebuilding. Thus youth, schools, and the larger community must be exposed to and aware of the possibilities to reconcile and move beyond the hate and anger they may be holding against each other, whether they are directly or indirectly impacted by political and social divides.

Teachers are the key in this proposed process of rebuilding nations in post-conflict settings. They can continue teaching "power politics" or they can take a new path and teach values and practices of forgiveness and reconciliation. It is a teacher's decision to engage in conflict transformation or reproduce the cycle of violence; thus, it is critical to understand teachers' roles and reasoning in addressing skills and modeling behaviors and attitudes to students including their rationalization about their decision to forgive or not.

## Background on linking forgiveness and reconciliation

In the field of peacebuilding, the debate on links between forgiveness and reconciliation can be simplified as a distinction between forgiveness as a necessary condition in achieving full reconciliation and forgiveness as unnecessary for achieving reconciliation. Spiritual and religious frameworks on reconciliation emphasize that forgiveness is an act that allows a person to internally reconcile with himself and, as a result, be able to externally reconcile with his enemies. Lederach and others who support the transformational approach in peacebuilding emphasize that mercy and forgiveness are integral parts of the reconciliation process (see Lederach 1997).

The field of forgiveness research has been gaining more attention in recent years, especially the examination of factors such as personal attributes, religious identity, ethics, and individual and collective perceptions that allow for forgiveness (Nasser and Abu-Nimer 2016). According to Thornton (2011), "Forgiveness is a concept that spans many cultures. Great persons from the likes of Mahatma Gandhi in India to Desmond Tutu in South Africa to Martin Luther King Jr. in the United States, have used this concept to reunite entire nations. These leaders were able to help people in their countries gain their independence after periods of apartheid and segregation" (245). For many who are involved in violent conflicts, the vision and prospect of forgiveness and reconciliation might seem impossible, however history shows that from the darkest and most difficult realities, individual leaders can call for a new path of reconciliation. Mahatma Gandhi and Martin Luther King Jr. led their followers and eventually their entire societies to believe in the power of reconciliation and accept a new reality in which they would live with their oppressors and perpetrators of violence.

Many intractable conflicts in our world will not end until those involved adopt processes of reconciliation and forgiveness. However, for these processes to be effective there is a need for institutional arrangements to be in place to guarantee peaceful and just transitions, including those related to rule of law, good governance, economic and social development, reformed security sectors, and a shift in educational policies and content to reflect the new direction of reconciliation and forgiveness.

Western scholars define forgiveness in various ways while emphasizing the roles and responsibilities of the individual to reach the decision to forgive. For example, according to McCullough and Witvliet (2002) forgiveness can be perceived as a "response, a personality disposition and as a characteristic of social units" (447). Forgiveness is also defined as a way to ameliorate and reduce the destructive cycle of conflict and violence between individuals and groups (Ahmed and Braithwaite 2005). Forgiveness is "the emotional replacement of (1) hot emotions of anger or fear that follow a perceived hurt or offense, or (2) ridding of the unforgiveness that follows ruminating about the transgression, by substituting positive emotions such as unselfish love, empathy, compassion, or even romantic love" (Worthington 2001: 8). Regardless of the above definitions, to end a violent conflict the management process has to include the above principles, values, and mechanisms to allow true ending of the destructive conflict dynamics.

Some of the leading scholars on forgiveness, Enright, Gassin, and Wu (1992) maintain that forgiveness is an act of mercy and "can occur independently of the wrongdoer expressing any remorse" (99). According to Enright (2001), forgiveness reduces anger, depression, and anxiety, and allows people to be more peaceful, also making peace with others more possible. On the other hand, there is clarity in the literature about what forgiveness is not, and according to Zembylas and Michaelidou (2011) forgiveness should not be confused with pardoning, apology, forgetting, or reconciliation. Thus, there is a special distinctive set of attitudes, perceptions, and behaviors associated with the process and outcomes of forgiveness. For example, the belief that the damage caused by the perpetrator cannot be fully repaired; letting go of the grudge against the perpetrator is possible; an individual can only forgive his part, but society might need other mechanisms to forgive; justice can be achieved even if one individual forgives; skills of forgiveness can be learned; there is a risk and price to be paid by the individual when deciding to forgive; etc. For example, when a Muslim leader in the Central African Republic took shelter from sectarian violence against Muslims in his city for six months in the house of a Christian religious leader during the civil war, both leaders took huge risks with their communities.[1] Nevertheless, there is evidence that forgiveness and education for forgiveness is culturally situated and takes different forms and shapes in various contexts (Abu-Nimer 2009; Zembylas 2012).

Forgiveness as a value belongs in the field of education as part of a life-skills set important for any learning process and social interactions in schools. It also has an appeal and an important role to play in the socio-emotional aspects of learning that are also critical for success in life and in schooling. For example, forgiveness education may contribute to the reconciliation processes around bullying when the environment and the parties are ready and willing. The ability and willingness to forgive is closely aligned with the ability to be empathetic and generous with others. A study by Macaskill, Maltby, and Day (2002) suggests a close correlation between both constructs and their contributions to socio-emotional learning and well-being. In a testimony by Lebanese religious leaders who decided to promote reconciliation and forgiveness in post-civil war reality, the three leaders emphasized the role of expressing empathy with those victims from the other religious and ethnic groups.

They also highlighted the enormous feelings of pain that they discovered in the other side.[2] Similar feelings were expressed by the Imam and the Pastor from Nigeria who engaged in a mutual process of reconciliation (Channer 2006). Those examples and many others illustrate the often-missing dimension in international conflict-management processes that focuses on negotiating interests and securing temporary agreements but fails in repairing societal and across-community relationships.

When considering the emotional and cognitive aspects of forgiveness, Enright and the Human Development Study Group theorized that forgiveness is a process that moves through six stages parallel to Kohlberg's 1976 moral development model (Langholtz 1998). The stages start with conditional steps of revengeful and conditional forgiveness because the person forgives if the perpetrator is punished. The middle stages are expectational and lawful expectational, where forgiveness is expected from both parties engaged. The highest stages are social harmony and love (Borris and Diehl 1998), where forgiveness is neither conditional nor expected from others.

---

**Textbox 9.1  Teachers' attitudes toward forgiveness and reconciliation in Arab region conflict-afflicted states**

The "Arab Spring" and its revolutions that swept the Arab region starting in 2011 left several nations in the grip of bloody civil war that exasperated divisions between ethnic and religious groups in addition to the already protracted political sides of the conflicts. Such changes affected everyone's lives in those states afflicted with these ongoing conflicts.

In this context a study was developed to examine the role of attitudes and rationale for teachers toward teaching forgiveness, where forgiveness is defined as "a cognitive and emotional decision-making process in which the 'victim' frees the offender from the burden of the responsibility to address his or her claims." How can teachers present such concepts to students in conflict areas and what is their cognitive reasoning and rationalization for so doing?

The study by Nasser and Abu-Nimer (2016), surveyed 590 Arab teachers from Iraq, Lebanon, Jordan, Palestine, and Egypt during the Arab Spring, which started in 2011. The survey included 12 hypothetical forgiveness dilemmas that included conflicts stemming from the cultural contexts of the participants. Participants were asked to explain their decisions to forgive, maybe forgive, and not forgive. The study's focus is to identify the rationale for the teachers' decision to forgive.

Some key findings were:

- Unconditional forgiveness was more likely in circumstances when it was felt that the situation was beyond the perpetrator's control.
- In examples where the teachers chose to forgive under certain conditions, many expressed the importance of justice in forgiveness.
- In examples where teachers chose not to forgive, many were in situations when they felt perpetrators went too far, such as in instances with family separation among Palestinians.

In Kohlberg's moral development stages, the model follows a certain order of reasoning that moves from the immediate and punitive to the more abstract and spiritual thinking about morality. The same with forgiveness; it moves from revenge to conditioning the act of forgiveness to selfless and loving behaviors of forgiveness. Hence the human being can move through these identified stages and educators will do so to support youth and their growth and development towards unconditional and non-revengeful behaviors. On a collective level there are procedures and mechanisms that can be instituted to emphasize and experience such stages of forgiveness and reconciliation – for example, memorials for victims from all sides; celebrating stories of cross-community peacemaking; revising historical narratives to illustrate compassion, love, and mercy as applied by people from during and post wars. International conflict management processes can integrate or introduce such discourse as part of the political-agreement process.

## Contending approaches to reconciliation

Post-conflict, many scholars and practitioners argue that pragmatic reconciliation can take place by agreeing on conditions and mechanisms that guarantee peaceful problem-solving and stable future relations among and between former enemies. Some of these pragmatic mechanisms include the establishment of good governance, a reliable system of rule of law, reforming the security and military institutions in a way to serve the public and not one sector, insuring equal economic and social development opportunities, etc. Scholars who discount the need for forgiveness and reconciliation argue that if such mechanisms are in place, individual or collective processes of forgiveness are not required for achieving agreement (Kriesberg and Dayton 2016). While this approach in international conflict management currently remains dominant, the history of human conflict and the field of peacebuilding provide many examples of failed international pragmatic conflict-management arrangements. Parties in conflict tend to repeat the same destructive behaviors if their relationships are not genuinely repaired and reconciled. The cycle of violence in Israel/Palestine has continued despite the signing of Oslo Accords in 1993, after more than 75 years of conflict. Similarly the Balkan Wars produced the Dayton agreement in 1996, yet the communities continue to be divided and remain under threat of a repeat cycle of violence. The 18 different Lebanese ethnic and sectarian religious groups live in community enclaves with continued tension between them despite the existence of the political agreement that was reached in Tae'f in 1991. The threat of civil war is looming with every major political shift. In fact, many of these agreements were mediated by external foreign powers who in many cases imposed certain conditions and economic and security arrangements to ensure that the agreement holds and stops the fighting on the ground.

Although international conflict management and pragmatic agreements can be largely imposed, facilitated, or mediated, reconciliation and forgiveness processes cannot be effectively imposed by outside agencies. Cultural and political contexts of the conflict should obviously determine people's collective and individual capacities to engage in such processes of forgiveness and reconciliation. The Ubunto process of reconciliation in South Africa is an integral cultural process that only South Africans can relate to. The Sulh processes in the Arab context is a cultural practice that can only be endorsed and adopted by members of Arab societies. The role of traditional dispute resolution (tribal and social mechanisms to settle conflicts) can be both a facilitating and an obstructing factor in promoting forgiveness and reconciliation. Scholars, especially anthropologists and conflict resolution experts such

Abu-Nimer (1996, 2003), have identified limitations and obstacles for social change based on tribal and traditional dispute resolution. Due to the pragmatic nature of these processes and their function in restoring the status quo and a balance of power relations that serves dominant groups, knowledge and practice of such processes can create confusion with transformative reconciliation and forgiveness processes. Teaching and learning aspects of forgiveness may provide an opportunity to teach the life skills needed to initiate a process that exists alongside the traditional and tribal methods. In many cases, traditional dispute resolution is led by male figures and the elderly; it is time for such practices to become more inclusive.

It is not up to parties to define the nature, sequence, timing, and extent of forgiveness processes, especially when such processes are derived from outside. Nevertheless, reconciliation processes in South Africa, Northern Ireland, and the United States (in the area of race relations), as well as in Australia and New Zealand concerning indigenous peoples' relations with the government and dominant white majorities, point to the necessity of deepening reconciliation acts beyond pragmatic and formal negotiated political agreements. A common obstacle for reaching genuine reconciliation in such processes has been the lack of societal and institutional transformation due to the lack of justice in the proposed reconciliation arrangements. Many of these agreements fall short in responding to deeply rooted grievances and a long history of a sense of victimhood and injustice. For example, restoring the rights and achieving justice for Native Americans or African Americans cannot be achieved by equality acts without a single reference to the history of 200 years of slavery and dispossession and victimhood. It is extremely challenging and, some argue, unrealistic to expect oppressed groups such as Native Americans, African Americans, Palestinians, Kashmiris, blacks in South Africa, Catholics in Northern Ireland, etc., to consider forgiving and letting go of the burden of victimhood that lasted for centuries. Especially when the international conflict-management procedures did not produce satisfactory agreements and did not respond to their sense of injustice.

A form of conditional forgiveness is consistently adopted by a majority of the victims in such conflicts. It is termed "conditional" because the person will not consider engaging in forgiveness or reconciliation unless a set of measures for justice are fulfilled. For example, a Palestinian refugee who lived in Lebanon since 1948 will not consider forgiveness and reconciliation without gaining his right to return to his land; on the other hand, Israeli victims of war and violence will not consider forgiveness unless their conditions are met. It is rare that we encounter unconditional acts of individual or collective forgiveness by victims in such contexts. The burden of historical injury and injustice remains at the center of the relations in such societies. Thus the call for unconditional forgiveness is perceived as weakness, selling out, or betrayal of the cause, and such acts are often countered by exclusion and excommunication or the belittling of the act or the actor. For example, the Imam who took shelter in the Bishop's house in the Central African Republic was excommunicated by his community and was publically accused of treason. However, due to the complexity of applying these processes on the collective and societal levels, it is clear that the link between reconciliation and forgiveness can be better understood in terms of interpersonal and small-group relations rather than collective and macro-level relations. When a conflict between a husband and wife takes place and their relationship is threatened, an act of unconditional forgiveness offered by one of them (especially the victim) can be a powerful step to restore harmony and genuine reconciliation. Such an act can also take place between people who do not necessarily belong to the same family or community. There are plenty of examples documented of such forgiveness cases, such as The Forgiveness Project and the Fetzer report on forgiveness in American Society.[3]

Although, as discussed previously, forgiveness and reconciliation are difficult processes and practices in which to engage, they can be acquired and learned through intentionally constructed spaces such as formal and informal education settings. A challenging question related to educating for forgiveness is: What are the required qualifications of a social change agent, such as teachers in the education system? Should this agent be expected to believe in and internalize the concept of unconditional and conditional forgiveness? Can teachers in societies experiencing deep-rooted intractable violent conflicts train and educate for forgiveness and genuine reconciliation?

## Education for forgiveness and reconciliation in international conflict management

Education for forgiveness may be included as part of the civic education curriculum common in many school systems, whether in formal or non-formal settings. It may also be part of a peace education curriculum. Teachers in North America and other places express their desire to teach and engage in dialogue, conflict resolution, and critical thinking as part of the curriculum, but very often they lack the skills needed to address these topics that may be difficult even in societies that are considered peaceful (Bickmore 2014). Due to the historical complexity and the nature of deeply rooted dynamics of victimhood in the Middle East, it seems necessary to include these types of activities and content as part of a larger restorative peace-building education agenda that is much-needed to move forward beyond the conflicts.

When addressing forgiveness perceptions in schools, there is a clear understanding of conditional versus unconditional forgiveness, although Zembylas (2012) highlights the existence of gray areas where teachers may fail to teach and preach for forgiveness. In the Middle East, this resistance is expressed in the constant reference to the issue of justice that teachers brought up in previous studies by Abu-Nimer and Nasser (2013). Many teachers expressed the importance of justice in forgiveness, which immediately makes the ability to forgive conditional. The individualistic, interpersonal approach to teaching forgiveness is more problematic in conflict-ridden areas, especially since some may jeopardize their jobs and safety if they introduce forgiveness education.

### *Arab teachers' perception of forgiveness affected by their cultural and religious context*

In the recent study of teachers in the Middle East referenced earlier, differences were found between the various countries in teachers' views and perceptions of forgiveness and forgiveness education. In fact, data analysis suggested significant differences across communities and religions. For example, participating teachers from Jordan and the West Bank showed less willingness to forgive, especially in situations related to family and close relationships, while teachers in Lebanon and Egypt showed higher tendencies to forgive in these circumstances. There were no significant differences in demographics such as gender, age, education, or marital status (Nasser and Abu-Nimer 2016).

In explaining their rationale for forgiving perpetrators, the teachers' responses can be classified in several major themes:

1   **The intentionality or unintentionality** of the action affected the willingness to forgive. Teachers repeatedly indicated that they might forgive if they knew the action was not

done intentionally. They disregarded forgiveness as a possibility when the act was intentional or even maybe intentional. Along with this theme, there was the rationalization that confession and apology may also result in forgiveness regardless of whether the act was intentional or not.

2   **Religious teachings encourage and require forgiveness** despite the wrongdoing. This theme was also repeated by many in the sample. It was mentioned as a reason for forgiving that stemmed from personal convictions about religion and religious teaching.

3   **Friendship and interpersonal ties** play a factor in forgiveness or lack thereof. In this theme, teachers considered forgiving when they had a close relationship with the wrongdoer. At the same time, betrayal and lack of trust in friends or others who may not be trustworthy are determinants in not forgiving.

4   **Uncontrollable situations** are more likely to be forgiven. This theme was expressed by teachers in situations that were beyond their ability to judge or choose to forgive. For example, in cases where property and material items such as expensive furniture and cars were damaged as part of the scenario, teachers saw the possibility for forgiveness as the destruction was beyond teachers' control.

5   **Forgiveness is conditional**, depending on the extent of harm. People are prone to recognize that making mistakes is part of human nature when the injury or damage from the perpetrator was not "too close to home," for example when it dealt with property damage and not honor or religion. Based on the previous themes, four main central factors are used by teachers to decide on forgiveness and, maybe as a result, to engage in the reconciliation process:

- Intentionality vs. unintentionality of the action;
- Closeness, commitment, and loyalty to family and close relationships;
- Religious beliefs and faith as motivators;
- Social and cultural beliefs as factors, such as in the case of good hospitality.

Although these factors were central in all the countries (Egypt, Iraq, Jordan, Lebanon, and Palestine), there were a few responses to scenarios that differed from one country and community to another or were more visible and mentioned more in one community versus another. Table 9.1 illustrates the more-specific rationalization of forgiveness based on each country. The specifics in each country are partly due to the different social and political contexts of each. (These contextual differences relate to tribal social fabric; level of inter-religious and interethnic interactions in each country; exposure of teachers to such topics; military and occupation, etc.) For example, in Palestine, where loss of land because of the occupation is prevalent, the scenario on property sends a strong message of unforgiveness. In the case of Egypt, there was agreement between all participants about the importance of fate and submission to God.

Table 9.1 demonstrates the importance of cultural and religious values with some variation that relies on the specific conditions in each country context. The table also affirms the themes highlighted in the analysis of the responses to questions on reasoning about the willingness to forgive or not. Teachers interviewed were honest about their willingness to forgive as well as their boundaries.

*Table 9.1* Country-Specific Rationalizations of Forgiveness

| Most important (most-recurring themes) | Reason/Reasoning about scenario |
|---|---|
| Palestine | Property in the case of the "building a wall" scenario is valued and might affect forgiveness, as neighbor relations are important. |
| Lebanon | Repeated statements such as, "I forgive to free myself. Forgiveness is liberating. Forgiveness to avoid conflicts and the freedom to do as you please" were prevalent in several scenarios. May be explained by the civil war experiences. |
| Jordan and Palestine (West Bank) | Repeated statements such as, "Honor can't be negotiated." Can't grant forgiveness, especially in the scenarios related to family and close friends were prevalent suggesting a collective sense of family honor and dignity. |
| Egypt | Less forgiving when harm is done by same religion because they know not to. Repeated statements like, "Insulting my religion is personal. Belief in fate and submission to God's will." It is mostly related to material things such as the car, but not close relationships regardless if respondents were Christians or Muslims. |
| Iraq | Forgiveness is a virtue dictated by religious teachings. It is an act of fate and generosity. |
| Jordan, Egypt, Iraq | Forgiveness or lack thereof depends on the extent of the harm/how bad is the action. The forgiveness here is conditional and calculated. |

### Lessons and implications

The above results on the rationalization for forgiveness go together with the previous studies conducted by the authors (Nasser and Abu-Nimer 2016; Nasser, Abu-Nimer, and Mahmoud 2014), where the reasons that determined whether teachers will forgive or not followed a similar pattern of thinking. For example, the factor of intentionality where teachers are more willing to forgive if the act is not intentional, is unique to the teachers in our study, and has been a consistent factor in all responses and statistical analysis. Here again the focus is on reasoning; the teachers emphasized its importance by using it most to rationalize their willingness to forgive or not.

When examining the six stages of forgiveness identified in the literature by Enright et al. (1992) and the Arab teacher's responses (see Table 9.2), those teachers in most cases utilized similar rationalization processes to explain their decision to forgive, except for the rationalization to forgive because other people expect them to forgive. The wider community expectation also played a role in the decision whether forgiveness could be taken at the individual level. This factor was not explicitly articulated by the Arab teachers. However, it should be noted that social norms and values in the Arab cultural context often stress the role of the wider community's expectation, while also deeming it unacceptable for individuals to publicly express such influence because it suggests the person is weak and relies on others to decide for him or her.

Teachers' responses in the different countries considered forgiveness as a very personal attribute. Cultural and religious beliefs strongly influence reasoning about forgiveness. Teachers also shared similar views, but the intensity of the reasoning was different. Teachers from Jordan, Iraq, and the West Bank consistently expressed strong views about the willingness to forgive and under what circumstances. For example, there was less willingness to

*Table 9.2* Teacher Responses Based on Six Stages of Forgiveness

| Stages of forgiveness | Arab teachers' responses |
| --- | --- |
| 1 Revengeful forgiveness: I forgive only when I can punish. | Property and honor can't be negotiated (justice orientation). |
| 2 Conditional forgiveness: I forgive if I get back what I lost or if I feel guilty. | Intentionality vs. unintentionality |
| 3 Expectational: I forgive because other people expect it. | This stage was not evident. |
| 4 Lawful expectational: I forgive because my religion or similar institutions demand it. | Religion as a motivator to forgive; Commitment to family (culture/tradition) |
| 5 Forgiveness as social harmony: I forgive because it restores harmony or good relations in society. | Social and cultural beliefs; Extent of respect for guests and hospitality |
| 6 Forgiveness as love: I forgive because it promises a true sense of love. | Forgiveness is liberating. Forgiveness as virtue (religious belief also) |

forgive in the case of damage or threat to family honor than in other cases. Stronger family and tribal networks might explain different views; for instance, in the case of religion and honor, the social status of the individual is largely determined by his or her tribal and clan affiliation. Zembylas (2012) introduced the concept of ambivalent forgiveness where he suggests that in some contexts, forgiveness is very complex and twisted, especially in the dynamics between groups. In troubled societies, he claims, interpersonal forgiveness models don't work as forgiveness processes (cognitive and emotional) and don't follow a clean stage-like process but a more "intermingled one with positive and negative emotions at play at once" (19). It seems that this is the case in the Arab society's context too, especially taking into consideration the turmoil and extreme violence that children and their teachers and communities were experiencing during the time of the study.

The major value of forgiveness expressed by teachers in their context was viewed to reduce behavioral issues, bullying, and violence. Teachers did not make the link to wider macro-international or national conflicts but related it to their own immediate context of school-based violence, which is a daily reality facing teachers in such communities. Deploying concepts and skills of forgiveness was perceived as a possible set of tools to contribute to the reduction of such violence. However, the majority of the teachers claim to lack the skills, preparation, and resources to help them be effective in educating for forgiveness. When asked about the resources and knowledge of forgiveness, teachers emphasized that they derive their ideas about teaching for forgiveness mainly from their religious identities (regardless if they were Muslims or Christians). However, they are eager to learn innovative ways and methods to address this topic in their classrooms.

## Challenges and future directions

The earlier case study confirmed the notion that teachers in conflict areas will find it difficult to teach and educate for forgiveness and reconciliation regarding national and international conflicts, especially if they themselves are not trained or equipped to do so. There are a number of factors that must be taken into consideration, including the correlation of societal attitudes on a teacher's reasoning behind when, how, and under what conditions forgiveness should be granted. More needs to be invested not only into teacher training, but also into resources to better prepare teachers in conflict and post-conflict situations to be able to adequately incorporate forgiveness and reconciliation values in their classrooms.

In addition, when educational systems in countries in conflict and post-conflict states such as those in the study are not including or incorporating values of forgiveness and reconciliation in their curriculum, it is highly unlikely that the new generation in such contexts will take the risk to explore transformative approaches to solve their conflicts. The cycle of violence and revenge is not challenged when students in K-12 and universities are not exposed to or able to learn about these topics throughout their formative years.

The lack of public awareness for the need to incorporate forgiveness and reconciliation in peacebuilding processes hinders its application. Thus, for international conflict management frameworks to be effective (transformative) in such a setting, it requires taking into consideration the level of public awareness of the need to reconcile with the enemy in a forgiving way, particularly in protracted conflicts with long histories. In fact, in political conflicts such as between Israel and Palestinians or relationships between post-colonial and historically colonizing states (i.e., France, Britain, and Italy), the concepts of reconciliation are taboo and completely out of the public dominant discourse, thus posing an even greater challenge to teaching forgiveness and reconciliation. However, concerning internal, national, or religious conflicts, the possibilities to explore forgiveness and reconciliation are more realistic and feasible; unfortunately, there is no preparation for such processes in the education system. Teachers and their leadership are kept away from such educational initiatives and frameworks, as they are not on the radar of education systems as necessary goals of education. Finally, the case study also illustrates the necessity of taking the role of cultural and religious values and norms into serious consideration in any international conflict-management intervention; obviously, such rule applies beyond conflicts in the Arab region and should be extended to any conflict context.

Forgiveness and reconciliation processes are necessary components of transformative conflict-management intervention. Through these processes, parties and third parties can ensure sustainability of political agreements. They are also necessary to pave the path for peaceful transition from violent conflict into a peaceful coexistence between conflicting parties. The lack of integration of these processes is evident in most of the international conflict-management approaches adopted by politicians and negotiators who operate from a power paradigm framework, especially those focusing primarily on pragmatic and immediate arrangements to end the violence or bring to a temporary ceasefire, such as the 1996 Dayton Accords or the 1993 Oslo Accords.

For forgiveness and reconciliation processes to be integrated in international management processes, there is a need to prepare the societies in conflict for such a possibility. Education systems are essential institutions in every society to introduce these values and practices from K-12. Within this context, teachers are central agents who can be pioneers in introducing forgiveness and reconciliation into their societies. The willingness and attitudes of teachers are crucial factors in this process.

As discussed earlier, this process is challenging not only because teachers lack the tools to carry out such roles, but despite the willingness and eagerness of teachers to introduce forgiveness in their schools, it is highly unlikely that the formal ministries of education in the Arab world will adopt plans to mainstream such a theme in schools. In conflict areas, especially in deep-rooted and intractable conflict contexts, integrating or mainstreaming forgiveness and reconciliation in educational systems is a nationally sensitive topic. Examples of such difficulties can be seen in local and national educational policies in post-conflict areas such as Northern Ireland, South Africa, United States, Canada, and Australia, who at best avoid such themes in the national curricula. Forgiveness education requires a more comprehensive approach that addresses related life skills (soft skills such as socio-emotional learning skills) and not only forgiveness, as this will be partial and not as effective in transforming attitudes and behaviors.

Nevertheless, through history there are many concrete examples and evidence that pragmatic (non-transformative) forms of reconciliation failed to achieve genuine reconciliation. However, when forgiveness is introduced into the process the relationships are reconciled and personal and collective healings are achieved, especially on interpersonal level. In general, applying conditional forgiveness (based on criteria of nature of relationship, justice and intentionality) seems to be the most popular position. However, when cases involve ethnic, racial, tribal, and religious differences, new challenges and obstacles are introduced in the process, making the process of forgiveness more difficult to achieve and even unrealistic in the views of the parties.

The study and research of the link between forgiveness and reconciliation and international conflict management remains in its infancy, especially in the field of peacebuilding. There are many questions that ought to be explored to develop solid theoretical framework that can guide our understanding of these process and people's decisions to engage in such processes. Some of these questions include: Are there major differences between adult and children in the decision to engage in forgiveness? If yes, what are they? How do such differences evolve? What are the obstacles facing processes of forgiveness and reconciliation on both collective and individual levels? Are religious values and beliefs necessary for engagement in forgiveness processes on individual and collective levels? What are the motivations and dynamics of unilateral and unconditional forgiveness decisions?

## Questions for further discussion

1   When examining your own educational journey, what did you learn about forgiveness and reconciliation? What were your teachers' attitudes and perceptions on this topic?
2   In your own personal life, have you engaged in any reconciliation or forgiveness processes? What was the main challenge in such an experience?
3   What examples can you identify from history in which reconciliation and forgiveness processes were successfully applied?
4   What is the role of culture and religion in the process of reconciliation and forgiveness?
5   What national or international conflicts are you aware of in which the process of reconciliation and forgiveness is needed? What are the challenges in integrating these processes in the current or existing conflict-management approaches?

## Suggested resources

1   Abu-Nimer, Mohammed. 2003. *Nonviolence and Peace Building in Islam*. Gainesville, FL: University Press of Florida.
2   Borris, Eileen R. 2003. "The Healing Power of Forgiveness." Occasional Paper No. 10. Institute for Multi-Track Diplomacy. http://imtd.org/wp-content/uploads/2017/03/op-10.pdf.
3   Crow, Karim Douglas. 2009. "Forgiveness in Muslim Thought and Practice: Response to Augsburger's 'The Practice of Forgiveness and Reconciliation in Conflict Transformation'." In *Peace-building by, Between, and Beyond Muslims and Evangelical Christians*,

edited by Mohammed Abu-Nimer and David Augsburger, 13–18. New York, NY: Lexington Books.

4    de Gruchy, John. 2002. *Reconciliation: Restoring Justice*. Minneapolis, MN: Fortress Press.

5    Film: An African Answer: www.anafricananswer.org/ – This film is a sequel to The Imam and the Pastor and illustrates an African initiative for fostering healing and reconciliation.

6    The Forgiveness Institute: https://internationalforgiveness.com/.

7    Stanford Forgiveness Project: www.hawaiiforgivenessproject.org/Stanford.htm.

## Become engaged!

1    Get involved in a range of activities related to reconciliation through the International Fellowship of Reconciliation: www.ifor.org/#mission.

2    Forgiveness project and research at Salam Institute for Peace and Justice: http://salaminstitute.org.

3    Mind and Life Institute: www.mindandlife.org/.

## Notes

1  Testimony based on KAICIID (International Center for Intercultural and Interreligious Dialogue) workshop for peacebuilding in Central Africa Republic on August 13, 2017.

2  Personal testimonies by Lebanese religious leaders in Beirut in a workshop for interreligious dialogue May 18, 2015.

3  See www.theforgivenessproject.com/stories; https://backend.fetzer.org/sites/default/files/resources/attachment/%5Bcurrent-date%3Atiny%5D/Survey%20of%20Love%20and%20Forgiveness%20in%20American%20Society%20Report.pdf.

## References and further reading

Abu-Nimer, Mohammed. 1996. "Conflict Resolution Approaches: Western and Middle Eastern Lessons and Possibilities." *American Journal of Economics and Sociology* 55 (1): 35–52.

———. 2003. "Toward the Theory and Practice of Positive Approaches to Peacebuilding." In *Positive Approaches for Peacebuilding*, edited by Cynthia Sampson, Mohammed Abu-Nimer, and Claudia Liebler. Washington, DC: PACT Publications.

Abu-Nimer, Mohammed, and David Augsburger, eds. 2009. *Peacebuilding by, Between, and Beyond Muslim and Evangelical Christians*. Lanham, MD: Lexington Books.

Abu-Nimer, Mohammed, and Ilham Nasser. 2013. "Forgiveness in the Arab and Islamic Contexts: Between Theology and Practice." *Journal of Religious Ethics* 41 (3): 474–94.

Ahmed, Ramadan, Fabiola Azar, and Etienne Mullet. 2007. "Interpersonal Forgiveness Among Kuwaiti Adolescents and Adults." *Conflict Management and Peace Science* 24 (3): 159–70.

Ahmed, Eliza, and John Braithwaite. 2005. "Forgiveness, Shaming, Shame and Bullying." *Australian and New Zealand Journal of Criminology* 38 (3): 398–23.

Bickmore, Kathy. 2014. "Peacebuilding Dialogue Pedagogies in Canadian Classrooms." *Curriculum Inquiry* 44 (4): 553–82.

Borris, Eileen, and Paul F. Diehl. 1998. "Forgiveness, Reconciliation, and the Contribution of International Peacekeeping." *The Psychology of Peacekeeping*, edited by Harvey Langholtz, 207–22. Westport, CT: Praeger Publishers.

Channer, Alan, dir. 2006. *The Imam and the Pastor*. London: FLTfilms.

de Waal, Frans B.M. 2000. "Primates: A Natural Heritage of Conflict Resolution." *Science* 289: 586–600.

Enright, Robert. 2001. *Forgiveness Is a Choice: A Step-by-Step Process for Resolving Anger and Restoring Hope*. Washington, DC: APA LifeTools.

Enright, Robert, Elizabeth Gassin, and Ching-Ru Wu. 1992. "Forgiveness: A Developmental View." *Journal of Moral Education* 21 (2): 99–114.

Kriesberg, Louis, and Bruce Dayton. 2016. *Constructive Conflicts: From Escalation to Resolution*. London: Rowman & Littlefield Publishers.

Langholtz, Harvey. 1998. *The Psychology of Peacekeeping*. Westport, CT: Praeger Publishers.

Lederach, John Paul. 1997. *Building Peace: Sustainable Reconciliation in Divided Societies*. Washington, DC: United States Institute of Peace.

Macaskill, A.J. Maltby, and L. Day. 2002. "Forgiveness of Self and Others and Emotional Empathy." *The Journal of Social Psychology* 142: 663–65.

MacLachlan, Alice. 2009. "Practicing Imperfect Forgiveness." In *Feminist Ethics and Social and Political Philosophy: Theorizing the Non-ideal*, edited by Lisa Tessman, 185–204. Dordrecht, The Netherlands: Springer.

McCullough, Michael, and Charlotte VanOyen Witvliet. 2002. "The Psychology of Forgiveness." In *Handbook of Positive Psychology*, edited by C.R. Snyder and S.J. Lopez, 447. New York, NY: Oxford University Press.

Morrison, Brenda, and Dorothy Vaandering. 2012. "Restorative Justice: Pedagogy, Praxis, and Discipline." *Journal of School Violence* 11 (2): 138–55.

Nasser, Ilham, and Mohammed Abu-Nimer. 2016. "Examining Views and Attitudes About Forgiveness Among Teachers in the Arab World: A Comparison Between Five Communities." *Journal for Social Change* 41 (2): 194–220.

Nasser, Ilham, Mohammed Abu-Nimer, and Ola Mahmoud. 2014. "Contextual and Pedagogical Considerations in Teaching for Forgiveness in the Arab World." *Compare: A Journal of Comparative and International Education* 44 (1): 32–54.

Thornton, Bevelynne. 2011. "Try Forgiveness." *The Family Journal: Counseling and Therapy for Couples and Families* 19 (3): 245.

Worthington, Everett. 2001. *Five Steps to Forgiveness: The Art and Science of Forgiving*. New York, NY: Crown.

Zembylas, Michalinos. 2012. "Teaching About/for Ambivalent Forgiveness in Troubled Societies." *Ethics and Education* 7 (1): 19–32.

Zembylas, Michalinos, and Andri Michaelidou. 2011. "Teachers' Understandings of Forgiveness in a Troubled Society: An Empirical Exploration and Implications for Forgiveness Pedagogies." *Pedagogies, an International Journal* 6 (3): 250–64.

# Part III

# Cross-cutting themes in international conflict management

# 10 Civil society and conflict management

*Thania Paffenholz*

## Introduction

Contemporary conflict management is a collective enterprise that requires broad participation by a multitude of local and international actors. Since the 1990s, there has been a shift in thinking among conflict-management scholars and policymakers from a traditional understanding of peacebuilding as a matter purely for states to a general acceptance that civil society has a constructive role to play therein. Yet even as late as 2014, discussions in the research community and among practitioners remained trapped in a binary debate arguing for or against the inclusion of civil society instead of considering how effective it has been in conflict management and what more should be done for it to be further constructive.

In the last few years, however, civil society inclusion in both practice and normative frameworks has become standard practice. Despite its positive implications, such inclusion faces resistance in practice, especially in Track I negotiations, due to the fear that enhanced participation greatly complicates the consensus-building process and makes it more difficult to reach a peace agreement. Furthermore, mediators often treat such inclusion purely as a normative issue. This means that they do not see it as a necessary condition to reach an agreement and set precedence for a more inclusive society but as a principle that has been agreed upon internationally and is not relevant to their contexts. As a consequence, they prefer inclusion modalities further away from the negotiation table, thus limiting civil society inputs to consultations with no real participation. In addition, even when civil society actors are included (whether at the negotiation table or otherwise), this does not necessarily mean that they have influence over the proceedings and outcomes of the negotiations. Actors' inclusion in and influence over a given peace process are largely constrained by context factors such as lack of political buy-in, lack of support to meet expectations of a representation mandate, and lack of receptivity of negotiators to collaborate with the diversity of civil society.

With this in mind, this chapter aims to explore what "civil society" is, clarify the various functions played by civil society actors in the area of collective conflict management, present different modalities for including these actors in high-level negotiations, and determine the challenges and dilemmas associated with their meaningful participation. The chapter concludes by exploring how policymakers can better utilize civil society actors in conflict management in order that they can contribute to ending wars, sustaining peace, and managing political transitions.

## Background/history of civil society in international conflict management

The launching of "An Agenda for Peace" in 1992 made preventive diplomacy an important theme in the global policy discourse. For almost two decades since then, with prevention in mind, an important link between inclusion and peacebuilding was forged. In only a few years, this link was highlighted as a priority for global policy action, and the once neglected topic of civil society inclusion in conflict management (Paffenholz 2014b) thus became the fashion of our times. There has never been a more conducive set of normative international frameworks that together highlight the importance of inclusion in peacebuilding and, by extension, conflict management. These include the 2030 Agenda and the Sustainable Development Goals (SDGs), particularly Goal 16; the work on UNSC Resolution 1325 on Women, Peace and Security (WPS); and UNSC Resolution 2250 on Youth, Peace and Security. Perhaps the most comprehensive normative framework emphasizing inclusion has been the Prevention Agenda, including both the UN Sustaining Peace Resolutions, as well as "Pathways for Peace," the 2018 UN-World Bank conflict-prevention report. All of these frameworks state that without inclusion there is no prevention of violence, mediation, or peacebuilding, and therefore no sustainable political system. Against this backdrop of an inclusion discourse, this section sheds light on the two terms *civil society* and *conflict management*, their interrelationship, and what they mean for the inclusion debate.

*Conflict management* in this chapter is considered to be an umbrella term covering various types of collective interventions carried out in order to end armed conflict or negotiate political transitions in the short-, medium-, or long-term. What civil society can contribute to conflict management varies depending on these different phases. One thus has to distinguish between its role in the short-term (often referred to as "peacemaking") and the long-term (mostly referred to by the UN as "peacebuilding"). Civil society actors use the term "peacebuilding" more broadly.

*Civil society* is generally understood as the arena of voluntary, collective actions of an institutional nature around shared interests, purposes, and values that are distinct from those of the state, family, and market. Civil society consists of a large and diverse set of voluntary organizations and comprises non-state actors and associations that are not purely driven by private or economic interests, are autonomously organized, show civil virtue, and interact in the public sphere (Spurk 2010). More differentiations and nuances of the term will be highlighted in the succeeding discussion.

It is important to note that civil society is not a homogenous actor solely comprising the "good society" that contributes to dialogue and democratization (Orjuela 2003). Rather, research has found that inclusive, civic, bridging, and pro-peace organizations often work alongside exclusivist, sectarian, and occasionally xenophobic and militant groups (Belloni 2001; Ikelegbe 2001; Orjuela 2003; Paffenholz 2010).

In light of a range of classifications (see Pearce 1998; Carothers 1999–2000; Belloni 2008; Orjuela 2003; Pouligny 2005; Paffenholz 2010; Aall 2007; Chigas 2007; Bartoli 2009), it is possible to identify the following non-mutually exclusive categories of civil society actors:

- Special interest groups (trade unions; professional associations for teachers, farmers, and journalists; minority and women's organizations; and veterans' associations)
- Faith-based organizations (churches, Islamic associations, and others)
- Traditional and community groups (youth groups, councils of elders, women's and mother's groups, radio listener's clubs, and user groups)
- Researchers and research institutions (local and international think tanks, universities, and individual researchers)
- Humanitarian or development-service delivery organizations (which include both local and international, "modern" and "traditional;" or religious organizations, like humanitarian aid NGOs, churches, or Islamic charities)

- Human rights and advocacy organizations (which can also be clustered under "special interest groups")
- Conflict resolution and peacebuilding NGOs and INGOs (which might also be advocacy or training-service organizations, depending on their mandate)
- Social and political movements (which can take the form of broad-based public movements around a common cause, such as the Arab Spring; or longer-term movements, like environmental, women's, or peace movements)
- Business associations (associations of entrepreneurs or journalists, independent of their profit-making side of business)
- Networks (which generally represent a larger number of organizations from any of the categories specified above, such as a network of religious councils)

Islamic charities are a good example of how these categories sometimes overlap. They can be both faith-based organizations and provide development or humanitarian services to the poor.

An important debate in the civil society discourse concerns its origins and its developments in different geographical contexts (see Spurk 2010). A closer look into the history of civil society also sheds light on some current terminological debates. Historically, the notion of civil society has been an almost purely Western concept, tied to the political emancipation of European citizens from former feudalistic ties, monarchies, and the state during the eighteenth and nineteenth centuries. This has given rise to a debate as to whether the concept of civil society is transferable to non-Western contexts (Lewis 2002). Nevertheless, there has always been some form of civil association in all geographical and historical contexts. In this respect, a number of context-specific discourses can be observed (see Spurk 2010; Crocker 2015 for more on these geographical distinctions).

## Contending approaches to civil society inclusion in conflict management

In recent years, there have been differing strands of research on inclusion and participation of civil society in conflict management. These could broadly be categorized under four themes: (1) top-down approaches to inclusion, (2) social movement theory-inspired frameworks that develop bottom-up approaches, (3) approaches that focus on radical mass actions, and (4) approaches that combine the aforementioned strands of arguments.

Top-down approaches refer to invited or organized spaces where the top (e.g., mediators, conflict parties, donors, or other official authorities) offers (voluntarily or pressured from outside or inside the country) participation spaces to civil society in different modalities. (*Modality* for the purpose of this chapter refers to a particular form in which civil society participation in conflict management occurs – representatives at the negotiation table, observers, etc.) This literature has for a long time been stuck in a binary debate on exclusion versus inclusion, by focusing on who should or should not be at the negotiation table for various kinds of reasons. The development of inclusion modalities (Paffenholz 2014b, 76–89) shifted the debate from the *who* to the *how* of inclusion and participation, revealing that inclusion does not only take place at the negotiation table. Instead, inclusion also occurs in negotiation processes with short- and long-term institutional arrangements such as inclusive commissions or governance structures. Practice thus combined top-down with bottom-up approaches.

Inspired by social movement theory, bottom-up claims of participation for change are based on case study research. Vogel (2016), for example, contends that peace processes have become more open to civil society organizations' participation, but argues that such openness might be misleading. With reference to the Cyprus peace process, she explains that different agendas of civil society organizations and the international community often sideline civil society organizations, meaning that certain opinions are not properly represented during peace negotiations. By exploring the cases of Kenya and Liberia, Zanker (2014) argues that the presence of civil society organizations during peace negotiations does not necessarily enhance the legitimacy of the discussions, since organizations are not always representative of and accountable to the public.

Another category of research focuses on social movements and negotiations, i.e., on citizen demands for increased political participation expressed in demonstrations, occupations, and other kinds of radical action central to the repertoire of social movements (Butcher and Apsan Frediani 2014). Here, scope and access are not "given" from above as in invited spaces, but develop between activists and state authorities in open, at times conflicting processes. Spector, for example, argues that negotiations are becoming more inclusive, but that these negotiations do not necessarily take place "at the table," but can materialize following a more disorganized approach accompanied by disjointed dialogues, media, and other spaces related to new communication technologies that allow outsiders to become more influential (Spector 2015). Older studies such as the one of Hickey and Mohan point here to the importance for participatory spaces to be embedded in strong social movements as a source of counter-hegemonic power (Hickey and Mohan 2005).

A final category combining the two aforementioned strands (bottom-up and radical mass actions) is still fairly underdeveloped. In doing so, the inclusion modalities framework developed by Paffenholz recognizes that mass mobilization is an important participation model but does not provide for a debate as to what the merging of the two perspectives entails for civil society inclusion in peace negotiations. A joint reflection project stipulating global online conversations among civil society actors about inclusion[1] comes to the conclusion that despite all the normative talk about inclusion, civil society itself seems to be skeptical of the potential of the inclusion hype to bring about social and political change.

## Civil society functions in international conflict management

In the literature, various roles and functions are attributed to civil society in conflict management. The following seven functions present the most comprehensive overview of what civil society can contribute: protection, monitoring, advocacy, socialization, social cohesion, facilitation, and service delivery (Paffenholz and Spurk 2006, 2010).

### *Protection*

Protection of citizens and communities against the despotism of the state and encroachment of extra-state armed groups is highly necessary in any situation. During and after an armed conflict, protection becomes almost a precondition for fulfilling other functions, given that regular life is interrupted by security concerns. The main protection-related activities are international accompaniment, watchdog activities, creation of "zones for peace," and human security initiatives like demining. Protection by specialized NGOs has been more effective when it was systematically combined with monitoring and advocacy campaigns, and when there was cooperation between international and local Civil Society Organizations (CSOs). During Nepal's civil war, for example, a number of local human rights organizations monitored violations by the army and the Maoists and systematically channeled all information to the National Human Rights Commission, the media, and to Amnesty International (AI). AI, in suit, used the data to successfully lobby at the international level for the establishment of a UN monitoring mission.

### Monitoring

Monitoring is, in general, a precondition for protection and advocacy. Monitoring is highly relevant to holding governments accountable and putting pressure on the conflict parties. Supervising and verifying the implementation of peace agreements are also key elements of monitoring activities, but they have often been neglected. The impact of monitoring has been greater when activities were designed to reinforce protection and advocacy initiatives. For example, the International Crisis Group (ICG) monitors situations in conflict countries and provides political analysis and recommendations to decision-makers. Due to high quality of analysis and international network and media coverage, it has become an influential monitoring institution.

### Advocacy

Advocacy is a core function of civil society. The strongest form of advocacy is public mobilization, when masses of people go to the streets to demand the end of authoritarian rule or armed conflict, as recently seen in the Middle East and North Africa, or in Nepal in 2006. The main activities within this function are agenda-setting by CSOs, such as bringing themes to the national agenda in conflict countries; lobbying for civil society involvement in peace negotiations; and applying public pressure by way of protests or demonstrations of support. Also important are international advocacy campaigns that lobby, for example, against land mines, blood diamonds, or the abuse of children as soldiers. Advocacy initiatives become more effective when organizations have campaigning know-how and base their advocacy on results of monitoring initiatives. International attention enhances their impact. For example, in Northern Ireland civil society groups managed to successfully lobby for the integration of human rights provisions into the Good Friday peace agreement.

### Socialization

Socialization realized through the active participation of citizens in various associations, networks, or movements is key to embedding democratic values in society. Socialization takes place only within groups, not between former adversary groups (which is social cohesion, discussed later); it focuses on strengthening in-group bonding ties. For example, more and more international NGOs are working on each side of the Israel/Palestine conflict separately in order to strengthen each group in their peace efforts and understanding. Socialization initiatives have been less effective overall because they have mostly worked in the short-term and outside of the key influential institutions that have the power to socialize people. The key institutions in society that influence how people learn democratic and also conflict behavior are families, schools, religious groups, secular and cultural associations, and the workplace. Yet, in most conflict countries, these socialization spaces tend to reinforce existing divides. In Israel, for example, education in schools reinforces the Jewish and Zionist identity and, to a lesser extent, liberal democratic values. However, in-group socialization of marginalized groups has often been effective. For example, in-group education of the Maya in Guatemala by the Catholic Church helped empower a generation of civic leaders by allowing for the construction of a pan-Maya identity across the twenty-four distinct language groups.

### Intergroup social cohesion

Social cohesion aims at (re)building "good" social capital that was destroyed during war. Therefore, it is crucial to build "bridging ties" across adversarial groups rather than "bonding ties" within specific groups (Putnam 2000). As explained previously, divided societies have many strong socialization institutions, including families, schools, and religious organizations that preach hatred and formulate enemy images over a long period (usually generations). In Somalia, for example, clan-based organizations worked to reinforce social cleavages and to weaken national cohesion. Therefore, bridging these gaps is crucial for peacebuilding. In addition, problem-solving workshops tend to select English-speaking elites as representatives, people who are often already "converted" to the idea of positive images of the other group. Evidence of this was found in an evaluation of a series of workshops in Cyprus that assessed attitudes of participants prior to and after the program. The evaluation revealed that most participants already had a positive attitude toward the other group prior to the workshops (Cuhadar and Kotelis 2010).

### Facilitation

Civil society can function as a facilitator to help bring parties together in a peace or transition process. Facilitation takes place both on the local and the national level. For example, in Afghanistan during Taliban rule, traditional mediation was the only resource for facilitating peace between the Taliban and various Afghani communities. The Tribal Liaisons Office helped organize local peace jirgas with religious and local leaders to explore options for peacebuilding. On the national level, facilitation is often done by prominent civil society leaders, whose legitimacy often determines the fate of negotiations. In Nigeria, the government nominated a Catholic priest as chief mediator between Ogoni groups due to this reason.

### Service delivery

During armed conflict, the provision of aid services through civil society actors (mainly NGOs, but sometimes associations as well) increases tremendously as state structures are either destroyed or weakened. There is no doubt that this function is extremely important to help the war-affected population and to support reconstruction. However, service delivery can only have an impact on conflict management if agencies create entry points for other functions such as protection and social cohesion, especially when large-scale violence ends. For example, in Somalia, the total absence of a state for almost two decades made service delivery the main preoccupation of civil society. In this instance, Islamic charities were especially successful in creating entry points for peacebuilding by extending networks across clan and regional lines.

## Seven modalities of civil society participation in international conflict management

On the question of how to involve civil society in conflict management, this section presents seven modalities of inclusion through which the seven functions described earlier are achieved; they focus primarily on short-term conflict management and look at means to broaden participation in formal Track I negotiations (Paffenholz 2014b). The seven

---

**Seven Modalities of Inclusion**

1. **Direct representation at the negotiation table**
   a. Inclusion within negotiation delegations
   b. Enlarging the number of negotiation delegations i.e. including a separate women's delegation
   c. National Dialogues (peace- and constitution-making, reforms)
2. **Observer status or advisors**
3. **Consultations**
   a. Official Consultations
   b. Non or semi-official Consultations
   c. Public Consultations
4. **Inclusive commissions**
   a. Post-agreement commissions
   b. Commissions preparing/conducting peace processes
   c. Permanent Commissions
5. **High-level problem solving workshops**
6. **Public decision-making** (i.e. referendum)
7. **Mass action**

---

*Figure 10.1* Seven Modalities of Inclusion

modalities – ranging from the most direct representation to the least direct – are set out in Figure 10.1. Please note that these are not mutually exclusive nor are a tick box.

### Modality 1: direct representation at the negotiation table

The modality of direct representation refers to the presence of civil society at the negotiation table, either on its own or as part of another actor's delegation, according civil society with the same status as the main conflict parties. However, the greater the number of groups present at the table, the more complex and challenging it becomes to reach an agreement. In order to address this, mediators in the 1999–2002 Inter-Congolese Dialogue resorted to sub-working groups as a way to break up great numbers of participants (Wanis-St. John and Kew 2008). It is important to note that direct participation of civil society at the negotiation table rarely happens.

### Modality 2: observer status or advisors

Civil society groups or international and local NGOs can be granted observer status that does not entail an official role, but enables direct presence during negotiations (Paffenholz

2014a), as happened in Liberia (2003), Sierra Leone (1996), the Solomon Islands (1991), and Burundi (1996–98) (Inclusive Peace & Transition Initiative 2017).

Observers act as critical watchdogs, advise the conflict parties and mediators, and form alliances with other observers to facilitate the agreement. They have also been able to lobby for new issues to be added to the negotiation agenda. The risk of being co-opted and the issue of underrepresentation due to the small and exclusive number of observers chosen are some challenges associated with this.

### Modality 3: consultations

Consultations may take place prior to, in parallel with, or after official negotiations. Consultations can either be elite-based, broad-based, or public. Any of these formats can be either an official part of the negotiation architecture or an informal initiative by one of the negotiating parties, by the mediator or the facilitator, or by groups wishing to influence the negotiations in some way.

Consultations can also be officially-endorsed, unofficial, or public. Officially-endorsed consultations aim to channel local people's demands into a formal peace process and to better understand how the public evaluates the substance of ongoing negotiations, including what may be widely perceived as missing from the official agenda. Unofficial consultations are sometimes used to generate pressure for the commencement of negotiations or in cases where the main parties refuse official consultations. Public consultations have been used both to disseminate the results of a negotiation process and to invite suggestions from the public. The latter involves collecting proposals and opinions from the broader society to be included in the formal negotiation agenda (i.e., agenda-setting) as a means of developing public ownership of a peace process (i.e., boosting overall process legitimacy) and of furthering the long-term sustainability of a negotiated agreement.

In general, conducting consultations avoids the problem of multiplying the number of actors at the main negotiation table while including a broad set of perspectives that gives the process more legitimacy. They can also help facilitate the discussion on difficult issues and provide an alternative channel for negotiations if official talks stall. On the other hand, they come at the cost of more distance from the negotiation table. Despite its mandate, a consultative forum can be ignored, sidelined, or dismissed by the principle negotiators. In order to ensure civil society input, regular communication has to take place between the mediation/facilitation teams of the official negotiation and the consultation. UN-led mediations in Guatemala (1994–1996) and in Afghanistan (for one week in December 2001) are some examples of successful officially endorsed consultative forums where civil society groups were able to bring crucial issues to the negotiation agenda that would have otherwise been left out.

### Modality 4: inclusive commissions

Inclusive commissions (official bodies authorized to implement a peace agreement) are most commonly found in the post-agreement stage, but they are occasionally used to set up or run part of the negotiation process. There are three types of commissions: a) commissions preparing/conducting a peace process; b) post-agreement commissions such as transitional justice mechanisms, ceasefire monitoring, or constitution-drafting commissions; and c) commissions set up as permanent constitutional bodies like the interethnic commission in Kyrgyzstan (2013), which was responsible for ensuring equal rights for all ethnic groups in the country.

The inclusion of civil society in various post-agreement mechanisms aims at strengthening democratization as well as the sustainability of the agreement. The main function of this modality is monitoring. Many peace agreements include provisions for the inclusion of civil society in implementation mechanisms, ranging from general to very specific (Bell and O'Rourke 2007). Some peace agreements also include provisions for civil society to raise awareness about the agreement among the population. In Somalia, for example, the 1993 agreement included a provision stipulating that civil society delegations would travel to all parts of the country to drive up awareness of the agreement.

### Modality 5: high-level problem-solving workshops

Problem-solving workshops or private facilitation initiatives aim at strengthening the impact of negotiations, providing facilitation, and, depending on the case, advocating for specific issues to be included in the agreement.

Problem-solving workshops are unofficial and generally not publicized. They bring together representatives close to the leaders of the conflict parties and offer them communication channels without pressure to reach an agreement (Fisher 2007). Such initiatives can last up to several years and are generally organized and facilitated by INGOs or academic institutions (sometimes in cooperation with local partners). They are also an option when belligerents refuse to meet publicly (Paffenholz 2014b).

The Schlaining Process in the Georgian-Abkhaz conflict demonstrates the use of these workshops. Though the Schlaining Process came to an end in 2007, it fostered a generation of ideas and communication channels across the conflict divide.

### Modality 6: public decision-making

Public decision-making processes are standard features of democracies. Peace agreements and/or new constitutions can be submitted for ratification by the population, and the results are usually binding. A binding endorsement of a peace deal also seeks to protect the negotiated agreement, provide democratic legitimacy to the process, and ensure public support and sustainability of the agreement. Mediators can also increase their understanding of the population's needs and expectations by conducting referenda, public hearings, and opinion polls. However, a decision to put a negotiated peace deal to a public vote needs to be carefully considered. A vote against the agreement blocks its implementation and usually places the entire process on hold.

### Modality 7: mass action

Mass action by citizens mobilizes large numbers of people, mostly in the form of public demonstrations. As global events of the last decade have confirmed, mass action remains a very powerful instrument of public pressure on established powers and incumbent political elites, particularly when used effectively in combination with social media and mass media, such as live satellite broadcasts of mass action. Most mass action is often the result of grassroots, bottom-up dynamics and centers on a common goal of national interest, such as political reforms to end authoritarian rule, the cessation of war or armed conflict, and/or the signing of a peace deal (Paffenholz 2014b). Mass demonstrations can be both pro-peace (Nepal 2006) and anti-peace (Sri Lanka 2000).

---

**Textbox 10.1    Syria: women and civil society inclusion in the third round of Geneva Peace Talks (2016)**

In 2012 and 2014, at the first and second rounds of peace talks on Syria in Geneva, no civil society or women's groups were included or consulted, a fact that flew in the face of UN Security Council Resolution 1325. Hence these groups mobilized to put pressure on the conflict parties and the mediation team for broadening participation in the talks.

As a result, in January 2016 in Round three, Special Envoy de Mistura invited 12 women from diverse backgrounds to formally contribute to the peace talks through the Syrian Women's Advisory Body (WAB). The Special Envoy also established a civil society support room (CSSR) consisting of rotating numbers of 10–20 civil society representatives from Syria. In practice, the WAB and the CSSR did not directly participate in the negotiations but rather separately met with the UN Special Envoy to submit papers on common positions and make recommendations. The intention was to provide both a gendered perspective to the talks as well as a different path of negotiating opposing, entrenched positions in circumstances where the main actors to the peace talks refused to even be in the same room as each other.

As the first of its kind in official peace negotiations, the WAB was lauded for its historic symbolism. However, in practice both WAB and CSSR had little influence on the negotiations and have also been criticized for not being representative, influential, or even legitimate (see Alzoubi 2017; Hellmuller and Zahar 2018). These bodies were not involved in initial stages of the peace talks, including the design and preparation stages of the process, so they had little influence on even administrative or logistical elements and agenda-setting. The peace talks took place in Geneva, creating logistical barriers to broader women and civil society participation (such as travel and accommodation costs). Further, there was little transparency in how the 12 women of the WAB were selected; certain minority, religious, class, political, and non-state actor groups were not represented; age groups not reflected; and there was too high a proportion of women supporting the government or from the elite. To their benefit, one must however say that the peace talks themselves were not really taking off the ground and women and civil society could not compensate for this. In that sense, it is also hard to talk about the impact of the WAB or the CSSR on the peace talks – as there were sadly never real peace talks happening in Syria.

---

### Challenges and future directions

Civil society is divided along the same lines of power, hierarchy, ethnicity, and gender as the greater society, displaying moderate as well as radical behavior. In general, civil society organizations are dominated by male leadership from influential groups within society, with the exception of women's and minority organizations. Hence, civil society can be "uncivil" (Spurk 2010), exclusivist, sectarian, and occasionally even xenophobic as well as inclusive, civic, bridging, and pro-peace (Belloni 2001; Ikelegbe 2001; Orjuela 2003; Paffenholz 2010).

Further, in polarized political settings, excluded civil society and parties to the conflict often criticize negotiation processes for not inviting them to be part of it rather than demanding their space to take part and influence the outcomes. Mediation actors sometimes only see inclusion as the fulfillment of a normative principle without thought for the appropriate design of inclusion in the context of a particular peace process. This leads to inclusion designs that are not sensitive to prevailing cleavages and therefore affect the legitimacy of the process, especially in the eyes of the parties concerned. Therefore, any design that includes civil society in negotiations must take into account these preexisting divides and be inclusive to the maximum possible extent for legitimacy.

Additionally, "NGOization" of civil society due to international donor agendas that prefer NGOs over membership-based civil society groups and associations is transforming these groups into professional service delivery NGOs, limiting their conflict-management potential because they become less political and often more accountable to the donor than to their own constituency (Orjuela 2003; Kaldor 2003; Kasfir 1998; Pouligny 2005; Belloni 2001; Belloni 2008; Paffenholz 2010). Added to this is the issue of increased focus of civil society on training to be fit for the eventual invitation for inclusion, which limits its potential to organize and rally behind important causes. When civil society is invited to take part, its ability to create pressure and momentum for change is limited since the focus is more on fulfilling technicalities to get invited instead of using the space to contest decisions. This lack of momentum thus curbs the impact civil society can make on conflict management.

The main context factors that enable or constrain civil society's impact in conflict management are the level of violence, behavior of the state, performance of the media, behavior and composition of civil society itself (including diaspora organizations), and the influence of external political actors and donors (Paffenholz 2010). With regard to the seven functions of civil society, more research needs to be done to evaluate its impact and to identify the appropriate phase to use them in a negotiation process. When designing such involvement, one must take into account the different impact potential of civil society actors. For instance, international and local NGOs can be particularly effective in providing protection and in conducting targeted advocacy campaigns, while mass-based organizations such as unions or other professional associations as well as schools and families have far greater potential to promote socialization and social cohesion than NGOs. Traditional and local entities can be effective in facilitation and protection, while eminent civil society leaders and conflict management NGOs can be effective in preparing the ground for national facilitation and in helping parties break out of a stalemate in negotiations. Yet broader change requires uniting of all available multiple change-oriented mass movements (Paffenholz 2010).

It is important to note that certain functions of the civil society are favored over others for manifold and complex reasons. They include the availability of funds; the often reactive mode of changing donor priorities; poor planning procedures on the part of NGOs that do not factor in the likelihood of changing context when designing initiatives; a limited set of theories of change (impact assumptions) on what works and what does not work in conflict management, which has led to more competencies in some areas (e.g., peace education, dialogue) than in others (protection, monitoring); and the lack of linkages between human rights (i.e., protection) and peace-related work (Paffenholz 2014a).

The growing role of civil society participation in international conflict management is important on multiple fronts: it democratizes the negotiation process and by extension the outcome; ensures inclusion of a broad range of voices, especially of the marginalized such as women and minority groups; and most importantly elevates the position of the "citizen" within the polity by creating more robust frameworks for citizen participation in the decision-making processes.

Despite these positive implications at the normative level, in practice, civil society participation in negotiations is fraught with problems ranging from under-representation of important groups to limited influence due to lack of political buy-in. Overemphasis on the fulfillment of donor agendas and non-acknowledgment of the limits of civil society have resulted in "NGOization" of civil society and an undermining of the civil society's potential to effect change respectively. Apart from these external factors that limit its potential, civil society also has horizontal inequalities between different groups that at times result in silencing voices of certain groups that lie at the bottom of the civil society power hierarchy.

The seven modalities presented in the chapter highlight different ways in which civil society participation in negotiations occurs. An important point to note is how civil society is often left out of Track I negotiations, thus clearly indicating that despite increased focus on inclusion, civil society is still treated as an outsider to a formal peace process. Policymakers should strengthen civil society participation mandates in negotiations in order to both legitimize the process and to avoid civil unrest by continuously neglecting important voices.

## Questions for further discussion

1   Consider all the organizations and individuals that influence the lives of people in your community.

   o   What are the different functions they perform?
   o   Are they state sponsored or private?
   o   Based on the above, what do you consider to be civil society?
   o   Is there diversity within civil society?

2   Select a case study of your choice.

   o   Identify civil society in this case, paying attention to the form of association, functions they perform, and their intended impact.
   o   Can you identify the civil society performing any of the functions described in this chapter?
   o   If there is a formal peace process in the selected case, identify the different ways in which civil society participates in the negotiation process. What modalities for inclusion (as described in the chapter) do you identify?
   o   Considering the political forces at play and conflict dynamics in the given case study, do you see the civil society applying pressure to participate in negotiations or being invited to join? What are the pros and cons of the two situations?
   o   What tensions do you identify within the civil society? Do you see some less powerful voices within civil society being co-opted?

## Suggested resources

1   Conciliation Resources. n.d. *Navigating Inclusion in Peace Processes*. www.youtube.com/watch?v=d5mefgIXeTM.
2   Carnegie Endowment for International Peace. 2019. "Civic Research Network." https://carnegieendowment.org/specialprojects/civicresearchnetwork/?lang=en.
3   www.inclusivepeacebuilding.org. Provides the most elaborate guide, and reflection and navigation tools concerning civil society, peacebuilding and inclusion. This includes multiple videos and online links including many short videos by Thania Paffenholz describing the functions of civil society).
4   Paffenholz, Thania, ed. 2010. *Civil Society and Peacebuilding: A Critical Assessment*. Boulder, CO: Lynne Rienner Publishers.

5   Stephen, Monica. 2017. "Partnerships in Conflict: How Violent Conflict Impacts Local Civil Society and How International Partners Respond." *International Alert, OXFAM*. https://policy-practice.oxfam.org.uk/publications/partnerships-in-conflict-how-violent-conflict-impacts-local-civil-society-and-h-620359.

## Become engaged!

1   CIVICUS: www.civicus.org/.
2   GPPAC: https://gppac.net/.
3   Alliance for Peacebuilding: https://allianceforpeacebuilding.org/.
4   UNOY Peacebuilders: http://unoy.org/en/.
5   Young peacebuilders: https://youngpeacebuilders.com/.
6   Build Peace: https://howtobuildpeace.org/.
7   Inclusive Peace: www.inclusivepeace.org/.
8   Mediation Networks: www.inclusivepeace.org/content/map-international-mediation-networks.

## Note

1   See www.peacedirect.org/civil-society-and-inclusive-peace/.

## References and further reading

Aall, Pamela. 2007. "The Power of Nonofficial Actors in Conflict Management." In *Leashing the Dogs of War: Conflict Management in a Divided World*, edited by Chester Crocker, Fen Osler Hampson, and Pamela Aall, 477–94. Washington, DC: United States Institute of Peace Press.

Alzoubi, Zedoun. 2017. "Syrian Civil Society During the Peace Talks in Geneva: Role and Challenges." *New England Journal of Public Policy* 29 (1): Article 11.

Appiagyei-Atua, Kwadwo. 2002. "Civil Society, Human Rights and Development in Africa: A Critical Analysis." Peace, Conflict and Development No. 2, University of Bradford. Accessed August 1, 2019. https://pdfs.semanticscholar.org/0149/92340667baaf88813129d7aef7257dd08456.pdf.

Babajanian, Babken, Sabine Freizer, and Daniel Stevens. 2005. "Civil Society in Central Asia and the Caucasus." *Central Asian Survey* 24 (3): 209–24.

Bartoli, Andrea. 2009. "NGOs and Conflict Resolution." In *SAGE Handbook on Conflict Resolution*, edited by Jacob Bercovitch, Victor Kremenyuk, and I. William Zartman, 392–412. London: Sage Publications.

Bell, Christine, and Catherine O'Rourke. 2007. "The People's Peace? Peace Agreements, Civil Society, and Participatory Democracy." *International Political Science Review* 28 (3): 293–324.

Bell, Christine, and Jan Pospisil. 2017. "Navigating Inclusion in Transitions from Conflict: The Formalised Political Unsettlement." *Journal of International Development* 29 (5): 576–93.

Belloni, Roberto. 2001. "Civil Society and Peacebuilding in Bosnia and Herzegovina." *Journal of Peace Research* 38 (2): 163–80.

———. 2008. "Civil Society in War-to-Democracy Transitions." In *From War to Democracy: Dilemmas of Peacebuilding*, edited by Anna K. Jarstad and Timothy D. Sisk, 182–210. Cambridge: Cambridge University Press.

Butcher, Stephanie, and Alexandre Apsan Frediani. 2014. "Insurgent Citizenship Practices: The Case of Muungano Wa Wanavijiji in Nairobi, Kenya." *City: Analysis of Urban Trends, Culture, Theory, Policy, Action* 18 (2): 119–33.

Carothers, Thomas. 1999–2000. "Civil Society: Think Again." *Foreign Policy* 117 (Winter): 18–29.

Chigas, Diana. 2007. "Capacities and Limits of NGOs as Conflict Managers." In *Leashing the Dogs of War: Conflict Management in a Divided World*, edited by Chester A. Crocker, Fen Osler Hampson, and Pamela Aall, 553–82. Washington, DC: United States Institute of Peace Press.

Crocker, Chester A., Fen Osler Hampson, and Pamela Aall, eds. 2007. *Leashing the Dogs of War: Conflict Management in a Divided World*. Washington, DC: United States Institute of Peace Press.
———, eds. 2015. *Managing Conflict in a World Adrift*. Washington, DC: United States Institute of Peace Press.
Cuhadar, Esra, and Andreas Kotelis. 2010. "Cyprus: A Divided Civil Society in Stalemate." In *Civil Society and Peacebuilding: A Critical Assessment*, edited by Thania Paffenholz, 181–206. Boulder, CO: Lynne Rienner Publishers.
Donais, Timothy, and Erin McCandless. 2017. "International Peace Building and the Emerging Inclusivity Norm." *Third World Quarterly* 38 (2): 291–310.
Fisher, Ronald. 2007. "Interactive Conflict Resolution." In *Peacemaking in International Conflict: Methods and Techniques*, revised edition, edited by I. William Zartman, 227–72. Washington, DC: United States Institute of Peace Press.
Hellmuller, Sara, and Marie-Joelle Zahar. 2018. "Against the Odds: Civil Society in the Intra-Syrian Talks." Issue brief. New York, NY: International Peace Institute.
Hickey, Sam, and Giles Mohan. 2005. "Relocating Participation Within a Radical Politics of Development." *Development and Change* 36 (2): 237–62.
Ikelegbe, Augustine. 2001. "The Perverse Manifestation of Civil Society: Evidence from Nigeria." *Journal of Modern African Studies* 39 (1): 1–24.
Inclusive Peace & Transition Initiative. 2017. "Women in Peace and Transition Processes." Accessed October 9, 2019. https://www.inclusivepeace.org/content/women-peace-and-transition-processes.
Kaldor, Mary. 2003. *Global Civil Society: An Answer to War*. Cambridge: Polity Press.
Kasfir, Nelson. 1998. "Civil Society, the State and Democracy in Africa." *Commonwealth and Comparative Politics* 36 (2): 123–49.
Lanz, David. 2011. "Who Gets a Seat at the Table? A Framework for Understanding the Dynamics of Inclusion and Exclusion in Peace Negotiations." *International Negotiation* 16 (2): 275–95.
Lewis, David. 2002. "Civil Society in African Contexts: Reflections on the Usefulness of a Concept." *Development and Change* 33 (4): 569–86.
Merkel, Wolfgang. 1999. *Systemtransformation: Eine Einführung in die Theorie and Empirie der Transformationsforschung*. Opladen, Germany: Leske and Budrich.
Orjuela, Camilla. 2003. "Building Peace in Sri Lanka: A Role for Civil Society?" *Journal of Peace Research* 40 (2): 195–212.
Paffenholz, Thania, ed. 2010. *Civil Society and Peacebuilding: A Critical Assessment*. Boulder, CO: Lynne Rienner Publishers.
———. 2014a. "International Peacebuilding Goes Local: Analysing Lederach's Conflict Transformation Theory and Its Ambivalent Encounter With 20 Years of Practice." *Peacebuilding* 2 (1): 11–27.
———. 2014b. "Civil Society and Peace Negotiations: Beyond the Inclusion-Exclusion Dichotomy." *Negotiation Journal* 30 (1): 69–91.
———. 2015a. "'Broadening Participation Project' Briefing Paper." Centre on Conflict, Development and Peacebuilding. Geneva: The Graduate Institute of International and Development Studies. Accessed August 1, 2019. http://graduateinstitute.ch/files/live/sites/iheid/files/sites/ccdp/shared/Docs/Publications/ briefingpaperbroader%20participation.pdf.
———. 2015b. "Civil Society and Peacebuilding." In *Development Dialogue*, 108–9. The Dag Hammarskjöld Foundation.
Paffenholz, Thania, and Christoph Spurk. 2006. "Civil Society, Civic Engagement and Peacebuilding." Conflict Prevention and Reconstruction Paper No. 36, 27–33. Social Development Papers. Washington DC: World Bank.
———. 2010. "A Comprehensive Analytical Framework." In *Civil Society and Peacebuilding: A Critical Assessment*, edited by Thania Paffenholz, 65–76. Boulder, CO: Lynne Rienner Publishers.
Pearce, Jenny. 1998. "From Civil War to 'Civil Society': Has the End of the Cold War Brought Peace to Central America?" *International Affairs* 74 (3): 587–615.
Pinkney, Robert. 2003. *Democracy in the Third World*. Boulder, CO: Lynne Rienner Publishers.
Pouligny, Beatrice. 2005. "Civil Society and Post-Conflict Peacebuilding: Ambiguities of International Programmes Aimed at Building 'New' Society." *Security Dialogue* 36 (4): 495–510.

Putnam, Robert. 2000. *Bowling Alone: The Collapse and Revival of American Community*. New York, NY: Simon and Schuster.

Ruffin, M. Holt, and Daniel Waugh, eds. 1999. *Civil Society in Central Asia*. Baltimore, MD: Johns Hopkins University Press.

Spector, Bertram I. 2015. "Citizen Negotiation: Toward a More Inclusive Process." *International Negotiation* 20 (1): 89–108.

Spurk, Christoph. 2010. "Understanding Civil Society." In *Civil Society and Peacebuilding: A Critical Assessment*, edited by Thania Paffenholz, 3–28. Boulder, CO: Lynne Rienner Publishers.

Vogel, Birte. 2016. "Civil Society Capture: Top-Down Interventions from Below?" *Journal of Intervention and Statebuilding* 10 (4): 472–89.

Waal, Alex de. 2017. "Inclusion in Peacemaking: From Moral Claim to Political Fact." In *The Fabric of Peace in Africa: Looking Beyond the State*, edited by Pamela Aall and Chester A. Crocker, 165–86. Montreal: McGill-Queen's University Press.

Wanis-St. John, Anthony, and Darren Kew. 2008. "Civil Society and Peace Negotiations: Confronting Exclusion." *International Negotiation* 13 (1): 11–36.

World Bank. 2007. "Civil Society and Peacebuilding: Potential, Limitations and Critical Factors." Report no. 36445-GLB. Washington DC: World Bank.

Zanker, Franzisca. 2014. "Legitimate Representation: Civil Society Actors in Peace Negotiations Revisited." *International Negotiation* 19 (1): 62–88.

# 11 Information and communication technologies for peace

## A primer for the peacebuilding community

*Madhawa "Mads" Palihapitiya, Pasan M. Palihapitiya, and Joseph G. Bock*

## Introduction

If the printing press was a game-changer in centuries past, Information and Communication Technologies (ICTs) are causing a similar transformation in today's global context. ICTs have disrupted the way we think, act, and behave. They affect every aspect of our lives, including the way we socialize, conduct our business, and engage in politics (Mehan 2014). No single entity controls, manages, or even has the ability to comprehend the amount of information that ICTs generate on a daily basis. An incident in one corner of the world is seen in another part of the world within a matter of seconds. This interconnectedness allows for smaller, unrepresented, or underrepresented entities to gain visibility. Traditional media (such as television and radio) no longer have such dominating control over information and communication (Carty and Onyett 2006). ICTs foster global networks, offering "unique mobilizing strategies" (Carty and Onyett 2006, 230).

ICTs provide important benefits for managing conflict. The first and most obvious benefit is that ICTs can facilitate communication regardless of nation-state boundaries. A second advantage is speed. ICTs allow people to spread messages around the world within seconds. A third advantage is the ability to store, retrieve, and analyze large data sets, including historical data, images, and videos. Scholars and activists can identify patterns with which to predict, preempt, or resolve conflicts. A fourth advantage is that ICTs can help geographically track exactly where a conflictual event takes place.

ICTs are a double-edged sword, however. On the positive side, people can stay abreast of political and military developments anywhere they have access to the World Wide Web (Mehan 2014). The connected world ensures that information on global conflict is provided from multiple perspectives. Sometimes that diversity of information impacts foreign policy decisions (Howard 2011). For example, when news surfaced that the oppressive Mubarak regime of Egypt was cracking down on telecommunications networks, policy makers and technology companies acted to provide clever workarounds, enabling activists to continue their nonviolent campaign demanding regime change. On the negative side, technology also became a tool for tracking activists during the height of the Arab Spring.

This chapter considers the use of ICTs for managing international conflicts. The following section discusses the history of ICTs in international conflict management and then evaluates how Internet freedom can provide openings for citizens and organizations to utilize technology to promote peace, but can be thwarted by governments attempting to oppress these voices. Next, the chapter considers how various ICTs can be used to map conflicts and to provide early warnings for conflict escalation. Finally, the chapter concludes with a discussion of the key challenges posed by ICTs, but also the opportunities they provide for managing international conflicts.

## Background/history of the use of ICTs for international conflict management

ICTs have become an extension of political space. While there are many definitions of *political space*, for the purposes of this chapter, it is understood as satisfying these three conditions: 1) the ability to assemble freely; 2) the ability to express freely; and 3) the ability to participate freely (Tkacheva, Schwartz, and Libicki 2013). With the advent of ICTs, political space is now partly online, even to some degree in countries experiencing war or undemocratic rule, where all other types of political space have been stymied.

The phrase *New Social Movements (NSMs)* denotes an activist network that is, in the traditional sense, without an organization (Shirky 2008). For example, the Black Lives Matter movement, which was originally spawned by the African American community, took off as an international movement with the popularity of the #BlackLivesMatter hashtag on Twitter

---

### Textbox 11.1   Cyberactivism in the Arab Spring

On January 25, 2011, Egyptian activists used Facebook and Twitter to mobilize a popular uprising against government corruption and the three-decade-old rule of then Egyptian President Hosni Mubarak. Protestors were also expressing dissatisfaction with deteriorating social conditions, including acute poverty and unemployment (Al Jazeera 2011). Three days later, Egyptian authorities started blocking access to Facebook and Twitter. They also disrupted mobile phone networks. The government's attempt to block the use of social media backfired, however. It drove people onto the street, increasing the size of the crowds protesting.

In direct response to the government's censorship, Google relaunched their speak-2tweet technology that allowed people in Egypt to send Twitter messages without access to the Internet by leaving a voicemail on three specific phone numbers provided by the search engine giant (Arthur 2011). As pressure on the regime mounted, Hosni Mubarak dismissed his entire cabinet and started releasing political prisoners. Yet protestors in Cairo's Tahrir Square continued to call for Mubarak's resignation. After days of avoiding the inevitable, Mubarak resigned on February 11, 2011, bringing an end to a longstanding authoritarian regime in a matter of days.

Prior to the ousting of Mubarak, Tunisian activists had similarly used ICTs to help oust longtime authoritarian leader Zine el-Abidine Ben Ali (Lowrance 2016). The successful overthrow of Egypt's Mubarak and Ben Ali of Tunisia was aided by cyberactivism. Cyberactivism can again be observed during the Arab Spring in Libya, Syria, and Yemen (Khamis and Vaughn 2013). These copycat revolutions learned from each other, though the outcome varied from country to country (Howard 2011).

While cyberactivism played a role in these political changes, it is difficult to measure how substantial of an influence ICTs had in successfully overthrowing what were assumed to be powerful leaders. Was it the ease of communication made possible by social media? Was it the use of nonviolent strategies? Was it the sharing of experience by young people involved in overthrowing dictators in the Balkans with young people in the Middle East (Rosenberg 2011)?

and Facebook. Similarly, the #BlueLivesMatter counter-movement and hashtag, though limited in reach, framed the issue as a movement to protect law enforcement officers from hate crimes.

*Cyberactivism*, which Howard has defined as the "act of using the internet to advance a political cause that is difficult to advance offline" (2011, 145), is supported by a complex array of interconnected technology platforms (including, but not limited to, Facebook, Twitter and Snapchat). They enable social movements to take advantage of political uncertainties and rising public anxieties to influence public opinion. Over time, social movements can use this influence to undermine the infrastructure that supports war and armed conflict. As Carty and Onyett (2006) point out:

> As theories of NSMs highlight, collective identities and grassroots mobilization, in conjunction with an awareness of structural level issues, are critical to understanding the re-emergence of the peace movement . . . The networks and coalitions of the peace movement are built on an identity politics in a global formation, with a demand that values such as dignity, compassion and a sense of sharing a common fate be considered in international relations.
>
> (2006, 245)

Yet the expansion of this political space has also resulted in violent backlash from oppressive regimes that view ICT-based political activism as undermining their authoritarian power. And while direct violence is always a threat, oppressive regimes and violent actors are increasingly turning to ICTs themselves to counter cyberactivism and mislead the public (Tkacheva et al. 2013).

According to the democracy and human rights watchdog Freedom House, at least thirty countries have used ICTs to disseminate falsehoods and manipulate their populations (2018). China and Russia regularly use paid commentators, trolls (people who deliberately cultivate quarrels), bots (computer programs that perform functions or disseminate information on the Internet, or both), false news sites, and propaganda outlets. Russia, China, Iran, and even terrorist groups such as the Islamic State of Iraq and Syria (ISIS) have troll armies or web brigades dedicated to manipulating information online (Eordogh 2018).

ICTs also have inherent technical weaknesses that peacebuilders need to keep in mind. The Internet hides many threats. These threats, as recent United States election interference by Russia have demonstrated, can endanger democratic institutions. If you are a human rights defender, journalist, or conflict resolution practitioner, and your government opposes your activism, government operatives could hack your computer or mobile device in order to identify who is providing you with information, to identify your network of local and international activists, or to find out what compromising information you might have of them on your computer or mobile device. In a recent example, a low-tech phishing operation, allegedly conducted by the Chinese government, successfully targeted pro-democracy and human rights activists in the Tibetan community. This incident further exposed the technological vulnerabilities of modern-day activism (The Citizen Lab 2018). In fact, digital spying attacks against activists have increased, and when such attacks happen these activists have very little recourse (Braga 2018).

Many who work in the field of conflict management are unaware of ways to safeguard their digital data, and have little or no access to computer or network security tools to counter these attacks and digital espionage activities. In the case of conflict early warning systems operating within conflict zones, for example, it is inevitable for both state and non-state actors to be curious about the information being collected, analyzed, and disseminated. Gathering information about movements of military forces or rebel groups, for instance, and sending that to a centralized early warning program headquarters can leave the people sending the information in a vulnerable position, such as when their phones are confiscated at checkpoints. However, many community-based early warning systems focus solely on publicly available data,

ICTs can help propagate dangerous content from organizations with divisive and sometimes violent political and religious ideologies. Al Qaeda and ISIS, for instance, use ICTs to recruit followers online. They encourage the use of violence either as a part of the terrorist NSM or military arm, but also cultivate "lone wolf" style attacks all over the world, where individuals or small groups embrace extremist ideology to a point where they feel the need to use violence. For example, in November 2015, Anwar Abu Zeid, a 29-year-old Jordanian police captain who was radicalized by messages on Twitter and WhatsApp, shot dead five people in a police training facility in Amman, Jordan. Days before the incident, Anwar had hinted of his intentions on WhatsApp (Al-Khalidi 2015).

It has become evident that Internet Service Providers (ISPs – such as Safaricom in Kenya, BSNL in India, and Comcast in the United States, among many others) may need to curate the content posted by third-party users. The curation or moderation of content by ISPs and content providers, such as Facebook and Twitter, compromises Internet freedom and violates data privacy. Despite this violation of privacy, content providers like Facebook are increasingly taking steps to curate or moderate content. For example, in 2018, Facebook contracted the cybersecurity company FireEye to help identify and eliminate misinformation, including fake profiles (Conger and Frenkel 2018).

While social media platforms like Facebook and Twitter have cracked down on terrorist propaganda, including recruitment videos and other related content (Lomas 2018), Freilich contends that "social media companies have generally employed a 'laissez-faire approach' [to not intervene] to preventing terrorists from using their platforms to promote their illegal agendas" (2018, 676). Peacebuilders may find themselves at both ends of this argument. For example, those wanting to curtail the spread of dangerous speech might argue for some content moderation or censorship, while those favoring a free flow of information from a particular conflict zone (for an early warning and early response program aimed at preventing mass atrocities, for example) might prefer the elimination of Internet censorship altogether.

## Democratization of the Internet

For the most part, advances in digital technology have assisted the democratization of the Internet. In many parts of the world, mobile communication service providers are making Internet an affordable service, and, as a result, Internet penetration has grown exponentially. In 2013, the number of cell-phone subscriptions in the world was roughly the same as the world population of that year. By that same year, there were 63 subscriptions for every 100 people in Africa, and 105 subscriptions per 100 people in Arab states (Himelfarb 2014). These developments enhance the potential for cyberactivism, but they can also trigger a struggle for Internet control by governments.

Moore's Law, which describes how semiconductors and other digital technology nearly double their speed each year, and other similar projections dictate that Internet access will get cheaper and faster, as will the devices we use to access it (Tkacheva et al. 2013). By

2013, around 2.4 billion people, or 34 percent of the world's population, had direct access to the Internet, and in the last decade alone, Internet access in the Middle East and Africa grew by 2,634 and 3,607 percent respectively (Himelfarb 2014). This means that Internet access would become cheaper along with the quality, security, and speed of the devices we use to access the Internet, making cyberactivism affordable and safe for billions of people, not just a handful of activists. It could also potentially help propagate cyberactivism and create a global community of concerned citizens as more and more people get online and share information about conflicts, human rights abuses, and other harmful activities. On the flipside of this democratization would be the manipulation of content by troll armies or those on the payroll of oppressive regimes or terrorist groups who could also use the Internet to spread false rumors, misinformation, and harmful ideologies. ICTs can also result in alienation from society in general, leading to a fragmented civil society.

## ICTs and Internet freedom: contending approaches to peacebuilding

A broad definition of *Internet freedom* is the ability to post and share information at will, without governmental restriction. Cultural differences, however, create parameters on what is acceptable regardless of regulation (Bambauer 2010). There is not a consensus on what should be allowed on the Internet. There *is* consensus, however, that Internet freedom is under siege. As of 2017, Freedom House reported a seven-year steady decline in Internet freedom around the world. This decline is due to various actors, primarily governments, engaging in disinformation tactics, disruptions to mobile Internet services, and physical and technical attacks on human rights defenders and independent media (2018).

Internet freedom is particularly important to people living in countries with limited civil liberties and disrespect for human rights, and especially for young people (Pew Research Center 2014). Eight in ten Russians between the ages of 18 and 29, for instance, say they want an uncensored Internet (Nicks 2014). In places with such limited civil liberties, the battle for Internet freedom becomes a struggle for democracy, human rights, and conflict resolution.

Oppressive regimes may cut off access to the Internet or drastically reduce Internet usage by increasing prices or by dramatically reducing Internet speeds, usually to restrict cyberactivism and engagement within political space online. The government of Syria, for example, drastically reduced Internet connection speeds on an already low-Internet using population to censor cyberactivists from sharing stories about its atrocities (Tkacheva et al. 2013). As a result, many living inside conflict zones in Syria found it difficult to convey accurate information about atrocities committed by the regime, or the early signs of an impending civil war, hindering chances of international intervention. While it is dubious to assume accurate, timely, early warning of atrocities will result in effective early response, there is clearly hope that the two will coalesce as in "if we warn them, they [that is, international peacekeepers] will come."[1]

However, oppressive regimes can spread malicious software to track cyberactivists. The Syrian government launched malware in the guise of Internet security suites to track down and infect the computers of cyberactivists (Tkacheva et al. 2013). If more regimes like Syria develop technical capability to track activists using ICTs, it will further endanger Internet freedom by exposing the activists themselves or their networks (Freedom House 2018). While ICTs are neutral, who uses them and for what purpose is often a political question.

In August 2018, the Ethiopian government shut down the Internet in the tense eastern region of Oromia as violence against ethnic minorities escalated, a tactic the government has used in the past (Fick and Mohammed 2018). As this Ethiopian case highlights, regimes may censor or partially shut down the Internet to avoid information about atrocities committed against a minority getting out to its populace or to the international community. When such shut downs occur, peacebuilders engaged in violence prevention have difficulty accessing information from an entire region and are unable to ascertain the gravity of the atrocities being committed. The Ethiopian example again highlights the significance of Internet freedom to the peacebuilding field.

Peacebuilders must educate themselves about workarounds to Internet censorship by oppressive regimes. Online privacy tools like *Tor*,[2] which many cyberactivists around the world use to protect their privacy online, can be employed to circumvent these obstacles. However, as in the case of Ethiopia, governments can install systems to block Voice Over Internet Protocol (VOIP) services like Skype and WhatsAPP (Lardinois 2012). Virtual Private Networks (VPNs) can help cyberactivists gain access to the Internet and restricted sites by evading censorship through encryption technologies.[3] A more expensive option is to provide free Internet access to activists through high-power antennas from outside those countries where full internet outage or censorship is being implemented (Tkacheva et al. 2013).

## Preventing violence between pastoralists and agriculturalists in Nigeria

In many parts of the world, population growth combined with environmental changes lead to growing tension between pastoralists, who graze cattle along traditional migratory pathways, and farmers, who grow crops. Violence that erupts in Nigeria between Hausa farmers and nomadic Fula or Fulani herdsmen in Nigeria routinely claims the lives of hundreds of people. In 2014 alone, these conflicts claimed approximately 1,200 lives, causing damage to both livestock and farms estimated to be at least US $13 billion (Gaffey 2016). This violence and economic loss can potentially be avoided if the Fulani, using Global Positioning System (GPS) devices, keep track of where they are grazing their herds, avoiding land held by farmers.

Tensions between pastoralists and farmers are exacerbated by a growing problem of cattle rustling. Organized crime syndicates and random banditry, combined with automatic weapons, bring even greater insecurity as they enhance the lethality of conflicts (Olaniyan and Yahaya 2016). Global Positioning System (GPS) devices alongside another technology developed in Kenya called *Chipsafer*,[4] a microchip inserted into each individual animal, can mitigate cattle rustling by providing law enforcement agencies with real-time data on cattle movements as well as a way of tracing ownership at cattle auctions.

The example in Figure 11.1 shows a cluster of events from northern Nigeria that were tracked using Google Maps on an early warning platform called *Waayama* that was developed for the Interfaith Mediation Center in Kaduna, Nigeria.[5] The map shows the "hot spots" where large concentrations of conflictual activities such as cattle rusting and armed attacks have occurred, followed by a detailed breakdown of incidents in the dashboard below it.

Figure 11.2 shows how the system tracks the locations of the events on Google Maps using the Google Pin feature. Events data linked to the geo-located pin can be accessed from the relational database with one click. In this instance, conflict early warning experts and trained peacebuilders from the IMC send in daily situation reports from all over northern Nigeria. They report on not only conflictual events like armed attacks and cattle rustling, but also on peace-promoting events like mediations and peace negotiations.

The main body that coordinated the early warning and early response actions at the IMC was the Community Peace Action Network (CPAN), comprised of the Community Peace Coordinating Centre (CPCC), the Conflict Mitigation and Management Regional Councils (CMMRCs), and Community Peace Observers (CPOs). The early warning situation reports sent in by CPOs via email, texts, or calls were stored in an encrypted cloud-based conflict early warning database called Waayama. Waayama turns the situation reports into geospatial

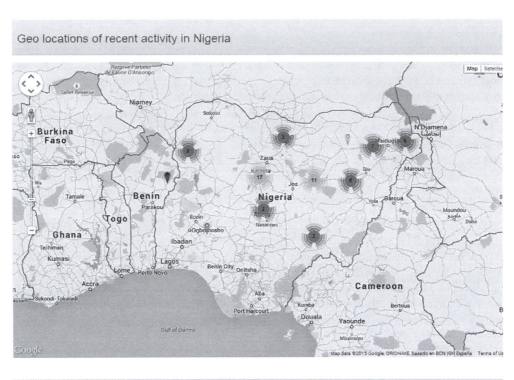

Geo locations of recent activity in Nigeria

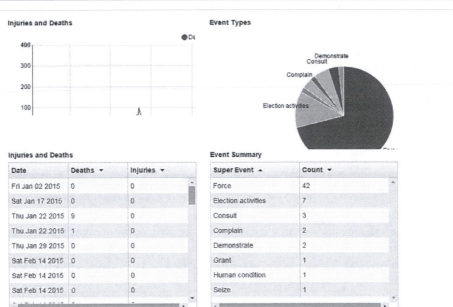

**Injuries and Deaths**

**Event Types**

**Injuries and Deaths**

| Date | Deaths ▾ | Injuries ▾ |
|---|---|---|
| Fri Jan 02 2015 | 0 | 0 |
| Sat Jan 17 2015 | 0 | 0 |
| Thu Jan 22 2015 | 9 | 0 |
| Thu Jan 22 2015 | 1 | 0 |
| Thu Jan 29 2015 | 0 | 0 |
| Sat Feb 14 2015 | 0 | 0 |
| Sat Feb 14 2015 | 0 | 0 |
| Sat Feb 14 2015 | 0 | 0 |

**Event Summary**

| Super Event ▴ | Count ▾ |
|---|---|
| Force | 42 |
| Election activities | 7 |
| Consult | 3 |
| Complain | 2 |
| Demonstrate | 2 |
| Grant | 1 |
| Human condition | 1 |
| Seize | 1 |

*Figure 11.1*  Waayama Dashboard and Event Geo Locations

## Geo locations of recent activity in Nigeria

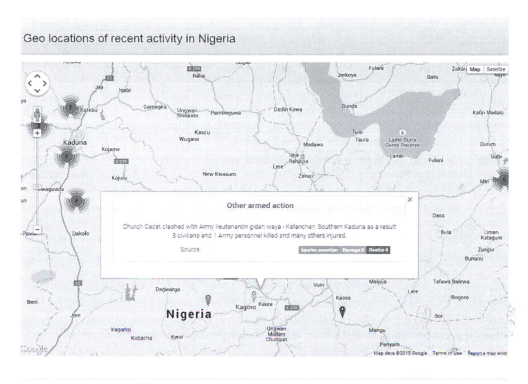

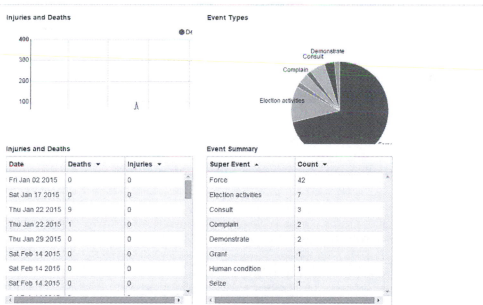

**Other armed action**

Church Cadet clashed with Army lieutenantin gidan waya - Kafanchan, Southern Kaduna as a result 3 civilians and 1 Army personnel killed and many others injured.

Source:

| Date | Deaths | Injuries |
|------|--------|----------|
| Fri Jan 02 2015 | 0 | 0 |
| Sat Jan 17 2015 | 0 | 0 |
| Thu Jan 22 2015 | 9 | 0 |
| Thu Jan 22 2015 | 1 | 0 |
| Thu Jan 29 2015 | 0 | 0 |
| Sat Feb 14 2015 | 0 | 0 |
| Sat Feb 14 2015 | 0 | 0 |
| Sat Feb 14 2015 | 0 | 0 |

| Super Event | Count |
|-------------|-------|
| Force | 42 |
| Election activities | 7 |
| Consult | 3 |
| Complain | 2 |
| Demonstrate | 2 |
| Grant | 1 |
| Human condition | 1 |
| Seize | 1 |

*Figure 11.2* Waayama Geo Locations Pin-drop and Events Data

data with an analysis presented on a dashboard. The result is a historical presentation and real-time analysis of an incident, with particular reference to where the incidents occurred, who was involved, on what date and at what time it occurred, with an assessment of the positive or negative results, as well as a record of who did or did not respond to the incident.

### Geographic information systems, SMS, and conflict management

Apart from geolocation systems, as in the case of the Google Maps in Waayama, Geographic Information Systems (GIS) can be used to map topology, vegetation, human settlements, administrative boundaries, natural resources, and human behavior, including violent hot spots. GIS can be used to identify incident locations and movements of belligerents. With widely available systems such as Google Maps, BingMaps, Apple Maps, and OpenStreet-Map, scholars and activists can accurately monitor the extent or the spread of behavior patterns, such as attacks by the Janjaweed militia in the Darfur region of western Sudan.

An alternative, low-cost ICT tool is the Short Messaging Service (SMS) for sending texts, available in almost all corners of the world, even where there is no access to the Internet. Text messaging has evolved as a powerful tool for conflict management, particularly with the addition of web-based text messaging tools like FrontlineSMS[6] that enable bulk texting.

Web-based text messaging platforms like FrontlineSMS can also be integrated with other technology platforms for tackling complex tasks. As in the case of Waayama, text-messaging technologies can be used synergistically with digital mapping platforms like *Ushahidi* (meaning "testimony" in Swahili) to enable near real-time crowdsourcing and triangulation of geospatial and events data. Ushahidi was first developed in 2008 to track election irregularities and associated violence in Kenya (see www.ushahidi.com). Crowd-sourcing allows people in a "crowd" to send information into a centralized entity, such as Ushahidi, as a way of contributing to a joint enterprise, in this case helping prevent or manage conflict. Texts can go directly to an individual or to groups for wider dissemination. These services, unlike the voice calls we place, have an added advantage in that they have a workaround against congestion. Congestion happens when mobile base stations get overloaded by voice calls.

For all of its potential benefits, it is important to remember that text messaging is volatile. The spread of unverified information on Instant Messaging (IM) and social media platforms can cause violence. IM platforms can help propagate dangerous speech or misinformation as in the case of the child abductions rumor and lynching in India, or even terrorism, as in the case of the radicalized Jordanian police officer mentioned earlier.

### Big data

Conflict early warning increasingly involves mining of big data, in which governments, civil society groups, and multi-lateral organizations look for trends and patterns to develop predictive analytics to help mitigate violent conflict. In the civil society sector, the Umati project and Ushahidi sought to predict dangerous speech online and to prevent election violence using crowdsourced data and big data analysis. The project monitored tweets, status updates, comments, posts, blog entries, videos and pictures generated daily by English and vernacular Kenyan blogs, online forums, online newspapers, Facebook, and Twitter.[7]

The US Department of Defense, under the banner of the Information Volume and Velocity program, also developed technologies to gather and analyze large amounts of data from the internet, particularly from social media to "deliver real-time situational awareness through accurate and actionable information for the strategic decision-making process" (Defense Information Systems Agency 2012). Similarly, the Global Pulse program of the United Nations uses big data analysis to "accelerate discovery, development and scaled adoption of big data innovation for sustainable development and humanitarian action."[8]

Attempts are being made to involve local people in big data analysis and content verification. This is consistent with approaches used in Asia and Africa involving crowdsourcing of conflict and election violence data, like in the case of Ushahidi. The idea behind the involvement of local people in generating big data, and in flagging, moderating, or removing harmful content can help further democratize the Internet while ensuring that local populations have a say in what content gets distributed. This is particularly useful for conflict resolution professionals who wish to engage local populations to contain or avoid violence in a conflict zone.

A model example of engaging local populations is the partnership between Samasource, a non-profit helping to outsource digital work to unemployed people in developing countries, and CrowdFlower, a private enterprise helping tech companies outsource micro-tasks like checking and verifying images to people living in the developing world.[9]

## Grassroots mapping

Grassroots mapping can also be used for conflict management (Yoo Warren 2010). Traditionally practiced by stitching together digital images taken by a camera attached to a weather balloon, increasingly, grassroots mapping now includes the use of civilian drones and kite mapping. As these technologies have become cheaper and freely available, they have become more affordable and accessible. Balloon mapping kits are relatively inexpensive, and images can be stitched together using open source software to create a comprehensive view of a particular area.

These participatory community-mapping processes can be used by conflict management practitioners to create a comprehensive view of a geographic area where a violent conflict, such as a riot, weapons attack, or even a mass atrocity is taking place. Such technologies and processes can provide an alternative narrative to what a state or non-state actor may provide to its population or the international community. This may help prevent or mitigate violence. It can also assist in holding perpetrators accountable.

Over the course of recent history, images and videos have been used to both vindicate the waging of war, and to justify the ending of it (Zenko and Welch 2012). Images and videos have helped create empathy for victims of war and political violence, and acted as evidence against those who have committed atrocities against humanity. Civilian drones were widely used in Syria to assess the destruction of eastern Aleppo and the movement of civilians from the conflict zone.[10] They are a cost-effective and low-risk option to sending an actual aircraft into a conflict area. Drones, balloons, and kites are also quite discreet compared to aircraft and can stay airborne over a particular area for longer periods, contributing to community mapping initiatives.

Over time, these grassroots cartography technologies will acquire capabilities that their larger, more expensive cousins now possess. An example is Light Detection and Ranging (LiDAR) technology that is used to map geographical formations, and to create 3-D images. These technologies can be used to add or remove certain attributes like vegetation to obtain a clearer image of a particular geographic area. LiDAR can map tiny physical features or changes on the surface of a certain area that can help locate evidence of conflict and its aftermath (such as mass graves). LiDAR mounted drones are currently being used by archeologists. These drones could help human rights activists detect mass graves or even signs of bombing or artillery strikes against civilians.

## Challenges and future directions

The fluid and changing dynamics of today's violent conflicts are a healthy reminder of the need to focus on Information and Communication Systems (ICTs) as a force for social mobilization, political activism, and peacebuilding. However, ICTs have been both a boon for peacebuilding, as well as a challenging propagator of misinformation and political manipulation. While ICTs have democratized global communication and amplified and empowered grassroots actors to define human security and participate in social movements against war and human rights violations, they have also become the tools of the oppressor.

ICTs are susceptible to politics and political control. The threat to Internet freedom and net neutrality is an indicator of the politicization of technology use, which poses a challenge to the way we conduct peacebuilding, particularly in emerging democracies and developing countries experiencing war, oppression, and violence. In essence, ICTs have become a double-edged sword forcing peacebuilders to approach it, not as a silver bullet to solving violent conflicts, but as a developmental tool that has great benefit if used appropriately.

Those in the peacebuilding field must lead the development and testing of these appropriate peacebuilding technologies and processes in participation with those at the frontlines of today's global conflicts. The peacebuilders of today, and certainly of tomorrow, need to develop a technological literacy that will enable them to operate in this challenging era where Internet freedom is being challenged.

In this context, numerous collaborations have emerged where technology solutions-providers, grassroots activists, and public and private enterprises have combined to address challenging global conflicts and the encroachment of ICTs by actors with crude political agendas. Together, they have utilized existing technology in innovative ways and have introduced pioneering new technologies to help those at the frontlines of peacebuilding, human rights, and democratization. They have helped amplify the voices for peace and activism for democracy and human rights and to undermine the rhetoric and oppressive actions of violent actors throughout the world. They are also banding together to resist the encroachment of ICTs by hostile actors through activism, public policy formulation, and political mobilization.

## Questions for further discussion

1   How could a comprehensive ICT-based peacebuilding strategy be developed that can increase the utilization of ICTs as a peacebuilding tool while limiting manipulation by malicious actors?
2   How can one create civic, public and private technology-based partnerships, tools, and resources to address complex and challenging global conflicts?
3   Is it the role of governments to regulate ICTs so that "news" is distinguished from "editorial"?
4   What are some ways to counter the potency of malicious social media posts designed to incite violence?
5   How important are Internet freedom and net neutrality to the use of ICTs for international conflict management?

## Suggested resources

1  Ushahidi: www.ushahidi.com/ is a digital mapping platform that crowdsources data and allows users to analyze trends. Ushahidi provides guidance on how to use their platform: www.ushahidi.com/support.
2  OpenStreetMap: www.openstreetmap.org is a platform that allows "the crowd" to create up-to-date maps, often used in humanitarian operations.
3  FrontlineSMS: www.frontlinesms.com/ allows for dissemination of messages to a wide group of people. TextIt: https://textit.in/ is similar.
4  The ICT4Peace Foundation: https://ict4peace.org was launched in 2004. It offers perspectives on a vast range of challenges, including on how to maintain Internet freedom, and how to use artificial intelligence for enhancing peace.
5  International Institute for Democracy and Electoral Assistance (International IDEA) has an ICT for Elections Data Base: www.idea.int/data-tools/data/icts-elections.
6  Search for jobs available to people knowledgeable about how to use ICT for humanitarian relief and development and conflict management. For instance, look for jobs on Devex.com, ICT4Djobs.com, and LinkedIn.

## Become engaged!

1  Learn how to use an ICT platform by watching YouTube videos. For instance, you could learn how to build a map that tracks sexual harassment, following the lead of a group of enterprising women in Egypt who created Harassmap: https://harassmap.org/en/. Here is an introductory video about their work: www.youtube.com/watch?v=FDHMuqEWvD4.
2  Consider volunteering with the Standby Task Force, an international network of technical experts and activists who respond to humanitarian disasters. Here is their website: www.standbytaskforce.org/.
3  Join the International Network of Crisis Mappers, which hosts an annual conference. Here is the network's Facebook page: www.facebook.com/crisismappers/.
4  Liberation technology is a view that ICTs can be instrumental in enabling people to improve their lives – in other words, liberating so-called beneficiaries to help themselves. Read about Stanford's Program on Liberation Technology at https://cddrl.fsi.stanford.edu/libtech/docs/about_libtech.

## Notes

1  Unfortunately, intervention in time to prevent large-scale violence by international peacekeepers has a disappointing record (Langille 2016).
2  "Tor." Accessed August 30, 2018. www.torproject.org/.
3  A VPN works by encrypting the communication from your device and puts it in a different protocol, presumably a protocol that is not blocked by the government, and sends it to the end device where data will be decrypted.
4  *Chipsafer*. Accessed August 27, 2018. www.chipsafer.com/.
5  "Waayama Early Warning." *Early Warning Nigeria*. Accessed August 30, 2018. www.earlywarning nigeria.org/.
6  *FrontlineSMS*. Accessed August 28, 2018. www.frontlinesms.com/.
7  "Umati Final Report Released." *Ushahidi*. Accessed August 28, 2018. www.ushahidi.com/blog/2013/06/28/umati-final-report-released/.
8  *United Nations Global Pulse*. Accessed August 28, 2018. www.unglobalpulse.org/about-new.
9  "Samasource." Accessed August 28, 2018. www.samasource.org/; see also Janah 2017.

10  "Drone Footage Shows Scale of Destruction in Eastern Aleppo – Video." 2016. *The Guardian*, September 27. Accessed August 28, 2018. www.theguardian.com/world/video/2016/sep/27/drone-footage-shows-scale-of-destruction-in-eastern-aleppo-video.

## References and further reading

Al Jazeera. 2011. "Timeline: Egypt's Revolution." *Al Jazeera*, February 14. Accessed August 22, 2018. www.aljazeera.com/news/middleeast/2011/01/201112515334871490.html.

Al-Khalidi, Suleiman. 2015. "Jordanian Killer Was on a Journey to 'Paradise or Hell'." *Reuters*, November 11. Accessed February 8, 2019. www.reuters.com/article/us-mideast-crisis-jordan-insight-idUSKCN0T029720151111.

Arthur, Charles. 2011. "Google and Twitter Launch Service Enabling Egyptians to Tweet by Phone." *The Guardian*, February 1. Accessed August 22, 2018. www.theguardian.com/technology/2011/feb/01/google-twitter-egypt.

Bambauer, Derek. 2010. "The Enigma of Internet Freedom." *Information Policy*, August 9. Accessed August 29, 2018. www.i-policy.org/2010/08/the-enigma-of-internet-freedom.html.

Braga, Matthew. 2018. "When Activists and Human Rights Groups Are Targets of Government Hackers, Where Can They Turn for Help?" *CBC News*, July 30. Accessed February 7, 2019. www.cbc.ca/news/technology/civil-society-phishing-hacks-online-threats-help-berkeley-1.4765264.

Carty, Victoria, and Jake Onyett. 2006. "Protest, Cyberactivism and New Social Movements: The Reemergence of the Peace Movement Post 9/11." *Social Movement Studies* 5 (3): 229–49.

Citizen Lab, The. 2018. "Spying on a Budget: Inside a Phishing Operation With Targets in the Tibetan Community." April 16. Accessed February 7, 2019. https://citizenlab.ca/2018/01/spying-on-a-budget-inside-a-phishing-operation-with-targets-in-the-tibetan-community/.

Conger, Kate, and Sheera Frenkel. 2018. "How FireEye Helped Facebook Spot a Disinformation Campaign." *New York Times*, August 23. Accessed July 25, 2019. www.nytimes.com/2018/08/23/technology/fireeye-facebook-disinformation.html.

Defense Information Systems Agency. 2012. "Information Volume & Velocity (IV2)." *Federal Business Opportunities*, Solicitation Number: DTOMC35011_SS_IV2, Procurement Directorate, Location: DITCO-NCR. Accessed August 28, 2018. www.fbo.gov/index?s=opportunity&mode=form&id=6fda262f46fab5f5273c18b1607e079d&tab=core&_cview=0.

Eordogh, Fruzsina. 2018. "The Russian Troll Army Isn't the Only One We Need to Worry About." *Forbes*, April 12. Accessed August 29, 2018. www.forbes.com/sites/fruzsinaeordogh/2018/04/11/the-russian-troll-army-isnt-the-only-one-we-need-to-worry-about/#4550a94e2334.

Fick, Maggie, and Omar Mohammed. 2018. "Internet in Eastern Ethiopia Shut Down After Regional Violence." *Reuters*, August 8. Accessed February 8, 2019. www.reuters.com/article/us-ethiopia-internet-idUSKBN1KT0T4.

Freedom House. 2012. "Bahrain: Freedom on the Net 2011." October 15. Accessed February 7, 2019. https://freedomhouse.org/report/freedom-net/2011/bahrain.

———. 2018. "New Report – Freedom on the Net 2017: Manipulating Social Media to Undermine Democracy." Accessed August 29, 2018. https://freedomhouse.org/article/new-report-freedom-net-2017-manipulating-social-media-undermine-democracy.

Freilich, Jaime. 2018. "Section 230's Liability Shield in the Age of Online Terrorist Recruitment." *Brooklyn Law Review* 83 (2): 675–99.

Gaffey, Conor. 2016. "The Nigerian Conflict You've Never Heard of." *Newsweek*, June 7. Accessed August 27, 2018. www.newsweek.com/nigerias-herdsmen-and-farmers-are-locked-deadly-underreported-conflict-450293.

Himelfarb, Sheldon. 2014. "Can Big Data Stop Wars Before They Happen?" *Foreign Policy*, April 25. Accessed August 28, 2018. https://foreignpolicy.com/2014/04/25/can-big-data-stop-wars-before-they-happen/.

Howard, Philip N. 2011. *The Digital Origins of Dictatorship and Democracy: Information Technology and Political Islam*. Oxford: Oxford University Press.

Janah, Leila Chirayath. 2017. "Samasource and CrowdFlower in Haiti: Rebuilding After a Crisis." *The Huffington Post*, December 7. Accessed August 28, 2018. www.huffingtonpost.com/leila-chirayath-janah/samasource-in-haiti-rebui_b_426311.html.

Khamis, Sahar, and Katherine Vaughn. 2013. "Cyberactivism in the Tunisian and Egyptian Revolutions: Potentials, Limitations, Overlaps and Divergences." *Journal of African Media Studies* 5 (1): 69–86.

Langille, Peter H. 2016. *Developing a United Nations Emergency Peace Service Meeting Our Responsibilities to Prevent and Protect*. New York, NY: Palgrave Macmillan.

Lardinois, Frederic. 2012. "Ethiopian Government Bans Skype, Google Talk and All Other VoIP Services." *TechCrunch*, June 14. Accessed August 24, 2019. https://techcrunch.com/2012/06/14/ethiopian-government-bans-skype-google-talk-and-all-other-voip-services/.

Lomas, Natasha. 2018. "Twitter Claims More Progress on Squeezing Terrorist Content." *TechCrunch*, April 5. Accessed August 29, 2018. https://techcrunch.com/2018/04/05/twitter-transparency-report-12/.

Lowrance, Sherry. 2016. "Was the Revolution Tweeted? Social Media and the Jasmine Revolution in Tunisia." *Digest of Middle East Studies* 25 (1): 155–76.

Mehan, Julie E. 2014. *Cyberwar, Cyberterror, Cybercrime & Cyberactivism: An In-depth Guide to the Role of Standards in the Cybersecurity Environment*. Cambridgeshire: IT Governance Publishing.

Nicks, Denver. 2014. "Russia's Youth Want Internet Freedom, Widening 'Censorship Gap'." *Time*, March 19. Accessed August 29, 2018. http://time.com/29255/russias-youth-want-internet-freedom-widening-censorship-gap/.

Olaniyan, Azeez, and Aliya Yahaya. 2016. "Cows, Bandits, and Violent Conflicts: Understanding Cattle Rustling in Northern Nigeria." *Africa Spectrum* 51 (3): 93–105.

Palihapitiya, Madhawa. 2013. "Ethnic Violence: A Case Study on Ethnic Riots in Sri Lanka." *Asian Journal of Public Affairs* 6 (1): 95–111.

Pew Research Center. 2014. "Emerging and Developing Nations Want Freedom on the Internet." *Global Attitudes Project*, March 19. Accessed August 29, 2018. www.pewglobal.org/2014/03/19/emerging-and-developing-nations-want-freedom-on-the-internet/.

Rosenberg, Tina. 2011. "Revolution U." *Foreign Policy*, February 17. Accessed July 24, 2019. https://foreignpolicy.com/2011/02/17/revolution-u-2/.

Shirky, Clay. 2008. *Here Comes Everybody: The Power of Organizing Without Organizations*. New York, NY: Penguin Books.

Tkacheva, Olesya, Lowell H. Schwartz, and Martin C. Libicki. 2013. *Internet Freedom and Political Space*. Santa Monica, CA: RAND Corporation.

Yoo Warren, Jeffrey. 2010. *Grassroots Mapping: Tools for Participatory and Activist Cartography*. PhD Thesis, Massachusetts Institute of Technology, Cambridge.

Zenko, Michah, and Emma Welch. 2012. "Imagery and Atrocity: The Role of News and Photos in War." *The Atlantic*, July 20. Accessed August 28, 2018. www.theatlantic.com/international/archive/2012/03/imagery-and-atrocity-the-role-of-news-and-photos-in-war/255275/.

# 12 Gender and international conflict management

*Debarati Sen, Loubna Skalli Hanna, and Nicole Junker*[1]

## Introduction

As humans, the most fundamental binary through which we make sense of the world around us is by identifying as a woman or man even before we begin to make sense of our biology. As we develop from childhood to adulthood, this binary only gets reinforced through the steady enculturation into powerful gender ideologies communicated to us through what Louis Althusser (1971) identifies as "ideological state apparatuses" (also knows in social theory as ISAs): our family/families, schools, media, state, and now corporations.

Very few things in life influence human activities as much as gender. From the moment we rise in the morning to the moment we fall asleep, our lives are heavily influenced by not only our gender, but by the gender of those around us. Gender can affect the choices we make in absolutely everything we do from what profession we choose to what clothes we wear and everything in between. Chances are that if a person were to put on a critical gender lens to analyze his or her activities throughout the day, he or she would see that gender plays a role in nearly every decision made. This cross-cutting nature makes the study of gender incredibly important in the understanding of human activities, including international conflict. Two of the most powerful forces in social theory that enable us to make sense of how gendered beliefs and practices shape our everyday lives and also influence the course of war, peace, and development are Feminist Theory and Feminist Methodology. In order to understand how to apply gender theories to the field of international conflict management, one must first understand what exactly gender is. A person's gender is not defined by biological sex. This means that someone's gender is not determined by being born with male or female sex organs. Gender is instead related to the concepts of masculinity and femininity and the social constructs that align with these definitions. Furthermore, those analyzing conflicts through a gendered perspective should ensure that they do not view gender as only having two categories: male and female. Gender, unlike sex, does not exist as a dichotomy. It is instead measured along a spectrum with hyperfemininity on one end and hypermasculinity on the other. In order to properly analyze anything through a gendered lens, one must consider the full spectrum of gender. In examining gender, the characteristics of an individual, group, activity, or institution signal a social construction that determines where on the gender scale such a unit would fall. For example, perhaps the most prominent social construction of gender is the invocation of masculinity as a representation of power, autonomy, rationality, and the public sphere while femininity is associated with weakness, dependence, emotion, and private sphere (Connell 2005; Tickner 1997). This association of masculine and feminine qualities can be seen in examining how gender norms and tropes are operationalized during international conflict. The strong, brave man becomes a soldier to protect his homeland (including his wife and child) from the enemy. Similarly, wives and daughters of the "enemy" may be seen as spoils of war, targeted for rape or other abuse as a sign of conquest.

These are just a few examples of the many ways that gender affects conflict and vice versa. Awareness of socially constructed gender norms may increase one's ability to understand the events leading up to, during, and following conflict. Therefore, a gendered perspective is a lens by which those analyzing a conflict can both explain and predict the events of a conflict.

This chapter discusses the role of gender in international conflict management, introducing the reader to the concept of gender analysis before reviewing the history of women's inclusion (or not) in the study of war, conflict, and peace. Providing examples of how attention to gender can improve the success of conflict management efforts, the chapter illustrates how a gender lens involves more than just adding women, but rather requires critical evaluation of power relations that affect conflict and influences the knowledge production about peace, conflict, and related processes.

## Evolution of gender analysis in international conflict management

When many people are asked to consider gender issues, their minds automatically go to thinking about women's issues. However, this assumption is problematic. As previously mentioned, gender encompasses both masculinity and femininity, meaning that in considering gender one must look at not only both men and women in conflict, but how their conflict-related activities are guided by their gender and how their gender affects their experiences during conflict. Furthermore, the relationship between gender and conflict is not a one-way street. Just as gender affects how conflict is carried out, conflict affects gender norms and roles in ways that often carry through following the conflict. When analyzing anything through a gendered lens, one must understand that the social constructions related to gender can vary by culture and have changed throughout history. However, as a social construct, gender can be, and often is, reconstructed by changes in social organizations. One example of such a shift is the case of the Yezidis during the ISIS insurgency in Iraq and Syria beginning in 2012 (see Textbox 12.1). In this case, the media attention of the cases of Yezidi women who had been held in captivity by ISIS increased the social standing and, ultimately, the social capital of women in the Yezidi community. Young women who, prior to the insurgency, would not have been considered for the role of spokesperson for the entire community suddenly became wielders of international power to shape the international understanding of the Yezidis. In the end, Yezidi women went from holding positions of little power within their communities to becoming incredibly powerful international actors helping push for significant social change, such as the recognition of genocide against the Yezidis.

### *Feminist research on war*

Many of the first ventures into studying gender in conflict were done in an effort to understand how women experienced conflict. Feminist scholars drove this expansion of knowledge by beginning to gather information from those who had not previously been given a voice in the study of war, including women. Prior to this endeavor, the accounts of international conflict focused almost entirely on the experience of men and their perceptions about world politics. These accounts observed conflict through the lenses of international relations, military science, and history, all of which were primarily focused on the actions of men. Most of this literature was also written by men, leaving out a key factor in the history and management of conflict: women. It is this dilemma that led feminist researchers to ask, "Where are the women?" in security studies.

**Textbox 12.1    Gender shifts in the Yazidi community**

In September 2014, the Islamic State of Syria and the Levant (ISIS) attacked Mt. Sinjar in the Kurdistan region of Iraq. This strategic push was part of a campaign by ISIS to eliminate the Yazidis, an ethnic and religious minority that lives mainly in Kurdistan. During the campaign, gender played a key role in the strategy of ISIS in what has since been deemed genocide of the Yazidi people. Immediately upon taking each village in the region, ISIS separated women from men and young from old. The men were killed while women were given a choice. They could convert to Islam and become the "wife" of an ISIS fighter or be sold as a slave to ISIS fighters (Cetorelli et al. 2017). Many of the women remained in captivity for months before they either escaped or were ransomed back to their families. Prior to the ISIS attack, women who had had relationships with non-Yazidis were at risk of being targeted in "honor killings." A lack of consent on the behalf of the woman was not factored into consideration in these cases of honor-based violence. Therefore, there was great concern on the part of the international community as to what would happen to these women upon return to their community from ISIS. However, once the women began to return to the Yazidi community following their captivity, the head Yazidi religious figure, Baba Sheik, made a decree that the women would not only be welcomed back into the Yazidi community, but they would be treated as war heroes. Women who returned were, for the most part, treated as such. They underwent a religious ceremony in which they were "re-purified" and many were married to Yazidi men (Foster and Minwalla 2018). Furthermore, Yazidi women who had returned from captivity gained a sort of power within their community as the public spokespeople for pushing for the recognition of the genocide committed by ISIS. Nadia Murad, one such woman who had been held by ISIS, became an internationally known public figure. Murad testified in front of countless delegations throughout the world, met with state leaders, and became the United Nations Ambassador on Human Trafficking. Nadia Murad went on to win the Nobel Peace Prize in 2018 (Morris 2018). This case is an interesting example of how conflict and gender interplay and affect one another. Not only did gender play a large role in the events of the conflict, but the conflict forever changed gender constructs within the Yazidi community.

*Inclusion of women in international conflict management*

Involving women in security, war, and peace, whether through gender mainstreaming or other methods, has shown to have lasting implications. Gender mainstreaming, which is a concept first explored by the United Nations in its efforts to achieve gender equality, is the process of involving a gendered analysis of policies at every stage from creation to implementation (Barrow 2009). Research has shown that there is a definite relationship between the status of women and the likelihood for peace following armed conflict, whether the conflict be intranational or international (Detraz 2012; Tickner and Sjoberg 2013). For example, Margit Bussman's work provides empirical evidence in the analysis of 110 conflicts between 1985 and 2000, illustrating that gender equality leads to a greater chance at domestic peace (Bussman 2007, 1). Gender equality is also a factor in the occurrence and conditions of war. In 2001, a study was conducted which produced empirical evidence that as gender equality increases in a state the severity of violence enacted by those states in international crises decreases (Tickner and Sjoberg 2013). In a publication for Inclusive Security, Mary O'Rielly analyzed statistical data on 80 years of international crises, which included findings from such organizations as UN Women, The Danish Institute for International Studies, The Rand Corporation, The Norwegian Nobel Committee, and dozens of independent scholars showing that there is overwhelming evidence that the inclusion of women in peace processes leads to a longer sustained peace following the end of conflict (O'Reilly 2015).

Keeping in line with these findings, the United Nations Security Council (UNSC) realizes the importance of development and empowerment of women to minimize the occurrence of war. This was solidified in the creation of UN Security Council Resolution 1325, which "reaffirms the important role of women in the prevention and resolution of conflicts, peace negotiations, peace-building, peacekeeping, humanitarian response and in post-conflict reconstruction and stresses the importance of their equal participation and full involvement in all efforts for the maintenance and promotion of peace and security" (UNSC 2000).

Although there is evidence that the inclusion of women in international conflict management leads to more sustainable peace, there is also contradictory evidence. In a study of post-conflict Liberia, Anne Theobald found that even though women were heavily involved in the peace process in Liberia, women did not achieve a gender-balanced peace in the post-conflict reformation, and women did not continue to play a leading role in international affairs for the nation following this specific period (Theobald 2014). Findings such as these are in line with what scholars have pointed out as flaws with gender mainstreaming.

### Gendered agency in conflict

In conflict, women are overwhelmingly stereotyped as being the helpless victims of violence. The scenario that is most often presented in conflict analyses is one in which men commit the violence willingly while women are the recipients of violence without having any choice in the matter (Helms 2013). While this notion is true in many cases, it is important to understand that women are also agents of violence. There are a number of recent studies of women who have been the agents of violence in conflict as soldiers, suicide bombers, and supporters of insurgencies (Sjoberg and Gentry 2007; Narozhna and Knight 2016). For example, the Chechen "Black Widows," many of whom had suffered the loss of their husbands or other family members at the hands of Russian forces, were known for utilizing terrorist tactics. Similarly, many women were members of the Liberation Tigers of Tamil Eelam (LTTTE) in Sri Lanka and were responsible for violent attacks – including the assassination of Indian Prime Minister Rajiv Gandhi in 1991. Women are also active agents in creating peace and in anti-war movements (Cockburn 2012; Cohn 2013). War also makes changes for women's agency on the domestic front as well. For example, American women found themselves called into the workforce at an unprecedented pace during World War II (Weatherford 2008; Hegarty 2008). While scholars disagree as to the lasting impact of the gender shifts that occurred at this time, there can be no argument that this change in daily responsibilities and labor sectors introduced women to experiences of labor and socialization which had, prior to the war, not been an option for American women (Honey 1984; McEuen 2011).

## Applying gender to international conflict management

How can academics and practitioners use a gendered lens to manage international conflict? The first step in any conflict management strategy is to conduct an analysis of the conflict and its actors. One part of this analysis should be focused on gender. A gender analysis of a conflict should take into consideration existing gender roles and norms of a conflict's parties and how those roles and norms play into the management of a conflict. For example, scholars have shown that gender-based violence often attributed to conflict is simply a magnification of gender norms present during peacetime among conflicting parties (Oriola 2017, 115). Therefore it is important to first analyze what a society's gender norms in peacetime are.

From this point, one can analyze shifts in gender norms and repercussions of gendered characteristics in conflict actors from the period prior to the outbreak of conflict to the current time or through the peace process for past conflicts. A gender analysis should include a comparison of experiences of men and women prior to and during a conflict while, as previously mentioned, organizing the information on a spectrum of gender rather than as a dichotomy. Though there are a myriad of guides for conducting a gender analysis, in the end a gender analysis should include information categorized by gender on societal power dynamics, the legal rights and status of women and men under local law (communal, national, religious, etc.), motivations and cultural priorities and daily activities (UNDP 2016).

As previously mentioned, it is important to stress that a gender analysis is not simply a look of how a conflict affects women. While this is certainly an important piece of the puzzle, failing to look at how gender influences the activities of all parties to the conflict will leave the analysis incomplete and will set the management strategy up to fail. Furthermore, a gender analysis must consider that there is not just one type of woman or one type of man in a conflict. An actor in a conflict will have additional characteristics that will affect his or her gender roles. Religion, economic status, ethnicity, and age all play deciding roles in how one experiences conflict. However, gender is a piece of this multifaceted identity that determines how individuals experience war, and it must be considered.

### Case study: problematic purity in Nigeria

Gender norms, and the disruption of them, can lead to further turmoil for communities experiencing armed conflict both during and following the conflict. During the period of active insurgency by Boko Haram in Nigeria, thousands of women were kidnapped by the insurgent organization. These women were usually taken by insurgents from their home villages to areas in the forests of Nigeria, where Boko Haram controlled territory. The women were often married off to Boko Haram soldiers and held for anywhere from a matter of days to years. Though some women were able to escape and return to their communities, the issue of their diminished purity quickly became problematic for these women. In many of the cultures from which these women came, their sexual purity is tied into notions of family and community honor (Oriola 2017). Once the women had returned, their communities often rejected them as "Boko Haram Wives," leaving them without the support necessary to overcome the challenges of reintegration (Matfess 2016). Often times, if the woman was married prior to being taken into captivity, the woman's husband no longer considered them married and rejected the woman as well (Spyra 2016). The situation facing these women was compounded if they had become pregnant or given birth to a child while in captivity. In short, the gender norm of women as symbols of purity had been violated, creating a new dimension to the conflict (Matfess 2017). The situation that develops upon the rejection and

ostracization of "dishonored" women and the children who are born in such conditions c
lead to a breakdown in social bonds, making it difficult to rebuild communities followi
conflict. Therefore, the problem is not just for the women and children directly affected by
these conditions, but for the entire community and the security of the region. Unfortunately,
the case in Nigeria is not uncommon in many of today's conflicts. This is one reason it is key
to understand the potential issues that can arise in a conflict when gender roles and norms,
such as expected purity of women, are broken.

### Case study: masculinity of ex-combatants in Colombia

Just as women face specific issues due to their gender and the normalized gender roles in their
communities, men face internal conflicts during and following war due to their perceived
gender roles in a society. When armed conflict moves toward a peace process, governments
and international organizations often turn to the process of Disarmament, Demobilization,
and Reintegration (DDR). In Colombia, the role of masculinity in ex-combatants became
apparent quickly to those involved in the DDR process after the insurgent war, bringing
gender to the forefront of the problems faced by the country. In order for soldiers to take on
the identity necessary to engage in armed conflict, the process of hypermasculinization, or
militarized masculinity is often engaged. This identity allows soldiers to engage in activities
that would be considered not only extremely violent, but criminal in peacetime. But when
war ends, how do ex-combatants return to their previous identities? In her work on masculinity and the DDR process in Colombia, Kimberly Theidon (2009) found that not enough
attention had been paid to reconstructing what it meant to be masculine for ex-combatants
who had to suddenly put down their weapons and cease engaging in activities that had driven
their masculine identities. Furthermore, other aspects of masculinity besides violent behavior
were tied into the ex-combatants' identities as soldiers, including social mobility, community
respect, and financial income. Since many of the ex-combatants in Colombia had joined
armed groups as young men living in poverty with little chance at a respectable career, the
opportunities afforded them as soldiers were very desirable. Consequently, the DDR process
was more than simply laying down arms; it involved laying down esteem and identity traits
deemed desirable by former combatants. Thus, the DDR process created a hostile environment that ex-combatants were not prone to accept. This situation is not unique to Colombia.
Many of the reintegration processes throughout the world, including the United States in
the wake of the Vietnam War and the wars in Iraq, fail to address the issue of reconstructing
"what it means to be a man" for ex-combatants returning home from war.

Apart from Latin America, where particular forms of hegemonic masculinities are apparent, militarized subnational identities have been mobilized in India's northeast, specifically
the border district of Darjeeling, by India's Nepali diaspora to entrench their demands for
respectful belonging within the Indian nation (Sen 2012, 2019). Young Nepali men distinguish themselves from marginal male youth in other border regions of India (like Kashmir)
through military labor in the Indian army.

### Using cyber activism to combat GBV in North Africa

The ways in which we look at international conflict and how to manage it continue to
develop. Methods for management are reflective of rapid growths in technology and
interconnectedness. New issues related to cyber terrorism, social media usage, and military use of technology are some of the fields that the international conflict management

community has begun to grapple with as it changes the realities of the problems we attempt to solve. However, technology has also proven to be a useful tool in both preventing and reacting to violence in conflict and there is a growing sphere of Internet and Communication Technology (ICT) tools being developed and used in conflict and post-conflict societies. For example, the ability to share vast amounts of information, including images and video, worldwide in real time has opened up a new avenue for awareness-building of Gender Based Violence (GBV). This technology is currently being utilized by activists in North Africa to not only educate the world about the realities of sexual harassment women face in the region, but to raise awareness among their own communities of issues which are rarely spoken about in public due to societal honor codes and victim blaming. Cellular technology, social media, and other Internet-based communication platforms have introduced the world to the issue of GBV faced by women in North African countries and just how prevalent and undermining sexual harassment for women is in these areas. The conversations surrounding the use of ICTs gained prominence during the Arab Spring when videos, pictures, and testimonies of victims of GBV made it to the world stage via social media platforms like Twitter, YouTube, and Facebook. In the wake of the Arab Spring, the same technologies that had been used haphazardly to spread awareness of the problem found a home with young activists who engaged crowdsourcing to continue their activism against GBV. In Egypt, Harassmap is an ICT tool that is mobilizing change through the sharing of data on the details and frequency of attacks of sexual harassment faced by women in Egypt (see also Chapter 11 on ICTs). The data is crowdsourced by volunteers who send text messages regarding experiences of sexual harassment, which enables Harassmap to monitor "hot spots" for sexual harassment. This data enables an assessment of different areas of the city to determine levels of necessary intervention or awareness-building.

In Morocco, *Women-Shoufouch* uses online platforms to change the discourse surrounding sexual harassment and to open up avenues for knowledge, experience, and solutions to be shared. The initiative originally began as a Facebook page where women and men could share their experiences and join in a call of action against the daily acts of aggression they experienced and witnessed. Both Harassmap and *Women-Shoufouch* have been incredibly successful in their use of ICT to fight sexual harassment. Though these initiatives are heavily focused on ending sexual harassment in North Africa, the underlying framework of using ICT to build awareness and generate a response to GBV can be applied to a much wider arena on international conflict management and the increased levels of GBV in conflict. These initiatives should provoke practitioners and academics alike to think creatively about how similar initiatives could be used to document GBV in conflict, or even gather data to prevent GBV in some cases.

## Challenges and future directions

There are a number of challenges in engaging a gender focus in international conflict management. These include the issue of ensuring that women are involved in conflict management and post-conflict transition and that gendered analyses are part of any conflict analysis done prior to engaging in conflict management strategy. Unfortunately, although there have been many efforts to include women in the securitization of post-conflict spaces, there is still a failure on the part of those involved in peace processes to fully engage women. Between 1990 and 2017, only 8 percent of negotiators for peace treaties were women, and a miniscule 2 percent of mediators for peace agreements were women (CFR and UN Women 2019).

The United Nations Security Council (UNSC) has made very public efforts to promote the inclusion of women in international security with the publication of UNSC Resolution 1325. It calls for the equal participation of women in security and urges the mainstreaming of gender perspectives into peacekeeping operations (UNSC 2000). The Resolution also calls for appointing and including more women in security-related activities and mentions this in several articles throughout the Resolution. However, as of yet, this call seems to have gone largely unanswered.

One of the most common struggles in engaging gender in international conflict management is working with other stakeholders to ensure that gender is given consideration by all who are involved. It is important for all involved to recognize that culturally held views on gender may not be shared by all, or even any, of the stakeholders involved in a conflict management strategy. However, no party or individual works alone in conflict management, and these differences will need to be identified and addressed if a strategy is to be successful. One method of engaging government stakeholders is to align gender-related conflict management strategies with the country's doctrine on women's issues. Many countries have National Actions Plans (NAPs) related to women's empowerment, strategies on the elimination of violence against women, or conventions on the inclusion of women in politics. While these documents may be little more than lip service, they will assist practitioners in aligning goals with the public positions of governments that may assist in obtaining buy-in from stakeholders.

"Gender and conflict" as a field of inquiry would not exist without the academic activism of feminist scholars over the decades. Further, students and practitioners of conflict management must also understand that one of feminism's key preoccupations in the current moment is to continue to underscore how violence and conflict are integral to knowledge production itself. Noted black feminist scholars like bell hooks and Beverly Guy-Sheftall have remained outspoken about the total disregard for race in white middle-class liberal feminist engagements with gender-based research.

One way in which this type of violence manifests itself in academic settings is in epistemic form first, but with consequences for representational politics, and, ultimately enabling hetero-patriarchy to dictate academic success. The most visible evidence of this trend is manifest in the discipline of Political Science, which is also a closely related field of conflict management. It took until 2019 for one of the most established social science disciplines to hand over editorial leadership of its prominent journal *American Political Science Review* *(APSR)* to a slate of women editors. According to recent media reports on this "historic" moment, a private research organization, Santa Fe Institute, writes of APSR: "only about 2 percent of articles in the flagship [APSR] between 2000 and 2015 focused on gender or sexuality, and only about 4 percent on ethnicity or race" (Todd 2019). In the same article where this statistic is quoted, Sara Todd writes:

> since editorial leadership at APSR was traditionally dominated by white men, the journal, established in 1906, evolved to favor the methodologies (quantitative analysis, as opposed to qualitative research) and subject areas (voting and elections) that tended to appeal to white men in the field. This is representative of a broader sociological phenomenon known as the "Matthew effect," in which people who are perceived as higher status accumulate more advantages. Identity, in other words, factors into what the APSR has typically included as well as what it has left out.

The field of conflict management, which still remains largely neopositivist (Tickner 2016), is often dismissive of feminist scholarship. Not only has this trend been noted by scholars like Anne Tickner in gender and conflict research, it surfaced in another recent controversy over the representational politics of the International Studies Association's "Sapphire Series" panels, leading to responses from the scholarly community like in this article published in 2018: "Feminist labour [sic] at the ISA: *White manels, the politics of citation and mundane productions of disciplinary sexism and racism*" (Åhäll et al. 2018).

The irony is that feminist scholars of conflict are not surprised by these moments of disruption since they are well aware of discourse of standard social science textbooks where words such as *exploratory* are often used to describe advanced qualitative research. In addition, the scholarship of non-western academics doing research in their own countries is labeled as "backyard research" (Sen 2017, 38). In our collective reflection on the field of gender and conflict research (of which gender and conflict management is a part) one should also observe citation politics. For instance, *intersectionality* is a much thrown-around term in gender-based research; however its black feminist origins in the work of legal activist Kimberle Williams Crenshaw is often forgotten in liberal-feminist and policy research. This has necessitated a cross-disciplinary campaign in academe under the hashtag #citeblackwomen.

The phenomena outlined previously in bringing attention to the violence and conflict in knowledge production has another related manifestation which is best described by Cathrine Rottenberg (2018) in her recent book *The Rise of Neoliberal Feminism*. Rottenberg details the history of feminisms in the US with specific focus on white middle class liberal feminists' complicity with free market forces on the one hand and neoconservative forces on the other. This emerging form of feminism is deeply non-intersectional with no attention to issues or race and privilege, beaming in self-proclaimed leadership roles, and is notably antiradical in its politics. Often these new pop-feminist formations are "unsettlingly unmoored from those key terms of equality, justice and emancipation that have informed women's movements and feminism since their inception" (Rottenberg 2018, 11). Rottenberg further uses data from the research of sociologist Sara Farris (2017) to show cross-continental patterns of US neoliberal feminism. Theresa May, the ousted British PM, proudly proclaims herself as feminist but according to Rottenberg (2018, 12) supported "every single one of the austerity measures that make the lives of poorer women much harsher." The same could be said of Ms. Ivanka Trump's brand of entrepreneurial feminism, which is the epitome of US neoliberal feminism. Rottenberg (2018, 12) underscores that these kinds of brand-based, market-logic-driven feminisms are hypocritical in denying structural gender oppression in the US while trying "to justify imperialist interventions in countries with majority Muslim populations halfway across the globe."

Further, the strategic use of social media not only exposes sexual harassment "on the street" (see our previous discussion of *Harassmap*) but also underscores entanglements of sexual harassment and powerplay in the process of knowledge production itself. The work and activism of multiple groups of young Indian feminists based both in India and the Indian diaspora in the US (such as Raya Sarkar, Thenmozhi Soundararajan, Inji Pennu, and others) have generated lively debates about the silence of mainstream Indian feminists on issues of caste-based, gender-based oppression in academe, once again centering on the violence inherent in knowledge production. Reflecting on these emerging engagements, Rukmini Sen, a feminist sociologist from India argues that these forms of violence and associated criticisms like #metoo have to be seen in the context of changes in Indian higher education as well (Rukmini Sen 2019). In Indian feminism #metoo exposed generational, caste, and class-based inequities in access to knowledge and power, much like the work of black and Latina feminists in the US.

These examples demonstrate why a well-rounded exposure to the field of conflict management must include meaningful exposure to contextual histories of feminism, within which gender and conflict research will always be embedded. The teaching of conflict management must educate newer generations about the politics of knowledge production, which has been a feminist concern over the last 50 years, if not more. Such a focus should enable a more grounded and reflexive approach and move beyond liberal underpinnings of gender-based thinking and analysis, where the "add women and stir" approach still dominates policy, practice, and diversity initiatives within academe. Such business-as-usual forms of gender and conflict research pay lip service to feminist ideals with no real respect for radicalism, social change, and structural inequities.

## Questions for further discussion

1  What are some of the common stereotypes about gender roles and norms during conflict? Give examples of how these stereotypes have been countered in past conflicts.
2  Describe the current presence of women in peace negotiations. How does this presence effect peace negotiations and resulting peace treaties?
3  Why is it important to focus on both men and women when conducting a gender-focused analysis of any conflict?
4  How can scholars and practitioners engage in research that builds knowledge on vulnerable populations while avoiding endangering research subjects?
5  What empirical evidence exists on the link between gender and the proliferation of conflict?

## Suggested resources

1  For more on the role of women in the Boko Haram insurgency, see: Matfess, Hilary. 2017. *Women and the War on Boko Haram: Wives, Weapons, Witnesses*. London: Zed Books. ISBN 978-1-78699-1481, 270 pages. For more on the reconstructing of masculinities in the Colombian DDR process see: Theidon, Kimberly. 2009. "Reconstructing Masculinities: The Disarmament, Demobilization, and Reintegration of Former Combatants in Colombia." *Human Rights Quarterly* 31 (1) (February): 1–34.
2  For more information on Harassmap and *Women-Shoufouch* see: Skalli, Loubna Hanna. 2013. "Young Women and Social Media Against Sexual Harassment in North Africa." *The Journal of North African Studies*. DOI: 10.1080/13629387.2013.858034
3  Cohn, Carol. 2013. *Women and Wars: Contested Histories, Uncertain Futures*. Cambridge: Polity Press.
4  Disney, Abigail E., Pamela Hogan, and Gini Reticker. "Women, War and Peace." New York. Thirteen Productions. Available through the Public Broadcasting Service (PBS) at www.pbs.org/wnet/women-war-and-peace/. Goldstein, Joshua S. 2001. *War and Gender: How Gender Shapes the War System and Vice Versa*. Cambridge: Cambridge University Press.
5  Saferworld, Colette Harris (SOAS, University of London) and the Uganda Land Alliance (ULA). "Gender Analysis of Conflict: Why Is it Important?" YouTube Video. 4:07. Posted July 5 2016. https://youtu.be/sI2AZdl-2O8.
6  Strochlic, Nina. "A Woman's War." *National Geographic*. Accessed March 1, 2019. www.nationalgeographic.com/culture/2018/10/women-war-conflict-nigeria-peru-iraq-philippines-international-day-of-girl/.

7    UN Women. "Commission on the Status of Women." United Nations. Accessed March 1, 2019. www.unwomen.org/en/csw.

## Become engaged!

1    United States Institute for Peace (USIP): USIP has an extensive gender-focused resource section that includes ongoing projects, publication opportunities, grants and fellowships, and a blog. More information can be found on their website at www.usip.org/issue-areas/gender.
2    United Nations (UN) Gender Internship Program: "The UN Women Internship Programme offers outstanding students the opportunity to acquire direct exposure to UN Women's work in areas such as strategic partnership, communications, advocacy, policy, evaluation, human resources, programme planning, research and data, finance, and ICT." For more information visit: www.unwomen.org/en/about-us/employment/internship-programme.
3    The Consortium on Gender, Security and Human Rights Internship Program: The Consortium on Gender, Security and Human Rights is a non-profit organization dedicated to expanding knowledge on the role of gender in peace and security. For more information visit: https://genderandsecurity.org/internships.

## Note

1    The authors contributed equally to the writing of this chapter; Dr. Debarati Sen is the corresponding author.

## References and further reading

Åhäll, Linda, Sam Cook, Roberta Guerrina, Toni Haastrup, Cristina Masters, Laura Mills, Saara Särmä, and Katharine A.M. Wright. 2018. "Feminist Labor at the ISA: White Manels, the Politics of Citation and Mundane Productions of Disciplinary Sexism and Racism." Accessed August 1, 2019. https://thedisorderofthings.com/2018/06/26/feminist-labour-at-the-isa-white-manels-the-politics-of-citation-and-mundane-productions-of-disciplinary-sexism-and-racism/.

Althusser, Louis. 1971. *Lenin and Philosophy and Other Essays*. New York, NY: Monthly Review Press.

Barrow, Amy. 2009. "'[It's] Like a Rubber Band': Assessing UNSCR 1325 as a Gender Mainstreaming Process." *International Journal of Law in Context* 5 (1): 51–68.

Bussmann, Margit. 2007. "Gender Equality, Good Governance, and Peace". Paper presented at the General Polarization and Conflict (PAC) Meeting, Gaillac, France, June 2007.

Cetorelli, Valeria, Isaac Sasson, Nazar Shabila, and Gilbert Burnham. 2017 "Mortality and Kidnapping Estimates for the Yazidi Population in the Area of Mount Sinjar, Iraq, in August 2014: A Retrospective Household Survey." *PLoS Medicine* 14 (5): 1–15.

Cockburn, Cynthia. 2012. *Anti-Militarism: Political and Gender Dynamics of Peace Movements*. New York, NY: Palgrave Macmillan.

Connell, R.W., and James Messerschmidt. 2005. "Hegemonic Masculinity: Rethinking the Concept." *Gender and Society* 19 (6): 829–59.

Council on Foreign Relations (CFR) and UN Women. 2019. "Women's Participation in Peace Processes." *CFR*. Accessed March 1, 2019. www.cfr.org/interactive/womens-participation-in-peace-processes.

Detraz, Nicole. 2012. *International Security and Gender*. Cambridge: Polity.

Dharmapuri, Sahana. 2011. "Just Add Women and Stir?" *Parameters: US Army War College* 41 (1): 56.

Farris, Sara. 2017. *In the Name of Women's Rights: The Rise of Femonationalism*. Durham, NC: Duke University Press.

Foster, Johanna E., and Sherizaan Minwalla. 2018. "Voices of Yazidi Women: Perceptions of Journalistic Practices in the Reporting on ISIS Sexual Violence." *Women's Studies International Forum* 67 (March): 53–64.

Hegarty, Marilyn E. 2008. *Victory Girls, Khaki-Wackies, and Patriotutes: The Regulation of Female Sexuality During World War II*. New York, NY: New York University Press.

Helms, Elissa. 2013. *Innocence and Victimhood: Gender, Nation, and Women's Activism in Postwar Bosnia-Herzegovina*. Madison, WI: University of Wisconsin Press.

Honey, Maureen. 1984. *Creating Rosie the Riveter: Class, Gender, and Propaganda During World War II*. Amherst, MA: University of Massachusetts Press.

Matfess, Hilary. 2016. "Nigeria: Boko Haram's War on Women." *Newsweek Middle East*, February 17. Accessed March 1, 2019. http://newsweekme.com/boko-harams-war-on-women/.

Matfess, Hilary. 2017. *Women and the War on Boko Haram: Wives, Weapons, Witnesses*. London: Zed Books.

McEuen, Melissa A. 2011. *Making War, Making Women: Femininity and Duty on the American Home Front, 1941–1945*. Athens, GA; and London: University of Georgia Press.

Morris, Loveday. 2018. "Nobel Prize Winner Nadia Murad's Story Is One of Unbelievable Bravery: It's Also One of Thousands." *The Washington Post*, October 5.

Narozhna, Tanya, and W. Andy Knight. 2016. *Female Suicide Bombings: A Critical Gender Approach*. Toronto: University of Toronto Press.

O'Reilly, Marie. 2015. "Why Women? Inclusive Security and Peaceful Societies." *Inclusive Security*. Accessed July 30, 2019. www.inclusivesecurity.org/publication/why-women-inclusive-security-and-peaceful-societies/.

Oriola, Temitope B. 2017. "'Unwilling Cocoons': Boko Haram's War Against Women." *Studies in Conflict & Terrorism* 40 (2): 99–121.

Rottenberg, Catherine. 2018. *The Rise of Neoliberal Feminism*. New York, NY: Oxford University Press.

Sen, Debarati. 2012. "Illusive Justice: Subnationalism and Gendered Labor Politics in Darjeeling Plantations." In *New South Asian Feminisms: Paradoxes and Possibilities*, edited by Srila Roy, 131–50. London: Zed Books.

———. 2017. *Everyday Sustainability: Gender Justice and Fair Trade Tea in Darjeeling*. Albany, NY: State University of New York Press.

———. 2019. "A Gorkha Never Betrays: Media, Militarized Identities and Subnational Movements in Contemporary India." Paper presented at the Cultural Studies Association Annual Meetings, Tulane University, New Orleans, July. www.culturalstudiesassociation.org/files/2019%20FINAL%20PROGRAM(1).pdf.

Sen, Rukmini. 2019. "Intimacy, Transgression, Ethics: Scripts and Silences in Gendered Academia." Draft Paper International Symposium on Comparative Perspectives of #MeToo, April 8–9, University of Kentucky, Lexington.

Sjoberg, Laura, and Caron E. Gentry. 2007. *Mothers, Monsters, Whores: Women's Violence in Global Politics*. New York, NY: Zed Books.

Spyra, Andy. 2016. "The 'Wives' of Boko Haram." *Foreign Policy*, March 31. Accessed March 1, 2019. https://foreignpolicy.com/2016/03/31/the-wives-of-boko-haram-fighters-nigeria-captives-escape/.

Theidon, Kimberly. 2009. "Reconstructing Masculinities: The Disarmament, Demobilization, and Reintegration of Former Combatants in Colombia." *Human Rights Quarterly* 31 (1): 1–34.

Theobald, Anne. 2014. *The Role of Women in Making and Building Peace in Liberia: Gender Sensitivity Versus Masculinity*. Stuttgart, Germany: Ibidem Press.

Tickner, J. Ann. 1997. "You Just Don't Understand: Troubled Engagements Between Feminists and IR Theorists." *International Studies Quarterly* 41 (4): 611–32.

Tickner, J. Ann. 2016. *A Feminist Voyage Through International Relations* (Oxford Studies in Gender and International Relations) 1st edition. Oxford: Oxford University Press.

Tickner, J. Ann, and Laura Sjoberg. 2013. "Feminist Perspectives of International Relations." In *Handbook of International Relations*, 2nd edition, edited by W. Carlsnaes, T. Risse, and B.A. Simmons, 170–94. London: Sage Publications.

Todd, Sara. 2019. "A Top US Political Science Journal Ignored Race and Gender – Until 12 Women Took Over." *Quartz at Work*, July 31. https://qz.com/work/1679115/the-top-us-political-science-journal-will-now-be-led-by-12-female-professors/?utm_source=facebook&utm_medium=qz-organ ic&fbclid=IwAR2FDtQVifdSBORkskPaw7fhazL7kOuirwNhgbx-Fdm3jLHCj8ox2_xOaCE.

United Nations Development Programme (UNDP). 2016. "How to Conduct a Gender Analysis." *United Nations*, October. Accessed March 1, 2019. https://info.undp.org/sites/bpps/SES_Toolkit/ SES%20Document%20Library/Uploaded%20October%202016/UNDP%20Guidance%20 Note%20how%20to%20conduct%20a%20gender%20analysis.pdf.

United Nations (UN) Security Council, Security Council Resolution 1325. 2000. [On Women and Peace and Security], October 31, S/RES/1325 (2000).

Weatherford, Doris. 2008. *American Women and World War II*. New York, NY: Facts on File, 1990; Castle Books.

Wibben, Annick T.R. 2016. *Researching War: Feminist Methods, Ethics and Politics*. Abingdon, OX: Routledge.

# 13 Ethnicity, religion, and international conflict management

*Charity Butcher and Kathleen Kirk*

## Introduction

Ethnic and religious identities are often seen as drivers of conflict, and thus are important issues to consider within the broader international conflict management field. This chapter discusses how ethnicity and religion may lead to conflict, may exacerbate or escalate conflict, and also how these factors can be prevented, mitigated, and managed. In addition, the chapter considers how religion and religious organizations have contributed to the process of peacebuilding in many countries.

Ethnicity and religion are interrelated concepts, and this chapter focuses on each of these concepts individually as well as their interconnectedness. Religion and religious groups as discussed here include groups of people who self-identify with those specific religions (such as an individual identifying as Jewish, Catholic, or Hindu). Identifying as part of a specific religious group is not necessarily tied to levels of religiosity (or having a strong religious belief), or even to how frequently one openly attends religious services or practices religious traditions. Rather, it is about the specific identity that a person might hold as part of a larger religious group. Further, while religious beliefs and doctrine are clearly different between different religious sects, there is also variation within religions regarding beliefs. This variation can be the source of conflict within and among religious groups, but may also potentially serve as a mechanism for conflict resolution. Ethnicity and ethnic groups are defined quite broadly in this chapter and refer to groups of people who identify as the same group based on shared ancestry, language, history, customs, culture, and/or religion. Thus, while religion is part of how people may identify themselves within a certain ethnic group, it is also often an identity separate from ethnicity.

Following the end of the Cold War, major ethnic conflicts in places such as the former Yugoslavia and Rwanda gave the impression that ethnic conflict was increasing. Further, arguments like Samuel Huntington's "Clash of Civilizations" (1993), which suggested that in the post-Cold War period, conflicts would be cultural (between "civilizations"), rather than ideological, fueled fears that ethnic conflicts would increase and escalate worldwide. However, evidence clearly suggests that these fears were misplaced. Since the mid-1990s, there has actually been a decline in the number of ethnic civil wars (Gurr 2000; Cederman, Gleditsch, and Wucherpfennig 2017), – a key point to remember throughout the discussion of the drivers of ethnic conflict.

However, while ethnic civil wars are in decline, it is generally true that they are more common than other types of civil conflicts. As such, considering the causes of such conflicts, and ways to prevent, manage, and mitigate these conflicts, is extremely important. The next section focuses on the causes of ethnic and religious conflicts, followed by a discussion of the theories and practices that help in preventing ethnic conflicts from starting (or reoccurring) and help manage and mitigate these conflicts when they are underway. Finally, the chapter concludes with a discussion of some of the key challenges in dealing with ethnic and religious conflicts and areas for optimism moving forward.

## The causes of ethnic and religious conflict

Why do groups that have lived peacefully alongside one another for years erupt into violent conflict with one another? There are three primary schools of thought on the formation of ethnic identity and the relationship between ethnicity and conflict. First, primordialism sees ethnicity as "biologically given," something that is inherited at birth. Ethnicity for primordialists is an ancient and natural phenomenon. From this perspective, individuals are born into a certain ethnic group, sharing its language, culture, and customs. In addition, primordialists tend to view kinship ties as strong among individuals within the same ethnic group due to this shared sense of identity. For primordialists, conflict between ethnic groups is a function of these ethnic differences. Different groups push for their own interests (at the expense of others), leading to inevitable conflict between groups. However, this primordial approach has a difficult time explaining why ethnic and religious groups often live in peace and has largely been discredited. Constructivism, a second perspective, views ethnic identities as socially constructed, and therefore assumes ethnic identities change over time and are not fixed. Because constructivists see ethnic identities as a product of interactions between groups, they do not see conflicts between ethnic groups as inevitable. Jenkins (2008) takes a similar view of ethnicity, but more fully emphasizes the sociological nature of identities. For Jenkins, "*identity* denotes the ways in which individuals and collectivities are distinguished in their relations with other individuals and collectivities" (Jenkins 2008, 18). Thus, identity is based on social interactions with others. Similar approaches to ethnicity are discussed in the next section. Finally, instrumentalism sees ethnic identity as something that is easily manipulated by elites to serve their own political ends. In this approach, elites capitalize on existing ethnic identities, often creating or exacerbating ethnic differences and grievances, potentially leading to conflict between groups. Themes from each of these various approaches are evident in the discussion of the various theoretical causes of ethnic and religious conflict.

### *Social identity theory*

The connection between group identity and violence derives from the term *ethnocentrism*, which is the belief in the superiority of one's ethnicity over others (Sumner 1906). Ethnocentrism often begins with individuals creating social categories and forming groups (Brewer 2001, 19). From there, group members begin to see themselves with positive attributes. As a result of this social categorization and in-group positivity, intergroup comparison and out-group hostility sometimes occur.

In response to the horrors of the Holocaust, theorists coined the term *Social Identity Theory (SIT)* to further explain one's need to identify with a group in order to reduce uncertainty and increase security and self-worth (Tajfel and Turner 1986). Building upon ethnocentrism, the inclusion of "competition" may be a possible intermediary step linking comparison and hostility. How in-group members assess their status depends on a comparison of themselves to the out-group. If in-group members view themselves more favorably than out-group members, in-group positivity increases. As a result, intergroup discrimination can occur as groups attempt to gain a sense of superiority. Other steps characterizing members of the out-group might include depersonalization and dehumanization, such as the Nazi depiction of Jews as rats (Tajfel 1981, 240). This constitutes a shift from comparison to competition.

While competition can beget conflict, this step is not automatic. Depending on perceptions between in- and out-groups, a group's strategy could range anywhere from assimilation to conflict. Members of the respective groups may see group boundaries as permeable or impermeable, status differences as legitimate or illegitimate, and the nature of these as stable or unstable. Social mobility can occur if group boundaries are permeable, but if boundaries are impermeable, members consider a change in in- and out-group relationship as the only way of improving social identity. In an effort to enhance self-worth, groups may attempt to reframe any negative attributes or resort to violence. Consider the immigration policy in France. The country has a strong sense of cultural heritage and, to maintain this, has adopted a policy whereby immigrants should assimilate. While immigrants adapt to French culture, they also wish to maintain their own sense of cultural identity. This has come to a head in recent years with influxes from the Middle East and North Africa (MENA). In 2011, France instituted a law banning face covering (e.g., burqas and niqabs). Subsequent fines and arrests led to rioting in the streets of Toulouse. As this case illustrates, France sees its boundaries as impermeable when it comes to face covering. In order for MENA immigrants to consider a change in status between in- and out-group relationship, they are faced with assimilation as it pertains to this law, or else public demonstrations or riots to frame their status in a positive light.

## Ethno-symbolism

Ethno-symbolism focuses on the importance of ethnic attachments, such as symbols, myths, and traditions that form and sustain entities ranging from ethnic groups to nations. Though such attachments are malleable and socially constructed, the deep emotional connection that often comes with them provides an indicator of their persistence (Demmers 2016). The salience of ethnic symbols is one reason that they are easily invoked during conflict and may help foster and intensify ethnic tensions.

Studying myths and symbols as they relate to identity, John Armstrong (1982) argues that ethnic consciousness has existed since antiquity. To understand the emergence of a group, one must observe changes that appear over an extended time. Groups define themselves and their differences with others using this history. Factors allowing for the persistence of symbols as identity-defining include a group's way of life (e.g., nomadic or sedentary), religion, and language, as well as how people tend to congregate in neighborhoods with others of their own background and the role of elites in transmitting myths to justify their political purposes.

Others expand on the ethno-symbolic approach, arguing that ethnic components are crucial to nation-building, creating a shared historic territory, myths, and common culture, economy, and legal rights (Smith 1986). Certain events can change cultural components of ethnic identities, such as war, exile, migration, and religious conversion, but communities engage in religious reform, cultural borrowing, and myths of being the "promised ones" to ensure cultural survival.

While ethnic attachments such as myths and symbols allow groups and nations to form by codifying group identity, such attachments can also heighten and escalate conflict between groups. Ethnic out-groups often lack a sense of belonging, political representation in government processes, and, where relevant, religious expression. Sometimes leaders use ethnic attachments for political means. For example, Russia has utilized the plight of Russians in

Crimea as justification for interventions into Ukraine. Political appropriation of such attachments can lead to ethnic wars, heightening group emotions rather than addressing group needs (Kaufman 2001). Consequently, hostility based on these myths may lead groups to follow extremist leaders, who often use violent conflict in their quest for ethnic domination. Further, since ethnic identities are often quite salient, conflicts surrounding such identities may be particularly intractable.

### Economic and political grievances

Socioeconomic inequality and ethnic discrimination are often noted as potential causes of conflict between ethnic groups. Often, economic resources and political power are not evenly distributed, which creates grievances within a society. In many cases, this inequality is found along ethnic or religious lines. Colonialism greatly contributed to the unequal distribution of resources and power within much of the world, as colonial powers often favored one ethnic group over another, most usually based on arbitrary physical characteristics or economic factors – such as differentiating between pastoralists and cultivators. These problems were even more pronounced when the favored group was also a minority group within a particular territory or space. Through such practices, colonial powers often created increased competition between ethnic groups that had not necessarily experienced intense competition prior to colonization. Ethnic conflicts in Rwanda and Burundi demonstrate the role that this unequal distribution of resources and power can play in exacerbating ethnic tensions within society. In these countries, Hutu are the largest ethnic group (comprising around 85–90 percent of the population of each country) and Tutsi are a minority, comprising around 10–14 percent of each country. However, in both countries, the Tutsi minority has at times been the dominant group, creating unequal distribution of resources and political grievances between these groups. These differentials have led to conflict in both countries.

While many groups within a society may have economic or political grievances, ethnic groups may have more opportunities to redress these grievances. This can particularly occur when governments and majority populations have treated minority groups unequally, or when governments cannot make credible commitments to protect ethnic groups (Lake and Rothschild 1996), leading to ethnic conflict. Since ethnic groups are often concentrated in the same geographic areas, they may have an easier time mobilizing to address their concerns (Denny and Walter 2014). Similarly, ethnic kinship provides an additional network for mobilizing supporters. For example, Kurdish organizations opposing governments (such as in Turkey and Iraq) often capitalize on the shared Kurdish identity to gain support from Kurdish populations. Thus, grievances shared by ethnic groups may be more likely to lead to conflicts between these groups and the government than grievances held by other types of sociopolitical or economic groups.

However, while ethnic conflicts may seem common, it is important to note that research also suggests that ethnic and religious diversity is not absolutely associated with violent conflict. Fearon and Laitin (2003) find that state weakness due to poverty, large populations, and political instability are more likely to lead to civil war than ethnic and religious grievances. Thus, the relationship between ethnicity and conflict is not always direct, and instead, ethnicity and religion might be factors that escalate or exacerbate already exiting grievances or provide the organizational means for addressed grievances. Consequently, ethnicity itself is not necessarily a source of conflict, as primordialists might suggest, but rather, conflicts are tied to a variety of motives and opportunities, some of which may also interact with ethnic and religious identities. At the same time, given the often salient nature of ethnic and religious identities, conflicts that have ethnic or religious dimensions may be intense and protracted, particularly when they do not address the sources of conflict and when leaders rely heavily on ethnic or religious symbols to perpetuate conflict.

---

**Textbox 13.1   China's persecution of its Uighur people**

Ethnic conflicts in places like China illustrate the role that ethnicity can play in a conflict but also demonstrate how economics and politics can play a role in instigating so-called ethnic conflict. The ethnic minority Uighur live in the far western Chinese province of Xinjiang. Being Muslim in practice and Turkic in ethnic and linguistic origin, this minority of approximately 11 million stands in unique contrast to mainstream Mandarin China, which espouses conformity, downplays religion, and encourages allegiance to the communist government. Adding to this complexity is the contested nature of the minority's origins (Bovingdon 2010). While the Uighur claim to be the one ethnicity indigenous to Xinjiang, the Chinese government argues they are ancient migrants from Mongolia. Using the pretext of combatting extremism, China created detention camps called "reeducation centers" in 2014 to detain Uighur Muslims, but activists point to economic factors underpinning this ongoing human rights violation. China's Belt and Road Initiative is an extensive development plan spanning through Asia and Europe, and Xinjiang's strategic location acts as the lynchpin for the initiative's success. Despite the strategic location, the government sees the minority Uighur population as a roadblock. With resources being diverted to the project, the Uighur are left disenfranchised. Realizing the potential for rebellion, the government uses detention camps to suppress potential dissidents. Since 2016, arrests have increased under a new Communist Party Secretary in Xinjiang. With the 2018 BBC exposé revealing satellite imagery of the area, the public gained proof of the extent of such camps, which fueled an outcry from various human rights groups and governments (Sudworth 2018). By July 2019, 22 governments signed a joint letter to the UN Human Rights Council calling for China to close the camps, while other governments like Saudi Arabia and Russia applaud China's alleged efforts against anti-extremism. As of 2019, an estimated 1.5 million Uighur are being detained without charges (Maizland 2019). While world leaders remain divided among their support, the underlying needs of China's government and the Uighur people lie within the realm of economy and identity. Acknowledging the Uighur's unique identity might allow them to gain a sense of belonging within the community, which could allow for China to expand its western development project with added buy-in from its Uighur citizens.

---

*Territory and ethnic conflict*

In addition to political and economic grievances, many ethnic groups have grievances related to territorial control. This is particularly pronounced when groups are geographically tied to a specific piece of territory regarded as their homeland. As Toft (2003) notes, territory can be both *divisible* and *indivisible*. Territory is divisible in that it is a physical object that can be quantified. The resources in and on the territory can be measured and valued. In these ways, territory could be divided between various interested parties. On the other hand, some territory may also be considered indivisible. In this sense, territory is sometimes closely linked to ethnic and religious identity in a way that makes it difficult to just divide between groups. Jerusalem is a good example of indivisible territory – multiple groups claim a fundamental religious connection to this city and as such, conflicts over the territory cannot easily be resolved just by dividing it up. When ethnic or religious identities become closely tied to territory, conflicts become much more difficult to resolve and are more likely to lead to violent conflict. Thus, ethnicity and religion are not necessarily the causes of conflict in these instances, but rather serve as an additional factor that exacerbates and escalates conflict.

Secessionist movements are often built on the idea of an ethnic homeland, particularly when an ethnic or religious group is concentrated within the territory that it considers its historical homeland. For example, many Kurds live in a fairly concentrated area between Turkey, Iran, Iraq, and Syria and refer to this area as Kurdistan. Kurdish groups in different countries have pushed for independence and to create an independent country within the territory of Kurdistan. Basques in Spain and Tamils in Sri Lanka are additional examples of groups that have sought autonomy and independence while being concentrated in a particular piece of territory. Further, some countries struggle over control of territory that they view as part of their historical homeland. Somalia claims portions of Ethiopia, Kenya, and Djibouti as part of "Greater Somalia" due to historical ties and the fact that ethnic Somalis live in these regions. The Ogaden War between Somalia and Ethiopia was directly tied to one such region of Ethiopia so claimed by Somalia. Given these examples, it is clear that territory and ethnicity are closely tied together and can increase the likelihood of conflict.

## Theories related to managing ethnic and religious conflicts

While the previous section outlined many of the theoretical causes of ethnic and religious conflict, not all ethnic grievances and issues lead to protracted and violent conflict. In fact, ethnic conflicts can be managed and transformed in ways to prevent the outbreak of war and recurrence of armed conflict. The next section focuses on the various theories of how to manage ethnic and religious conflict.

### *Contact theory*

Track II diplomacy is built on contact theory, which stipulates that interaction between groups experiencing conflict can increase tolerance (Allport 1954). As discussed in Social Identity Theory, prejudice results from generalizations made by one group about the other. Interpersonal contact can reduce prejudice, bringing about a reconceptualization of group categories. This theory distinguishes between negative contact (e.g., insulting and committing acts of violence), and positive contact (e.g., cooperation). In order to achieve positive contact, the following conditions should be present: equal status among group members, common goals, intergroup cooperation, and support of authorities.

Other theorists have proposed methods to explain how contact reduces prejudice. One example is the "four processes of change," which entails learning about the out-group, changing behavior, generating affective ties, and in-group reappraisal (Pettigrew 1998). From here, positive contact expands to other members of the out-group after initial contact. Specifically, such ongoing positive contact could reflect a three-stage model that extends over time to enhance positive contact and generalization: de-categorization of "us versus them," positive generalization, and re-categorization from "us versus them" to "we." In the case of Rwanda, a de-categorization of "us versus them" would consist of "Tutsis versus Hutus." A positive generalization might entail an interaction between individuals from both groups and news of this spreading among groups. A re-categorization to "we" could be "Rwandans."

As Marc Ross (2001) notes, the challenge for conflict theorists lies in utilizing identity dynamics to manage ethnic conflict constructively (174). While groups may use in- and out-group identities to create competition and eventually conflict, one potential approach focuses on reinventing group narratives with new metaphors to create possibilities for positive inter-group cooperation. According to Vamik Volkan (1988, 1997) and Joseph Montville (1991), a crucial step in the process involves mutual acknowledgement of loss and means of collective mourning. In addition, Herbert Kelman (1987, 1992) stipulates that groups should also acknowledge that the other's right to exist is not mutually exclusive to their own. Another potential strategy is Track II diplomacy, whereby facilitated interaction between civil society members from both groups builds understanding and trust, which could lead to solutions to the conflict (Cuhadar and Dayton 2011). However, as Miles et al. (2014) note, the results of intergroup contact in a post-conflict society can be difficult to predict. Conflict theorists should work to best track the benefits and limitations of extended contact to leverage group identity in a path toward reconciliation.

While positive contact has proven to improve ethnic intergroup relations, timing and context are not always ideal for such intervention. Specifically, during times of civil war or violent conflict, contact between groups might be too dangerous. Because of this, group leaders should carefully consider other means of establishing initial contact, such as Track II diplomacy.

### Ethno-symbolism and conflict management

While ethnic symbols can create and exacerbate ethnic conflict, they can also provide the source of post-conflict identity building and help in preventing the recurrence of conflict. Decisions on governance structures come from assumptions about identity and group boundaries (Keranen 2014). In post-conflict nation-building, historical and recently invented symbols can be deployed to construct a sense of belonging that lends to identity building. However, while identity-building projects may help specific groups, the number of projects may undermine peacebuilding efforts (2014). For instance, if multiple international and local identity-construction programs advance different visions of community and belonging, this can slow reconciliation efforts (129).

Another strategy for understanding and applying ethno-symbolism is the concept of large-group psychology surrounding shared trauma and images (Volkan 2013). Here, groups should acknowledge the "time expansion" between more recent events and historical ones through understanding and feeling how such mental representations of traumas have transformed into group identity markers. Through this process, groups may gain insight and empathy for the other in order to promote coexistence. To support this process, Volkan recommends the collaborative development of "concrete actions, programs, legal changes, and institutions" using insight from psychoanalysts and buy-in from diplomats (242–3). In addition to diplomacy and economic incentives, theorists point to the peacebuilding efforts of nongovernmental organizations working to change the attitudes of a population at all levels (Kaufman 2001).

### Government institutions and solutions for ethnic and religious conflict

Unequal distribution of political power and economic resources (i.e., grievances) is one of the potential causes of ethnic conflict. Thus, dealing with these issues is important in order to prevent the recurrence of conflict. Changes to the institutional and governing structures of a country are one potential way to address these various inequalities. In particular, demo-cratic institutions have been cited as important for balancing the interests of various ethnic groups with the interests of state elites (Gurr 2000). Without such considerations, groups will continue to be dissatisfied. Some scholars argue that the decline in ethnic conflict since the mid-1990s is more generally tied to specific government policies of accommodation, specifically providing additional guarantees to minority groups, including decreasing dis-crimination, protecting minority rights, increasing political autonomy, and providing more power-sharing opportunities (Gurr 2000; Cederman et al. 2017). For example, Kurds in Iraq have increasingly received autonomy and the Kurdish Regional Government largely controls the Kurdish portion of Iraq. Such accommodations are useful ways to redress ethnic and religious grievances and help make societies more equal for all groups, thereby decreasing the likelihood of conflict.

Other studies have also found connections between democratic practices and a reduction in ethnic conflict. For example, competitive elections have been associated with a lower likelihood of ethnic conflict, particularly when ethnic groups are large (Cederman, Gleditsch, and Hug 2012). Further, proportional representation has also been linked to a reduction in ethnic violence (Saideman et al. 2002). Consociationalism, which is a democratic form of government where power is shared and divided among various groups, has also been sug-gested as a possible solution to ethnic conflicts. However, consociationalism has not proven to reduce conflict in all divided societies, with some countries, such as Lebanon and Cyprus, having less success with this structure than Belgium (Wolff 2012).

### Separation as a solution to ethnic conflict

While many authors argue that ethnic conflicts can be prevented or managed through a vari-ety of measures, some scholars argue that sometimes ethnic conflicts so shatter societies that states cannot be fully restored to the status quo ante (Kaufmann 1996). Further, ethnic divi-sions often create divisive issues that are difficult to accommodate within the existing state. In particular, symbolic demands of groups are not easily compromised (Horowitz 1985). Instead, such scholars argue for separation of ethnic groups, suggesting that even though ethnic identities may be socially constructed, it may be extremely difficult to reconstruct these identities after a major conflict in a way that prevents conflicts from recurring. Violent conflict often hardens identities, regardless of their origin. In particular, after very intense ethnic conflicts, it becomes difficult for majority groups to guarantee the safety of minority groups. One way to deal with this dilemma is to separate groups into different defensible regions. This separation could be in the form an independent new state like in South Sudan, or could result in an autonomous region, like the Basques in Spain, the Tamils in Sri Lanka, and the Kurds in Iraq.

There are some key critiques of the idea of separation. Logistically, separation can be dif-ficult. Although planned population transfers can be safer than forced migration and refugee problems, when populations are highly intermixed, such separation will likely be exception-ally difficult. Further, separation will not necessarily create peace between groups. In the case of the India-Pakistan partition, for example, an ethnic security dilemma became an international security dilemma between two states – now with nuclear capabilities.

### Role of religion in peace and peacebuilding

While religious differences may help perpetuate conflicts between groups and even states, religion has also been used to peacefully resolve conflict as well as for promoting peacebuilding after conflict. Some religious groups, such as the Quakers, Mennonites, and Church of the Brethren, are known for their peace advocacy. However, peace approaches can be found in other branches of Christianity, Islam, Hinduism, Buddhism, Baha'ism, and other major world religions. Further, individuals, such as Martin Luther King Jr. and Mahatmas Gandhi were known for their faith-inspired nonviolence movements (see Chapter 5 on Non-violence Resistance for more information). Some have noted that religion provides social, moral, and spiritual resources during a peacebuilding process and that religious leaders may often have the moral legitimacy to appeal to populations in conflicts related to religion (Abu-Nimer 2001). Many faith-based humanitarian organizations, such as Islamic Relief World-wide, Christian Aid, and Catholic Relief Services, are key actors in sending humanitarian aid to war-torn places. In many cases, religious organizations may have more legitimacy among local populations than non-religious groups to provide relief and discuss peaceful approaches to resolving conflict.

Further, there are many examples of interfaith movements dealing with conflicts in socie-ties. The Parliament of the World's Religions, created to promote peace and justice in the world and harmony among the world's spiritual communities, first convened in Chicago in 1893. Organizations such as Religions for Peace and the World Council of Churches also have interfaith missions. Interfaith efforts can be found around the globe, including in places with conflicts that have religious dimensions, such as the Israeli-Palestinian conflict. For example, the Interfaith Encounter Association, located in Jerusalem, works to build connec-tions between Jews, Muslims, and Christians. Other interfaith organizations, such as Kid-s4Peace and the Center for Religious Tolerance, are located outside of Israel and Palestine, but are also committed to supporting peace and interfaith connections within Israel and Pal-estine. While religion may be part of the conflict in many places, religion can also be lever-aged in such cases for peace as well.

## Case study of ethnic conflict and conflict management – the Rohingya in Myanmar

The primarily Muslim Rohingya are an ethnic group comprising approximately 1.1 million individuals who inhabited the primarily Buddhist country of Myanmar as early as the eighth or ninth century (Human Rights Watch 2000). Their population speaks Rohingya, an Eastern Indo-Aryan language noticeably different from others spoken in Myanmar, but similar to a Bengali dialect spoken in the southern part of Bangladesh bordering Myanmar. However, activists point to a history of exclusion as crucial for understanding the current genocide happening in Myanmar (International Human Rights Clinic 2015). Between 1824 and 1948 the British colonized the area, forcing many laborers from today's India and Bangladesh into modernday Myanmar, administrating it as an Indian province. Although the British did not think this migration significant, locals viewed the influx of outside laborers negatively. After Myanmar's independence in 1948, the government called the migration illegal and refused citizenship to a majority of Rohingya (HRW 2000). The Union Citizenship Act (UCA) iden-tified which ethnicities had a right to citizenship, excluding the Rohingya (UCA 1948). Ini-tially, the government provided identity cards for those living in the country for at least two generations, including citizenship and representation in parliament.

After the 1962 military coup, the government of Myanmar began requiring citizens to apply for national registration cards and provided fewer and fewer Rohingya with this documentation (Irish Centre for Human Rights 2010). Instead, the government provided Rohingya with foreign identity cards, thereby limiting their access to jobs and educational benefits (HRW 1996). This denial of citizenship escalated in 1982 when a new Citizenship

Law was passed that required individuals to show proof of fluency in one the national languages as well as evidence that their family lived in Myanmar before 1948. Many Rohingya lacked documentation, which left many Rohingya stateless (Albert 2018).

Since the late 1970s, a number of government crackdowns have forced hundreds of thousands of Rohingya in Rakhine State to flee to Bangladesh, Malaysia, Thailand, and other Southeast Asian countries (HRW 1996). According to the Human Rights Watch (HRW), during such forced displacement, refugees reported torture, arson, rape, and murder. When nine border officers were murdered in October 2016, the government claimed the culprits to be an armed Rohingya group (HRW 2016), leading to another security crackdown on the Rohingya severe enough that UN official John McKissick condemned the government for conducting ethnic cleansing (Aljazeera 2016).

In 2017, Myanmar's military launched a campaign of persecution, committing mass killings, rampant arson, and sexual violence in Rakhine, home to the largest Rohingya population. This has led to a mass exodus of over half a million by the Rohingya to the neighboring Bangladesh. The United Nations (UN) called this military offensive "a textbook example of ethnic cleansing" (UN 2017). Myanmar denied this, claiming that their target was Rohingya militants, not civilians. According to the HRW, at least 362 villages have been destroyed since the latest 2017 military campaign against the Rohingya (2018).

According to the United Nations High Commissioner for Refugees (UNHCR), over a million Rohingya have fled Myanmar since the late 1970s, more than 168,000 of them since 2012 (UNHCR 2017a; UN 2018). In addition, more than 650,000 Rohingya have fled to Bangladesh and over 112,000 have fled to Malaysia by boat between 2012 and 2015 (UNHCR 2017b). In November 2017, Bangladesh and Myanmar signed an accord for the return of 650,000 Rohingya refugees (Reuters 2017). Each state agreed to complete a voluntary repatriation in two years. In April 2018, the UNHCR and Bangladesh finalized a Memorandum of Understanding (MOU) regarding the voluntary return of refugees to Myanmar. The MOU stipulates their return only when conditions in Myanmar are conducive, meaning the environment must be safe, dignified, and sustainable (UNHCR 2018). The responsibility of such conditions remains in the hands of Myanmar authorities. Refugees in Bangladesh indicate that before considering return, there should be definitive progress toward their ability to attain legal status and citizenship, security, and access to basic rights (UNHCR 2018). The UNHCR and UN Human Rights Council (HRC) continue to call on Myanmar to take these concrete measures. The HRC's latest report documents human rights abuses in Kachin, Rakhine, and Shan States as well as violations of international humanitarian law and recommends a restructuring of the armed forces, a cessation of unlawful military operations, and a halt to sexual and gender-based violence perpetrated by armed forces (HRC 2018).

### Theoretical application

Ethnicity and religion lie at the core of this ongoing conflict in Myanmar. The Rohingya's contested ethnicity – at least on the part of Myanmar – has caused the latter to categorize the former as the outsider according to Social Identity Theory (SIT). Intergroup comparison occurred with Myanmar's 1948 Union Citizenship Act and 1982 Citizenship Law. This legislation acted to both a) distinguish in-group (ethnicities recognized by Myanmar) from out-group (excluded ethnicities like the Rohingya) and b) designate superiority to the in-group in the form of rights and citizenship. This erupted into out-group hostility in multiple military campaigns against the Rohingya (e.g., 1978, 2016, 2017) that resulted in arson, murder, and rape. Further, the process created clear grievances among the Rohingya by excluding them politically and socially within the country.

In terms of ethno-symbolistic indicators, the cleavage seems to stem from differences in language, religion, and shared history. While such ethnic components are crucial for nation-building, the Rohingya's attributes are deemed foreign. Exacerbating this is the fact that their language is not only different, but of a separate language branch from others in Myanmar. At this point, their persecution has now lasted two generations, which has created a shared history that is separate from the rest of Myanmar. If and when Myanmar repatriates the Rohingya refugees, the government could incorporate Rohingya language into street signs and provide safe locations for prayer. This would show a good faith effort to incorporate the Rohingya into their national identity as well as provide the beginnings of a sustainable path forward.

SIT and contact theory both suggest intergroup cooperation as a possibility to build sustainable relations between groups. While cooperation or a reconceptualization of group categories has yet to be realized, there is hope in the repatriation plan. To demonstrate good will, the UNHCR suggests Myanmar provide the UNHCR and other actors with full access to the refugees' places of origin in Rakhine State, which would allow the latter to assist the Rohingya with updates on their places of origin and assist with their return. The UNHCR also recommends Myanmar ease restrictions on movement of internally displaced individuals, which would help build confidence among refugees in Bangladesh and demonstrate a commitment to a sustainable solution (2018). Such steps could build trust and understanding, which could create a better view of Myanmar officials by the Rohingya. In turn, this might facilitate positive contact experiences between groups. Though it is a distant hope, SIT, ethno-symbolism, and contact theory point to the potential for both groups to unite behind the common goal of restructuring a national identity that is inclusive of the Rohingya. Hopefully, this reframing of the conflict into a shared problem will situate both groups in the mindset to work toward a common goal, one that can leave a lasting legacy. That said, the first step lies in the safe repatriation of the Rohingya refugees.

Further, changing governmental institutions to better incorporate minority rights for the Rohingya and to provide some level or autonomy and/or power-sharing may help alleviate fears among the group. The parliamentary republic has a legislative branch that provides an equal number of representatives elected from Regions and States. Perhaps the government could provide seats to Rohingya so that their population is represented properly from the Regions and States they inhabit. Overall, without changes in governmental policy, the relationship between groups is unlikely to change.

## Challenges and future directions

One of the key challenges regarding ethnic and religious conflicts is that they tend to recur and are often viewed as intractable. The Rwandan case shows that once grievances are present, they become difficult to resolve, particularly when the underlying problems of inequality between groups is not addressed. Another key challenge in dealing with ethnicity and religion is that ethnic and religious identities are particularly salient. This often means that it becomes more difficult to find compromises to situations when people feel their very identities are threatened. In addition, many religious beliefs are considered nonnegotiable by those who hold them, which can lead to problems, particularly if these nonnegotiable beliefs are in conflict with those of another religion. Further, the salience of ethnic and religious identities makes them particularly susceptible to politicization. Ethno-nationalist sentiments and xenophobia increase the likelihood of violence, and recently there has been an increase in these sentiments, particularly in the wake of the movement of refugees throughout the world.

Relatedly, ethnic conflicts also often have "spillover" effects that make such conflicts prone to spread. In addition to the spread of refugees, ethnic divisions in one country may mirror those in a neighboring country. When ethnic conflict erupts in one of these countries, there is an increased likelihood that the conflict will also have implications for neighboring states. The conflict in Rwanda is a good example. Burundi has a similar ethnic composition and colonial history (though different historical power dynamics), and conflicts in one certainly fed and affected conflicts in the other. Similarly, refugees fleeing these conflicts into the Democratic Republic of Congo also created tensions and disrupted power balances between various ethnic groups.

However, while ethnic and religious conflicts are difficult to resolve, there is reason to be hopeful. As mentioned above, evidence suggests that ethnic conflict is actually declining. More importantly, it appears that such declines are linked to government efforts to change policies in the interest of inter-ethnic coexistence. Governments are increasingly expanding regional autonomy, protecting minority rights, providing power-sharing options, and otherwise working to accommodate ethnic minority voices into the structures of the state. While increased nationalism and xenophobia are found in parts of the world, there are also many examples of accommodationist policies that decrease the grievances that might lead to conflict between ethnic and religious groups. Thus, there is reason to remain optimistic about the future of preventing, managing, and transforming ethnic and religious conflicts.

## Questions for further discussion

1   How might increased contact between groups help prevent ethnic conflict? In what ways might this contact approach be unsuccessful?
2   Choose a recent ethnic conflict and discuss how the various causes discussed in the chapter might be applied to that conflict. Which conflict management theories and techniques might be useful in this conflict?
3   What are the pros and cons of separation as a solution to ethnic conflict? What are some current examples of situations where separation might be considered an option? How well would separation work in these examples?
4   In your daily life or on a local level, what examples of ethnic or religious conflict are salient? What approaches might help mitigate such conflict?
5   In what ways might interfaith dialogue be utilized during times of conflict? In what scenarios might religion be useful in peacebuilding efforts?

## Suggested resources

1   United Nations Office on Genocide Prevention and the Responsibility to Protect: www.un.org/en/genocideprevention/about-responsibility-to-protect.html.
2   United States Institute of Peace. "Religious Engagement in Peacebuilding: A USIP Fact Sheet." www.usip.org/publications/2018/05/religious-engagement-peacebuilding.
3   Check out these handbooks related to Ethnic Conflict: Butcher, Charity. 2019. *The Handbook of Cross-border Ethnic and Religious Affinities*. London: Rowman & Littlefield Publishers; Cordell, Karl, and Stefan Wolff. 2016. *The Routledge Handbook of Ethnic Conflict*. Abingdon, OX: Routledge; and Landis, Dan, and Rosita Albert, eds. 2012. *Handbook of Ethnic Conflict*. New York, NY: Springer.

4  The following datasets provide data related to ethnicity around the world: Ethnic Power Relations (EPR) Datasets: https://icr.ethz.ch/data/epr/, PRIO: Ethnic Composition Data: www.prio.org/Data/Economic-and-Socio-Demographic/Ethnic-Composition-Data/, and Minorities at Risk Project: www.mar.umd.edu/.

5  Ethnologue: Languages of the World: www.ethnologue.com/ – a source outlining all current languages found in every country around the world.

6  Council on Foreign Relations: Global Conflict Tracker: www.cfr.org/interactives/global-conflict-tracker#!/global-conflict-tracker.

7  Parliament of the World's Religions: www.parliamentofreligions.org/.

8  Hotel Rwanda (2004) – A film about a hotel manager in Rwanda who helped house Tutsi refugees fleeing from Hutu militia.

## Become engaged!

1  Find an internship on race and ethnicity in your area or volunteer for an organization that promotes ethnic and religious equality in your area.

2  Religions for Peace: https://rfp.org/.

3  Consider engaging with or contributing to religious mediation or interfaith organizations that align with your own beliefs. Examples might include the International Center for Ethno-Religious Mediation (ICERM): www.icermediation.org/, The Interfaith Peace Project: www.interfaithpeaceproject.org/, the Interfaith Peace Initiative: For Peace and Human Rights in Israel-Palestine: www.interfaithpeaceinitiative.com/, or the World Council of Churches: www.oikoumene.org/en.

4  Help your university's Philosophy and Religious Studies department arrange interfaith panels among local religious leaders and religious campus organizations.

5  Think globally and act locally. Attend local civil and human rights activist meetings to expand your knowledge of issues affecting local minority groups. See how you can get involved.

## References and further reading

Abu-Nimer, Mohammed. 2001. "Conflict Resolution, Culture, and Religion: Toward a Training Model of Interreligious Peacebuilding." *Journal of Peace Research* 38 (6): 685–704.

Albert, Eleanor. 2018. "Rohingya Crisis." *Council on Foreign Relations*. Accessed September 22, 2018. www.cfr.org/backgrounder/rohingya-crisis.

*Al Jazeera*. 2016. "Rohingya Face Myanmar 'Ethnic Cleansing': UN Official." Accessed October 29, 2018. www.aljazeera.com/news/2016/11/rohingya-face-myanmar-ethnic-cleansing-official-161125065731036.html.

Allport, Gordon. 1954. *The Nature of Prejudice*. Cambridge, MA: Addison-Wesley Publishing Company.

Armstrong, John A. 1982. *Nations Before Nationalism*. Chapel Hill, NC: University of North Carolina Press.

Aung, Thu, and Yimou Lee. 2017. "Myanmar, Bangladesh ink Rohingya return deal amid concern over army's role." *Reuters*. Accessed October 29, 2018. www.reuters.com/article/us-myanmar-rohingya/myanmar-bangladesh-to-ink-rohingya-return-deal-amid-concern-over-armys-role-idUSKBN1DN0HA.

Bovingdon, Gardner. 2010. *The Uyghurs – Strangers in Their Own Land*. New York, NY: Columbia University Press.

Brewer, Marilynn. 2001. "Ingroup Identification and Intergroup Conflict: When Does Ingroup Love Become Outgroup Hate?" In *Social Identity, Intergroup Conflict, and Conflict Reduction*, edited by Richard Ashmore, Jussim Lee, and David Wilder, 17–41. Oxford: Oxford University Press.

Cederman, Lars-Erik, Kristian Skrede Gleditsch, and Simon Hug. 2012. "Elections and Ethnic Civil War." *Comparative Political Studies* 46 (3): 387–417.

Cederman, Lars-Erik, Kristian Skrede Gleditsch, and Julian Wucherpfennig. 2017. "Predicting the Decline of Ethnic Civil War: Was Gurr Right and for the Right Reasons?" *Journal of Peace Research* 54 (2): 262–74.

Cuhadar, Esra, and Bruce Dayton. 2011. "The Social Psychology of Identity and Inter-group Conflict: From Theory to Practice." *International Studies Perspectives* 12 (3): 273–93.

Cumming-Bruce, Nick. 2019. "China Rebuked by 22 Nations Over Xinjiang Repression." *The New York Times*. Accessed July 14, 2019. www.nytimes.com/2019/07/10/world/asia/china-xinjiang-rights.html.

Demmers, Jolle. 2016. *Theories of Violent Conflict*. Abingdon, OX: Routledge.

Denny, Elaine K. and Barbara F. Walter. 2014. "Ethnicity and Civil War." *Journal of Peace Research* 51 (2): 199–212.

Fearon, James D., and David D. Laitin. 2003. "Ethnicity, Insurgency and Civil War." *American Political Science Review* 97 (1): 75–90.

Gurr, Ted Robert. 1994. "Peoples Against States: Ethnopolitical Conflict and the Changing World System." *International Studies Quarterly* 38 (3): 347–77.

———. 2000. "Ethnic Warfare on the Wane." *Foreign Affairs* 79 (May-June): 52–64.

Hewstone, Miles, Simon Lolliot, Hermann Swart, and Ed Cairns. 2014. "Intergroup Contact and Intergroup Conflict." *Peace and Conflict: Journal of Peace Psychology* 20 (1): 39–53.

Horowitz, Donald. 1985. *Ethnic Groups in Conflict*. Berkeley, CA: University of California Press.

Human Rights Council. 2018. "Report of the Detailed Findings of the Independent International Fact-Finding Mission on Myanmar." *Ohchr.org*. Accessed November 11, 2018. www.ohchr.org/Documents/HRBodies/HRCouncil/FFM-Myanmar/A_HRC_39_CRP.2.pdf.

Human Rights Watch. 1996. "Burma: The Rohingya Muslims: Ending a Cycle of Exodus?" *Hrw.org*. Accessed October 29, 2018. www.hrw.org/reports/pdfs/b/burma/burma969.pdf.

———. 2000. *Hrw.org*. Accessed September 22, 2018. www.hrw.org/reports/2000/burma/burm005-01.htm.

———. 2013. "All You Can Do Is Pray: Crimes against Humanity and Ethnic Cleansing of Rohingya Muslims." *Hrw.org*. Accessed September 22, 2018. www.hrw.org/report/2013/04/22/all-you-can-do-pray/crimes-against-humanity-and-ethnic-cleansing-rohingya-muslims.

———. 2016. "Burma Military Burned Villages in Rakhine State." *Hrw.org*. Accessed October 29, 2018. www.hrw.org/news/2016/12/13/burma-military-burned-villages-rakhine-state.———. 2018. "Burma Scores Rohingya Villages Bulldozed." *Hrw.org*. Accessed October 29, 2018. www.hrw.org/news/2018/02/23/burma-scores-rohingya-villages-bulldozed.

Huntington, Samuel. 1993. "The Clash of Civilizations?" *Foreign Affairs* 72 (3): 22–49.

Irish Centre for Human Rights. 2010. "Crimes Against Humanity in Western Burma: The Situation of the Rohingyas." Accessed October 29, 2018. http://burmaactionireland.org/images/uploads/ICHR_Rohingya_Report_2010.pdf.

Jenkins, Richard. 2008. *Social Identity*, 3rd edition. London: Routledge.

Kaldor, Mary. 1999. *New and Old Wars: Organized Violence in a Global Era*. Stanford, CA: Stanford University Press.

Kaufman, Stuart J. 2001. *Modern Hatreds: The Symbolic Politics of Ethnic War*. Ithaca, NY: Cornell University Press.

Kaufmann, Chaim. 1996. "Possible and Impossible Solutions to Ethnic Civil Wars." *International Security* 20 (3): 136–75.

Kelman, Herbert C. 1987. "The Political Psychology of the Israeli-Palestinian Conflict: How Can We Overcome the Barriers to a Negotiated Solution?" *Political Psychology* 8: 347–63.

Kelman, Herbert C. 1992. "Acknowledging the Other's Nationhood: How to Create a Momentum for the Israeli-Palestinian Negotiations." *Journal of Palestine Studies* 22 (1): 18–38.

Keranen, Outi. 2014. "Building States and Identities in Post-Conflict States: Symbolic Practices in Post-Dayton Bosnia." *Civil Wars* 16 (2): 127–46.

Lake, David A., and Donald Rothchild. 1996. "Containing Fear: The Origins and Management of Ethnic Conflict." *International Security* 22 (2): 41–75.

Maizland, Lindsay. 2019. "China's Crackdown on Uighurs in Xinjiang." *Council on Foreign Relations*. Accessed July 13, 2019. www.cfr.org/backgrounder/chinas-crackdown-uighurs-xinjiang.

Montville, Joseph. 1991. "Psychoanalytic Enlightenment and the Greening of Diplomacy." In *The Psychodynamics of International Relationships*, edited by Vamik Volkan, Joseph Montville, and D.A. Julius, 177–92. Lexington, MA: Lexington Books.

Ojea Quintana, Tomás. 2010. "Progress Report of the Special Rapporteur on the Situation of Human Rights in Myanmar, U.N. Doc No. A/HRC/13/48." U.N. Human Rights Council. Accessed October 29, 2018. http://www2.ohchr.org/english/bodies/hrcouncil/docs/13session/A-HRC-13-48.pdf.

Pettigrew, Thomas F. 1998. "Intergroup Contact Theory." *Annual Review of Psychology* 49 (1): 65–85.

Ross, Marc. 2001. "Psychocultural Interpretations and Dramas: Identity Dynamics in Ethnic Conflict." *Political Psychology* 22 (1): 157–78.

Saideman, Stephen M., David J. Lanoue, Michael Campenni, and Samuel Stanton. 2002. "Democratization, Political Institutions, and Ethnic Conflict: A Pooled Time-Series Analysis, 1985–1998." *Comparative Political Studies* 35 (1): 103–29.

Smith, Anthony D. 1986. *The Ethnic Origins of Nations*. Oxford: Basil Blackwell.

Special Correspondent. 2018. "A Summer Vacation in China's Muslim Gulag." *Foreign Policy*. Accessed July 13, 2019. https://foreignpolicy.com/2018/02/28/a-summer-vacation-in-chinas-muslim-gulag/.

Sudworth, John. 2018. "China's hidden camps." *BBC News*. Accessed July 13, 2019. www.bbc.co.uk/news/resources/idt-sh/China_hidden_camps.

Sumner, William G. 1906. *Folkways and Mores*. New York, NY: Schocken Books.

Tajfel, Henri. 1978. *Differentiation Between Social Groups: Studies in the Social Psychology of Intergroup Relations*. London: Academic Press.

———. 1981. *Human Groups and Social Categories*. Cambridge: Cambridge University Press.

Tajfel, Henri, and John Turner. 1986. "The Social Identity Theory of Intergroup Behavior." In *Psychology of Intergroup Relations*, edited by Stephen Worchel and William Austin, 276–93. Chicago, IL: Nelson-Hall.

Tausch, Nicole, and Miles Hewstone. 2010. "Intergroup Contact and Prejudice." In *The Sage Handbook of Prejudice, Stereotyping, and Discrimination*, edited by J.F. Dovidio, M. Hewstone, P. Glick, & V.M. Esses, 544–60. Newburg Park, CA: Sage Publications.

Toft, Monica Duffy. 2003. *The Geography of Ethnic Violence*. Princeton, NJ: Princeton University Press.

UNHCR. 2017a. "Rohingya Likely Fled Myanmar Since 2012." *Unhcr.org*. Accessed October 29, 2018. www.unhcr.org/news/latest/2017/5/590990ff4/168000-rohingya-likely-fled-myanmar-since-2012-unhcr-report.html.

———. 2017b. "UNHCR Distributes Aid to Rohingya Refugees Ahead of Bangladesh Winter." *Unhcr.org*. Accessed October 29, 2018. www.unhcr.org/en-us/news/briefing/2017/12/5a3399624/unhcr-distributes-aid-rohingya-refugees-ahead-bangladesh-winter.html.

———. 2018. "Bangladesh and UNHCR Agree on Voluntary Returns Framework for When Refugees Decide Conditions Are Right." *Unhcr.org*. Accessed October 29, 2018. www.unhcr.org/en-us/news/press/2018/4/5ad061d54/bangladesh-unhcr-agree-voluntary-returns-framework-refugees-decide-conditions.html.

Union Citizenship Act. 1948. Accessed October 29, 2018. www.ibiblio.org/obl/docs/UNION_CITIZENSHIP_ACT-1948.htm.

United Nations. 2017. *News.un.org*. Accessed September 22, 2018. https://news.un.org/en/story/2017/09/564622-un-human-rights-chief-points-textbook-example-ethnic-cleansing-myanmar.

Volkan, Vamik. 1988. *The Need to Have Enemies and Allies: From Clinical Practice to International Relationships*. New York, NY: Aronson.

———. 1997. *Bloodlines: From Ethnic Pride to Ethnic Terrorism*. New York, NY: Farrar Straus Giroux.

———. 2013. "Large-Group-Psychology in Its Own Right: Large-Group Identity and Peace-making." *International Journal of Applied Psychoanalytic Studies* 10 (3): 210–46.

Wolff, Stefan. 2012. "Consociationalism: Power Sharing and Self-Governance." In *Conflict Management in Divided Societies: Theories and Practice*, edited by Stefan Wolff and Christalla Yakinthou, 23–56. London: Routledge.

Yale Law School International Human Rights Clinic. 2015. *Fortify Rights*. Accessed October 29, 2018. www.fortifyrights.org/downloads/Yale_Persecution_of_the_Rohingya_October_2015.pdf.

# 14 Economic issues in international conflict management

*Marcus Marktanner, Almuth D. Merkel, and Luc Noiset*

## A brief history of international conflict arising out of economic thought

It has been evident to economists since at least World War II that competitive and equal opportunity market systems both within and across nations are a necessary condition for sustained peace and development. Since World War II many countries have experienced an unprecedented period of peace in large part because of the interwoven free-markets that connect the prosperity of one to the prosperity of the other. The evolution of the economic paradigm of the modern developed world can be traced through three important historical periods. The first is the mercantilist period, from the sixteenth through the eighteenth centuries. The second is the laissez-faire capitalism period from the late 1800's to the early 1900's. The third is the retreat from laissez-faire capitalism, which took place during the inter-war period, roughly 1919 to 1939. In each of these periods, there occurred economic failings that, each in their own way, contributed to the international conflicts of the day (Cameron 1993; Di Vittorio 2006; Clark 2008). This chapter highlights the lessons learned from the sixteenth century to modern times, and in doing so argues that the competitive and equal-opportunity market mechanism, tempered by the social-market economy ideals of equitable access to market opportunities, can provide a peacebuilding formula to help today's conflict-prone regions of the world to flourish, as have Europe, North America, Japan, and the rest of the developed world since the end of World War II.

## Mercantilism

The mercantilist ideology asserts that trade between countries is a zero-sum game, meaning that the gain of one country occurs at the expense of another, an ideology that economists now know is incorrect, but which, nevertheless, continues to be promoted by modern day politicians. According to mercantilist thinking, countries should focus on producing goods for export and should import as little as possible. Yet, importing goods or services at a lower cost than they can be produced domestically can only benefit an economy. Moreover, when all countries work to expand exports and block imports, they are working against each other, and mercantilism becomes a formula for international conflict.

Two prominent advocates of mercantilism were Oliver Cromwell (1559–1658) and Jean Baptiste Colbert (1619–1683). Oliver Cromwell was responsible for England's 1651 Navigation Acts, which restricted shipping services related to commerce with England. England was a global hegemon with lucrative colonies around the world. Before the Navigation Acts, other countries could provide shipping services between England and its colonies. The Netherlands was one such country. The Dutch had a considerable fleet and their own colonies in the Caribbean and the Dutch East Indies (modern-day Indonesia). The Navigation Acts, however, mandated that all trade activities between England and her colonies needed to be administered by English shipping, since the overall objective of English mercantilism was to capture as much of the profit of trade as possible. This economic attack on the interests of the Dutch led to a series of Dutch-Anglo wars during the seventeenth and eighteenth centuries (Di Vittorio 2006; Jones 2013).

Jean Baptiste Colbert summarized the ingredients for a "successful" mercantilist strategy in three principles: trade coercion, military superiority, and agricultural self-sufficiency (Colbert 1882). Mercantilist thinkers knew about the inherent international conflict potential of colonial exploitation. Thus, it was clear that a mercantilist strategy was only sustainable as long as it was backed by a strong military. Agricultural self-sufficiency was required to prevent food dependencies on other countries in times of conflict. The fact that, to this day, most industrialized countries protect their agricultural sectors can be seen as a remnant of mercantilism, which in more recent history has led to substantial agricultural trade-related tensions between developed and developing countries.

## The first modern globalization wave (1870–1914)

The first modern wave of globalization was facilitated by the secular political liberalization of the late nineteenth century, first in England and then in continental Europe. Political liberalization, in turn, facilitated economic freedom, such as private business ownership and labor mobility, which led to the industrial revolution. By this time, many former colonies had gained their independence. The former colonial trade coercion of the mercantilist era was now turned into voluntary trade relationships. The northern hemisphere specialized in the production of capital-intensive manufactured goods, and the southern hemisphere specialized in the production of land-intensive agricultural goods. Trade between the North and the South began to flourish, and international trade no longer appeared to be a zero-sum game, but instead a positive sum, "win-win," relationship (Collier and Dollar 2002). There were, of course, winners and losers within each country, but as a whole, the world was becoming more prosperous, and the lives of many were improving.

Although trade became a major driver of international economic relations and the world economies were becoming interdependent, the benefits from trade did not substantially trickle down to the working citizens of trading partners. Industrialists largely benefitted from trade in the northern hemisphere while landowners largely benefitted in the Global South. Workers did not generally benefit as much from this first modern globalization wave. This led to an increase in income inequality between industrialists and workers in the North and between landowners and workers in the South.

In search for better living conditions, many Europeans migrated to the United States, Canada, Australia, and New Zealand. The exodus of some 60 million Europeans escaping hardship between 1870 and 1914 increased Europe's labor scarcity. The loss of workers migrating abroad empowered remaining workers and forced European politicians to consider social and economic reforms. The introduction of social safety nets and land reforms in Europe can be traced back to this period (Palier 2010). Workers' living conditions in Europe began to improve and the distribution of income became more equal. In Latin America and Africa, landless peasants faced greater economic and cultural barriers to migrate north. Migration in the Global South was largely domestic, from rural to urban areas, which is one of the reasons why there are relatively larger cities in the Global South, particularly in Latin America, and greater urban poverty in general (Beattie 2009). With fewer opportunities to migrate, workers were less empowered to spur social and economic reforms, and the distribution of income and wealth in the South remained more unequal than in the Global North.

As the first modern globalization wave proceeded, the industrializing Global North was put on a firm path that led to Europe's social-welfare states and public policy debates around a political center that sanctioned a more equitable sharing of the fruits of economic prosperity. The Global South, with its greater focus on agriculture, was set on a path of greater domestic socioeconomic tensions and politics between the extreme right, which tended to protect the landowners, and the extreme left, which called for land redistributions.

These different political configurations between the North and South also led to international conflicts. When left-leaning policies gained the upper hand in the South and attempted to carry out land redistribution policies, this was often detrimental to the economic interests of the North, which profitably traded with the landowners in the South. In the Western Hemisphere, for example, the United States was already establishing itself as a regional hegemon with the Monroe Doctrine of 1823, which, in effect, claimed all of Latin America as within the US sphere of influence. In Honduras, Nicaragua, and many other places in Central America and the Caribbean, American commercial interests such as the United Fruit Company motivated the American government to use its military might to maintain peace and stability for the benefit of the commercial interests. The phrases *Banana Wars* and *Banana Republic* were coined to cast dispersions on these activities of the American government in concert with the Central American governments of the early 1900s.

Another important example of America's economic interests leading to conflicts over land in the South is the intervention by the US in support of Panama's separation from Colombia in 1903, thereby securing the land for the Panama Canal Zone (McPherson 2016). The Panama Canal was needed to advance the global trade ambitions of the United States, and the Panama Canal Zone itself ultimately became sovereign territory of the United States and stayed that way until a treaty to transfer control was signed in 1977, with formal transfer occurring in December 1999.

## The interwar period – retreat from laissez-faire capitalism

After World War I, Europe was economically and morally weakened and politically divided. The United States was economically and morally strengthened and politically unified (Galbraith 2009). The United States enjoyed the roaring 1920s, while Europe fell into an economic depression. This was particularly true for Germany, which was burdened by the reparation payments mandated by the Treaty of Versailles after World War I. Reparation payments took away the vast majority of the government's tax revenue and prevented the government from providing basic government services. The German government resorted to printing money to finance government spending, resulting in the German hyperinflation of 1923, which decimated the German economy even more. After Germany's economy hit rock bottom, international aid entered to ease the unsustainable burden of reparation payments (Dawes Plan), but as Germany was beginning to recover, the 1929 stock market crash and Great Depression brought back the specter of economic hardship and misery. The German people were left morally and psychologically crushed and vulnerable to nationalistic and xenophobic ideology (Borchardt 1991).

After the 1929 stock market crash, countries around the world slid into recession, and unemployment was rampant. To fight unemployment many countries retreated from international trade and globalization and instead pursued nationalistic policies that resembled a return to mercantilism. Tariffs were increased to reduce imported goods in the hope that domestic production would replace imports and create new domestic jobs. As countries became more protectionist, exports to other countries decreased throughout the world and jobs that were created to replace imports were lost in the sectors that had been exporting. Protectionist policies did not create more jobs, but all countries lost the gains from trade and specialization that they had begun to enjoy earlier in the century (Madsen 2001; Friedman and Schwartz 2008).

The Great Depression led to a questioning of the efficiency of free markets and the capitalist model of worldwide economic growth and prosperity. The distrust of international capitalism and a return to mercantilist thinking led to the portrayal of other countries as enemies and helped alternative, misguided political ideologies such as fascism and totalitarianism gain popular acceptance. The Nazis rose to power in Germany, leading to one of history's most horrific crimes against humanity, the Holocaust, and ultimately another devastating world war. Likewise, Stalinism led to devastating socialist doctrines in Russia and surrounding countries. These extreme political ideologies, born out of economic misery and hardship, led to government interventions that eschewed free-market incentives and principles, leading to the destruction of livelihoods and the starvation of millions of people. The Soviet Union's annexation of the Ukraine and China's experiment with its Cultural Revolution, for example, led to two of the most severe famines and human rights violations ever recorded (Snyder 2011).

### The post-war economic reforms

After suffering through the ravages of World War II, leaders of the world, especially in Europe, dedicated themselves to the task of establishing an international economic order built on the humanist principles of freedom, equal opportunity, and solidarity, and positioned on top of the fundamental foundations of competitive free-market economics. This vision called for all countries to have equal access to the markets of other countries. To create a complementary international infrastructure, several international treaties were established. These included the General Agreement on Tariffs and Trade (GATT), which evolved into the World Trade Organization (WTO), the International Bank for Reconstruction and Development (the World Bank), the International Monetary Fund (IMF), the International Labor Organization (ILO), and many others.

### The competitive market as a foundational mechanism for international peace and stability

In the organization of competitive market economies, economists see both a mechanism for the efficient allocation of scarce resources and the foundation of a peacebuilding formula. The economist's classic model of perfect competition is an economic structure that requires the following conditions: The economy contains many markets and each market structure is atomistic, meaning that all economic actors on both the demand and the supply side face so much competition that no individual actor has power to manipulate prices. In other words, each economic actor, whether buyer or seller, is but a tiny, insignificant part of the market in which it participates. There can be no monopolies, cartels, or dominant businesses within a market. Each actor, whether producer or consumer, is a price-taker – one who accepts prices as they are and manages a consumption or production plan in accordance with those prices. The invisible hand of the market generates the price that emerges for any good. In a perfectly competitive market, each consumer has a price she is willing to pay for a certain good or service, and each producer knows the price which she is willing to accept to sell the good or service. The invisible hand of the market matches consumers and producers until no consumer is left whose willingness to pay exceeds the price required by producers to cover costs of production. The market has cleared and is said to be in equilibrium when the amount supplied per period by producers is equal to the amount demanded per period by consumers (Smith 1987, 2010; Marshall 2009; Samuelson 1948).

In a world of perfectly competitive markets, the potential for economic conflict is eliminated. The reason for this is that there is no advantage to be achieved in one business over another. All participants are doing the best they can and if they want to do another activity, they are not restricted from doing so. In the real world it is often restrictions or barriers to take part in a particular economic activity that allow the few in that activity to make abnormally high profits and motivate outsiders to try to break the rules to acquire some of those profits for themselves. In other words, it is the deviations from the perfectly competitive model that are the sources of economic conflict in the real world.

History has seen episodes when the economic system was closer to the ideal of perfect competition and periods when it was further away from this ideal. In the United States, for example, the early days of independence until the end of the nineteenth century were characterized by relatively high levels of competition, before after the mid nineteenth century trusts emerged that undermined the perfectly competitive ideal. Fortunately, the United States was able to correct some of these anticompetitive developments through antitrust legislation and competition policy, such as the Sherman Act of 1890. Very often, however, governments fail to prevent competition from killing competition, which then sows the seeds for conflicts among economic producers and between consumers and producers. Thus, the better policymakers understand the peacemaking potential of competitive markets and the closer the world can move toward the competitive, free-market, equal opportunity paradigm, the less room there will be for economic conflict. Once in place, of course, a competitive free-market system also requires institutions, such as anti-monopoly agencies that level the playing field and protect competitive markets from anticompetitive forces.

Whenever firms gain the ability to manipulate prices (called "market power" by economists), they can generate abnormally high profits. In perfect competition, abnormally high profits do not exist, in the sense that each producer is earning the same as every other producer both within an industry and even across industries. When firms have no market power, they also have no political power to thwart competition and amass profits.

International conflicts also often result when multinational firms use their market power to influence political decisions in countries where the rule of law is weak. Multinational companies might bribe governments to get special treatment, for example. Such special treatment may include requests that governments exempt multinational companies from liability to compensate citizens for damages to the environment. Multinational companies may also lobby against the introduction of social standards or the opening of markets, keeping potential competitors out even when such policies would benefit the population. Therefore, when international market power meets weak political institutions, conflict and political violence are often preprogrammed into the relationships (Grossman and Helpman 1994; Shaffer 1996).

One long-existing example of this type of relationship is the controversial Freeport-McMoRan mining operation in the Papua province of Indonesia, where for decades the company has been dumping mine waste into the Ajkwa River system. The local population there has little political clout with the central government thousands of miles away across the archipelago in Jakarta, but has been demanding for decades, to no avail, that the company stop polluting their homeland and disrupting their communities. The company pays hundreds of millions of dollars per year to the government for the right to mine in the area and appears to have the central government on its side.

The potential for national and international conflict is less likely in competitive, equal-opportunity economies because competition both in national and international markets provides the best solution to societies' production and resource use problems, while at the same time giving full sovereignty to consumers and producers. All economic actors are doing what they want to do, and if they would like to do something different or even something that someone else is doing, they are perfectly free to do so. Casual observation suggests this conclusion, when one notes the relative stability of competitive modern market economies such as in North America, Europe, and Japan, as compared to countries such as Venezuela and the former Soviet Union countries that have yet to fully adopt market-based reforms.

The subsequent sections argue that the economic issues that are the sources of conflict are usually the result of an economic order that falls short of the perfectly competitive model, and that these sources of conflict can be eliminated, or at least greatly diminished, with policies that help move a society closer to a perfectly competitive, free-market paradigm.

## Competitive markets as an international conflict management mechanism

Economists use simple graphical models to highlight core concepts that are generalizable to human interactions across the world stage. Three elementary tools are particularly useful to help make the general case that competitive free markets tend to diminish opportunities for conflict and promote peaceful development. These are Economic Welfare Analysis, Comparative Cost Advantage, and the Prisoner's Dilemma.

### Economic welfare analysis

In perfect competition, all economic actors enjoy costless entry into and exit out of any industry. This implies that there is equal opportunity and the absence of market power. This is true because if there are profits to be made that are higher than elsewhere, firms will enter until profits are the same everywhere, and if there are losses firms will exit. In this way, abnormally profitable or powerful firms will never exist.

A perfectly competitive market can be described with demand and supply diagrams. Imagine that demand is a lineup of consumers according to their willingness to pay from highest to lowest. In Figure 1, there are six consumers labeled "A" to "F." Consumer "A" is willing to pay $9 for the good, "B" is willing to pay $8, and so on. The supply is a lineup of producers according to their willingness to sell from lowest to highest accepted selling price. In Figure 14.1, there are six suppliers labeled "a" to "f." Supplier "a" has a reservation selling price of $3, "b" has a reservation selling price of $4, and so on. In a free market, exactly four units will be sold at a "market-clearing" price of $6.

The important thing to note is that consumers "A," "B," and "C" were each willing to pay more than $6, and producers "a," "b," and "c" were each willing to accept less than $6, but the price is $6 for all in a free market. Consumer "A" was willing to pay $9 but only pays $6, so she enjoys what economists call a "consumer surplus" of $3. Consumers "B" and "C" enjoy a consumer surplus of $2 and $1 respectively, whereas consumer "D" just breaks even. Consumers "E" and "F" will not be participating in this market because their willingness to pay is less than $6.

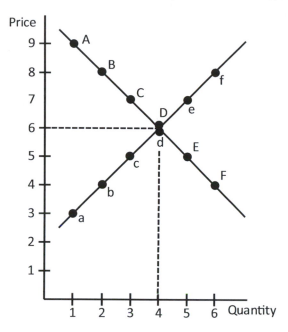

*Figure 14.1* Perfectly Competitive Equilibrium

Likewise, "producer surplus" is calculated as the difference between the $6 market price and what the producer was willing to accept. Producers "a," "b," and "c" receive producer surplus of $3, $2, and $1 respectively, whereas producer "d" breaks even. Producers "e" and "f" will not participate in this market because their reservation selling price is higher than $6. Adding up the total consumer and producer surplus sums to a "total surplus" of $12 for this market.

Next, assume that producers "a" and "b" have political clout to prevent producers "c" and "d" from competing in this market. Producers "a" and "b" supply only two units and are able to sell these two units at a clearing price of $8. In this situation, consumer surplus would equal $1 since consumer "A" is willing to pay $9 and consumer "B" breaks even. Total producer surplus is now $9, since producer "a" was willing to accept $3, but gets $8 and producer "b" was willing to accept $4 and also gets $8. Total surplus in the market is reduced from $12 to $10, which economists call a "loss of economic welfare" or "deadweight loss." At the same time two market participants "a" and "b" are made better off at the expense of all the other market participants, including consumers and the other producers.

A distortion of competition occurred when producers "c" and "d" were cut out of the market and producers "a" and "b" remained. When this occurs, corruption, criminal activity, conflict, and violence tend to follow as the powerful devote efforts to capturing high profits and the losing interests, like firms "c" and "d," fight to take it back from them. This tendency toward conflict occurs simply because of a disruption of the competitive order in free and open equal-opportunity markets. It is the responsibility of government to ensure that there are no such restrictions on free-market competition, but sadly it is often government, manipulated by special interests, such as firms "a" and "b," that interferes in markets by imposing restrictions on free and open competition.

### The theory of comparative cost advantage

The theory of comparative cost advantage is the foundation of the economic liberal peace theory, which suggests that countries that trade with one another do not tend to engage in conflict with each other (Kant 1996; MacMillan 1998).

The reason for this is best illustrated with an example. Consider two countries, Pattyland and Bunland. Pattyland has three workers, and each worker can produce either two beef patties or one bun. Bunland has nine workers, and each worker can produce either one patty or two buns. Consumers in each country only consume hamburgers, meaning that patties and buns should be produced in equal numbers, since an overproduction of either will just go to waste.

Figure 2 illustrates graphically Pattyland's and Bunland's production possibility frontiers (PPF) resulting from all possible allocations of workers towards the production of patties or buns. Bunland is able to produce 9 patties or 18 buns or some combination of the two along its PPF. Pattyland is able to produce 6 patties or 3 buns or some combination of the two along its own PPF. Suppose that when the two countries don't trade, Pattyland chooses to produce (and consume) 2 hamburgers and Bunland chooses to produce (and consume) 6 hamburgers (Points A and B respectively).

Notice, however, that in Pattyland the production of a bun requires the foregoing of two patties, while in Bunland the production of a bun requires foregoing only one half of a patty. Alternatively, one could say that a patty costs Pattyland one half of a bun but costs Bunland two buns. Now imagine that the two countries agree to trade as follows: Pattyland produces six patties and zero buns (Point C), while Bunland produces four patties and ten buns (Point D). This increases the two countries' total hamburger production from eight to ten. If the two countries now agree that each country will consume one extra hamburger, Pattyland and

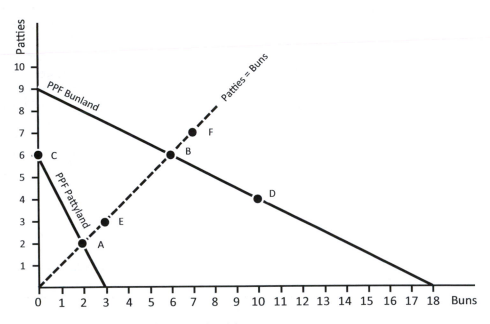

*Figure 14.2* The Theory of Comparative Advantage

Bunland can consume three and seven hamburgers (respectively Points E and F), one more each than in the case where they did not trade. To achieve this, note that Pattyland would need only to trade three patties in exchange for three buns from Bunland. The key point here is that both countries are better off when they have a friendly economic relationship and agree to trade with each other. If they were to get into a conflict and stop trading, they would both be worse off. This simple example highlights the key economic foundation of the liberal peace theory: Free and open trade creates gains for all, which tends to serve as deterrent to international conflict (Ricardo 1891).

### Prisoner's Dilemma

The final tool, the Prisoner's Dilemma (introduced in Chapter 3), can be used to illustrate why a decision to restrict trade might seem individually beneficial but can lead to a collective "rationality trap," in which all parties are looking after their own interests but collaboration and cooperation would have been better for all. Table 14.1 shows a non-cooperative game between two countries, A and B. In this example, each country has two strategies available, either to impose or not impose a tariff. There are thus four possible combinations. The pay-offs for each combination of actions are shown in the cells, with the first payoff in each cell belonging to Country A and the second to Country B.

If Country A thinks that Country B will impose a tariff, Country A's best strategy is also to impose a tariff, since -1 is better than -2. If Country A thinks that Country B will not impose a tariff, then Country A's best strategy is again to impose a tariff, since +2 is greater than +1. Imposing a tariff is what economists call a "dominant strategy" for Country A because it is the best thing to do no matter what country B does. The game is symmetric, so it is easy to see that Country B also has a dominant strategy to impose a tariff. The solution of this game (a so-called Nash equilibrium) is that both countries impose tariffs and live with -1, -1 pay-offs. The payoff is higher for a country when it imposes a tariff and the other one does not because this allows the country to replace imports by domestic production and employment without losing employment in the export sector. Similarly, the payoff is lowest when a country keeps its own markets open but the other country imposes a tariff.

A more careful inspection of the diagram, however, indicates that both countries would be better off if they would cooperate and commit to a no-tariff relationship. In this case, the payoffs are +1 and +1. The previous solution, the Nash equilibrium, occurs when countries try to improve their own well-being at the expense of other countries. This can obviously lead to a buildup of international hostilities. The Prisoner's Dilemma highlights the importance of economically informed policy for international peace and development. Countries that fail to communicate or have insufficient economic knowledge are more likely to fall into an international destabilizing Prisoner's Dilemma. As the benefits of international trade and

*Table 14.1* Prisoner's Dilemma – Tariffs

|  |  | *Country B* | |
| --- | --- | --- | --- |
|  |  | *Impose Tariff* | *Not Impose Tariff* |
| Country A | Impose tariff | −1, −1 | +2, −2 |
|  | Not impose tariff | −2, +2 | +1, +1 |

economic relationships are recognized and understood, countries open up their borders and markets to participants from other countries. These economic relationships inevitably lead to cultural exchanges, partnerships, and a buildup of trust that help to establish widespread economic prosperity and a long-lasting peace.

---

**Textbox 14.1   The social market economy as Europe's post-World War II peacebuilding formula**

After World War II, Europe needed to overcome the legacy of conflict between Germany and its neighbors. A concern was that Germany would again become a threat to worldwide peace and stability. As opposed to the isolationist policy imposed on Germany by the Treaty of Versailles after World War I, which failed to prevent Germany from again becoming a threat, post-World War II European leaders saw establishing a common market as the solution for restoring lasting peace with Germany. This process began with the 1951 Treaty of Paris that created the European Community for Steel and Coal (ECSC), which were the markets most relevant to the military sector. The ECSC was as much a means to promote economic integration among the signatory states as it was a means to monitor Germany's commitment to peace and stability in Europe. The fast success of the ECSC in building trust between Germany and its neighbors was then quickly expanded to the creation of the European Economic Community, established by the 1957 Treaty of Rome. Since then, Europe has become ever more integrated. The preliminary climax of this integration process is the 2007 Treaty of Lisbon, which transformed the European Economic and Monetary Community into a political union, known today simply as the European Union (EU). This treaty also defined the Social Market Economy as Europe's economic vehicle to support peace and the well-being of the Europeans. After World War II, the EU has almost exclusively been free from armed international conflicts. Without the economic dividends associated with the establishment of a European competitive market system, the peace dividend that Europe has enjoyed would have been barely imaginable. The establishment of a competitive common market has generated gains from specialization and trade, access to larger markets, and harmonized and transparent rules and regulations. In light of the tremendous economic benefits resulting from Europe's competitive economic integration process, the incentives to resort to armed hostilities have been dramatically reduced.

---

## Pillars of a social-market economic peacebuilding formula

The Social Market Economy model combines the principles of competitive free-market capitalist systems with equitable social development as a peacebuilding formula. It is an economic philosophy that distinguishes itself from pure laissez-faire capitalism and socialism in three areas: the principle of the socially conscious human, a thoughtful concept of justice, and a clearly outlined role of the state (Müller-Armack 1956; Glossner 2010).

## The socially conscious human

In the classic laissez-faire capitalism model, the human being is assumed to be guided by pure self-interest. In the socialist model, solidarity and brotherhood characterize the ideal human. Both of these taken too far will lead to violence. Under laissez-faire capitalism, a shock or imbalance can lead to uprisings among those who suffer economically. Under socialism, the state will have to repress those who seek to advance their own economic status above that of their fellow citizens. Social Market economists view individuals as characterized by both self-interest and solidarity. As explained by Wilhelm Röpke (1960, 91):

> [T]he market economy is not everything. It must find its place in a higher order of things which is not ruled by supply and demand, free prices, and competition. It must be firmly contained within an all-embracing order of society in which the imperfections and harshness of economic freedom are corrected by law and in which man is not denied conditions of life appropriate to his nature. Man can wholly fulfill his nature only by freely becoming part of a community and having a sense of solidarity with it. Otherwise he leads a miserable existence and he knows it.

Social market economists assume that people assign a weight to both self-interest and solidarity, with the self-interest's weight being greater than solidarity's. The implication of this understanding of the human nature calls for a market economy in which people can pursue their self-interest, but also for a government that assures each individual a level playing field and a social safety net whenever vulnerable persons have exhausted their means to help themselves (Röpke 1960).

This notion of the socially conscious human is more than just an intellectual construct. It is in fact strongly supported by psychological and experimental economic research. In so-called ultimatum games, for example, individuals have an opportunity to split a sum of money in a number of different ways, including keeping all the money for themselves. Numerous repeated experiments have demonstrated that humans across cultures treat themselves best, but also have varied emotions that motivate them to share with others (Oosterbeek, Sloof, and De Kuilen 2004). These emotions include sympathy, social responsibility, and solidarity, and the findings suggest that human beings are not only guided by self-interest, but do have a strong social impulse. The lessons from such experiments are that an economy that either restrains self-interest too much or creates too wide a gap between the haves and the have nots, will likely be rejected by its populace, leading to tension, conflict, and ultimately violence.

## The concept of justice

Justice systems generally involve three interdependent concepts: (1) efficiency justice, (2) distributive justice, and (3) equal opportunity justice. Efficiency justice means that those who choose to contribute to the production of a pie deserve a slice of pie equal to their productive contribution. Distributive justice means that everybody gets their fair share, but this can mean anything from everybody gets an equal slice (as for example in pure communism) to everybody gets at least some pie and some people deserve to get more than others. Equal opportunity justice means that everyone has the same opportunity to contribute to the making of the pie.

Pure laissez-faire thinkers and social-market economists believe strongly in efficiency justice, but tempered differently by equal opportunity justice. Pure laissez-faire thinkers tend to view equal opportunity as eventually arising as a natural outcome of socio-economic forces. The free market will ultimately provide every economic actor with the same opportunities, so any final distribution of income must therefore reflect people's free choices about how to react to those opportunities. Under laissez-faire capitalism, the distribution of income may be unequal, but it is always just.

Social-market economists place greater weight on the possibility that opportunities to access market success are not equally distributed. Equal opportunity justice is not a natural state, but it is possible in a market system. Social-market economists are particularly concerned with the acquisition of market-access capabilities, such as health, education, and financial services. Government can create equal opportunity justice, and once this is accomplished, efficiency justice leads to distributive justice because all differences in income are due to free choice.

### The role of the state

From the previous discussion it is clear that the role of the state differs under socialism, laissez-faire capitalism, and social market economics. Laissez-faire capitalism has been derisively accused of advocating a "night-watchman state" (Von Mises 1991) that merely protects property rights. Socialism abolishes private property and manages peoples' lives through a "central-planner state" (Engels 1999, 66, referring to the work of Henri de Saint-Simon 1770–1825; Marx and Engels 2008, 35). As alluded to earlier, both of these models of the state tend to lead to violent conflict: the first because of the harsh vicissitudes of the market, and the second because it conflicts with the natural human desire for individual economic freedom.

The social market economy state is an enabler and referee. It is concerned with the removal of barriers for the individual acquisition of market-access capabilities. The objective of public investments into the promotion of individual market-access capabilities is not to create a welfare state, but to prevent one (Beattie 2009; De Soto 2000). As referee, the state does not participate in the game, but lays down the order and the rules of the game (Erhard 1958, 102). In other words, the social market economy state is not an economic actor, but an institution that is responsible for maintaining a competitive and equitable economic order. A social safety net is essential and a system of equal economic opportunity for all is needed to promote peaceful coexistence among all members of society.

## Challenges and future directions

A first economic challenge for international conflict management involves correcting inequitable development. Developing perfectly competitive markets alone is not necessarily a safeguard against the emergence of national and international conflict. The importance of social safety nets in combination with a competitive international market economic order has become particularly apparent in the context of the transformation process from a central planner to a market economy. This was a process of transforming an entire labor force from an inefficient state sector into an efficient private sector. Yet, because during the transformation process inefficient workers in the state sector are laid off faster than they can be absorbed by an efficient private sector, the popular frustration potential steadily increases.

The failure of providing the temporary losers from the transformation process with sufficient social safety nets can then lead to an economic reform blockade, or even a reversal. A blockade or reversal of economic reforms can also bring back new international hostilities. Countries that fail to successfully manage their economies often try to distract from their economic problems by engaging in armed international conflict adventurism, leading to what many term "diversionary wars." Two examples in this regard are Russia's 2014 annexation of the Crimea or, earlier, Iraq's 1990 invasion of Kuwait. Both military acts seem much less likely if either country had economically prospered and been well-integrated into the productive international division of labor.

A second economic challenge for managing international conflicts may also result from the fact that a political leadership resists economic reforms even if the economy is ailing. Often, the government is maintaining a socialist, fascist, or theocratic ideology that is not compatible with market economic reforms. Political power-clinging then leads to even greater socioeconomic hardship, popular unrest, and in the worst case a humanitarian catastrophe. Once a humanitarian catastrophe unfolds and government begins suppressing its own citizens, external military interventions can become an international humanitarian responsibility.

The liberation of Germany from the Nazis or Afghanistan from the Taliban might be seen as examples of a humanitarian interventionist responsibility. More often, however, the world community fails to live up to a humanitarian interventionist responsibility. Examples for this might be seen in the failure to prevent the massacres on the Bosnian people during the Bosnian War (1992–1995) or the 1994 Rwandan genocide.

Of course, external military interventions in the name of humanitarian responsibilities are rarely completely detached from political objectives. Eventually, every humanitarian crisis also becomes an international security concern, especially when humanitarian crisis situations become breeding places for terrorism. Accordingly, an unfolding humanitarian crisis in a country that is ideologically opposed to another country makes external military intervention much more likely. The prime example for international interventions to contain a spreading terrorism problem is the emergence of the so-called Islamic State in the context of the 2010 Arab uprising.

A third economic challenge to international conflict management relates to resource-rich states, since irrespective of political factors, a country's economic structure can become a major impediment to the development of perfectly competitive markets and lead to international conflict. The so-called resource curse makes economic diversification more difficult than in countries that have no other choice but to rely on income from developing diversified sectors of the economy. It also promotes the development of a rentier state, which is where the government relies on income from the sales of natural resources rather than taxing citizens. The rentier state is closely related to the authoritarian bargain, in which citizens trade their right for representation and political voice for low taxation. Authoritarian structures are more likely in resource rich states. The authoritarian bargain is a fragile arrangement that often leads to domestic conflict when resource price shocks reduce government revenues. Depending on the social structure and constellation of international relations, international actors may interfere in domestic conflicts. A prime example of a country where an authoritarian bargain collapsed in response to falling commodity prices is Venezuela. Since oil prices decreased in 2010, Venezuela can no longer finance its promises from its Bolivarian revolution, but the country's government clings onto power despite an unfolding humanitarian crisis, threats of a civil war, and international interventions.

## Questions for further discussion

1   What is the main argument of economists that makes the perfectly competitive economic model a peacebuilding formula? In answering this question, make sure that you emphasize the assumptions of atomistic market structure, price-taking behavior, and free entry and exit.
2   Explain why mercantilism led to war. What were the assumptions of mercantilism regarding trade, and why were these assumptions flawed when compared to modern trade theory?
3   Expand the game-theoretical framework of a Prisoners' Dilemma to show that cooperative multilateralism is more conducive to peace and prosperity than nationalistic unilateralism.
4   What are the main differences between socialism, laissez-faire, and a social market economy regarding the nature of the human being? Discuss possible conflict situations arising when the actual nature and government's idea of a human being are not aligned.
5   Discuss how competitive markets, open trade, and social market economy ideals apply to Europe's post World War II peace process.

## Suggested resources

1   Cato: www.cato.org/economic-freedom-world.
2   Fragility, Conflict, and Violence Website: www.worldbank.org/en/topic/fragilityconflict violence/overview.
3   International Monetary Fund: www.imf.org/external/index.htm.
4   The World Bank, Doing Business: www.doingbusiness.org/en/doingbusiness.
5   World Economic Forum: www.weforum.org/.

## Become engaged!

1   American Enterprise Institute Internships: www.aei.org/internships/.
2   Careers at the World Bank: www.worldbank.org/en/about/careers.
3   Konrad Adenauer Foundation Scholarships: www.kas.de/web/begabtenfoerderung-und-kultur/home.
4   Transparency International Internships: www.coalitionforintegrity.org/archive/who/jobs.html.
5   UNDP Jobs: https://jobs.undp.org/cj_view_jobs.cfm.
6   Young Leaders Program Heritage Foundation: www.heritage.org/node/23118.

## References and further reading

Beattie, Alan. 2009. *False Economy: A Surprising Economic History of the World*. New York, NY: Penguin Group.
Borchardt, Knut. 1991. *Perspectives on Modern German Economic History and Policy*. Cambridge: Cambridge University Press.
Cameron, Rondo E. 1993. *A Concise Economic History of the World: From Paleolithic Times to the Present*. New York, NY: Oxford University Press.
Clark, Gregory. 2008. *A Farewell to Alms: A Brief Economic History of the World*, Vol. 27. Princeton, NJ: Princeton University Press.

Colbert, Jean Baptiste. 1882. *Lettres, instructions et mémoires de Colbert: publiés d'après les ordres de l'empereur, sur la proposition de Son Excellence M. Magne, ministre secrétaire d'état des finances*, Vol. 1. Imprimerie impériale.

Collier, Paul, and David Dollar. 2002. *Globalization, Growth, and Poverty: Building an Inclusive World Economy*. New York, NY: Oxford University Press.

De Soto, Hernando. 2000. *The Mystery of Capital: Why Capitalism Triumphs in the West and Fails Everywhere Else*. New York, NY: Basic Civitas Books.

Di Vittorio, Antonio, ed. 2006. *An Economic History of Europe*. London: Routledge.

Engels, Friedrich. 1999. *Socialism: Utopian and Scientific*. Australia: Resistance Books.

Erhard, Ludwig. 1958. *Prosperity Through Competition*. New York: Frederick A. Praeger.

European Union. 2007. "Treaty of Lisbon." Accessed November 11, 2018. https://europa.eu/european-union/law/treaties_en.

Friedman, Milson, and Anna J. Schwartz. 2008. *A Monetary History of the United States, 1867–1960*. Princeton, NJ: Princeton University Press.

Fromm, Erich, Karl Marx, and Thomas B. Bottomore. 1961. *Marx's Concept of Man*. With a translation from Marx's Economic and Philosophical Manuscripts. New York, NY: Frederick Ungar Publishing.

Galbraith, John Kenneth. 2009. *The Great Crash 1929*. Boston, MA: Houghton Mifflin Harcourt.

Glossner, Christian Ludwig. 2010. *Making of the German Post-War Economy: Political Communication and Public Reception of the Social Market Economy After World War Two*. London: IB Tauris.

Grossman, Gene M., and Elhanan Helpman. 1994. "Protection for Sale." *The American Economic Review* 84 (4): 833–50.

Jones, James Rees. 2013. *The Anglo-Dutch Wars of the Seventeenth Century*. London: Routledge.

Kant, Immanuel. 1996. *Toward Perpetual Peace*. Cambridge: The Cambridge Edition of the Works of Immanuel Kant.

Keynes, John Maynard. 2017. *The Economic Consequences of the Peace*. London: Routledge.

Löwy, Michael. 2007. *The Marxism of Che Guevara: Philosophy, Economics, Revolutionary Warfare*. London: Rowman & Littlefield Publishers.

MacMillan, John. 1998. *On Liberal Peace: Democracy, War and the International Order*, Vol. 4. London: IB Tauris.

Madsen, Jakob B. 2001. "Trade Barriers and the Collapse of World Trade During the Great Depression." *Southern Economic Journal* 67 (4): 848–68.

Marktanner, Marcus. 2014. "The Social Market Economy – Assembled in Germany, Not Made in Germany." *The Euro Atlantic Union Review* 1: 77–113.

Marshall, Alfred. 2009. *Principles of Economics*, Unabridged 8th edition. New York, NY: Cosimo, Inc.

Marx, Karl, and Engels, Friedrich. 2008. *The Communist Manifesto (1848)*. Auckland, NZ: The Floating Press.

McPherson, Alan. 2016. *A Short History of US Interventions in Latin America and the Caribbean*, Vol. 9. West Sussex, UK: John Wiley & Sons.

Müller-Armack, A. 1956. Soziale Marktwirtschaft. In *Handwörterbuch der Sozialwissenschaften*, T. IX. Stuttgart, Tübingen, Göttingen: Vandenhoeck & Ruprecht.

Oosterbeek, Hessel, Randolph Sloof, and Gijs van De Kuilen. 2004. "Cultural Differences in Ultimatum Game Experiments: Evidence from a Meta-analysis." *Experimental Economics* 7 (2): 171–88.

Palier, Bruno, ed. 2010. *A Long Goodbye to Bismarck? The Politics of Welfare Reforms in Continental Europe*. Amsterdam: Amsterdam University Press.

Puehringer, Stephen. 2017. "The Success Story of Ordoliberalism as the Guiding Principle of German Economic Policy." In *Ordoliberalism, Law and the Rule of Economics*, edited by Josef Hien and Cgrustuab Joerges. London: Bloomsbury.

Ricardo, David. 1891. *Principles of Political Economy and Taxation*. London: George Bell & Sons.

Röpke, Wilhelm. 1960. *A Humane Economy: The Social Framework of the Free Market*. Chicago: Henry Regnery Company.

Samuelson, Paul. 1948. *Foundations of Economic Analysis*. Cambridge: Harvard University Press.

Schumpeter, Joseph. 2010. *Capitalism, Socialism and Democracy*. London: Routledge.

Shaffer, Edward. H. 1996. "Peace, War and the Market." *The Canadian Journal of Economics/Revue canadienne d'Economique* 29 (special Issue: Part 2): S639-S643.

Smith, Adam. 1987. *The Glasgow Edition of the Works and Correspondence of Adam Smith: VI: Correspondence*, Vol. 6. New York, NY: Oxford University Press.

———. 2010. *The Theory of Moral Sentiments*. New York, NY: Penguin Books.

Snyder, Timothy. 2011. *Bloodlands: Europe Between Hitler and Stalin*. New York, NY: Random House.

Von Mises, Ludwig. 1991. *Liberty and Property*. Auburn: Auburn University.

Yergin, Daniel, and Joseph Stanislaw. 1998. *The Commanding Heights: The Battle between Government and the Marketplace*. New York, NY: Simon & Schuster

# 15 Refugees and migration

*Brandon D. Lundy and Sherrill W. Hayes*

## Introduction

For people living in conflict zones, making the decision to leave home is never taken lightly. While planning to leave might involve envisioning greener pastures, new opportunities, and an improved life, in some circumstances, it also involves threats, vulnerability, and the high probability of never being able to return home again. This distinction can be explained as the difference in choosing to leave and being displaced. Consider the differences in moving into a new apartment because you are starting college and moving into a new apartment because your house burned. Although in both cases the end result is the same, the reasons why you left, the circumstances around leaving, and the ultimate impact of the situation under which you left are very different.

The process of moving from one location to another is called "migration." One could argue that since humans were hunter-gatherers before permanent settlements emerged that humans are migratory. The human urge to move has not diminished. During the "Age of Exploration," Europeans sought and settled new lands across the globe. The actions of these "voluntary migrants" are now better understood to have resulted in disastrous consequences for local populations, such as war, disease, slavery, and famine, which often resulted in groups of "forced migrants." For example, historians estimate that during over four centuries of the transatlantic slave trade alone, more than 17 million men, women, and children were deported from their homes and sold into slavery (UNESCO 2017). While oversimplified, this process of conquerors forcing out vanquished civilians to new lands and, in some cases, seeking to return to the homes they lost, even generations later, is too often repeated throughout human history. Mobility results from both forced (pushed out) and voluntary (pulled away) perspectives. One intention of this chapter is to show how international conflict management has a role to play in how people move, resettle, and eventually integrate, reintegrate, or return to a homeland.

Although migration is a central part of the global human experience, there remains confusion over and debates about the use of certain terminology related to it. In general, anyone who moves is a migrant; anyone leaving a home country is an emigrant; and anyone coming into a host country is an immigrant. Asylum seekers or asylees are immigrants who are seeking, but have not yet obtained, official status of refugee while residing in another country. People who are displaced from their homes but are still living inside their country's borders are known as Internally Displaced Persons (IDPs). The concept of a refugee, someone forced to flee her homeland into another country (i.e., seeking refuge), was codified into international law by the United Nations (UN) in the 1951 Convention on Refugees:

> Someone who owing to a well-founded fear of being persecuted for reasons of race, religion, nationality, membership of a particular social group or political opinion, is outside the country of his nationality, and is unable to, or owing to such fear, is unwilling to avail himself of the protection of that country.

This codification of the term *refugee* drives much of the international law and policy on how to deal with displaced persons across country borders since governments have obligations to accept political migrants fleeing persecution from other countries. People who are escaping crime, poverty, and natural disasters do not have the same legal protections in international law and are therefore are less likely to find safe passage between national borders. The distinctions between these two groups with similar problems but different status has ignited interest and controversy.

Ultimately, migration is a "conflict-space" characterized by complex potential for the intensification of conflict and violence in many forms (Rummel 1976; see also Sirkeci 2009). These "environments of human insecurity" are populated by armed conflict, lack of employment, poor infrastructure, discrimination, human rights abuses, fear of persecution, and miscommunication according to Ibrahim Sirkeci (2009, 8), who exposes two possible options for these conflict-induced migrants: they can either grin-and-bear-it by staying in bad situation, or leave. As you will see in the rest of the chapter, these decisions are difficult and sometimes not decisions at all, as migrants lose their agency or ability to choose what to do for themselves such as in the case of human trafficking. Migration is a complex phenomenon, from the reasons people migrate, to the process of migration itself, and finally to recovering, resettling, or repatriating. This chapter aims to show the ways that people are impacted by migration and how it has an impact on the places from which they leave and to which they migrate.

## International efforts to manage migration and refugees

The global community – including UN agencies, policy-makers, civil society, international organizations, nation-states, and the private sector – works to manage both the volume of displaced persons and to develop strategies to address the complex issues that create displacement. Some of the questions facing them include: where and how to draw lines or build walls; how to rethink the decisions around disaster aid and recovery; and how to support countries involved in conflicts without exacerbating war, endangering civilian lives, supporting regime change, or further politicizing human suffering? While exploring the answers to all these questions is beyond the scope of this chapter, the primary mechanisms for addressing current refugee and migrant issues are framed by the 1951 UN Convention Relating to the Status of Refugees, the 1967 Protocol Relating to the Status of Refugees, and individual countries' legislation such as the United States Refugee Act of 1980.

The 2018 United Nations High Commissioner for Refugees (UNHCR) report on displaced persons indicated that 30 people were displaced every minute in 2017 (Edwards 2018). A record 68.5 million people in the world were displaced as a result. The areas most affected by refugees were developing countries and those whose neighbors were suffering conflict, violence, and war. A full 85 percent of refugees and asylum-seekers were living in developing and underdeveloped countries, and 80 percent of migrants were still living next door to the troubled countries from which they had fled, such as Syria, Afghanistan, South Sudan, Myanmar, and Somalia. Refugees in 2017 equaled around 25.4 million people, up almost 3 million from the previous year, and those awaiting asylum application outcomes numbered over 3 million. In 2017, there were around 40 million asylum seekers. One in five refugees were Palestinians protected under the United Nations Relief and Works Agency;[1] the other 80 percent were administered by the UNHCR.

The UN outlines three durable solutions for refugees: (1) voluntary repatriation, (2) local integration, or (3) resettlement in a third country. These solutions were intended to offer a comprehensive approach that can fulfill the needs of different migrant situations. These durable solutions, however, remain strongly dependent on the will of the refugees themselves and stakeholder countries involved in these processes. Of the approximately 68.5 million displaced persons and the 25 million official refugees in 2018, less than 1 percent will file for resettlement or be resettled. These statistics demonstrate that most refugees are more likely to be repatriated home or locally integrated into a neighboring country. This puts enormous pressure on already-strained countries whose neighbors are in conflict and who receive a disproportionate amount of conflict-induced migrants. Furthermore, these durable solutions cannot address the invisible migrants' crisis such as those 20–30 million slaves in the world today. Although difficult to track, the US Department of State (2019) estimates that almost 1 million people are trafficked across international borders every year (see also UNODC 2019).

The United States has been the largest third-country resettler of refugees through the UN mechanism with approximately 3 million refugees since 1980, although many neighboring countries have much larger numbers of asylum-seekers and refugees waiting to be resettled in a third country. Unfortunately, this leaves millions of vulnerable people around the world stuck in camps and other precarious environments waiting for international assistance (in the form these three durable solutions outline by the UN), which rarely come.

Historically, countries like the United States, Canada, Australia, Sweden, and Norway accepted large numbers of the refugee population (by some UN figures up to 95 percent) who were seeking resettlement in a third country; however, these patterns are changing. For example, in 2018 the UN worked with third-party resettlement countries to try and place 81,300 refugees (UNHCR 2019). According to US Department of State statistics, however, the United States accepted only 33,000, the lowest number since 2003 (Connor and Krogstad 2018). This is problematic because the signatories to the UN Convention on Refugees in 1951 and 1967 have obligations to not return asylum-seekers and refugees to countries where they may be persecuted. This means that many refugees spend months or even years in refugee camps and other temporary arrangements in hosting countries that often do not have the political will or the resources for protracted settlement or permanent resettlement and integration. The international agreement not to re-endanger refugees is known as non-refoulement, in which signatories agree to protect the rights of those whom they "host." However, there are no universal rules governing the treatment of refugees and asylum-seekers; implementation of the convention is left to national level legislations.

Although resettlement and asylum have not been contentious issues historically, the situation in recent years has changed, becoming politicized due primarily to concerns about terrorism and the economic impacts of high numbers of migrants on strained economies. Readjusting the narrative has been difficult for lawmakers and advocates in signatory countries because these decisions are burdened by a large, unclear, and aging lexicon of politically polarizing terms such as *forced* versus *voluntary* migration, immigration, asylum, human security, and humanitarian space. Most researchers and practitioners understand migration in a more nuanced way than the public and even policy makers do. For example, the conflation of "refugee" and "migrant" in recent years has caused confusion and the mixing of ideas to create colloquial expressions like *economic refugee*. Economic migrants are by definition not refugees, since they could reasonably return to their homes, but disentangling the ideas in the public consciousness has proved challenging.

Refugees and their families are entitled to the freedoms and privileges specified in the Universal Declaration of Human Rights (UN 1948) and supported by the 1951 Convention Relating to the Status of Refugees. For example, Article 22 of the 1951 Convention affords "refugees the same treatment as is accorded to nationals with respect to elementary education" (UNHCR 1951), which means that school-aged refugee children are guaranteed to attend public schools in their countries of resettlement. In the United States, the 1980 Refugee Act outlines resettlement policy and procedures at the national level through the Office of Refugee Resettlement. The office was charged with developing an infrastructure and making resources and opportunities available for English language training, employment training, and placement to ensure economic self-sufficiency, cash assistance, and gender equality in all training and instruction. The Office provides grants for these projects, consults with state and local governments about sponsorship and distribution of refugees, and develops a data collection and monitoring system. Other countries have similar, although in many cases less sophisticated and experienced, government offices for refugee resettlement.

## Conflict-induced migration

The concept of "conflict-induced migration" promotes discourse about asylum-seekers, refugees, displaced persons, stateless individuals, undocumented persons, and other migrants who are fleeing something, but often lack an official status (Hayes, Lundy, and Hallward 2016). This concept recognizes that conflicts can take many forms, but most have direct impacts on livelihoods (Lundy and Adebayo 2016) and mobility. Examples can include armed conflict, political coups, environmental degradation (e.g., droughts and pollution), and natural disasters that create unlivable conditions.

Refugees and forced migrants can result from conflicts, such as the millions displaced in Syria and Myanmar. Such human displacement can also give rise to additional conflict, as evidenced in the European reactions to refugees since 2015, or the destabilizing effects displaced populations continue to have on their neighboring countries. For example, since the late 1970s hundreds of thousands of Muslim Rohingya have fled the predominantly Buddhist country of Myanmar, crossing into Bangladesh, Indonesia, Malaysia, and Thailand. Renewed violence in 2017 triggered further exodus and international charges of ethnic cleansing against Myanmar's security apparatus. At the same time, migration is as much about humanity's search for a better life as it is about power relations, identity politics, and indifference. Distinctions between migration push and pull factors, therefore, are not easy to separate and often conflate.

The European migrant crisis beginning in 2015 and the Mexico Border crisis of 2019 have each resulted in populist attacks on the asylum and refugee resettlement processes. These highlight a global humanitarian tipping-point in which both the real and perceived consequences of mobility are superseding human rights associated with the freedom of movement. The human tide is being corralled into "zones of humiliating entrapment" (Jansen 2009, 815) either in formal refugee camps (see the Kenya case in Textbox 15.1), at national borders through elaborate radar detection and document regimes (e.g., Frontex),[2] in transit countries that allow this tide to wash up on their shores for political and economic incentives, or in countries of origin to which people are deported back. For example, on March 18, 2016, the European Council and Turkey reached an agreement to stop the irregular flow of migration via Turkey to Europe, especially Greece. In exchange, Turkey gained broader access to Europe and European markets as well as funds from the EU to address social security needs and the refugee impact on Turkey.

Nation-states have begun to explicitly restrict paths to legal migration and asylum with greater emphasis placed instead on trying to manage, resolve, or transform conflicts in sending countries before displaced populations reach their national borders. Similar conflict issues, although fewer legal issues, exist when dealing with internally displaced people (IDP), who are individuals seeking safe places within their country of origin (Bohnet,

Cottier, and Hug 2018). Today, many displaced people seeking entry to a resettlement country without officially approved documentation such as identity cards, passports, proof of residency, bank statements, and visas are often termed "irregular migrants" who face legal challenges, political derision, economic impoverishment, and social ostracism (Torpey 2018).

Refugees can be understood as a liminal (betwixt and between) category where displaced persons are stuck between a homeland in disarray and a destination that has erected seemingly impassable barriers. A refugee camp is intended as a temporary accommodation for people who have been forced to flee their homes because of violence or persecution. These humanitarian spaces allow organizations like UNHCR to provide necessary assistance including security, food, and medical attention. According to UNHCR, there are more than 2.6 million refugees living in camps and many more millions in urban areas and informal settlements.

---

**Textbox 15.1   Life in refugee camps**

Kakuma refugee camp in Northwestern Kenya was established in 1992 for those fleeing the Sudanese civil war (1983–2005) and has a 2018 population of 184,550 (UNHCR Kenya 2018b). Kakuma also hosts refugees from Ethiopia, Burundi, Uganda, South Sudan, and Rwanda. Few resettlement opportunities present themselves for the hundreds of thousands of refugees in Kenya. Return is unlikely, especially to South Sudan with its ongoing violent conflict. How do these populations in camps like Kakuma demonstrate resilience and ingenuity in these precarious environments? Refugee camp inhabitants suffer from isolation and dependency. As such, some organizations are considering solutions to make camps more resource-efficient, climate-proof, socially inclusive, resilient, and self-regenerative (Rooij, Wascher, and Paulissen 2016). Although counter to the concept of providing "temporary solutions," introducing sustainability principles into refugee camps is necessary for the quality of life of thousands. The residents of these camps, alongside local communities and with assistance from abroad, including remittances, are investing in their own empowerment as well, creating opportunities to flourish in these long-term "temporary" spaces. These include the creation of pooled-resource cooperatives and women's groups, developing markets, educating adults and youth, and supporting peacebuilding and statebuilding efforts in both the host and home countries (Endale 2019; Odera 2016). After decades of existence, these settlements in Kenya now boast notable leaders placed around the world including professional athletes, academics, and supermodels. The 2016 Summer Olympics saw South Sudanese refugees hosted in Kenya compete with the first Refugee Olympic Team. While the world was captivated by these athletes' stories, many of these same athletes returned to untenable circumstances. Kenyan hosts are using popular security tropes to argue that these camps shelter terrorists, which justifies a push to have them shuttered. While international pressures and logistical challenges are keeping these camps open for now, many in Kenya continue to lobby for refugees to go, although where remains uncertain (Kibicho 2016). Compounding these population pressures, 2007–8 post-election violence in Kenya saw 650,000 locals displaced.

Two-thirds of refugees worldwide come from just five countries – Syria, Afghanistan, South Sudan, Myanmar, and Somalia (UNHCR 2018). Both South Sudanese and Somali refugees have found temporary homes in neighboring Kenya, which as of 2018 still had two of the ten largest and longest-running refugee camps in the world.

The Dadaab Refugee Complex in Kenya has a 2018 population of 235,269 (UNHCR Kenya 2018a). It was first established in 1991 to accommodate Somali refugees from the civil war in the early 1990s. The Federal Republic of Somalia, after a fifteen-year civil war (1991–2006), passed a provisional constitution in August 2012, ushering in a period of reconstruction. According to the UNHCR, there were 975,951 registered refugees from Somalia in neighboring states as of 2016 with an additional 1.1 million IDPs, the majority of whom are children, caused by armed violence, droughts, and other natural disasters. Interestingly, as of 2015, there were almost 10,000 registered refugees and more than 10,000 registered asylum-seekers in northern Somalia who had come from Yemen because of the Houthi insurgency.

Post-conflict countries, in an effort to develop economically, are now directly courting the involvement and return migration of their diaspora abroad. In Vietnam, for example, international remittances from the Vietnamese diaspora displaced during and after the Vietnam War (1955–1975) have significant impacts on families, communities, and the country as a whole "with international remittances at around $12 billion a year and accounting for 6 percent of its GDP" (Small 2018, 20). Similarly, Endale (2019) found that everyday engagement from the diaspora including entrepreneurship, education, and return migration are having direct impacts on peacebuilding and stability efforts, in this case, in post-conflict Ethiopia. A right of return formulated through the 1948 Universal Declaration of Human Rights, the 1948 Fourth Geneva Convention, and the 1966 International Covenant on Civil and Political Rights has now been enshrined in international law. As such, it has been argued that the right of return has passed into customary international law, making it binding to all signatories and non-signatories to these conventions. This statute guarantees every person's right to voluntary return or re-entry to his or her country of origin or citizenship, including after forced displacement. Existing document regimes, however, can make these repatriation efforts difficult as people who fled their homelands with nothing are asked to demonstrate their origins and citizenship rights through documentation.

## Contending approaches to explaining migration

The multifaceted issues that surround conflict-induced migration across the globe have attracted the attention of researchers from a wide range of academic disciplines, practitioners from across many human service and legal fields, and policy-makers. Each of these fields brings a unique set of theoretical perspectives and contending approaches to an understanding of migration and refugees. For example, conflict-induced migration has many drivers – violence, war, environmental degradation, deprivation, fear, identity politics, and economic insecurity – which all invite explanation from a broad spectrum of ideas, theories, and research. Conflict managers must consider the lived experiences of refugees fleeing from violence, their adaption to new countries, cultures, and languages, and how they deal with the aftermath of their experiences to create new lives for their families and children. There are also complex international legal and economic treaties, policies, and intergovernmental finances that offer another approach to studying migration. Although space does not allow full consideration of all these issues, three perspectives central to conflict management provide a foundation for understanding and explaining research and practices around migration and refugees: (1) human needs, (2) human rights, and (3) security perspectives.

## Human needs

When examining the drivers of migration and refugee resettlement, the first perspective that must be acknowledged is basic human needs, which focuses on how unmet needs such as identity recognition, safety and security, and personal development could be drivers of conflicts. While space will not allow a comprehensive review of the different treatises on basic human needs, Galtung (1969, 2005) and Burton (1990) have best articulated the conflict management perspectives on these areas. Both of these authors acknowledge the foundational work by Maslow (1954), who divided needs hierarchically from physical to psychological. Both of these scholars viewed needs theory as an objective basis from which conflict management research and practice could focus on human development rather than more transactional international relations approaches. These drives to satisfy basic needs for welfare, freedom, and meaning suggest a desire strong enough that people are willing to sacrifice other desired ends for it. This suggests that conflict management and resolution must include the attainment of these needs such as the location of a safe and secure place to live and thrive.

In effect, a refugee is someone who fled because he or she feared that personal needs, physiological and psychological, were not being or could not be met. Physiologically, refugees are bodily attacked, such as in sexual assault; denied food, water, and shelter; or deprived of their physical freedoms. Psychologically, refugees may be unable to fulfill their identity needs due to belonging to a particular ethnic, religious, or social group (Lundy, Adebayo, and Hayes 2018). For example, Jewish German citizens during the Third Reich were denied the right to work due to their cultural identity. As discussed previously, the UN's three durable solutions also focus on ensuring that both physical and psychological needs are met by first, ensuring that the refugee makes the decision on either repatriation or resettlement (non-refoulement) and second, protecting the life and dignity of refugees by finding a safe and satisfying place to locate them, whether back home or in a third party country.

## Human rights

Societies have developed systems of laws to ensure that basic human needs can be met without fear, unnecessary interference, or persecution. The foundation of these systems is rights. As with human needs, the scope and number of authors who have written on human rights is vast (see for example Alston and Goodman 2012); we focus specifically on Galtung and Wirak (1977) and Sen's (2004) theories of human rights because of their applications to conflict management and issues of migration and refugees.

The basic premise of these works (Galtung and Wirak 1977; Sen 2004) is that rights are rooted in culturally specific modalities that should be viewed as the foundation of all law. Further, it is the responsibility of governments to ensure that rights are protected equally for all citizens, especially ensuring that vulnerable groups are not ignored or unfairly targeted. Galtung and Wirak go further, prescribing that when applied correctly by governments, rights ensure both freedom and security. Sen asserts that human rights are more than written laws (which are primarily utilitarian); they are also moral and ethical obligations that cross national boundaries. In both cases, the discussions of rights moves into both "freedoms" (being provided opportunities to develop as an individual), and the "duties and obligations" of individuals to societies. Galtung and Wirak explore these ideas by contrasting "positive peace," which emphasizes not just one's right to avoid harm ("negative peace"), but that calls for living in a way that allows for development of human potential. While Galtung and Wirak may not see positive peace as a "right," the concept transcends any political boundary or legal system and should be extended to all people around the world. Sen believes we must intervene to ensure rights for all people suffering in oppressive regimes, even if that means providing mechanisms to move to safer locations where their rights can be protected.

In application to the issues of migration and refugees, these ideas assume that people have a legitimate right to be a citizen in their country of origin (citizenship), that their country will protect those rights (security), and if it does not, that there are ways available to them to enter a new country without violating the laws of their new country (process). Underlying this set of beliefs is the assumption that rights, ethics, and moral protections are founded on universal human dignity and should be available to migrants at all stages of the process.

By contrast, the use of common phrases like *status*, *undocumented*, *illegal*, and *irregular* all highlight how current application of rights-based perspectives tend to focus on the utilitarian legal aspects of rights instead of human dignity. In other words, should border security ensure lawful transitions between countries before individual human rights for safety, security, and freedom? In many cases, it is possible to see how both of the assumptions and application of human rights perspectives have been violated. For example, the Rohingya people are not officially recognized as citizens in Myanmar, which is their country of origin, because of their ethnic identity and Islamic faith. Although they share some ethnic and religious similarities with the majority of Bangladeshi people, they were not born in that country, so they are not recognized as citizens there either. In this case, no government is protecting their rights; they hold no official status, but remain human beings with unmet needs and claims to universal rights.

In places where national governments have been unable to or unwilling to ensure the rights of their citizens, there are pathways that ensure displaced people's rights are protected that are the result of international agreements and conventions (e.g., the 1951 UN Convention on Refugees and the 1967 Protocol removed previous temporal and geographic restrictions on the definitions of refugees). Once inside those countries that are signatories to these treaties, those laws should ensure their rights. Additionally, these international agreements provide options for international pressures and sanctions when violations occur, even when they take place in countries that are not signatories. While covering the national laws and procedures designed to protect these rights is beyond the scope of this chapter (see Acosta 2016 for a review), it is sufficient to note that there are many and varied pathways to leave one country and arrive in another that relate to citizenship rights and that are controlled by national governments (e.g., work visas, temporary residency). Equally, there are legal and protected paths back home once disputes are resolved and conflicts are managed.

### Security perspectives

The United Nations Universal Declaration of Human Rights states that all people are entitled to "security of person," which reinforces needs-based concepts of freedom from physical and psychological harm and creates a rights-based obligation for the state to provide such security. This combines two key elements of the security perspective: "human security" and "national security" (Hanlon and Christie 2016; Roberts 2008). Security seems to be the perfect synthesis of human needs and human rights (i.e., human security); however, the complication comes when the obligation extends to humans beyond specific political boundaries such as forced migrants and refugees.

Since World War II and especially the end of the Cold War, human security has been used as an explanation for military and humanitarian interventions in intrastate conflicts. If individuals' needs or rights are being infringed, is there not a moral obligation to act? In regards to migration and refugees, if displaced persons are fleeing from one country to another seeking asylum and UN protection, it activates an international system that involves many countries that may not be direct neighbors to the conflict. As in the case of Syria, a civil war created both a regional security issue for already distressed countries in the Middle East and an obligation for other countries to provide needs, protect rights, and legal pathways for those displaced individuals to potentially become citizens of those countries. It is easy to understand how this intrastate conflict easily became an international issue because of the complex web of international interests that exists between neighboring countries like Jordan, Iraq, and Iran among others. When considering the multiple ways that human security, regional security, and national security intersect with migration and refugee policies and practices, the possible debates about admissions' standards and how to evaluate rights' violations multiply significantly. Some of these are addressed in the remainder of the chapter.

## Application of conflict management approaches to migration and refugees

Conflicts often create mobility. Mobility creates challenges not only for those on the move, but for communities left behind and for those receiving migrants. These community impacts call for socially engineered conflict solutions (i.e., management, resolution, and transformation) since population movements can exacerbate and intensify latent conflict (Reuveny 2007). Managing the root causes and effects of human mobility becomes critical to development, peace, and security.

This section focuses on both the needs and the wants of migrants and those left behind with a particular emphasis on the application of peace and conflict management approaches to migrant- and refugee-sending and host communities. Successful international conflict management is based on accurate information, data-driven interventions, and sound policies. To illustrate this point, Bock, McMahon, and Haque (2017) surveyed the proliferation of information and communication technologies being developed for mobile phones to offer a plethora of refugee and migration services (see Chapter 11 in this volume).

In fact, refugees, migrants, and people surrounded by violent conflict have described the ability to maintain mobile phones as more essential than their other basic needs, including food and shelter (Benton and Glennie 2016).

Effective policies can also positively affect migration experiences and outcomes. National immigration strategies help focus resources, incubate institutions, and promote practices among the many stakeholders to enhance the integration efforts of foreign guests toward a more cohesive society. For example, the West African island nation of Cabo Verde enacted its first National Immigration Strategy on January 23, 2012, after several years of strained and sometimes-violent encounters between foreign guest workers from conflict-prone neighboring countries and domestic youth experiencing high levels of unemployment (Lartey and Lundy 2017; Lundy and Darkwah 2018). Its strategy focused on four pillars: (1) migratory fluxes; (2) dialogue, solidarity, and partnerships; (3) economic growth and social integration; and (4) coherence of migration policies. The national immigration strategy combines measures, initiatives, and policy responses to the challenges imposed by immigration that are based on a set of guiding topics such as regular migration, visas and residence, and labor migration needs. Examples of these effective interventions include community policing, adult literacy campaigns, and the granting of amnesty periods in which irregular migrants are assisted to acquire formal residency and work permits.

By 2015, just three years after the implementation of its first National Immigration Strategy, Cabo Verde experienced a decline in crime, especially in migrant communities (Lundy and Lartey 2017). Community policing efforts increased trust, found common ground, and created collaborative partnerships between law enforcement and the communities they served. Immigration offices were opened in local municipalities to explain immigration policies and to work with foreign guests to acquire work permits during amnesty periods. Additional efforts emphasized culture, religious practices, and tolerance, helping to satisfy frustrated local communities (Lartey and Lundy 2017). This example demonstrates how perceived injustices can be heaped onto migrant "others," blaming migrants for their difficult situations, sometimes leading to outright discrimination and violence. This can be intensified through nationalistic and xenophobic rhetoric and the ratcheting-up of feelings of intolerance, prejudice, and discrimination toward newcomers.

Ineffective policy can negatively affect migration experiences and outcomes. For example, policies and practices in the United States since Donald Trump's 2016 election as president have worsened the human security of migrants and refugees. Ruth Gomberg-Muñoz (2011, 2017) and many others working on immigration policy in the United States show these effects on workers and families. Undocumented workers are criminalized, leading to disappearing paths to resettlement, legal migration, work visas, and citizenship. There are now more than 10 million undocumented people in the United States whose precarious status leads to extreme hardships including a lack of access to quality education, healthcare, and employment. The implementation of these immigration and refugee policies have seen the separation of children from parents, long-term detentions of refugees and asylum-seekers, racial profiling, and mistaken deportation.

Civil society, state, and local governments are fighting back against the inhumane treatment of people on the move both inside countries and across state borders. One such organization, Welcoming America, is attempting to create welcoming cultures that can reform the policies and institutions of cities and states around the world through a network of welcoming and sanctuary initiatives. Launched in 2009, this nonprofit organization promotes the welcoming of new immigrants and the inclusion of all residents in policy decisions. Welcoming America's national and international network helps nonprofit and government partners elevate their communities into more welcoming and hospitable places for all people, through economic, social, and civic engagement.

The current and ongoing debate over "sanctuary cities" is in fact a debate over immigration federalism, or the role of states and municipalities in making and implementing immigration law and policy, and it has become an increasingly relevant issue for organizations like Welcoming America (Rodriguez, McDaniel, and Ahebee 2018). These "sanctuary" localities (cities, counties, states, etc.) purposefully limit their cooperation with federal immigration enforcement agents to shield "low-priority" immigrants from deportation proceedings. This does not mean that these same municipalities do not enforce serious crimes, including turning over undocumented persons who have committed felonies to US Immigration and Customs Enforcement (ICE). Being undocumented is a civil offense, not a crime. Furthermore, unlawful holding of immigrants past the point at which time they should be released is also unconstitutional. Local-federal immigration law ambiguity often leads to immigrant fear of law enforcement with negative documented outcomes (Becerra et al. 2016; Ciancio 2017).

## Challenges and future directions

The record number of people displaced in the past decade has highlighted some critical issues for refugees and migrants in the realm of conflict management and development: How are issues of national securitization beginning to trump relieving human suffering? What continues to drive conflict-induced or survival migration? How can development, peace-building, and policy-reform initiatives break the cycles of population displacement? These are just a few of the key challenges that remain essential to better understanding the conflict-migration nexus.

Conflicts, natural disasters, political disagreements, and economic necessity create real and perceived insecurity for people, and these insecurities often lead to migration. The migration context changes over time, which can influence the migration process including further travel, return migration, or decisions to stay in the host country. At each of these stages, conflict management and resolution interventions – alternative dispute resolution, indigenous approaches, peacebuilding, diplomacy, early warning and response – can influence the nature of human mobility.

Critically, prevention is always more economical than intervention after migration has occurred. The loss and separation experienced by migrants and refugees is associated with depression and other mental health problems as well as identity crises, which can lead to things like gang affiliation and violence. English proficiency, close relationships with supportive adults and peers, and developing a multicultural identity have been associated with better integration outcomes in the United States (Hayes and Endale 2018). Multicultural policies to encourage early integration such as those adopted in Cabo Verde should translate into preventing future issues related to effective settlement of foreign guests.

Studying migration from multiple perspectives including the migrants' and host communities' presents opportunities to understand complex human relations around intercultural contact – from welcoming to dehumanizing the "other." These challenges are compounded as environmental pressures (including climate change) mean more frequent natural disasters, more conflict, and more displacement. This means that migrants may need to move two and three times before finding a welcoming and hospitable place to call home (Lopes and Lundy 2014). These more frequent movements necessitate several changes including the recognition of social citizenship, in which those acculturated into locales are deemed to belong, whether or not they hold certain legal credentials of state citizenship (Lundy 2011).

Furthermore, the establishment and maintenance of global migrant-friendly networks, such as Welcoming America, will remain an essential ingredient to encourage receptivity, positive integration, and managing difficult transitions for people on the move. Further, better tools and models for understanding how successful community integration, family, and individual development happens are critical (Hayes and Endale 2018; Lundy and Darkwah 2018). Strategically incorporating technology into the process will help ensure the effective mobilization of populations undergoing conflict. Identified technology uses for managing conflict-induced migration include asylum processing, information gathering and dissemination, family reunification, accessing government services, education, language training, skill development, healthcare, cash assistance and transfers, job acquisition, business creation, and communication (Bock et al. 2017). Finally, new and emerging research at the intersection of conflict management and migration must also focus on resilience and positive adaptation through language learning, formal education for children, and the development of new and multifaceted identities. But at the end of the day, establishing viable channels for post-conflict homeland engagement including remittances, peacebuilding, statebuilding, and economic development alongside return migration and repatriation options will help deter future outbreaks of conflict and associated conflict-induced migration. "As individuals who survived persecution, violence, and succeeded in overcoming multiple challenges associated with flight and resettlement, they have the unique opportunity to understand the value of peace" (Endale 2019, 127).

## Questions for further discussion

1 How might climate change affect population movements around the world?
2 Who gets to travel across international borders by choice, and who does not? Why do you think that is?
3 As human populations have grown over time, how do their responses to conflict change?
4 How do migrants and refugees use communication technologies? Why are these so essential to effective travel and resettlement?
5 Does deportation make sense for people raised in a particular country, but not born there? What are possible alternatives?

## Suggested resources

1 Church World Service (CWS): https://cwsglobal.org/our-work/refugees-and-immigrants/; HIAS: www.hias.org/; International Rescue Committee (IRC): www.rescue.org/; Lutheran Immigration and Refugee Service: www.lirs.org/; US Committee for Refugees and Immigrants (USCRI): http://refugees.org/; World Relief: www.worldrelief.org/. These resources are important international refugee resettlement organizations.
2 Frontex – European Boder and Coast Guard Agency: https://frontex.europa.eu/. This is Europe's border protection agency.
3 *God Grew Tired of Us*. 2007. www.godgrewtiredofus.com/. A documentary about the resettlement of Sudanese refugees in the United States.
4 Migration Policy Institute: www.migrationpolicy.org/. An important migration research center.
5 PRIO (Peace Research Institute Oslo) – Migration research group: www.prio.org/Research/Group/?x=1. An important migration research center.
6 7 videos guaranteed to change the way you see refugees: www.unhcr.org/innovation/7-videos-guaranteed-to-change-the-way-you-see-refugees/. Short documentaries promoted by UNHCR provide open access.
7 Southern Poverty Law Center: www.splcenter.org/. Provides lawyers to assist with a wide-range of US refugee issues.
8 UNHCR (United Nations High Commissioner for Refugees): www.unhcr.org/en-us/. An international refugee organization.
9 Welcoming America: www.welcomingamerica.org/. A non-profit organization working to promote migrant integration through the United States.
10 Community Dynamics in Clarkston: A Photovoice Project: www.photovoiceclarkston.com/. A project about refugee resettlement that showcases one of the most diverse communities in the United States.

## Become engaged!

1 Migration Policy Institute Internships: www.migrationpolicy.org/about/internships.

2   Internships at the International Organization for Migration: www.iom.int/internships-iom.
3   National Network for Immigrant and Refugee Rights Internships: www.nnirr.org/drupal/intern-projects.
4   Intern – World Relief: www.worldrelief.org/intern/.
5   UNHCR Internships: www.unhcr.org/en-us/internships.html?query=interns.
6   Homeland Security Careers: www.dhs.gov/homeland-security-careers/students.
7   The Migration Conference: www.migrationconference.net/.
8   Clarkston Community Center: https://clarkstoncommunitycenter.org/.
9   John Dau Foundation: www.johndaufoundation.org/.
10  Green Card Voices: www.greencardvoices.com.

## Notes

1   Following World War II, the United Nations became the first international agency to try to deal comprehensively with refugees through the founding of the International Refugee Organization (IRO) in 1947 and UNHCR in 1950. Preceding this was the United Nations Relief and Rehabilitation Administration established in 1944 to address the millions of people displaced across Europe because of the war. Then, in December 1949, the United Nations Relief and Works Agency for Palestine Refugees in the Near East (UNRWA) was formed to support the more than 5 million registered Palestinian refugees who fled or were expelled from their homes during the 1948 Palestine war as well as those who later fled or were expelled from the 1967 Six Day war. Aid is provided to operations in Jordan, Lebanon, Syria, the Gaza Strip and the West Bank, including East Jerusalem. In 2018, the United States government announced that it would be ceasing its funding to the agency, which makes up about a third of the annual budget (George 2018).
2   Frontex is the European Border and Coast Guard Agency headquartered in Warsaw, Poland and tasked with the border control of the European Schengen Area, which consists of 26 European countries of which 22 are European Union states.

## References and further reading

Acosta, Luis. 2016. "Refugee Law and Policy in Selected Countries." The Law Library of Congress, Global Legal Research Center. www.loc.gov/law/help/refugee-law/refugee-law-and-policy.pdf.

Alston, Philip, and Ryan Goodman. 2012. *International Human Rights*. New York, NY: Oxford University Press.

Becerra, David, M. Alex Wagaman, David Androff, Jill Messing, and Jason Castillo. 2016. "Policing Immigrants: Fear of Deportations and Perceptions of Law Enforcement and Criminal Justice." *Journal of Social Work* 17 (6): 715–31.

Benton, Meghan, and Alex Glennie. 2016. *Digital Humanitarianism: How Tech Entrepreneurs Are Supporting Refugee Integration*. Washington, DC: Migration Policy Institute.

Bock, Joseph G., Kevin McMahon, and Ziaul Haque. 2017. "Massive Displacement Meets Cyberspace: How Information and Communication Technologies Are Helping Refugees and Migrants and How We Can Do Better." In *The Migration Conference 2017 Proceedings*, edited by Fethiye Tilbe, Elif Iskender, and Ibrahim Sirkeci, 48–69. London: Transnational Press London.

Bohnet, Heidrun, Fabien Cottier, and Simon Hug. 2018. "Conflict-induced IDPs and the Spread of Conflict." *Journal of Conflict Resolution* 62 (4): 691–716.

Burton, John. 1990. *Conflict: Human Needs Theory*. New York, NY: Springer.

Ciancio, Alberto. 2017. *The Impact of Immigration Policies on Local Enforcement, Crime and Policing Efficiency*. PhD dissertation, University of Pennsylvania, PA. https://repository.upenn.edu/edissertations/2231.

Connor, Phillip, and Jens Manuel Krogstad. 2018. "For the First Time, US Resettles Fewer Refugees Than the Rest of the World." *Pew Research Center*, July 5. www.pewresearch.org/fact-tank/2018/07/05/for-the-first-time-u-s-resettles-fewer-refugees-than-the-rest-of-the-world/.

Edwards, Adrian. 2018. "Forced Displacement at Record 68.5 Million." *UNHCR*, June 19. www.unhcr.org/en-us/news/stories/2018/6/5b222c494/forced-displacement-record-685-million.html.

Endale, Etsegenet G. 2019. *Beyond Resettlement: The Role of Ethiopian Refugee Diaspora in Homeland Peacebuilding*. Ph.D. dissertation, International Conflict Management, Kennesaw State University, Kennesaw, GA.

Galtung, Johan. 1969. "Violence, Peace, and Peace Research." *Journal of Peace Research* 6 (3): 167–91.

———. 2005. "Meeting Basic Needs: Peace and Development." In *The Science of Well-Being*, edited by Gelicia A. Huppert, Nick Baylis, and Barry Keverne, 475–502. New York, NY: Oxford University Press.

Galtung, Johan, and Anders Helge Wirak. 1977. "Human Needs and Human Rights – A Theoretical Approach." *Bulletin of Peace Proposals* 8 (3): 251–58.

George, Susannah. 2018. "US Ends Funding of UN Agency for Palestinian Refugees." *Associated Press*, September 1. www.apnews.com/fc4de8bf22c7493ababa86e1e47f6448.

Gomberg-Muñoz, Ruth. 2011. *Labor and Legality: An Ethnography of a Mexican Immigrant Network*. New York, NY: Oxford University Press.

———. 2017. *Becoming Legal: Immigration Law and Mixed-Status Families*. New York, NY: Oxford University Press.

Hanlon, Robert J., and Kenneth Christie. 2016. *Freedom from Fear, Freedom from Want: An Introduction to Human Security*. Toronto, Canada: University of Toronto Press.

Hayes, Sherrill W., and Etsegenet Endale. 2018. "'Sometimes My Mind, It Has to Analyze Two Things': Identity Development and Adaptation for Refugee and newcomer Adolescents." *Peace and Conflict: Journal of Peace Psychology* 24 (3): 283–90.

Hayes, Sherrill W., Brandon D. Lundy, and Maia Carter Hallward. 2016. "Conflict-Induced Migration and the Refugee Crisis: Global and Local Perspectives from Peacebuilding and Development." *Journal of Peacebuilding and Development* 11 (3): 1–7.

Jansen, Stef. 2009. "After the Red Passport: Towards an Anthropology of the Everyday Geopolitics of Entrapment in the EU's 'Immediate Outside'." *Journal of the Royal Anthropological Institute* 15 (4): 815–32.

Kibicho, Karanja. 2016. "As the Kenyan Minister for National Security, Here's Why I'm Shutting the World's Biggest Refugee Camp." *Independent*, May 9. www.independent.co.uk/voices/as-the-kenyan-minister-for-national-security-heres-why-im-shutting-the-worlds-biggest-refugee-camp-a7020891.html.

Lartey, Kezia, and Brandon D. Lundy. 2017. "Policy Considerations Regarding the Integration of Lusophone West Africa Immigrant Populations." *Border Crossing* 7 (1): 108–21.

Lopes, Jessica, and Brandon D. Lundy. 2014. "Secondary Diaspora: Cape Verdean Immigration to the Southeastern United States." *Southern Anthropologist* 36 (2): 70–102.

Lundy, Brandon D. 2011. "Dearly Deported: Social Citizenship of Undocumented Minors in the US." *Migration Letters* 8 (1): 55–66.

Lundy, Brandon D., and Akanmu G. Adebayo. 2016. "Introduction: Sustainable Livelihoods, Conflicts, and Transformation." *Journal of Global Initiatives* 10 (2): 1–8.

Lundy, Brandon D., Akanmu G. Adebayo, and Sherrill W. Hayes, eds. 2018. *Atone: Religion, Conflict, and Reconciliation*. Lanham, MD: Lexington Books.

Lundy, Brandon D., and Kezia Darkwah. 2018. "Measuring Community Integration of Lusophone West African Immigrant Populations Through Needs Assessment, Human Security, and Realistic Conflict Theory." *Journal of International Migration and Integration* 19 (2): 513–26.

Lundy, Brandon D., and Kezia Lartey. 2017. "Deciding to Stay: Bissau-Guinean Labour Migrants in Cabo Verde, West Africa." In *The Migration Conference 2017 Proceedings*, edited by Fethiye Tilbe, Elif Iskender, and Ibrahim Sirkeci, 548–60. London: Transnational Press London.

Maslow, Abraham H. 1954. *Motivation and Personality*. New York, NY: Harper.

McKelvey, Tara. 2003. "Where Are the 'Lost Girls'?" *Slate.com*, October 3. www.slate.com/articles/news_and_politics/foreigners/2003/10/where_are_the_lost_girls.html.

Odera, Catherine A. 2016. "Peacebuilding in the Context of Displacement: Women's Groups in Internally Displaced Persons (IDPs) Settlements in Kenya." Ph.D. dissertation, International Conflict Management, Kennesaw State University, Kennesaw, GA. https://digitalcommons.kennesaw.edu/incmdoc_etd/4.

Reuveny, Rafael. 2007. "Climate Change-Induced Migration and Violent Conflict." *Political Geography* 26 (6): 656–73.

Roberts, David. 2008. *Human Insecurity: Global Structures of Violence*. London: Zed Books.

Rodriguez, Darlene Xiomara, Paul N. McDaniel, and Marie-Dominique Ahebee. 2018. "Welcoming America: A Case Study of Municipal Immigrant Integration, Receptivity and Community Practice." *Journal of Community Practice* 26 (3): 348–57.

Rooij, Bertram de, Dirk Wascher, and Maurice Paulissen. 2016. "Sustainable Design Principles for Refugee Camps (KB-25–005–005)." Internal Report, Wageningen Environmental Research, Wageningen University and Research.

Rummel, Rudolph J. 1976. *Understanding Conflict and War: Vol. 2: The Conflict Helix*. Beverly Hills, CA: Sage Publications.

Sen, Amartya. 2004. "Elements of a Theory of Human Rights." *Philosophy and Public Affairs* 32 (4): 315–56.

Sirkeci, Ibrahim. 2009. "Transnational Mobility and Conflict." *Migration Letters* 6 (1): 3–14.

Small, Ivan V. 2018. *Currencies of Imagination: Channeling Money and Chasing Mobility in Vietnam*. Ithaca, NY: Cornell University Press.

Torpey, John C. 2018. *The Invention of the Passport: Surveillance, Citizenship and the State*, 2nd edition. New York, NY: Cambridge University Press.

UN. 1948. "Universal Declaration of Human Rights." United Nations General Assembly. Accessed October 9, 2019. https://www.un.org/en/universal-declaration-human-rights/.

UNESCO. 2017. "Transatlantic Slave Trade." United Nations Educational, Scientific and Cultural Organization. www.unesco.org/new/en/social-and-human-sciences/themes/slave-route/transatlantic-slave-trade/.

UNHCR. 1951. "Convention Relating to the Status of Refugees." United Nations High Commissioner for Refugees. Accessed October 9, 2019. https://treaties.un.org/Pages/ViewDetailsII.aspx?src=TREATY&mtdsg_no=V-2&chapter=5&Temp=mtdsg2&clang=_en.

———. 2018. "Figures at a Glance." United Nations High Commissioner for Refugees. www.unhcr.org/en-us/figures-at-a-glance.html.

———. 2019. "Resettlement." United Nations High Commissioner for Refugees. www.unhcr.org/resettlement.html.

UNHCR Kenya. 2018a. "Dadaab Refugee Complex." United Nations High Commissioner for Refugees. www.unhcr.org/ke/dadaab-refugee-complex.

———. 2018b. "Kakuma Refugee Camp and Kalobeyei Integrated Settlement." United Nations High Commissioner for Refugees, www.unhcr.org/ke/kakuma-refugee-camp.

UNODC. 2019. "Global Report on Trafficking in Persons." United Nations Office on Drugs and Crime. www.unodc.org/documents/Global_Report_on_TIP.pdf.

US Department of State. 2019. "2019 Trafficking in Persons Report." www.state.gov/reports/2019-trafficking-in-persons-report/.

# 16 Environment, conflict, and peace

*Eric Abitbol and Valerie Puleo*

## Introduction

While the field of environmental peacemaking/environmental conflict resolution is relatively new, the intersection of environment, conflict, and peace dates back millennia. Equitable access to natural resources like land and water are among the reasons why communities and nations have gone to war. Resources have also figured prominently in peace processes and agreements. Thus, one cannot objectively assume that countries and nations will simply or necessarily go to war with their neighbors over natural resources. And, there is a rich history of agreement-building over natural resources.

Natural resources are generally devastated by armed conflict, where these same natural resources may have been the pretext or cause of escalations. For example, the 1991 Gulf War was launched by a so-called Coalition of the Willing, led by the United States (US), against the Iraqi regime of Saddam Hussein. The trigger for this war was clearly Iraqi forces crossing into, and then occupying, Kuwait. Strategically, occupying Kuwait nearly doubled Iraq's control over known global oil reserves (OPEC 2004). As it became clear that Saddam Hussein's army was no match for Coalition forces, Iraqi soldiers set more than 700 oil wells ablaze, burning about 4.6 million barrels of oil per day. This was one of the worst intentional, human-made environmental (but not natural) disasters in history. Throughout this conflict, hundreds of thousands of demonstrators from Washington, DC to Montreal to London marched with placards and chanted, "No Blood for Oil." This is a harsh but telling portrayal of the relationship between natural resources and armed conflict. It is, however, not the only one.

In 1932, the US and Canada created what is believed to be the world's first peace park, a conservation area spanning both countries, bringing together the US Glacier National Park and the Waterton Lakes National Park of Canada. In creating the Waterton-Glacier International Peace Park, these two countries affirmed their commitment to both conservation and peaceable international relations, for decades allowing visitors to cross the world's longest land border (at 5,525 miles) with relative freedom. The Park's management cooperated and coordinated many of their activities, with all sorts of joint projects on environmental education, vegetation restoration, wildfire suppression, and more. The Waterton-Glacier reflected and further cemented the strong Canada-US relationship, though it too has been subject to the totalizing discursive force of global threat and terror. In the wake of the attacks on September 11, 2001, American Glacier Park staff (notably park rangers) were retrained as border patrol officers, drawing precious resources that had formerly been invested in transboundary cooperative projects.

These are but a few of the many ways that the environment intersects with conflict and peace issues and processes. This is a rich and complex field that includes water wars and transboundary water agreements for shared and equitable utilization. It includes blood diamonds that have taken the lives of the young and hopeful working in insecure and brutalizing conditions to support armed conflict in the Democratic Republic of Congo (DRC), as well as global efforts to create transparency, accountability, and traceability in the diamond industry through the Kimberley Process. This intersection speaks to issues of Indigenous Rights, Children's Rights, Human Rights more generally, and climate justice.

In some respects, the environment is a resource like any other, given that much of its power derives from the political, discursive, economic, and other usages to which it is put. It is nonetheless different in that the water we drink, air we breathe, climate in which we live, and oceans that feed us are the basis of humans' ability to survive and thrive on planet Earth. There is also evidence to suggest that agreements are easier to reach over (at least some) natural resources (e.g., water) than national borders or the presence and location of security forces. This suggests that the environment and natural resources may serve as a gateway to resolution processes, creating space for yet more challenging issues to be addressed.

This chapter frames and discusses the intersection of environment, conflict, and peace, introducing the reader to its origins, literature, and debates. Two case studies are discussed in greater depth, on the water-food-energy nexus cooperation of Israelis and Palestinians as well as contemporary environmental conflict resolution processes involving the US government. Finally, this chapter will identify and touch upon emerging discourses for the future at the intersection of environment, conflict, and peace, in theory and in practice.

## Drivers, impacts, and approaches to conflict and peacebuilding involving the environment

### Environmental impacts of violence and armed conflict

This chapter opened with a reference to the burning oil fields of Kuwait in the early 1990s. Images from the round-the-clock news cycle that emerged are enduring, and the impact of the war did not stop there. The marine ecosystem was devastated, as between 1 and 1.7 million tons of oil spilled into the Persian Gulf (Taylor 2016). The climate in the Gulf, Kuwait, Iraq, Saudi Arabia and neighboring countries was negatively affected (Linden, Jerneloev, and Egerup 2014). This is but one of hundreds of examples of the detrimental environmental impacts of war.

For instance, the presence of landmines in Afghanistan and Cambodia has resulted in changing land use patterns, in addition to undermining agricultural and other livelihood practices (Biswas 2001). These weapons render large tracts of land unusable for farming and gathering resources, which lengthens the time required for ecosystems and nearby communities to recover from conflict. Similarly, the air-dropped and ground-based delivery of cluster bombs by artillery or rocket systems leaves behind unexploded ordnances, ultimately impacting communities for many years, irrespective of whether or not peace agreements have been put into effect, as the locations of the explosives are often unknown and it is difficult and costly to locate and remove them (GICHD 2016).

In Central African Republic (CAR) and elsewhere, displacement due to conflict as well as short-term conflict recovery programs can deplete and degrade natural resources. As individuals cope with displacement, they may undertake strategies such as cutting trees for fuel, which results in soil erosion and increased desertification (Friends 2014). Some militant groups engage in poaching as a tactic to self-finance, further enabling local and global criminal networks. It has been reported that poachers enter CAR, Chad, Cameroon, and other neighboring countries, resulting in mass killings of elephants to acquire ivory for sale on international black markets (Agger 2014). In such cases, the environment is itself a victim of violence and armed conflict, which impacts communities and entire societies, nationally and transnationally.

### Environment as a source of conflict

While the academic discussion and popular discourse on the environment as a source of conflict is longstanding, the academic field gained new footing with the groundbreaking work of Thomas Homer-Dixon throughout the 1990s. Scholarship during this time focused on resource scarcity and on the "resource curse." The "resource scarcity" thesis argued that scarcity and degradation of natural resources, and in particular in terms of equitable access to these resources (including land, water, and forests) is a cause of violent conflict. The resource curse thesis argued that abundance in raw material resources can lead to institutional weakening and increase the likelihood of conflict, decreasing the effectiveness of institutions to amicably or productively respond to conflict (Homer-Dixon 1999; Auty 1993).

Critics of this early scholarship argued that important factors were neglected in the resource scarcity/curse literature, pushing for a deeper understanding of the interplay between local communities and international companies, international financial institutions, national governments, and development assistance agencies (Gleditsch 1998; Levy 1995). Some scholars point to the pivotal permissive, even enabling, role of weak institutions in conflict environments, arguing that "environmental problems are most combustible when they exacerbate existing social tensions based on class, region, or ethnicity. When such tensions are triggered in the absence or weakness of social institutions that otherwise could mediate disputes or in the context of 'failing' states, it is said, violent conflict may be triggered or worsened" (Conca 2002; see also Theisen 2008).

In 1987, the report of the World Commission on Environment and Development (known as Our Common Future, or the Brundtland Report) highlighted the link between environmental sustainability and good governance. In response to growing consumer concern about resources fueling conflict worldwide, efforts emerged like the Extractive Industries Transparency Initiative (EITI), which promotes government accountability, and the Kimberley Process for tracing diamonds in an effort to certify them as conflict-free. These efforts were developed with the goal of improving governance and mitigating the catalytic effect of resources on conflict, particularly in the extractive industries. Similarly, the Forest Stewardship Council (FSC) is an institutional mechanism promoting sustainable environmental governance of the world's forests. It offers a certification program to ensure products come from responsibly managed forests. The ten principles in the certification program cover multiple criteria including compliance with the law, indigenous and community rights, and environmental integrity (e.g., healthy ecosystems, clean air and water, etc.).

### Environmental conflict resolution

Environmental issues are inherently complex because they are ever-changing, transboundary in nature, and often involve multiple levels of government with overlapping jurisdictions. The environment invokes different value systems for different individuals, communities, and cultures. Environmental issues are also subject to fluctuating political dynamics and social realities, most recently seen on a global scale with the enthusiasm, contestation, and uncertainties around the 2015 Paris Climate Agreement (Curtin 2018).

Governments and private institutions often look to technological innovation as a way to solve environmental challenges. Desalination and water recycling initiatives are two examples of how water scarcity is being addressed through technological means. However, technical solutions are not always the answer for environmental challenges, which often involve a multitude of stakeholders with different values and interests. For example, some stakeholders may be more likely to support strategies that promote local livelihoods, while others may prioritize conservation. The term *wicked problem* aptly describes the dilemma associated with confronting especially complex social policy issues that do not have a universally acceptable technical solution (Rittle and Webber 1973). A technically feasible solution that meets the needs of several groups may not be acceptable to others.

Environmental conflict resolution may be an effective approach for addressing such complexity. This is because solutions come from the stakeholders of such processes themselves rather than from outside experts who may not be impacted directly by the problem or the solution to be implemented. According to Fisher and Sablan (2018), when environmental issues "[divide] people into camps that are sharply delineated along values and positions, environmental conflict resolution can offer new ways to engage, to restore trust and relationships, and identify common and higher ground upon which to build innovative, collaborative solutions and decision-making processes."

The US Institute for Environmental Conflict Resolution, the federal government agency tasked with providing neutral third-party conflict resolution services, defines environmental conflict resolution as people with differing views and interests working together in a systematic and organized way to find workable solutions to shared problems about environmental issues. Central to this activity is a search for agreements by consensus (or modified consensus, with dissent) rather than majority rule (SPIDR 1997).

The basic foundational concept in environmental conflict resolution processes is the focus on interests rather than positions. Interests are defined as the reasons parties have a preferred solution or preferred outcome to a conflict. Focusing on the underlying concerns of the parties through interest-based negotiation increases the likelihood of agreement because the parties focus on mutually beneficial outcomes, rather than positional win/lose scenarios (Fisher, Ury, and Patton 1991).

Environmental conflict resolution can describe a variety of processes along a spectrum (Bean, Fisher, and Eng 2007; see Figure 16.1). The "upstream" end of the spectrum could involve collaboration, where parties may not yet be in formal conflict, but recognize the need to coordinate because of the potential for conflict. This may serve a conflict prevention function (Ramsbotham, Woodhouse, and Miall 2011). The "downstream" end of the spectrum could involve formal mediation processes where parties may already be in violent conflict but see the potential benefits of resolving differences through negotiated processes. This occurs when parties recognize that they stand to gain from negotiation – or lose through continued violence or litigation.

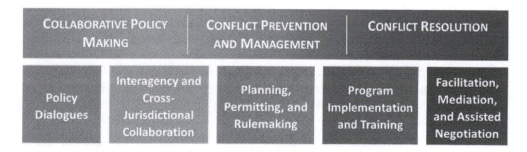

*Figure 16.1* Spectrum of Environmental Conflict Resolution

Processes might involve third-party facilitation or mediation, multi-stakeholder collaborative processes, and/or public policy dispute resolution. Joint fact finding (JFF) is one type of process that often involves a neutral third-party facilitator. This process is used to help parties reconcile different understandings of the technical dimensions of a problem. JFF involves pooling relevant information and enabling dialogue between technical experts, decision makers, and other key stakeholders. The process focuses on translating information so that it is understandable and accessible to all participants, and it "maps" areas of

---

### Textbox 16.1 Tri-state water wars in the United States

The conflict in the Apalachicola-Chattahoochee-Flint (ACF) river basin has been referred to as the "tri-state water wars" between the "ever-growing population of Atlanta, the ecological interests of Florida, and the municipal, industrial, and power uses of Alabama" (ABA 2012). The case involves disagreement over proper apportionment of water from an interstate river basin, with downstream stakeholders claiming that water withdrawals were made without regard to downstream interests. The case has been tied up in litigation for almost 30 years.

In 2008, a small group of stakeholders from the three states of the ACF basin, frustrated with the political stalemate, began looking at strategies and potential actions for sharing the water in the basin. The US Institute for Environmental Conflict Resolution served as the neutral third party to develop a process for working through differences between stakeholders at the grassroots level. Through a facilitated process, the ACF Stakeholders, Inc. (ACFS) was established. The agreed-upon process design resulted in a decision-making body made up of 56 members, representing 14 interest categories from 4 sub-basins.[1] Their goal was to achieve equitable water-sharing solutions among stakeholders that balanced economic, ecological, and social values, while ensuring sustainability for current and future generations. The 56 members of the ACFS Governing Board (the name of the decision-making body of the group) reached consensus on a Sustainable Water Resource Management Plan – the first water management plan that addresses water issues throughout the basin and incorporates broad and balanced perspectives from stakeholders from all three states (ACFS 2015).

The final decision on water allocation in this case is still pending in the Supreme Court (Supreme Court 2018). While the stakeholders came to consensus on a management plan, ACFS continues to seek adoption of the plan by the states. As such, this case illustrates the complicated way in which state and national politics, as well as legal processes, can influence and interact with stakeholder and public interests. In this case, perceived stagnation at the political level spurred creative alternatives that resulted in relationship building and conflict resolution efforts at the local, grassroots level. ACFS serves as the unified stakeholder voice in the ACF basin and a forum for the exchange of information and joint problem solving. At the same time, this case illustrates the limitations of environmental conflict resolution when situated in a broader political context involving different political actors with different interests.

agreement, disagreement, and uncertainty (McCreary et al. 2001). JFF has been used to resolve disagreements over which types of facilities are best suited to draw in seawater while minimizing impacts to marine species as part of California's desalination efforts (McCreary and Cowart 2016).

Collaboration and cooperative governance mechanisms are continuing to gain attention from policymakers as an alternative for addressing highly complex conflicts over water, land, and other resources. Such processes are pursued to favor equitable access and management of resources through negotiation, agreement making, JFF, mediation, or other processes. The substance of discussions and consideration of possible outcomes are stakeholder-driven. Environmental collaboration and conflict resolution processes result in cost reduction, improved relationships, and better outcomes that avoided litigation (ECCR 2018). These benefits come from the focus on win-win solutions and relationship building rather than having a winner and a loser. Agreement between divergent interests is likely to endure over the long term if a variety of voices have been involved in a decision.

### Environmental peacemaking and peacebuilding

Early conflict resolution literature typically referred to conflict and its resolution in a linear way. Conflicts were understood to move from formation to escalation and into endurance, with the hope that they would de-escalate and find resolution, often with the support of third parties. In the 1990s, the notion of conflict cycles entered the literature, rooted in the idea that conflicts could de-escalate and re-escalate before finding resolution or transformation and that multiple conflict cycles could exist within larger conflicts. With this growing sophistication in the field's framing and examination of conflicts, it became increasingly clear that conflict environments are complex, with conflictual and cooperative interactions operating simultaneously, by different actors and with different relational intentions and practices (Zeitoun and Mirumachi 2008).

Within conflict contexts, there is sometimes evidence of peaceable cooperation on environmental and natural resources management between different groups. Where high-level official actors intent on coming to formal agreement pursue such cooperation, it has typically been referred to as *environmental peacemaking*. Where undertaken by sub-national bodies, civil society organizations, NGOs, epistemic communities, and sometimes officials engaged in informal processes or non-official capacities, this has been understood as *environmental peacebuilding*. The literature aims to understand the extent to which environmental cooperation may contribute to transforming conflicts, how transformation takes place, and with what specific effects, while identifying the obstacles and challenges involved. While environmental peacemaking and peacebuilding may come from the same root, they have branched in separate though complementary directions.

### Environmental peacemaking

Multiple "pathways" of environmental peacemaking have been developed, based on a growing and continuously evolving understanding of how this takes place (Conca 2002). One pathway of environmental peacemaking is rooted in the notion that such cooperation can alter the strategic climate in which conflict parties situate themselves, extending the "shadow of the future" (i.e., the bargaining window), and creating new opportunities for high-level agreement on matters other than, or in addition to, environmental governance. A second pathway is rooted in the development of shared and/or overlapping identities of conflict parties, often through functional or neo-functional cooperative processes, the building of environmental security communities, and the like.

It must also be recognized that not all environmental cooperation can or should be understood as peaceable. Indeed, such cooperation operates within a context and between actors that are sometimes quite different in their sources and practices of power (e.g., in the Middle East, between Israel and the Palestinian Authority). In such cases, so-called cooperation may have the perverse effect of reproducing hegemonic, asymmetric relations (as argued in the hydrohegemony literature; see Zeitoun 2009). In other words, environmental *cooperation* should not necessarily be understood as environmental peacemaking or peacebuilding. It is important to examine whether cooperation is itself structured to transform relations between conflict parties or simply reproduce the relational status quo between them.

*Environmental peacebuilding*

Environmental peacebuilding may be defined as the pursuit of peaceable relations between conflict stakeholders through environmental cooperation. Typically, environmental peacebuilding is distinguished from environmental peacemaking in that it is undertaken by non-state actors (or in some cases, state actors acting in a non-official capacity), where the intention is not specifically to build official agreement (though this may spill into Track I diplomacy) and where considerations of environmental sustainability are central, if not paramount.

Environmental peacebuilding operates in multiple ways. While official discourses may construct enemy images of the other, cooperative environmental practices may contribute to the transformation of such images, a rehumanization of the other, bridging the divide and enabling trusting relations to develop. Transboundary environmental action may enable the development of shared identities that are layered upon uninational identities, again countering othering narratives and allowing for the production of emergent shared ones. Finally, environmental peacebuilding typically operates from the assumption of, and desire to transform, inequitable access to environmental resources (including conservation areas, ecosystem services, indigenous territories, etc.; this is discussed in the case study on the water-food-energy nexus in Israel/Palestine).

Finally, environmental peacebuilding entails an acute and reflexive sensitivity to issues of power, intent on transforming power and asymmetry (Abitbol 2012). Environmental peacebuilding is variably positioned to build equality and partnership between conflict parties and to enable equitable access to resources and material benefits. It ensures environmental sustainability while favoring ecosystemic benefits (e.g., preventing raw sewage from being dumped into transboundary streams). To ensure ongoing peaceable progress, environmental peacebuilding processes must ever be mindful of hydrohegemonic residues, well-intentioned processes that unwittingly re-produce asymmetric, even violent hegemonic relations. For example, if environmental peacebuilding processes happen only in the language and physical space of the more powerful actor, ostensible progress on environmental issues may also reproduce asymmetric relationships. In brief, environmental peacebuilding entails the production of just peace through environmental cooperation.

## Case studies in environmental peacebuilding and conflict resolution

Two case studies have been selected to illustrate the concepts discussed. The first case study focuses on the nexus of water-food-energy peacebuilding between Israelis and Palestinians.

The second focuses on the evolution of the field of environmental conflict resolution in the US federal government.

### *Israel/Palestine*

Contemporary peacebuilding efforts at the water-food-energy nexus involving Israelis and Palestinians are situated within the Israeli-Palestinian conflict. To understand the water-food-energy nexus work underway, it is essential to recognize the centrality of water in the conflictual Middle East.

A good place to start is understanding that there are both conventional and non-conventional water resources in the region. Conventional water resources include the Jordan River, whose natural flow is estimated between 1.24–1.476 Billion Cubic Meters (BCM), though with only 78–90 Million Cubic Meters (MCM) flowing into the Dead Sea today.[2] The other principal conventional water resource is the Mountain Aquifer, which is itself divided into three sub-aquifers, whose total available safe yield has been agreed on as 679 MCM (as per the Israeli-Palestinian Oslo Agreement). The largest of the three, the Western Mountain Aquifer yields some 300–450 MCM, the North-Eastern Aquifer some 130–200 MCM, and the Eastern Aquifer 151–250 MCM. The range of estimates reflects the assessment of different scientists, political bodies, and development organizations, given that water and even science are sometimes politically charged. Also, each sub-aquifer recharges and discharges its water in varying proportions in Israel and the West Bank. The question of whose water it is has become fraught with complexity (e.g., the Western Mountain Aquifer recharges largely in the West Bank while predominantly discharging in Israel – thus, whose water is it?). In addition, there is a Coastal Aquifer in both Israel and Gaza and other smaller aquifers in the South; they are less contentious than the Jordan River and Mountain Aquifer.

There are also non-conventional water resources in the region, derived from both desalination and wastewater recycling, which are important given the natural water scarcity in the region. Israel produces some 600 MCM/yr of desalinated water, which is slated to increase to 750 MCM by 2020. The Palestinians produce none, for a host of reasons (including the underdevelopment and fragility of conflict-affected Gaza, the Palestinians' only direct access to the sea). The anticipated Red Sea Dead Sea Water Conveyance is expected to increase supply to Jordan, Israel, and the Palestinians (who are slated to purchase some 32 MCM/yr from Israel). Israel recycles and reuses close to 90 percent of its wastewater for irrigation purposes, while the Palestinians recycle almost none (for technological, administrative, economic, political, and other reasons).

Any discussion of water issues between Israelis and Palestinians needs to be situated in historical context. Hydropolitical relations between Israel and the Palestinians were particularly violent and unjust in the period stemming from the 1967 Israeli occupation of the West Bank to 1995. For example, shortly after its occupation, Israel imposed a water-related regime of permits on the Palestinians in the West Bank, dramatically altering their water management practices. In other words, Israeli authorities issued permits to all Palestinians (as well as Israelis) for drawing and developing water resources (both in the West Bank and in Israel). Palestinians' ability to access water resources for agricultural purposes was severely curtailed during this time.

In the Israeli-Palestinian relationship, Israel is clearly the stronger power, compared to the occupied Palestinian – politically, economically, militarily, in terms of natural resource access, and in other ways. Among other things, the 1993–2000 Oslo process was meant to transform the hydropolitical relationship of Israelis and Palestinians. Most notably, the Oslo

II Accords, Article 40, provides an acknowledgment of Palestinian water rights and reflects the culmination of an environmental peacemaking component of a wider Israeli-Palestinian peacemaking process between Israel and the Palestinian Liberation Organization (PLO)/Palestinian Authority (PA). However, even the meaning of Palestinian "water rights" remains to this day disputed by the parties.

While the Oslo process collapsed in 2000, the water agreement between Israel and the Palestinians, including the Joint Water Committee (JWC), has persisted in the absence of something better. Today, the JWC serves as a coordinating body for water resources management in the West Bank, with Palestinian and Israeli representatives. While keeping the lines of communication open between the parties, it has also been perceived as a body that reproduces Israeli-Palestinian asymmetry; e.g., there is no mediating third-party presence at the JWC to temper the vastly superior technical, economic, security, and other resources of Israel as compared to the Palestinians.

Within this challenging hydropolitical context, there are a host of civil society organizations and private sector actors engaged in transboundary environmental cooperation. One organization that has intentionally framed its work as environmental peacebuilding is EcoPeace (formerly known as Friends of the Earth Middle East). Led by one Israeli, one Palestinian, and one Jordanian director, this organization has engaged in environmentally grounded peacebuilding work for more than 20 years in a multiplicity of ways.

At the core of its approach and engagement, EcoPeace has fundamentally sought to identify that which Israelis and Palestinians (as well as Jordanians) have in common in terms of the environment and to build upon it. With equal respect for Palestinian, Israeli, and Jordanian human rights and dignity, EcoPeace has ensured that all of its work and campaigns are led by at least one person from each community. Launched in 2001, in the midst of the Second Palestinian Intifada, the Good Water Neighbours (GWN) project built cross-border partnerships between Israeli and Palestinian communities (with more limited Jordanian involvement). The entire approach was rooted in a partnership that saw project leaders, municipal and community leaders, private sector actors, and young people and their parents engage one another across the 1967 border between Israel and the West Bank (known as the Green Line) in a vast array of activities. This included building ecological gardens, developing heritage initiatives, engaging in field trips, and more. At its root, the GWN project built upon and sought to further cultivate a shared bioregional identity on the premise that "Nature knows no bounds" (an EcoPeace slogan).

While EcoPeace has been overt in referring to its work as environmental peacebuilding, the Arava Institute for Environmental Studies (AIES) and the Palestinian Wastewater Engineers Group (PWEG) have been more reticent about referring to their work in such a way. These organizations, one Israeli and the other Palestinian, have worked together for some ten years in providing small-scale wastewater (and subsequently energy and food security) solutions to Palestinian community members in the Jericho Governorate. Palestinian beneficiaries of these efforts are off-grid, with their wastewater formerly flowing largely into unlined cesspits with a good portion of this wastewater seeping into the groundwater and/or dumped directly into valleys and then crossing from Palestine into Israel.

In delivering small-scale, off-grid wastewater treatment solutions, PWEG and AIES have provided direct and tangible benefits to Palestinians. Environmentally speaking, they are modestly preventing groundwater and surface-level pollution deriving from wastewater in Palestine. They are facilitating access to increased quantities of treated wastewater for irrigating gardens, fields, and date palms among farming communities. They are saving community members' money (i.e., the cost of tankers pumping wastewater, the cost of water for irrigation). All of this work contributes to a healthier environment. It has also supported date farmers from the community through greater access to a sustainable source of solar energy for irrigation pumps. Finally, it has been contributing to structured and sustained relationship-building between farming communities in the Jordan and Arava Valleys.

The vantage point and approaches of EcoPeace and PWEG/AIES are clearly different. Yet, what they have in common is the partnership development and practice they pursue, acknowledging the equality in rights and dignity of Palestinians and Israelis, but also operating from a critical stance against the inequities, injustice, and asymmetry of their conflictual circumstances and daily lives. While there is no universal definition of environmental peacebuilding, it may very well be understood as the *production* of a relationship rooted in equality, seeking equity and material benefit, pursuing environmental sustainability, and structured as partnership between community members ostensibly on opposite sides of the conflict divide.

### United States Government

Environmental conflict resolution in the United States has been used in a variety of capacities, from collaborative processes involving stakeholders to interagency collaboration issues involving multiple levels of government (federal, state, local, tribal) and the public.

Environmental conflict resolution is understood to have coalesced as a field of practice in the United States during the 1970s. Environmental conflict resolution came out of challenges related to implementing the National Environmental Policy Act (NEPA) as well as obstacles to consensus building in the context of a rigid legal system (Fisher and Sablan 2018). Early on, there were questions about the extent to which government collaboration with outside stakeholders was appropriate. There was also concern about agencies opening themselves up to risks by sharing decision-making power with the public, and the challenge of maintaining consistency in policy across the country (SPIDR 1997).

A key turning point in advancing the use of collaboration in the US government was the Office of Management and Budget (OMB) and the Council on Environmental Quality (CEQ) issuing a joint policy statement in 2005 that directed agencies to increase their use of environmental conflict resolution and their institutional capacity for collaborative problem solving. It also included a formal definition of *environmental conflict resolution* as "third-party assisted collaborative problem solving and conflict resolution in the context of environmental, public lands, or natural resources issues or conflicts, including matters related to energy, transportation, and water and land management" (OMB 2005). It was reinforced with the 2012 memorandum, adding collaboration as a key component (OMB 2012), as well as guidelines for agencies engaging in collaborative problem-solving. The memorandum increased the legitimacy of environmental collaboration and conflict resolution approaches in the federal government and helped standardize basic principles.

Environmental conflict resolution is used in many contexts in the United States, including between federal agencies and Native American tribes. This is challenging because in some instances, "the framing of the negotiations does not comport with the worldview of some of the parties" (Podziba 2018, 386). Negotiations often require transparency in order to talk through difficult issues, but "in the case of many sacred sites and resources, cultural and religious strictures may make it impossible for a tribe to reveal a site's exact location, times needed for sacred ritual, and specific use and purpose" (Podziba 2018, 389). Another complicating factor is that the laws that apply to the US government, such as the Freedom of

Information Act (FOIA), can result in making information public, therefore tribal decision makers are often unwilling to trust the promise of confidentiality that is often a key part of an environmental negotiation process.

One of the contemporary issues gaining attention is the management of wild horses, particularly as the White House administration contemplates changes to agency policy (Brulliard and Eilperin 2017). For many in the US, free-roaming horses represent the American West and the American spirit. However, there are conflicting narratives about whether or not they are native to North America. Differing interpretations of science and historical documents support one or the other narrative. Based on these conflicting narratives, there is fundamental disagreement among different stakeholders who value public lands in the United States for different purposes (e.g., recreation, cattle ranching, conservation, etc.) as well as members of the public about whether the horses are compatible with native ecosystems in the United States. This distinction drives conflicting views and a variety of concerns about appropriate management strategies. Some of the concerns affecting decision making include humane treatment of animals, genetic diversity, environmental resilience, habitat for other species, watershed protection, and equity for others who use the land.

The agencies charged with management of these horses include the Bureau of Land Management (BLM), an agency under the Department of Interior (DOI), and the US Forest Service, an agency under the Department of Agriculture (USDA). Both agencies are bound by multiple-use mandates, meaning they are required to manage public land for potentially conflicting purposes that include conservation, recreation, cattle grazing, energy development, extractive industries, and others. The 1971 Wild and Free-Roaming Horses and Burros Act (commonly referred to as the Wild Horse and Burro Act) was passed in response to public pressure for the federal government to protect the animals. The Act charged both the Forest Service and the BLM with protecting the horses under federal law, in addition to ensuring multiple uses of public lands.

The multi-jurisdictional challenges around wild horse management in the United States are vast, and often involve federal, state, and local agencies with authorities. Horses migrate between federal, state, and private land, which requires coordination around overlapping laws and regulations. Horses may also migrate onto adjacent tribal land, which is subject to its own legal system that is separate and different from the US government and differs for each Tribal Nation.

Because of all the complexities described here, environmental conflict resolution is a promising way for addressing ongoing challenges. There is a range of mechanisms that can be drawn upon in such a process. Any of these mechanisms or combinations of mechanisms could be used as elements of a larger multi-stakeholder collaborative effort or facilitated negotiation process. They include:

- Appreciative inquiry involves exploring a joint vision for the future. This can be helpful in framing and/or addressing conflicting narratives by moving groups toward a common narrative for the future.
- Mediation may involve two parties deliberating over a distinct sub-issue as part of the larger issue. There might be historic animosity and a specific legal issue between two stakeholder groups that needs to be addressed while the larger group deliberates on related topics.
- JFF involves reconciling competing science. One form this may take is having experts on both sides of an issue engage in direct deliberation while stakeholders observe.

The challenge for environmental conflict resolution practitioners is to create a process that can move parties toward an agreement. This means taking conflicting narratives, divergent interests, contradictory science, and complex legal stipulations and creating a process that is constructive and leads to joint problem-solving. As this topic continues to gain attention in the United States, collaborative efforts are underway, offering an opportunity for stakeholders with divergent viewpoints to address complex challenges. More often than not, environmental conflict resolution processes do not conclude with one strategy to endure over the long term. Rather, they are iterative and ongoing, as strategies are often revisited due to changing conditions.

## Challenges and future directions

One of the key issues of the twenty-first century, climate change, has introduced a new set of challenges to those working at the environment-conflict-peace nexus, given emerging and dynamic multifaceted, multilevel, and multisectoral realities and implications facing the world (see Ramsbotham et al. 2011, 293–304). Acknowledging that industrialized countries are responsible for 70 percent of global greenhouse gas emissions, it is now widely recognized that industrial development pathways of the last century have had major detrimental implications for the global environment, with still-rising emission levels causing widespread damage to our biospheric home. This is already having asymmetrically devastating consequences for communities in the Global South, and even more particularly for women and children (Díez 2008). Communities in the Global South are more directly dependent on natural resources for food and shelter. They are more vulnerable to climate patterns, including warming trends, and have legitimately sought greater climate justice, a reality that is likely to increase into the future (Stoett 2012).

Today, a few global organizations whose mandates have primarily been to address global environmental issues, including biodiversity, freshwater management, fisheries and coastal management, climate change, and more, are starting to take notice of the need to be much more intentional than they have been in the past of the conflict and peace implications of their work. Indigenous/tribal groups have typically criticized the field of conservation for failing to recognize their rights to land and resources and for rejecting their worldviews.

To begin addressing and transforming this history, among others, the International Union for the Conservation of Nature and Natural Resources (IUCN), through its Commission on Environmental, Economic and Social Policy (CEESP) has integrated the experience and knowledge of indigenous peoples alongside that of scientists to address challenges at the intersection of conservation, livelihoods, and environmental justice. A recently published Environmental Peacebuilding Training Manual by Conservation International provides some of the nuts-and-bolts of how to pursue concrete processes of environmental peacebuilding and transformation.

There also remains much work to be done to integrate gender into the field, in terms of the research and literature produced, methodologies pursued, and practices on the ground, and also recognize the immense contribution of women as leaders in this field. The ecofeminist work of Nobel Peace Laureate Wangari Maathai and the Green Belt Movement have inspired countless on the path of environment and peace, bridging the local and global in a partnership of men and women from the Global South and North. As deliberations continue over the future of the academic field and practice at the environment-conflict-peace nexus, it is important to draw further inspiration from this work, whose premise is that a transformation of our relationship with the environment *and* with one another go hand-in-hand and are in fact mutually constitutive. This is true of relations between Israelis and Palestinians, indigenous and non-indigenous communities, and between men and women, whether in deserts, cities, forests, on the banks of rivers, or at the hearts of bustling cities.

## Questions for further discussion

1   How are environmental issues similar to and also different from other issues at the intersection of conflict and peace?
2   How might environmental cooperation processes facilitate wider peace processes?
3   What motivates different conflict parties to move from conflictual to collaborative processes?
4   How can cooperative environmental processes and agreements address and cope with climate change or other unforeseen events?
5   Under what circumstances do you think environmental conflict resolution might not work or might not be appropriate at a given point in time?

## Suggested resources

1   Conca, Ken, and Geoffrey Dabelko. 2002. *Environmental Peacemaking*. Washington, DC: Woodrow Wilson Center Press with Johns Hopkins University Press.
2   Conservation International. 2017. *Environmental Peacebuilding Training Manual*. October. Available in multiple languages at: https://sites.google.com/a/conservation.org/peace/home/training.
3   Moore, Lucy. 2013. *Common Ground on Hostile Turf: Stories from an Environmental Mediator*. Washington, DC: Island Press.
4   Zeitoun, Mark. 2009. *Power and Water in the Middle East: The Hidden Politics of the Palestinian-Israeli Water Conflict*. New York, NY: IBTauris.

## Become engaged!

The following associations and organizations provide opportunities for engagement, including conferences, membership, internship, and relevant resources for further participation.

1   Association for Conflict Resolution's Environment and Public Policy Section (ACR EPP): www.acrepp.dreamhosters.com/.
2   Environmental Peacebuilding Association: https://environmentalpeacebuilding.org.
3   International Association for Public Participation (IAP2): www.iap2.org/.
4   IUCN Commission on Environmental, Economic and Social Policy (CEESP): www.iucn.org/commissions/commission-environmental-economic-and-social-policy/ceesp.

## Notes

1   Interest categories include navigation, recreation, water quality, water supply, farm and urban agriculture, industry and manufacturing, seafood industry, hydropower, thermal power, local government, environment and conservation, business and economic development, historic and cultural, and other. The four sub-basins are Apalachicola, Flint, Upper Chattahoochee, and Lower/Middle Chattahoochee.
2   The Dead Sea is the terminal lake of the Jordan River Basin.

# References and further reading

Abitbol, Eric. 2012. *Hydropolitical Peacebuilding: Israeli-Palestinian Water Relations and the Trans-formation of Asymmetric Conflict in the Middle East*. Ph.D Thesis. University of Bradford. Accessed October 5, 2019. https://ethos.bl.uk/OrderDetails.do?uin=uk.bl.ethos.600413.

ACFS Sustainable Water Management Plan. 2015. "Apalachicola Chattahoochee Flint (ACF) Stake-holders, Inc." Accessed July 29, 2019. http://acfstakeholders.org/wp-content/uploads/2015/05/ACFS-Sustainable-Water-Management-Plan-For-Release.pdf.

Agger, Kasper. 2014. "Behind the Headlines: Drivers of Violence in the Central African Republic." *Enough Project*, May 1. Accessed December 8, 2018. https://enoughproject.org/files/CAR%20Report%20-%20Behind%20the%20Headlines%205.1.14.pdf.

American Bar Association. 2012. "Lessons from the Tri-State Water War." October 23. www.americanbar.org/publications/state_local_law_news/2011_12/winter_2012/tri-state_water_war/.

Auty, Richard M. 1993. *Sustaining Development in Mineral Economies: The Resource Curse Thesis*. London: Routledge.

Bean, Martha, Larry Fisher, and Mike Eng. 2007. "Assessment in Environmental and Public Policy Conflict Resolution: Emerging Theory, Patterns of Practice, and a Conceptual Framework." *Conflict Resolution Quarterly* 24 (4): 447–68.

Biswas, Aswit K. 2001. "Scientific Assessment of the Long-Term Environmental Consequences of War." In *The Environmental Consequences of War: Legal, Economic, and Scientific Perspectives*, edited by Jay E. Austin and Carl E. Brush, 303–15. Cambridge: Cambridge University Press.

Brown, Harrison. 1954. *The Challenge of Man's Future*. New York, NY: Viking Press.

Brulliard, Karin, and Juliet Eilperin. 2017. "Wild Horses Could Be Sold for Slaughter or Euthanized Under Trump Budget." *Washington Post*, May 26. Accessed December 13, 2018. www.washingtonpost.com/news/animalia/wp/2017/05/26/wild-horses-could-be-sold-for-slaughter-or-euthanized-under-trump-budget/?noredirect=on&utm_term=.3864157c1033.

Brundtland, Gro Harlem. 1987. "Report of the World Commission on Environment and Development: Our Common Future." August 4. Accessed July 29, 2019. www.un-documents.net/our-common-future.pdf.

Conca, Ken. 2002. "The Case for Environmental Peacemaking." In *Environmental Peacemaking*, edited by Ken Conca and Geoffrey Dabelko, 1–22. Washington, DC: Woodrow Wilson Center Press with Johns Hopkins University Press.

Conservation International. 2017. *Environmental Peacebuilding Training Manual*, October. Available in multiple languages at: https://sites.google.com/a/conservation.org/peace/home/training.

Curtin, Joseph. 2018. "The Paris Agreement Versus the Trump Effect: Countervailing Forces for Decar-bonisation." *Institute of International and European Affairs*, March 12. Accessed July 29, 2019. www.iiea.com/publication/the-paris-climate-agreement-versus-the-trump-effect-countervailing-forces-for-decarbonisation/.

Díez, Jordi. 2008. "Globalization and Environmental Challenges Confronting the South." In *Global Environmental Challenges: Perspectives from the South*, edited by Jordi Díez and O.P. Dwivedi. Buffalo, NY: Broadview Press.

Federal Forum on Environmental Collaboration and Conflict Resolution. 2018. *Environmental Collaboration and Conflict Resolution (ECCR): Enhancing Agency Efficiency and Making Government Accountable to the People*, May 2. Accessed July 29, 2019. https://ceq.doe.gov/docs/nepa-practice/ECCR_Benefits_Recommendations_Report_%205-02-018.pdf.

Fisher, Micah, and Tina Sablan. 2018. "Evaluating Environmental Conflict Resolution: Practitioners, Projects, and the Movement." *Conflict Resolution Quarterly* 36 (1): 7–19.

Fisher, Roger, William Ury, and Bruce Patton. 1991. *Getting to Yes: Negotiating Agreement Without Giving in*. New York, NY: Penguin Books.

Friends Committee on National Legislation. 2014. *Central African Republic Crisis: Managing Natural Resources for Peace*. Accessed July 29, 2019. www.fcnl.org/documents/27.

Geneva International Centre for Humanitarian Demining (GICHD). 2016. *A Guide to Cluster Munitions*, 3rd edition, Geneva. Accessed October 4, 2019. http://www.clusterconvention.org/wp-content/uploads/2016/04/A-Guide-to-Cluster-Munitions.pdf.

Gleditsch, Nils Petter. 1998. "Armed Conflict and the Environment: A Critique of the Literature." *Journal of Peace Research* 35 (3): 381–400.

Hartmann, Betsy. 1998. "Population, Environment, and Security: A New Trinity." *Environment and Urbanization* 10 (2): 113–28.

Homer-Dixon, Thomas F. 1991. "On the Threshold: Environmental Changes as Causes of Acute Conflict." *International Security* 16 (2): 76–116.

———. 1994. "Environmental Scarcities and Violent Conflict: Evidence from Cases." *International Security* 19 (1): 5–40.

———. 1999. *Environmental Scarcity and Violence*. Princeton, NJ: Princeton University Press.

Innes, Judith E., and David E. Booher. 2007. "Consensus Building and Complex Adaptive Systems: A Framework for Evaluating Collaborative Planning." *Journal of American Planning Association* 65 (4): 412–23.

Levy, Marc. 1995. "Is the Environment a National Security Issue?" *International Security* 20 (2): 35–62.

Linden, Olof, Arnie Jerneloev, and Johanna Egerup. 2004. "The Environmental Impacts of the Gulf War 1991." *International Institute for Applied Systems Analysis (IIASA) Interim Report*, April. IIASA, Laxenburg, Austria: IR-04–019. Accessed December 10, 2018. http://pure.iiasa.ac.at/id/eprint/7427/.

McCreary, Scott, and Meredith Cowart. 2016. "Desalination in California: The California Coastal Commission/ Poseidon Water Joint Fact-Finding Process." *Joint Fact Finding in Urban Planning and Environmental Disputes*, edited by Masahiro Matsuura and Todd Schenk, 111–38. London: Routledge.

McCreary, Scott, John Gammon, and Bennett Brooks. 2001. "Refining and Testing Joint Fact Finding for Environmental Dispute Resolution: Ten Years of Success." *Conflict Resolution Quarterly* 18 (4): 329–48.

Moore, Lucy. 2013. *Common Ground on Hostile Turf: Stories from an Environmental Mediator*. Washington, DC: Island Press.

Organization of the Petroleum Exporting Countries (OPEC). 2004. "World Proven Crude Oil Reserves by Country, 1980–2004." Accessed December 10, 2018. www.opec.org/library/Annual%20Statistical%20Bulletin/interactive/2004/FileZ/XL/T33.HTM.

Osborn, Fairfield. 1953. *Our Plundered Planet*. Boston, MA: Little, Brown, and Company.

Parker-Follett, Mary. 2003. "Dynamic Administration: The Collected Papers of Mary Parker Follett." In *Volume 3 of Early Sociology of Management and Organizations, Kenneth Thompson*, edited by Henry C. Metcalf and Lyndall Urwick Harper. New York, NY: Taylor & Francis.

Podziba, Susan L. 2018. "Mediating Conflicts Over Sacred Lands." *Conflict Resolution Quarterly* 35 (4): 383–91.

Ramsbotham, Oliver, Tom Woodhouse, and Hugh Miall. 2015. *Contemporary Conflict Resolution: the Prevention, Management and Transformation of Deadly Conflicts*, 3rd edition. Cambridge: Polity Press.

Rittel, Horst W.J., and Melvin M. Webber. 1973. "Dilemmas in a General Theory of Planning." *Policy Sciences* 4 (2): 155–69.

Society of Professionals in Dispute Resolution (SPIDR). 1997. "Report and Recommendations of the SPIDR." *Environment/Public Disputes Sector Critical Issues Committee*. CNCR-Hewlett Foundation Seed Grant White Papers.

Stoett, P.J. 2012. *Global Ecopolitics: Crisis, Governance, and Justice*. North York, Ontario: University of Toronto Press.

Supreme Court. 2018. "Florida v. Georgia, No. 142." Accessed July 29, 2019. www.supremecourt.gov/opinions/17pdf/142%20orig_h3ci.pdf.

Tanner, Randy, Wayne Freimund, Brace Hayden, and Bill Dolan. 2007. "The Waterton-Glacier International Peace Park: Conservation Amid Border Security." In *Peace Parks Conservation and Conflict Resolution*, edited by Saleem H. Ali, 183–204. Cambridge: Massachusetts Institute of Technology Press.

Taylor, Alan. 2016. "Operation Desert Storm: 25 Years Since the First Gulf War." *The Atlantic*, January 24. Accessed December 10, 2018. www.theatlantic.com/photo/2016/01/operation-desert-storm-25-years-since-the-first-gulf-war/424191/.

Theisen, Ole Magnus. 2008. "Blood and Soil? Resource Scarcity and Internal Armed Conflict Revisited." *Journal of Peace Research* 45 (6): 801–18.

United States Congress. 2006. "The Wild Free Roaming Horse & Burros Act of 1971." Public Law 92–195 amended by Congress as of January 2006. Accessed December 11, 2018. www.blm.gov/or/regulations/files/whbact_1971.pdf.

United States Executive Office of the President. 2005. *Memorandum on Environmental Conflict Resolution*. Washington, DC: Office of Management and Budget and Council on Environmental Quality. Accessed July 29, 2019. www.udall.gov/documents/Institute/OMB_CEQ_Memorandum_2005.pdf.

———. 2012. *Memorandum on Environmental Collaboration and Conflict Resolution*. Washington, DC: Office of Management and Budget and Council on Environmental Quality. www.udall.gov/documents/Institute/OMB_CEQ_Memorandum_2012.pdf.

Ury, William. 1993. *Getting Past No: Negotiating in Difficult Situations*, revised edition. New York, NY: Penguin Books.

Zeitoun, Mark. 2009. *Power and Water in the Middle East: The Hidden Politics of the Palestinian-Israeli Water Conflict*. New York, NY: IB Tauris.

Zeitoun, Mark, and Naho Mirumachi. 2008. "Transboundary Water Interactions: Reconsidering Conflict and Cooperation." *International Environmental Agreements: Politics, Law and Economics* 8 (4): 297–316.

# 17  Conclusion

## Future challenges and opportunities in international conflict management

*Charity Butcher and Maia Carter Hallward*[1]

## Introduction

This book has considered a wide range of mechanisms for managing international conflict and has explored a variety of themes within the field of international conflict management. Each mechanism for international conflict management has its strengths and weaknesses. Negotiation is one of the most frequently used tools of international conflict management and has been successful in a variety of cases, including the negotiation of the Rome Treaty, establishing the International Criminal Court. At the same time, negotiations may not always lead to a successful outcome, as the Brexit negotiations under Teresa May demonstrate. Since international negotiation is a two-level game, both international and domestic considerations are at play, which make such processes very complex and difficult. Similarly, mediation has been successful in cases such as the Colombian peace process, but finding external mediators who are viewed as neutral can be difficult due to the complexity of the parties and issues involved. Nonviolent resistance has been shown to help lead to successful social change outcomes, but some argue that it is hypocritical to expect oppressed groups to use nonviolence while governments use force against them. Some ignore the strategic nature of nonviolent resistance and dismiss it as utopian fluff rather than a method more successful than violence at deposing authoritarian leaders. Though the United Nations peacekeeping failed to prevent the genocide in Rwanda and was unable to protect civilians in the UN-safe-area in Srebrenica, studies have shown that UN peacekeeping is generally effective at increasing the length of peace, and the UN has revised peacekeeping operations to better protect civilians. For example, in 2017 the peacekeeping mission in Cote d'Ivioire was successfully completed after thirteen years (United Nations Peacekeeping 2017). At the same time, UN peacekeeping forces have been accused of committing atrocities such as rape during their service, further highlighting the potential problems associated with peacekeeping missions, even while peacekeepers are expected to take on additional and more complex tasks in the course of their mandates. Despite these challenges, and the high cost of peacekeeping, it remains more cost-effective than some other forms of intervention.

Many in the field of international conflict management view peacebuilding as necessary for preventing the recurrence of conflict, but, like peacekeeping, it has experienced numerous failures, many of which are attributed to liberal principles promoted by Western countries. Peacebuilding, particularly as carried out by multilateral agencies and large donors, is often criticized for failing to fully consider local contexts and local actors within the peacebuilding process. Succeeding generations of peacebuilding have sought to further integrate the efforts of multiple actors and agencies and to focus on resiliency, but major challenges remain in achieving the potential of peacebuilding due to the complex interaction of conflict, violence, and fragility, and the challenge of developing true synergy across sectors, institutions, and actors. Transitional justice has emerged since the end of World War II to help address the gravest crimes committed during armed conflicts and to help countries and individuals gain justice for these crimes. Reconciliation, which can also be found in some transitional justice measures, also aims for individuals to be able to reconcile their grievances and move forward in a more peaceful world. However, these mechanisms also have their limitations. Transitional justice can take many forms, but often includes some element of amnesty for some perpetuators of war crimes, which does not allow for justice to be served. Reconciliation, while an ideal outcome, is extremely difficult to attain, as forgiveness following horrible human rights abuses and conflict is not easily given. In both approaches, local context is key, but Western requirements for transitional justice may force an external model or a quicker timeline than suits the local engagement necessary for an authentic process. Further, resource constraints can play a role in ensuring adequate and timely justice or adequate reparations for victims whose lives and livelihoods were destroyed by authoritarian regimes and/or decades of violent conflict.

While individual chapters have been dedicated to each of these mechanisms, there are also clear connections between the content of these chapters. While certain techniques for managing conflict might be most useful in some cases, in reality most conflicts are managed using multiple tactics. For example, nonviolence resistance may incentivize actors to come to the table to discuss peace; mediation and negotiation may be used as methods to help parties reach agreement once they have come to the table; while peacekeeping, peacebuilding, reconciliation, and transitional justice mechanisms may each help create the conditions for a sustainable and lasting peace. Further, these processes may not always be entirely distinct. For example, United Nations peacekeeping increasingly includes peacebuilding components, and some forms of transitional justice overlap with efforts at reconciliation and coming to terms with past injustices.

Many of the themes discussed in this volume are complex and often interconnected. For example, civil society plays an important role in a variety of processes and issues and is critical for the "local turn" in peacebuilding as well as Track II negotiation processes, nonviolence resistance efforts, and culturally relevant transitional justice processes. Thematic issues such as the environment, economics, refugees and migrants, and ICTs act in mutually impacting ways, in which the economy or the environment can create new waves of migrants and refugees, and ICTs can be used to track potential conflict from such migration. Further, migrants and refugees can have an environmental and/or economic impact, as can the resource extraction necessary for manufacturing the mobile devices and computers needed for linking up to the Internet. In all of these cases, context matters – the environment can serve as a common resource around which people and groups come together to resolve their conflicts, or environmental change can spawn conflict. Likewise, ICTs can be used for oppression and as tools for liberation. Conflict management scholars and practitioners must also bear in mind that not all individuals and groups experience and respond to conflict in the same manner. Chapters on gender, ethnicity, and religion remind readers of the importance of identity in both peace and conflict. For example, each of these issues is important to consider when discussing refugees and migration, where the intersectionality of gender, ethnicity/religion, and economic factors, along with refugee or migrant status, add greater complexity to situations.

## Future challenges for managing international conflicts

Because international conflicts are often quite complex and multifaceted, significant challenges face those seeking to manage, resolve, and transform them. Addressing the root causes of conflict, which can include structural, cultural, and interpersonal factors, is essential for preventing the recurrence of armed conflict. As chapters in this volume attest, processes such as peacebuilding, reconciliation, and transitional justice are intended to assist in breaking cycles of conflict; however, despite good intentions, bureaucratic processes, power politics, and a tendency to prefer professionalized Western NGOs as partners rather than local grass-roots actors pose key obstacles. Further, actors within conflicts hold a myriad of identities, interests, and grievances, and surface-level demands may mask underlying concerns or fears. As noted in Chapter 12 on gender, for example, the DDR process in Colombia felt like a threat to ex-combatants' identities by forcing them to return from a status of glorified fighter to impoverished slum dweller. It is insufficient to glorify the local and dismiss the state, however, since not all non-state actors are "civil," nor do traditional local practices always espouse practices inclusive of racial and ethnic minorities, youth, or women. Bypassing the state, however, has its own challenges, as states continue to be seen as legitimate actors in the international system, and states are the key parties to international bodies like the United Nations, and to the treaties and conventions associated with the international human rights regime.

Policy coherence of the many actors involved in international conflict management at all levels of analysis remains a key challenge, as does ensuring appropriate involvement and recognition of multiple stakeholders. While the circumvention of states has been viewed as problematic for peacebuilding processes, amnesty for the abuses of state actors or tacit acceptance of state abuses also cause obstructions for peace. Similarly, the exclusion of non-state actors deemed illegitimate, including groups that use terrorism, makes negotiations or mediation more difficult processes. When such actors are excluded, the interests and griev-ances of these actors cannot be fully addressed, making conflict recurrence more likely. The same is true for a host of other actors, such as Syrian women noted in Chapter 10 on civil society, and is reflective of broader patterns of exclusion and intersectional oppression noted in Chapter 12 on gender.

A second challenge for international conflict management involves actors with such oppo-sitional goals that compromises are not easily managed. For example, atavistic nationalist and populist movements around the world, which are on the rise, often utilize language that is highly divisive, pitting one group ("us") against another ("them"). These issues are par-ticularly present in situations where there are significant numbers of migrants and refugees; these groups may be labeled as "security risks" by portions of the population, while others in the same population emphasize the benefits, such as a labor and cultural diversity, that migrants, including refugees, bring to a country. When such divides are compounded by absolute presumption of "right" and vilification of differing views to the point of refusing to engage in meaningful conversation, traditional conflict resolution methods do not suf-fice. Further, theories, including realism, that view the state as a unified actor with a single national identity and national interest cannot account for such internal divides, and therefore their prescribed policy outcomes cannot be assumed.

A third challenge facing international conflict management involves the increased speed with which people, weapons, and information, can travel. As noted in Chapter 15, conflict can lead to increased flows of migrants and refugees, and said flows can also generate con-flict in third-party states. At the same time, ethnic tensions in one country can create similar conflicts in neighboring countries with analogous ethnic divisions. Conflicts in Rwanda and Burundi, as well as the Democratic Republic of Congo, have been closely linked. In addition, diaspora communities – real or imagined – can also play a role in stoking flames of conflict, particularly with the advent of numerous Internet and social media platforms. For example, the so-called Islamic State was able to recruit many foreign fighters who sympathized with its sophisticated messaging that appealed to a wide range of identity groups using tropes of humanitarianism, inclusion, and drawing on a range of cultural norms (Carter Center 2016). As this example indicates, conflict can also spread and intensify through the cascading involvement of external actors in what was originally an intrastate conflict, as happened in Syria and Yemen in the wake of the 2011 uprisings. The conflict in Yemen is largely a proxy war between the regional powers of Saudi Arabia and Iran, but builds on a history of exclusion and marginalization at the national and subnational levels, and is continued due to the lack of action from great power states such as the United States, which has sold arms to Saudi Arabia and conducted drone strikes to allegedly contain Al Qaeda in the Arabian Peninsula. The wide array of actors in these conflicts makes resolution significantly more difficult; further, the involvement of powerful states often exacerbates armed conflicts by escalating the level of violence or prolonging the conflict through the use of vetoes at the UN Security Council.

A fourth challenge is the continuation of power inequalities on the global stage, as the actions of powerful states often have repercussions for much of the international community. For example, the Joint Comprehensive Plan of Action (2015) was an agreement between Iran, the five permanent members of the UN Security Council (the US, UK, France, China, and Russia), and the EU to limit Iran's nuclear weapons potential in exchange for the removal of sanctions on Iran. However, the plan was quite unpopular with Republicans in the United States, and though Iran was viewed as being compliant by most authoritative accounts, including by the International Atomic Energy Agency (IAEA), the organization tasked with inspecting Iran's facilities for compliance, US President Donald Trump decided to withdraw from the agreement in 2018 and to reinstate sanctions on Iran. While Iran and the other key actors remained in the agreement, US sanctions led to increased tensions not only between Iran and the United States, but also between Iran and European actors. Similarly, the trade war between the United States and China, which began in 2018, has created problems and issues for countries and institutions around the world. Thus, the actions of major powers can create and exacerbate conflicts around the globe.

While there are many international institutions that can help in managing international conflicts, such as the United Nations, the World Trade Organization (WTO), and the International Criminal Court (ICC), states differ in their trust of these various organizations. While most countries are members of the UN and the WTO, many states, including the United States, are not party to the ICC and other major international agreements. Lack of membership by major powers reduces the effectiveness of various international agreements and institutions in providing conflict management mechanisms that can be successful. Further, states like the United States have often acted unilaterally outside of these institutions, such as the US's 2003 invasion of Iraq against the will of the UN Security Council. Such unilateral actions further weaken international institutions, their legitimacy, and their ability to successfully manage conflicts. At the same time, the structure of many of these international organizations is seen by many as reflective of the interests of the powerful, as evidenced in the Security Council veto of the Permanent Five members, or perpetuating the wealth of the Global North, as evidenced in the neoliberal policies of the Bretton Woods economic institutions. Lack of resources and the propensity of mainstream media coverage to favor certain news stories over others can also create a vicious cycle in which some conflicts receive international attention and others are ignored.

A fifth challenge, discussed in Chapter 16 on the environment, involves the devastating and unpredictable impact of climate disruption around the world. Shifts in weather and precipitation patterns, along with changes in water levels and propensity for major storms impacts conflict in many ways. Some suggest the Syrian conflict began in part due to drought-induced internal migration, and the depletion of natural resources that sustained Yemen's economy is a contributing factor to the conflict there as well.

Even as inequalities of power, resources, and access perpetuate and incur conflict, some of the same challenging dynamics can serve as potential opportunities for managing and transforming conflict.

## Opportunities for successfully managing international conflicts

While there are significant challenges in managing international conflict, there are reasons to be hopeful. First, there is an increasing acceptance that local approaches to peacebuilding, as well as civil society involvement in all stages of peacemaking and peacebuilding processes, are important for legitimate and sustainable peace (see Chapters 7 on peacebuilding and 10 on civil society). Nonviolent resistance movements have helped bring about changes to existing state structures without resorting to war, and new and creative methods of civil resistance have had an impact in places as diverse as South Sudan, Hong Kong, and Puerto Rico, where nonviolent movements for change are occurring at time of this writing. Thus, whereas traditional IR theories focused on states as the primary actors, an interdisciplinary approach provides additional lenses for conceptualizing the actors and mechanisms available for managing conflict and building peace.

Second, despite the increased visibility of nationalism and xenophobia, evidence suggests that ethnic civil war is actually declining worldwide (Gurr 2000; Cederman, Gleditsch, and Wucherpfennig 2017). This decline in ethnic conflict is largely linked to government efforts to change policies in the interest of interethnic coexistence and to more explicitly provide politics that are designed to decrease grievances that have led to ethnic and religious conflicts. For example, regional autonomy for Kurds in Iraq has reduced ethnic tensions in Iraqi Kurdistan, even while conflict persists between Kurds and other governments in the region that have not granted such accommodations. If these types of changes can be found in places where conflicts have been particularly intractable, there is hope that other societies will be able to resolve similar conflicts. The possibility of virtual exchange programs, such as the Soliya dialogue program, which brings together students from around the world for facilitated dialogue sessions through an innovative web-based platform, also helps build bridges across real and perceived differences, fostering dialogue in the place of ignorance. The proliferation of citizen journalists and other ICT-facilitated communication tools also help people around the world connect and work together to address harassment, oppression, and provide photo evidence to discredit the lies told by oppressive regimes.

Third, while major powers and actors in the international system have often instigated and perpetuated armed conflicts, such actors also have the power to help mediate such conflicts, particularly given the will to do so. Although they are problematic, institutions such as the International Criminal Court and the UN Peacebuilding Commission are indications of the importance with which the global community of states views transitional justice and peacebuilding efforts. Further, the inclusion of a dedicated Sustainable Development Goal to peace, justice, and strong institutions (Goal 16) in the 2030 agenda emphasizes the interconnectedness of peace and justice with sustainable development. The future of managing international conflicts is certainly still wrought with uncertainty and challenges. However, there are clear mechanisms within the international system to deal with conflicts, and civil society actors are working to hold states accountable to utilizing these mechanisms rather than armed violence to achieve their aims. Although the conflicts currently raging in various parts of the world may seem overwhelming, history shows that each individual has the capacity to enact change, and technological and social changes in the past 100 years provide more opportunities for humans to engage individually and collectively to transform violent conflict into peaceful change.

## Questions for further discussion

1 Choose a recent conflict in the world and discuss how various conflict management mechanisms discussed in this book (mediation, negotiation, nonviolent resistance, peacekeeping, peacebuilding, transitional justice, reconciliation) have been or might be used to help manage this conflict.
2 What are the various factors, or elements of a conflict that might impact how successful various conflict management mechanisms are in managing conflict? Under what circumstances might some mechanisms be more successful than others?
3 Given the variety of issues related to conflict and conflict management discussed in this book, what do you think is the biggest challenge to creating a more peaceful world?

## Note

1 The authors have contributed equally to this chapter and are presented in random order.

## References and further reading

Carter Center. 2016. *Countering Daesh Propaganda: Action-Oriented Research for Practical Policy Outcomes*. Atlanta, GA: Carter Center. Accessed July 31, 2019. www.cartercenter.org/resources/pdfs/peace/conflict_resolution/countering-isis/counteringdaeshpropaganda-feb2016.pdf.

Cederman, Lars-Erik, Kristian Skrede Gleditsch, and Julian Wucherpfennig. 2017. "Predicting the Decline of Ethnic Civil War: Was Gurr Right and for the Right Reasons?" *Journal of Peace Research* 54 (2): 262–74.

Gurr, Ted Robert. 2000. "Ethnic Warfare on the Wane." *Foreign Affairs* 79 (May-June): 52 64.

United Nations Peacekeeping. 2017. "Cote d'Ivoire Is Inspiring Example of UN Peacekeeping Success, Country's Leader Tells Assembly." Accessed July 31, 2019. https://peacekeeping.un.org/en/cote-divoire-is-inspiring-example-of-un-peacekeeping-success-countrys-leader-tells-assembly.

# Glossary

**Amnesty**  A pardon or legal protection from prosecution or other accountability measures.

**Anarchy**  Situation that lacks a central, coercive authority, such as the international system.

**Arab Uprisings**  Large-scale popular uprisings in many Arab countries in 2010 and 2011 that challenged the status quo and sought regime changes, also known as Arab Springs.

**Artificial intelligence**  The result of using computers to perform functions similar to humans by deriving meaning from data using associational logic.

**Asylee**  A displaced person who is seeking admission at a port of entry to apply for political protection or who is already present in a resettlement country seeking protection.

**Big data**  Large quantities of information that are either structured, as in columns and rows, or unstructured, as in tweets on the Internet, that must be processed rapidly for them to be useful.

**Bots**  Computer programs that perform functions or disseminate information on the Internet, or both.

**Boycott, divestment, and sanctions**  A nonviolent coercion method, for example the 2005 campaign of over 170 Palestinian civil society organizations that issued a call for BDS to increase global pressure on Israel until it complies with international law and universal principles of human rights.

**Brexit (short for "British Exit")**  The term used to identify the process by which the United Kingdom is leaving the European Union.

**Cartel**  A group of economic actors organized to manipulate prices and restrict competition in a particular market.

**Citizenship**  The status of a person recognized under the custom or law as being a legal member of a sovereign state or belonging to a nation.

**Climate justice**  A term used to frame global warming as an ethical and political issue, rather than only an environmental issue.

**Collective security**  A method of attaining security where states join together into a collective in which any aggressive act against any individual member will be met with collective force.

**Comparative advantage**  A phrase used to describe specialization advantages in production.

**Conflict-induced migrant**  Asylum seekers, refugees, displaced persons, stateless individuals, the undocumented, and other persons fleeing conflict.

**Congestion**  When a mobile phone station receives more voice calls than it can handle.

**Consumer surplus**  Consumer's valuation of a good over and above the market price.

**Constructivism**  A theory that focuses on the social constructed norms of the international system and how these norms shape the actions of actors.

**Contact theory**   The hypothesis that interaction between groups experiencing conflict can decrease discrimination and increase the likelihood of tolerance, collaboration, and friendship formation.

**Crowdsourcing**   When people in a "crowd" send information into a centralized source as a way of contributing to a joint enterprise.

**Data mining**   The practice of using mathematics, often involving artificial intelligence, to identify trends and patterns within data in the information fire hose.

**Internet freedom**   The ability to post and share information at will, without governmental restriction.

**Deadweight loss**   The loss in mutual gains from trade that occurs when markets are prevented from reaching a perfectly competitive equilibrium.

**Democratic Peace Theory**   A theory that suggests that democracies are unlikely to go to war with each other.

**Deportation**   The expulsion of a person or group of people from a place or country.

**Diaspora**   The dispersion of any people from their original homeland.

**Discursive analysis**   Analysis of written or spoken communication.

**Dominant strategy**   A strategy that appears to be the best choice no matter what strategy the opponent chooses to undertake.

**Dual Concern Model**   A model that sets forth approaches to conflict based on levels of concern for self and concern for others.

**Durable solutions**   Defined by the United Nations, the permanent settlement of refugees, whether in the host country, a third country, or repatriated to the country of origin.

**Economic interdependence**   A situation where states are mutually economically dependent upon each other, often through trade.

**Economic migrant**   A person who travels from one country or area to another in order to improve his or her standard of living and not primarily for fear of harm.

**Economic welfare analysis**   An analytical economic tool to assess and compare different markets and policies by analyzing and measuring total consumer and producer surpluses under varying scenarios.

**Emigrant**   A person who leaves his or her own country in order to settle permanently in another.

**Ethno-symbolism**   The importance of ethnic attachments, such as symbols, myths, and traditions that form and sustain entities ranging from ethnic groups to nations.

**European Community for Steel and Coal**   Europe's first post-WWII economic cooperation agreement.

**European Union**   Europe's post-WWII political and economic integration model created to ensure the free movement of capital, labor, and goods and services across Europe.

**Forced migration**   Movements of refugees and internally displaced people, especially those displaced by conflicts within their country of origin, by natural or environmental disasters, chemical or nuclear disasters, famine, or development projects.

**Fambul Tok**   A community-based tradition of conflict resolution in Sierra Leone.

**First Intifada**   A phrase literally meaning "shake off;" Palestinian attempt to rid themselves of Israeli occupation from 1987 to 1991, employing largely nonviolent methods.

**Forgiveness**   The ability to let go of hard feelings towards someone.

**Freedom of Information Act (FOIA)**   A law that requires the full or partial disclosure of previously unreleased information and documents controlled by the United States Government upon request.

**G7+**   An intergovernmental voluntary organization of 20 countries affected by conflict and fragility.

**Gacaca Courts**   A form of community justice in Rwanda.

**Gender**   A social construct that defines the continuum of masculinity and femininity within a given sociocultural context.

**General Agreement on Tariffs and Trade (GATT)**   The first post-WWII vehicle for the promotion of free trade.

**Geneva Conventions**   International agreements that codify humanitarian law.

**Hegemon**   Powerful actor that dominates the international system in terms of power.

**Homeland**   A person's or a people's native land.

**Human security**   An emerging paradigm for understanding global vulnerabilities arguing that the proper referent for security should be at the human level as a people-centered and multidisciplinary understanding of security ensuring "freedom from want" and "freedom from fear" for all persons.

**Human trafficking**   The trade of humans for the purpose of forced labor, sexual slavery, or commercial sexual exploitation.

**Humanitarian space**   An operational environment that allows humanitarian actors to provide assistance and services according to humanitarian principles and in line with international humanitarian law.

**Hybridity**   Term used to reflect complex processes of interaction and transformation occurring between different institutional and social forms and normative systems, such as the "local" and the "global."

**Hydrohegemony**   Control over transboundary waters.

**Immigrant**   A person who comes to live permanently in a foreign country.

**Immigration federalism**   The role of states and localities in making and implementing immigration law and policy.

**Integration**   The process by which immigrants become accepted into society, both as individuals and as groups.

**Interest-based negotiation**   A negotiating strategy in which both sides work to develop agreements that satisfy common interests.

**Internally displaced person (IDP)**   Someone who is forced to flee his or her home but who remains within his or her country's borders.

**International Bank for Reconstruction and Development**   Was created after WWII to finance the post-WWII reconstruction and has evolved into a major -lender for capital investment in less developed countries. Is one of the five members of the World Bank Group.

**International mediation**   A nonviolent conflict resolution process in which a third party (or parties) assists disputing states or intrastate actors as they seek to negotiate a resolution to their conflict.

**International Monetary Fund (IMF)**   Post-WWII institution created to help maintain a system fixed exchange rates and evolved, in a flexible exchange rate world, as a lender of hard currency to countries that have balance of payment shortages.

**Irregular migration**   Movement of persons that takes place outside the laws, regulations, or international agreements governing the entry into or exit from the state of origin, transit, or destination.

**Impunity**   Exemption from punishment. In relation to transitional justice, it is the commission of serious violations of human rights or international crimes without being held accountable.

**Intentional harm**   When someone hurts someone else intentionally, making it harder to forgive even if possible, to reconcile.

**Joint fact finding**   Strategy for resolving factual disputes, specifically technical and scientific disputes; process of engaging multiple stakeholders to interpret data.

**Laissez-faire approach**   A posture of non-intervention, sometimes referring especially to keeping the government from distorting markets.

**Laissez-faire capitalism**   A system of economic organization in which the sole role of government is to ensure the protection of property rights and protection from foreign aggression, allowing the price system to be the mechanism that organizes all other productive activities.

**Liberalism**   An international relations theory that focuses on the importance of cooperation and international institutions to create peace and stability in the world.

**Liberal Peace Theory**   The notion that democracy and cross-country trade diminishes tendencies for countries to engage in conflict with each other.

**Lustration**   The purging of party members and government officials associated with the previous regime.

**Market power**   The ability to control or manipulate a price.

**Mato Oput**   A forgiveness and reconciliation ritual used by the Acholi people in North Uganda and South Sudan.

**Memorialization**   The honoring of victims of human rights abuses through monuments, museums, and commemorations.

**Mercantilism**   An economic concept where countries promote trade, but also rely on protectionist strategies.

**Migrant**   A person who moves from one place to another, especially in order to find work or better living conditions.

**Monopoly**   A market in which there is only one seller or producer of a good.

**Multinational companies**   Generally, large, private, for-profit businesses that operate in a number of countries across the world.

**Nash Equilibrium**   A situation in which each economic actor has no desire or incentive to change what he or she is doing given what the other actors are doing.

**National Environmental Policy Act (NEPA)**   Law that requires the United States government to give proper consideration to the environment prior to undertaking any major federal action that significantly affects the environment.

**National security**   The protection of a nation-state, including its citizens, economy, and institutions, regarded as a duty of government.

**Negative peace**   The absence of armed conflict or war.

**Neutral third party**   Party that has no financial, official, or personal interest in a controversy, dispute, or issue in which it is requested to assist parties in resolving.

**New Social Movements**   Activist networks that do not have a formal organization.

**New Deal**   A 2011 agreement between fragile and conflict-affected states, development partners, and civil society to improve development policy and practice in fragile and conflict-affected states. It involved pursuing the five Peacebuilding and Statebuilding Goals (PSGs): legitimate politics, justice, security, revenue and services, and economic foundations.

**New wars**   A term associated with Mary Kaldor that describes conflicts in the post-Cold War period, involving both state and non-state actors, and including issues of identity.

**Noninterference**   The international relations principle that suggests states should not interfere in the domestic politics of other states.

**Non-refoulement** The practice of not forcing refugees or asylum-seekers to return to a country in which they are liable to be subjected to persecution.

**Nonviolence** Active approach to challenge oppression and war through collective action that is free of violence and the threat of violence. Also called people power, civil resistance, popular struggle, or unarmed insurrection.

**Oslo Accords** Set of agreements between the Government of Israel and the Palestine Liberation Organization (PLO).

**Peacebuilding** A process aimed at reducing the likelihood of relapse into armed conflict; includes a wide range of approaches.

**Peacekeeping** Efforts to preserve (negative) peace once active fighting has ceased, intended to help implement peace agreements.

**Perfect competition** An economic structure in which there are no barriers to competition and all market participants are small and react only to market prices, which they cannot alter or affect in any way.

**Peace enforcement** Authorized by the Security Council, these peacekeeping missions permit coercive measures, including use of military force.

**Political space** A political environment that allows for freedom of assembly, expression, and participation.

**Positive peace** The absence of all forms of violence, including structural violence, within society.

**Primordialism** An argument that views ethnic identities as ancient, natural phenomenon and suggests that individuals are born into a certain ethnic group.

**Prisoners' dilemma** A Nash equilibrium that is not the socially optimal outcome for the actors involved.

**Producers Surplus** The amount that a price received by a producer for a good or service is over and above the producer's reservation price for selling that good or service.

**Production possibility frontier (PPF)** All the possible production combinations of outputs for which an economy is at its maximum production capacity.

**Radical flank effect** A radical arm of a nonviolent movement that has more extreme goals, demands, or activities, sometimes with the use or threat of violence. Can make the mainstream movement look more reasonable or undermine the credibility of the whole movement.

**Realism** An international relations theory that sees states as seeking power and pursuing their self-interests in an anarchic world.

**Reconciliation** Making peace with someone who hurt you.

**Red Sea Dead Sea Water Conveyance** Planned project that would pipe water from the Red Sea to the Dead Sea.

**Refugee** A person outside his or her country of nationality who is unable or unwilling to return to his or her country of nationality because of persecution or a well-founded fear of persecution on account of race, religion, nationality, membership in a particular social group, or political opinion.

**Refugee camp** A temporary settlement built to receive refugees and people in refugee-like situations (i.e., displaced persons) who have fled their communities or home countries.

**Relative deprivation** When a party feels that they have less in comparison than other referent actors.

**Remittances** A transfer of money, often by a foreign worker to an individual or group in their home country.

**Reparation** Compensation for a loss, injury, or abuse related to a conflict. Reparations can include the restoration of lost property, monetary or in-kind compensation.

**Repatriation**   The return of someone to his or her own country.

**Resettlement**   The transfer of refugees from an asylum country to another state that has agreed to admit them and ultimately grant them permanent settlement.

**Return migration**   The voluntary or involuntary return of travelers and migrants to their place of origin.

**Ripeness**   Refers to the extent to which the parties are ready to come to the negotiating table due to the presence of a mutually-hurting stalemate as well as incentives or pressure from third-party states or international organizations (such as the United Nations).

**Sanctuary cities**   Municipal jurisdictions, typically in North America and Western Europe, that limit their cooperation with the national government's effort to enforce immigration law.

**Second Intifada**   Also known as the Al-Aqsa Intifada, a period of increased violence between Palestine and Israel from 2000 to 2005, largely shaped by internal struggle between Palestinian factions, Hamas' suicide attacks, and brutal Israeli responses, but nonviolent activities continued with some Israeli and Palestinian activists joining forces to end Israeli occupation.

**Security dilemma**   A situation where states attempt to make themselves more secure, but in the process make themselves more insecure.

**Sherman Act (1890)**   The first law passed in the United States that restricted anti-competitive behavior, limiting the ability of businesses to form monopolies or acquire excessive market power.

**Shuttle diplomacy**   When a mediator meets with each side's representatives separately while carrying messages or applying appropriate pressure or inducements for collaboration and compromise. This is common prior to the commencement of official mediation efforts.

**Social citizenship**   Those acculturated into locales are deemed to belong, whether or not they hold certain legal credentials of state citizenship.

**Social Identity Theory**   The human need to identify with a group in order to reduce uncertainty and increase security and self-worth.

**Social market economy**   An economic model originating during the inter-war period in Germany and coming into force after WWII, combining free-market principles with equitable social development and recognizing the important regulatory role of the state to create prosperous and peaceful society.

**Socialism**   An economic model that emphasizes central planning of economic activities and government ownership of the means of production.

**Sovereignty**   The idea that the supreme authority to rule within a state belongs solely to that state and its leader.

**Spectrum of Allies**   A tool developed by George Lakey used by nonviolent movements to identify allies, potential allies, and opponents to develop strategic action plans.

**Structural violence**   A term coined by Johan Galtung to describe how institutionalized structures and laws prevent marginalized groups from achieving their full potential and continue the oppression of certain segments of society.

**Total social surplus (Welfare)**   The sum of consumer and producer surplus in a market.

**Track I Diplomacy and Mediation**   Involves high-level political and military leaders working on issues of cease-fires, political boundaries, treaties, and peace agreements (Usip.org/glossary for more definitions).

**Track II Diplomacy and Mediation**   Involves dialogue and problem-solving interventions aimed at improving relationships between two or more countries, usually undertaken by influential leaders who are not members of the government, such as academics, religious leaders, non-profit organizations, business owners, and even well-known athletes or celebrities.

**Track III Diplomacy and Mediation**  Involves people-to-people efforts undertaken by individuals and small groups designed to build understanding and draw attention to important causes of international conflict such as refugees or the environment.

**Transitional justice**  The full range of processes and mechanisms associated with a society's attempts to come to terms with a legacy of large-scale abuses, in order to ensure accountability, serve justice and achieve reconciliation (UNSC S/2004/616).

**Triangulation**  Using multiple sources of information to enhance accuracy.

**Trolls**  People who deliberately cultivate quarrels.

**Truth commission**  A body tasked with uncovering the wrongdoings of a government in an effort to promote social reconciliation.

**Undocumented**  A person who is foreign-born and who does not have a legal right to be or remain in the host country.

**Unexploded ordnances**  Explosive weapons (bombs, land mines, etc.) that did not explode when they were employed and still pose a risk of detonation.

**US Civil Rights Movement**  Mass protest movements from the mid-1950s to the late 1960s to end racial segregation, discrimination, and disenfranchisement and give African Americans equal civil rights.

**Voluntary migration**  The migrant has a choice whether or not to migrate and where to move and if he or she should move at all.

**Wicked problem**  Confusing and complex, system-wide problem in which many actors with conflicting values are involved.

**Zero-sum**  A situation where what is gained by one actor will be lost by another actor.

# Index

Note: Page numbers in *italics* refer to figures or tables.

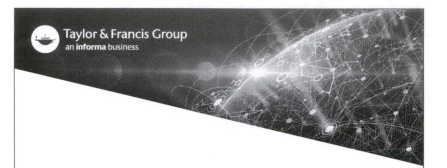